The Private
Secretary's Manual

Every man who knows how to read has it in his power to magnify himself, to multiply the ways in which he exists, to make his life full, significant and interesting.
—ALDOUS HUXLEY

THE PRIVATE
SECRETARY'S MANUAL

THIRD EDITION

by

Bernice C. Turner

Revised by the Editorial Staff of
Prentice-Hall, Inc.

PRENTICE-HALL, INC., Englewood Cliffs, New Jersey

Foreword

Secretaries are made, not born. It is for this reason that this completely new edition of *The Private Secretary's Manual* is published. We sincerely believe that this book will serve the needs of the private secretary and also of the secretary who wishes to become a private secretary.

A successful private secretary enjoys the feeling of being indispensable to an important man. No one who has not been a private secretary can know how completely a man relies on his secretary and how he appreciates the way she looks after his interests and protects him from outside annoyances and distractions. A career as private secretary is rewarding in many ways. It pays well, ranks high in job ratings, and, best of all, permits an unusually high degree of personal satisfaction.

The girl who wants to be a successful career secretary is generally one who is proud of her abilities and skills. She doesn't depend on personal attributes to excuse slovenly work in typing or stenography. She makes every effort to maintain the effectiveness of the various skills she learned in secretarial school, to develop new ones as they are needed, and to add to her knowledge and technical proficiency whenever possible.

She realizes that a secretarial career calls for the utmost in loyalty, understanding, and—perhaps most important—tact. Qualities such as these enable her to guide and lead her employer without becoming bossy and possessive; to keep her executive informed on attitudes and conditions throughout the office without stooping to talebearing and gossiping; to be utterly self-reliant but obedient to her employer's wishes and instructions; to stand her ground when necessary without becoming argumentative or opinionated.

The author has seen much need for a book that will guide the employer in helping his secretary develop into that most valued of employees—a private secretary, endowed with all the trust, respect, and responsibility that the term implies. Such a reward belongs only to the employer who consciously seeks to turn his secretary into a valued confidante and assistant. *The Private Secretary's Manual* is designed to be read to advantage by both the executive and the secretary. It gives information needed by the secretary on the job and also shows the executive how best to use his secretary's abilities; how to share more of his work with her; how to inspire her loyalty.

Because a good command of English is a prerequisite to success as a private secretary, several chapters in this book deal with grammar, sentence structure, punctuation and spelling. The ability to carry on a correspondence with her executive's business contacts also is a distinguishing characteristic of the private secretary, and so there are chapters on the art of writing both business and personal letters for your employer. The executive will be interested in the chapters describing how a competent secretary can handle details of such matters as insurance, banking, and stock investments for him. Other chapters are concerned with the personal qualifications that lead to success as a private secretary, and methods of making the office attractive. Basic secretarial skills have not been neglected, however, and there are chapters on stenography, typing, filing, receiving callers, and other office procedures.

The suggestions in this book will also help you to simplify your daily office routines. By so doing you will save time and energy and rid yourself of the irritating feeling that these everyday tasks are holding you back from working at top efficiency on more important matters.

This book is presented in as informal, readable, and interesting a manner as possible, rather than as a dictionary of office procedure and secretarial practice. This has been done in the hope that you may be more inclined to read it with enjoyment after work. When a busy day's work has been completed, few secretaries or businessmen have either the energy or the inclination to study a dictionary of business data. In the first edition of *The Private Secretary's Manual,* an effort was made to present this business information in a readable and interesting manner, with just enough humor interspersed to prevent the reading from becoming burdensome. Requests that the "human interest style" be retained in this revision have been gratifying indeed.

When you read this book, we hope it makes you feel as though you are sitting down with a friend to chat about your office problems.

In the present edition, additions and deletions have been made to bring material up to date. The list of individuals who have contributed helpful suggestions and information during the revision of this book is so long that specific acknowledgments cannot be attempted here. Especially helpful, however, have been the letters received from secretaries working in practically every state in the United States, as well as in Canada.

The stories and incidents cited to illustrate points in various chapters actually happened. They will indicate how general are the problems secretaries face from time to time.

Secretarial work, as practiced by top-flight private secretaries, calls for a vast store of general information and knowledge, aside from the basic skills of typewriting and shorthand. With this in mind, bibliographies are appended to each chapter that follows to help you find further information on a given topic. Included in these lists are the names of periodicals published exclusively for secretaries. Reading that deals specifically with the work performed by you and women all over the country will add much to your awareness of the common problems shared by everyone in your field.

You will note that quotations head each chapter. Here is one to close this foreword, which might well be the secretary's motto:

> If you work for a man, in heaven's name work for him! If he pays you wages that supply your bread and butter, work for him—speak well of him, think well of him, stand by him, and stand by the institution he represents.
>
> —ELBERT HUBBARD

Contents

Chapter **1**

The Secretary as a Stenographer

How do you tackle your work each day? Are you scared
of the job you find? Do you grapple the task that comes
your way with a confident, easy mind?
                                        —Edgar A. Guest

Shorthand skill is essential

Although a few secretaries are relieved of stenographic work,
shorthand is the written language of the profession. A slight knowledge of the subject will not suffice; you cannot afford to have less
than a thorough mastery of the principles of the system you write.
If you must stop to think how to write any appreciable number of
outlines, your speed will be retarded. No one speaks a language well
until he does away with all attempts at quick mental translations and
starts to think in that language. Only then does it become a direct and
easy vehicle for expressing his thoughts. In like manner, shorthand
must be made a vehicle for facile recording of what you hear; there
must be no pause for mental translations from longhand into shorthand. (Secretaries who use machines rather than notebooks for taking
dictation must maintain proficiency in their method of taking dictation.)

Brush up on your theory

Review your shorthand system from time to time in order that you
may not wander too far away from the principles it sets forth. This
practice is so important that most employment managers will not hire

1

a secretary who boasts that she writes her own system. One fast writer says that she goes through her manual once a month. If you try to get through yours once in six months, you will find that you will be able to speed up your work considerably. The manual is not a book to be studied for a certain period of time and discarded, as is done by so many students. You will be surprised to find that there are a large number of points you will readily absorb now that made no impression when you were first studying the text. As a student, you had no tangible experience upon which to base your learning. With working experience comes understanding of the theoretical problems you studied.

Textbooks to have at hand

Keep the manual, a shorthand dictionary, and a phrase book in your desk. Many times you will look into them to see how to write some new outline that you have not met before. Of course, when you take dictation, you will write the outline as you think it should be written, or you will make some hieroglyphic which you will be able to remember stands for the word. What a satisfaction to be able to turn to your shorthand dictionary when you are transcribing and find that you were right!

Increase your writing vocabulary

Your employer's vocabulary may be extremely limited and you may have a well-rounded knowledge of English, but he will commonly use some words that you do not even know. Consequently, you will be forced to learn new outlines to make your writing vocabulary conform to the dictator's speaking vocabulary. Often you may rely on your memory or a longhand scribble to recall a word or phrase your employer dictated, and for which you do not know the outline. But you cannot afford to let your stenographic ability lapse in this way. Shorthand quickly deteriorates to such an extent that one's ability to take the dictation of one man may not be an asset when taking dictation from a person in a different line or department.

Give yourself incentives

If you wish to study by yourself, get in touch with the publishing company sponsoring your system of shorthand. Very likely it publishes magazines, tests, contests, and other incentives to help a secretary keep up to date.

Evening schools and special shorthand classes attract thousands of efficient secretaries who are perfecting their knowledge of shorthand theory. In one school, a class is maintained for girls holding high-grade secretarial positions. They are given a little speed and much theory. A girl who entered this class attended for two years. When the personnel director of her company accidentally found out that she was enrolled in the school, he called her to his office and inquired: "You are the oldest girl here, in point of service, and the highest paid. What does this school work mean?" She replied: "I never had any trouble in getting the letters here, but I was often troubled over an outline. I decided to enroll for a few weeks and review my principles. Since I have mastered them, I continue in order not to forget. Maybe I pay tuition because I like the teacher, but I really do get something out of her classes each evening." You may find that the inspiration of a teacher and classmates one or two nights a week provides just the incentive you need to improve your knowledge of shorthand principles.

Penmanship affects outlines

One of the chief causes of poor transcription is poor penmanship. If you write Gregg, do your outlines flow along smoothly? If you use the Pitman method of shorthand, are you making a distinction between your light and heavy strokes and between your long and short strokes? Lack of uniformity puts too heavy a burden on your ingenuity. Time wastes away while you play at guessing games with your notes. Are your outlines approximately the size of those in the texts? Size of notes is one of the first things to consider in improving your writing.

The tools of your trade

The tools you use should be conducive to clear writing. Your pencils should be very sharp, so as to make outlines that are readable. If you use a pen, choose a good one that you can rely on. A pen has the advantage of keeping notes clear, regardless of the amount of handling to which they may be subjected. Pencil notes often become so blurred as to be illegible. Clear notes prevent eyestrain, a point worth recognizing in stenographic work. Reading pen notes, even over a long period and under poor light, will lessen that strain. As children, we learned to write with a pencil, forming careless habits because the main emphasis was put on the language aspect of writing. After we had learned to write fluently with a pencil, we were introduced to pens and told to do our very best work. The extra care exerted to make pen-writing better than ordinary pencil-writing usually brought good results, but there was a tendency to write more slowly.

Pen-writing, to be effective, should have been used from the very beginning of your shorthand work, in order that this tendency to write deliberately may not retard speed in taking notes. However, you can probably learn to use a pen quite successfully, even though you have used a pencil for many years.

Shorthand all the way

Time lost between outlines is usually the reason for slow writing. If you would become a speedy writer, try to minimize this time by going from one outline to the next without hesitation. Be sure that no pause is due to a fundamental lack of knowledge of the principles. Do not be too conscientious about writing every outline perfectly. Get something down for every word. Write names and addresses in shorthand, putting the longhand in above if necessary. A habit of writing proper nouns in longhand is poor, because the dictator usually reads on very quickly. Partial indication of an address in longhand often leads to errors. Proper names are not difficult to write in shorthand if you form the habit of indicating them in that way. If necessary, write the longhand spelling above a shorthand outline, but use only the shorthand outline for all repetitions of the name.

Do not erase shorthand notes or scratch them out with a needless number of movements of the pen, as this wastes time. An oblique line drawn through an outline is sufficient to indicate deletion.

Rate of dictation

Secretaries first going into business always ask how fast men dictate. Much depends on the man and on the type of work being dictated, but the final test is usually how fast you can take dictation. The average man finds some fascination in the speed with which his dictation can be taken. If he picks up something he can read, he is likely to forget that you are not a reporter and will read it at a very fast rate. These spurts of speed which test your ability usually do not last long. When a dictator is thinking as he dictates, he makes such long pauses that you will have to make a studied effort to keep your attention from wandering. The self-control which you must exercise not to tap your pencil, smooth your hair, or otherwise distract his attention will often make you so nervous that you will be almost ready to jump out of the window. However, refraining from showing annoyance is the price that you must pay for success. You will find it much easier to wait if you try to determine what you would say if you were dictating. You may be called on to furnish a word, but do not volunteer it unless you know that it will not distract the dictator. Pauses also offer you an opportunity to go back over your notes and improve those that probably would be hard to read in a few hours.

Developing and maintaining speed

Few positions furnish dictation fast enough over any period of time to increase a secretary's speed of writing. Any gain in speed which you make after leaving school will probably come from self-directed practicing of outlines, special dictation classes, and the general knowledge you will absorb about the particular business in which you are engaged. Special effort will have to be put forth to maintain a practical speed while working in some offices. On the other hand, what is often erroneously called speed is really not worth anything from a practical standpoint. People who are graduated from schools purporting to require a graduation speed of one hundred twenty words a minute often can neither take nor correctly transcribe fairly simple material dictated at forty words a minute. Your speed should be rated on the basis of your ability to take solid matter for at least five minutes. A short, simple business letter is not a true test of shorthand proficiency.

Interruptions call for tact

If you are not getting what your employer is dictating, do not hesitate to ask him to repeat. It is foolhardy to go on pretending you are getting everything when you are not, for incomplete notes will do you no good when you start to transcribe. A man has far more respect for the secretary who admits she is not getting his dictation than for one who tries to bluff through a letter. The employer knows what he wants to say and usually does not object to a little necessary repetition.

A woman who had been with one firm for a long time was compelled to move to another city. When she applied for a new position, the girls in the office heard her term herself a "crack stenographer." She was hired, and her first day there the president of the company, taking her at her word, dictated at his usual speed. Though the work was very technical, she never winked an eyelid while taking the dictation; nor did she ask him to repeat anything. As soon as she left his office, however, she began asking first one and then another of the secretaries to help her figure out what he might have said. After several interruptions, one of the girls refused to stop in the middle of her work again, saying, "I think 'cracked' instead of 'crack' would be the word to describe you." To an outsider, and even to a businessman, this might seem like an extreme case, but shorthand writers in any large office can cite numerous examples of these parasites who prey upon the time of others. Secretaries are usually very willing to help one another, but they have their own work to do and should not be called upon to worry about what an inept worker isn't able to figure out for herself.

When you do not understand the context, it is safe to wager that the recipient of the letter will not find it clear. You can help your employer by tactfully drawing his attention to lack of clarity. Even the work of professional authors is read by many people before it is submitted to the printer. Material which is perfectly clear to the writer may mean absolutely nothing to a reader. As you are the only person who can help your employer detect his failure to express any idea clearly, do not hesitate to offer him this service. Just be sure you do it respectfully and graciously, not in a way that makes him feel stupid.

When an employer interrupts to insert material in dictated matter, do not try to write it in above your notes, unless it is only a word or two. Write *Insert* in shorthand and put a ring around it. Then at a point below where the interruption occurred, draw a wavy line and write beneath it the part to be inserted. End with another wavy line.

Proper time to interrupt

The time to interrupt is usually a matter of discretion. Sometimes it is well to try to get an entire sentence and then go back and read it over until you come to the place where you missed a few words. Many men forget what they are going to say if there is an interruption in the middle of a sentence. Others prefer to stop at once. Learn which method suits your employer.

Holding a dictator responsible for his work

A man who dictates with a pipe in his mouth, who gazes out of the window, or who walks the floor, puts an unnecessary burden on the secretary to whom he is dictating. Unfortunately, such men are not always patient about repeating poorly enunciated passages. You will need to develop a keen sense of hearing in these cases, but it is only fair to hold such a dictator responsible for your getting the context.

Harsh methods are sometimes necessary to awaken a thoughtless employer to a sense of responsibility for his own work, especially if he refuses to give needed information, because he knows others will find for you what he is too lazy to get himself. You cannot afford to impose upon the good nature of others to hunt an address in their files or to look through several source books for the correct name of a firm.

The secretary to a junior officer, who would neither give her necessary information nor tell her where she could find it, always went to a busy vice president and got the data. Each time, she mentioned the senior officer's help when she handed the letter to her employer to sign, pretending she thought he would be interested in knowing these details. The young man became exasperated to think that his superior should be bothered and that his own ignorance of details should be revealed, with the result that he began to take great care to give the secretary any information she needed.

The gentle art of questioning

Many questions show a lack of initiative; one may be asking information to avoid searching for it. Of course, in any new work it is absolutely necessary to ask some questions in order not to waste time. An intelligent secretary will give some thought to cloaking her interrogations in the least objectionable form of question. For example, instead of continually repeating, "What?" "What did you say?" "Beg pardon?" or any of the other inane forms used to secure repetition, a wise secretary will say: "That name is new to me," "Where will I find Mr. Smith's title?" or "Would you mind repeating that sentence; the context is not clear to me?"

The art of wording a question is of prime importance; it is one of the ways in which you express your personality. A man who would complain bitterly about the extreme dullness of a girl who asks, "How do you spell 'Smith'?" might not think of her as particularly ignorant if, with a twinkle in her eye, she says, "Does that man *still* spell his name S-m-i-t-h?" Of course, if you are to be handed the correspondence to which your employer is replying, you will not have to ask how a name is spelled, but you should unobtrusively check to make sure that the names are clear in the signatures of the letters you are answering.

Try to make your questioning a means of checking your own judgment and memory. A customer, returning to a restaurant after a long absence, was made to feel very much at home by a waiter who said, "You take cream in your coffee, do you not?" If his guess had been wrong, he would have received the desired information just as readily as though he had asked, "Do you take cream in your coffee?" Train yourself to think before you ask a question.

Proper use of your notebook

A line should be ruled down the center of each sheet in your notebooks, if they are not already so ruled. Write on one half of a sheet; then go to the top of the second half. As you start down the second column, insert the left index finger under the sheet on which you are writing and with the thumb and index finger slowly move the sheet upward. When the page is finished, release the sheet and you can begin writing on the next page without loss of time.

Daily dating of dictation

Most secretarial practice books insist on dating each day's dictation, yet many secretaries neglect this, even after experience has taught them the value of this practice in locating back work. Form a habit of getting your notebook out to date it as soon as you come into your office each morning; this practice will not only prevent your forgetting to date your work but will, at the same time, make your notebook easily available for that first call to take notes.

Finding your place

A heavy rubber band should hold all transcribed work to the cover of the notebook. The secretary who cannot find notebook, pen, or place in a notebook usually finds a very impatient man, or else a portion of the first letter is dictated before she is ready to write.

Keeping track as you transcribe

Draw a horizontal line at the end of each letter dictated. This habit will enable you to determine at a glance the approximate length of any letter which you are transcribing. As you finish transcribing each letter, draw an oblique line from the upper left-hand corner to the lower right-hand corner. Do not transcribe letters in the order dictated, but pick out the most important ones first. The line drawn through transcribed letters will enable you to tell which ones you have finished. If you are not in the habit of transcribing all of your letters each day, write the date of transcription at the end of each letter in your notebook, in order to be able to find the dated file copy quickly.

Old notes and those written by others

The practice of letting transcription pile up is not advisable in many offices, because letters are expected to be dispatched with all possible haste; but in certain types of dictation, such as reports, immediate transcription is not so important as getting the notes down while events are fresh in the mind of the dictator. One medical secretary had ten notebooks full of work which she had not transcribed, having taken dictation steadily for three weeks. The doctors for whom she worked then went on a month's vacation, and she had plenty of time to write up the reports. Her writing is like the models in a shorthand textbook—small, compact, and correct—so she had no trouble reading notes that had been written several weeks before. It is in cases like this that memory can never displace a knowledge of shorthand principles.

Rare is the occasion when you might be asked to read someone else's notes—but it can happen. The secretary to the vice president of a large manufacturing firm was called on to read the minutes of an important meeting. At first she was overwhelmed at the thought of trying to read someone else's notes, but she reasoned that as she and the absent girl had studied the same shorthand system there couldn't be too much difference in their outlines. She was right about this, and had soon typed up a copy of the minutes to be sent to the chairman of the board, who was in Europe on business and anxious for a complete report of this meeting. The president of the firm was so pleased that he personally put through a salary increase for the secretary.

Typewriting skill

Typewriting is not merely an adjunct to shorthand; it is the means by which shorthand accuracy is expressed. You may be able to read your notes well, but if you cannot present a letter or report in attractive form, your employer will have no measure of that shorthand ability. Shorthand skill and typewriting skill should go hand in hand.

A secretary who was writing about one hundred seventy-five words a minute in shorthand was continually reminded of her poor typewriting. She joined a theory class when a new book was published in her system of shorthand and found that her outlines had deteriorated in the twelve years she had been employed. When her shorthand notes were more accurate and easier to read, she made fewer errors in typing. Seeming lack of typing ability may be due either to poor training and technique or to the inability to transcribe accurately because of poor shorthand notes.

Sometimes lack of concentration results in errors. Notice words and combinations of letters you always seem to have trouble with. Spend a few minutes a day typing these correctly and you will break the habit of always getting them wrong.

Your work determines your speed

The speed with which you type will be largely determined by the work you have to do. In many offices there is so little typing that the secretary cannot retain a high speed without doing some speed practice each day. In other places work is so heavy that an operator is pushed to her limit and gradually increases her speed. Speed in typing should equal at least half your speed in shorthand. If you take notes at eighty words a minute, you should type at the rate of forty words a minute; if you take dictation at one hundred twenty words, you should type at sixty.

Know your typewriter

Study your typewriter until you know you can use all its parts to advantage. A free booklet from the typewriter company will explain the uses of all improvements on your machine. If you are being transferred to another position, it is wise to do a little preliminary practicing on the strange machine before you start your work.

When you dust your machine each morning, do not neglect to dust underneath. Though not obvious to you, dust below a typewriter is quite visible to others in the room.

To clean the type, use a stiff brush or one of the commercial cleaners prepared from chemicals which will not soften the metal and cause pieces of type to chip off. A common pin is effective in removing dirt from type which has become clogged. Unclean type detracts from the appearance of any typewritten sheet, yet a survey of your morning's mail will show that many secretaries send out letters which are inferior in this respect.

Be sure the machine is covered or closed when you leave the office at night, so dust will not settle on it.

Fresh new ribbons make a difference

Learn to put a new ribbon on a typewriter quickly and without smearing ink all over yourself. The simple process of changing ribbons does not require a mechanic's services and is a dirty job only if you make it so. If the school you attended has not trained you to make this change of ribbon in less than a minute, you should take time to practice doing this. There is no excuse for sending out correspondence that is not clear because of a worn ribbon.

In most offices there is little use for the bichrome ribbon, since the plain black ribbon gives twice the service. However, in some accounting departments, advertising departments, and law offices, bichrome ribbons are indispensable. All shifting must be carefully done when a bichrome ribbon is used, for a letter struck before the shift key is totally depressed or totally released will cause the impression to be partly red and partly black. This makes an untidy piece of work.

A raised capital letter or a dropped lower-case letter in any writing is evidence that you are striking keys incorrectly. Be sure that you are not holding the shift key after it should be released. If the carriage is not returning to its normal position quickly, a repair man will be able to remedy this defect.

Position is everything

A secretary's position at the typewriter is of vital importance to her health, as well as to accurate writing. Sit back in your chair when typing, with hips touching the back of the chair and your body above the waistline away from the chair. Be careful not to sit on the edge of your chair or to wind your feet around the legs of either desk or chair. Aside from making you an ungraceful ornament for an office, such a position throws your entire weight on your arms, causing fatigue.

Even margins improve style

Listen for the bell at the end of each line in order to eliminate glancing up, with its attendant danger of losing your place in your notebook.

Care in placing the paper against the paper guide will make all margins uniform on any number of sheets. Long letters often betray extreme carelessness in this matter.

Marginal stops should be adjusted to harmonize with each letter written. Because some secretaries are prone to write from one edge of the paper to the other, a few business houses have an arbitrary rule that marginal stops must be placed at certain figures on the writing scale, say ten and sixty-five. This precludes having short letters occupy two or three seventy-five space lines. Of course, any real secretary will want to use discretion and artistry in placing each letter, even though she may have to conform to such a rule.

Keeping right-hand margins even often requires dividing words into syllables. Make frequent use of a dictionary to confirm your division of words. Do not divide dates, proper names, or figures. Never start a word when you cannot get at least two letters and a hyphen on the first line. Always finish a word, unless you have more than two letters to carry to the next line. Test yourself to see that you are striking the hyphen key by touch.

The right-hand margin on some work, such as programs and menus, should be even. Determine the last space upon which you wish to write. Set your machine one space beyond this point and backspace one space for each letter or space in the matter which you wish to have come out to the right-hand margin. If you backspace from the point where you want the last letter to appear, the line will be one space short.

Figures at your fingertips

Learn to write figures by touch. There is no reason why time and accuracy should be wasted by your having to look up to strike the fourth bank of keys. Because few schools give sufficient numbers practice, you may have to work several hours by yourself to complete your training in this respect. However, its accomplishment will save you much time and lend accuracy to your work.

Figures should be placed so they can be added easily. In sums of money, decimal points usually aid a secretary in placing columns correctly. When there is no decimal, space numbers so that the right-hand edge is even.

Roman numerals sometimes cause a secretary trouble, because they are not commonly used except in business. They are always capital letters; a capital I being the Roman *one,* and a lower-case l being an Arabic *one.* (I–1; X–10; L–50; C–100; D–500; M–1000). Remember that a small number placed *before* a larger number means that the smaller is subtracted from the larger, while small numbers placed *after* a larger number are added to that number. Thus XL is *forty* and LX is *sixty.*

If you must erase—do it well

The secretary who makes no errors is a myth. Many books and schools insist on absolute accuracy, allowing students to throw the paper away when a mistake is made. This training is often carried over into office work. Aside from the fact that paper costs money, nothing is more exasperating to a dictator who is waiting for a letter than to see the secretary jerk it out of the typewriter when it is almost finished and start all over again.

Learn to erase well. Experiment until you have found the eraser, or combination of erasers, best suited to the texture of the paper you are using. A medium soft eraser is best for erasing carbon. Place a protecting piece of steel eraser guard or celluloid eraser shield between the carbon paper and the copy sheet. The scale on many electric typewriters is an erasure guard. Erase from the original back through the carbon copies. Keep erasers clean by rubbing them on a clean surface.

There are several new types of erasers on the market. Among them are electric erasers and an eraser of special paper that covers errors with a white chemical. Try them out to see if one suits your needs.

Never let laziness stop you from erasing. Strikeovers are inexcusable. Erase with a rotary motion. Never press hard, as this causes the surface of the paper to curl up. A ring rubbed over the rough surface of a highly glazed paper will sometimes restore the polish. Be careful not to put your fingers on the area, as this causes smearing. Erase only the spot containing the error; there is no excuse for allowing an erasure to show on the larger part of a square inch, when only one small letter has been erased. Little celluloid cards with holes of different sizes prevent making unnecessarily large and unsightly erasures.

After making an erasure, strike the keys lightly. Most erasures show up plainly because a writer is annoyed at having made an error and, in starting to write again, gives vent to that annoyance by striking the correct letters very deliberately.

A safety-razor blade—used very gently—is an excellent tool for removing the tail from an unwanted comma and can be used on carbon work very effectively. When writing so near the bottom of a sheet that erasing carbons might disturb the alignment of your work, erase only the original copy and let the carbons go until you finish. With a razor blade you can remove the mis-struck letter—or letters— quite satisfactorily. Commercial artists use a razor blade extensively for removing lines.

Inserting omissions

When a letter has been omitted from a word, erase two letters and insert three letters in the two spaces. On most machines this may be done by using the backspacer or by holding the carriage in the proper position. If an extra letter has been inserted in a word, erase three letters and spread the two letters over the space in which you wrote three before. This spacing will not be perfect, but it can be so carefully done that a reader will not notice the change.

Train yourself to check each sheet carefully before releasing the paper from the machine. It is easy to roll the cylinder back and make a correction while the alignment is set; to reinsert the sheet and try to adjust the alignment, however, is quite another matter. Vertical alignment is adjusted by pressing the paper release and trying to find the exact position of some single letter. Horizontal alignment is gauged from the previous line by means of the variable line spacer. If you are not perfectly sure of the machine you are using, always test its alignment on another sheet of paper before reinserting a sheet for corrections. When many carbon copies must be corrected, it is usually safer to do each one separately. Put a small strip of carbon paper and a piece of the letterhead behind the ribbon guide. This will insure the inserted word's being in the proper position, and the carbon impression will be nearly like the original writing. If you try to correct several sheets at once, you will almost certainly find that only the word on the original copy is in position. Always move the carriage so that the spot to be erased is far from the ribbon guide. This will eliminate any need for rolling the cylinder back too far. It is especially important to do this if you are near the bottom of a sheet, for the alignment of some of the copies will be disturbed by moving the cylinder back any distance. When it is not advisable to roll the cylinder up a few spaces, erasing may be done, even on carbon copies, by shifting the spot to be erased as far as possible from the ribbon guide and then releasing the paper fingers. The sheet can then be turned down for erasure without disturbing the position of the carbon copies.

Spacing has its own rules

Much correspondence that comes over any office desk shows a lack of application of the fundamental rules of spacing. It will be well to check your work for these errors.

STANDARD RULES FOR SPACING

ONE SPACE:
> After a comma.
> After a semicolon.
> After a period following an abbreviation or an initial.
> After an exclamation mark used in the body of a sentence.
> Before and after "x" meaning "by."

TWO SPACES:
> After a colon. (A few authorities have adopted only one space after a colon.)
> After every sentence, whether followed by a period, an interrogation mark, or an exclamation point.

NO SPACING:
> Before or after a dash, which is two hyphens.
> Before or after a hyphen.
> Between quotation marks and the matter enclosed.
> Between parentheses and the matter enclosed.
> Between any word and the punctuation following it.

Punctuation should never be separated from the word it follows. For instance, do not put a dash at the beginning of a line just because you think you do not have room for it on the preceding line. Always strike punctuation marks lightly; period and comma keys are very sharp, and a severe pressure will sometimes puncture the paper. Turn a typewritten sheet over and run your hand over the reverse surface to see if you are striking punctuation marks too heavily. If the tension on period and comma keys is so tight that you cannot

overcome punching them through the paper, call a typewriter repair-
man and have him adjust those two keys to your touch.

Vertical writing tricks

Holding the space bar will prevent some machines from spacing.
Where one character is directly under or over another, hold the space
bar while you strike both, and you will not have to backspace. For
example, in striking an exclamation mark, press the shift key and the
space bar at the same time. Hold the space bar until both period and
apostrophe keys have been struck. The same is true of a star or an
asterisk, which is the small *v* struck over the capital *A*. In making
boxings with vertical dotted lines, hold the space bar and turn the
platen by hand. Use a period for an evenly spaced line and a colon
for an unevenly spaced line. Holding the space bar is much safer
than trying to remember to backspace each time. The same method
is used in making vertical lines with other characters.

Horizontal alignment

Lock your variable line spacer if writing on unevenly spaced material. You will not then unconsciously shift your machine with the line
space lever.

In writing on lined paper, the typewritten line should exactly follow the printed line. Many ruled forms are spaced for a standard typewriter, making it necessary to adjust only the first line to the machine.
However, do not neglect to adjust every line on forms not so ruled.
Where the blank space is not wide enough, it is better to omit spacing
after punctuation than to run the writing over into the printed matter.

Artistic arrangement

The real pleasure of typewriting comes from the opportunity it
affords to make work attractive. Even a happy message may have

some of its joy taken away by poor arrangement. Phrasing of different parts of a title on appropriate lines and proper spacing of inscriptions will be an index of your judgment and ability.

Centering without guessing

Too many secretaries guess at the center of their paper. Find the central point of your writing space; then backspace once for each two spaces, punctuation included, required to write the heading. This will place the machine in the proper position to start writing. A folded sheet the size of the one upon which you are writing will enable you to locate the central point without removing the paper from your machine. By once folding a correspondence sheet used in your office, you will discover some point on the letterhead, which will guide you in future centering.

It is sometimes desirable that short headings take up more space than ordinary writing of them would occasion. A space left after each letter and three spaces between words will make the heading stand out more clearly. A more artistic effect is gained by underscoring only the letters and leaving the spaces blank. Strike the underscore key lightly.

Artistic gains from legal work

Writing of bylaws, articles of incorporation, agreements, contracts, deeds, and wills offers excellent training in accurate and artistic work. Usually these are written by lawyers, but many business committees write them up in tentative form before submitting them to their lawyers. A secretary in a large organization recently received a bonus larger than her salary because she was able to type legal forms in an emergency. She had been studying this work just to get ideas for the artistic arrangement of her daily work. Any complete typewriting manual will give you suggestions for arrangement of legal work. Further information on legal points involved in secretarial work will be found in Chapter Eleven.

Covers for typewritten documents

So-called *legal covers* could be widely used if all secretaries realized the importance of protecting papers which must be handled constantly. Use a sheet of heavy paper, in color if you wish. Turn the bottom up to within an inch from the top and crease. Fold again. If you wish to type on the outside, put a tiny check mark on the upper *left*-hand corner of the folded section, open to the half-fold and insert in the typewriter so that the check mark is on the upper *right*-hand corner. Type the information you need for reference on the quarter to the right of the crease. The inch at the top can be folded over the paper or papers you wish to protect and stapled. Then fold to fit the creases you have already made in the cover.

Stenographic standards

Although this chapter on stenographic work may seem too detailed, an inspection of the work in a number of offices will reveal the need for such a condensed résumé of these points, which either have been forgotten or were never learned. In evening classes, the transcription work of secretaries who are improving their work shows a woeful need for a thorough checkup on general shorthand and typewriting technique. In the final analysis, stenographic technique is probably the foundation upon which most secretarial positions are built. Unfortunately, many workers become so involved in the other details of their work that they neglect skills. An ambitious secretary will profit much by studying the new books which are being published and by following magazines devoted to improving stenographic standards.

BOOKS THAT AID IN SHORTHAND AND TYPEWRITING

IMPROVEMENT

TEXTBOOKS:

Manuals of shorthand principles, shorthand dictionaries, phrase books, foreign-language adaptations, and special treatises on different lines of secretarial work, such as medicine, law, and other technical work. Apply direct to the company sponsoring your system of shorthand.

DICTATION MATERIAL:

Correlated Dictation Studies in Thomas Natural Shorthand, Bisbee & Thomas, Prentice-Hall, Inc., Englewood Cliffs, N.J.

Shorthand Speed Drills, Paul S. Moser, Pitman Publishing Corp., New York

Lightning Cuts to High Speed, Pitman Publishing Corp., New York

Guide to High Speedwriting, Pitman Publishing Corp., New York

Gregg Dictation Simplified, Gregg Publishing Division of The McGraw-Hill Book Co., New York

Gregg Transcription Simplified, Gregg Publishing Division of The McGraw-Hill Book Co., New York

Gregg Speed Building Simplified (home-study instruction manual), Gregg Publishing Division of The McGraw-Hill Book Co., New York

Note: Most dictation material is divided into groups of twenty words, either by a heavy, parallel straight line or by superior figures in the copy. In giving timed dictation, the reader must use a clock or watch with a second hand, because it is necessary to read each group of twenty words in a uniform number of seconds. Much practice is often required to gain the ability to read smoothly at any desired speed. At first, one must stop to wait or speed up the tempo of his reading at the end of each time unit in order to gauge the time correctly.

SCALE OF SPEED UNITS

60 words a minute—Twenty words in 20 seconds
80 words a minute—Twenty words in 15 seconds
100 words a minute—Twenty words in 12 seconds
120 words a minute—Twenty words in 10 seconds
140 words a minute—Twenty words in $8\frac{4}{7}$ seconds
160 words a minute—Twenty words in $7\frac{1}{2}$ seconds
180 words a minute—Twenty words in $6\frac{2}{3}$ seconds
200 words a minute—Twenty words in 6 seconds

CURRENT PERIODICALS:

Pitman Journal (a monthly publication), Pitman Publishing Corporation, New York

Today's Secretary (a monthly publication), Gregg Publishing Division of The McGraw-Hill Book Company, New York

TYPEWRITING:

Gregg Typing (college edition), Gregg Publishing Division of The McGraw-Hill Book Co., New York

Tested Timed Writings, Tidwell, Bell, Porter, Prentice-Hall, Inc., Englewood Cliffs, N.J.

Business Timed Writing, Fries, Nanassy, Prentice-Hall, Inc., Englewood Cliffs, N.J.

Speed Typing—Intensive Course, Blackstone, Prentice-Hall, Inc., Englewood Cliffs, N.J.

Technique, Speed and Accuracy Typing, Blackstone, Prentice-Hall, Inc., Englewood Cliffs, N.J.

Thirty Typing Tests, Pitman Publishing Corp., New York

Typing Speed Builders, Connelly and Porter, Prentice-Hall, Inc., Englewood Cliffs, N.J.

Chapter **2**

The Office Mail

Mails from the North—the East—the West—the South—
whence, according to some curious etymologists, comes
the magical word NEWS.

        —THOMAS DeQUINCEY

Importance of mail

One of the most universal of secretarial duties is caring for mail.
This may take the very limited form of sorting and preparing mail
which is brought to and taken from a private office by messenger boys
in a large organization, or it may involve complete charge of every
detail, even to dealing with the post office itself. In most cases, this
work is done in a rather haphazard fashion, as evidenced by the many
errors that are made. However, certain rules do help to systematize
this work, with resulting efficiency. Because mail is the lifeblood of
business, it demands painstaking consideration.

Incoming mail

Though mail is opened in a central department in most large
organizations, letters addressed to a private office, rather than to the
company itself, are generally delivered direct. If you do not have an
automatic or manually operated letter opener, stack the envelopes
with the flaps away from you and open them all before putting down
the letter opener. Date stamp the letters as you remove them from the
envelopes.

23

Sorting the mail

Make room on your desk for several piles, each of which can be devoted to one class of mail. In one pile, which will form the lowest tier of the final pile, will be circulars and bulky mail of lesser importance. Much of this can be thrown away or sent to other people. For instance, an advertisement on filing equipment will be sent to the purchasing department. The middle pile will contain mail of medium importance, but of a nature that can wait until more urgent communications have been taken up. In the third and top pile will be letters of pressing importance or of vital interest.

Some men prefer that their mail be arranged alphabetically. This enables them to go through their desk file easily. Although alphabetic sorting is especially valuable for certain types of mail, such as daily price lists and answers to questionnaires, to which only a cursory glance need be given before filing, an arrangement based on importance is probably better for most general correspondence.

Verifying enclosures

Take great pains to see that each envelope is completely emptied. Some employers demand that all envelopes be opened on three sides and used for scratch paper. This is done not to save paper but to make sure that all contents are removed from each envelope.

Check the enclosure notations on letters to see that everything is found. Some secretaries put a check mark through notations of enclosures to indicate that they were received when the letter was opened. Omissions should be carefully noted on a letter. Read the letter through hastily to see that all intended enclosures were noted at the bottom. Frequently enclosures that were meant to be sent are not included. A firm sent a letter of transmittal to cover a check for $25,-000 with which it was opening an account with a new bank. The secretary wrote the letter and dispatched it by special messenger, but did not include the check. Such a thoughtless error seems impossible, but some so-called secretaries are "keepers of secrets" only because they have neither life nor perception enough to know what they are doing most of the time. Their constant daydreaming causes them to do strange things. Surely a letter in which no item other than an enclosure is discussed ought to make some impression on the writer.

Attach enclosures to the top of the letter with a flat clip, if this has not already been done by the sender.

Checking remittances

Remittances should always be checked with the letter of transmittal to see that they are correct. Some notation should be recorded on the letter if you keep the check for deposit.

Attaching necessary data

If you find that other correspondence or data are needed to answer certain letters, make shorthand notes of the matter as you read through the mail. When you have finished sorting the mail, locate this material and clip it to the letters and put them in their proper place in the mail pile. Carbon copies of previous correspondence, figures of amounts on your books, and other information may be included among the data which will be necessary to answer some letters.

If an address or signature is not included, or if it might not be plain to the one answering the letter, copy the information clearly from the envelope or from some other source.

Making a digest of the mail

A summary of the contents of the day's mail is sometimes necessary, especially if the employer is away and will call you during the day. It is impractical in most cases to read an entire letter over the telephone, especially since a long letter can often be condensed into a few words. For instance, a two-page letter can be reduced to: "Mr. Harris has written you at length on conditions in his territory. He wants you to come out there next week." A digest which you make to read over the telephone may be mailed to an absent executive. (See Chapter

Eight on the business trip.) A few businessmen allow their secretaries to handle all mail, referring to a digest to inform themselves of its contents.

In reading mail, it is suggested by some books that all important parts be underscored to enable the busy man to glance through it quickly. Before attempting this, be sure your employer does not object to having mail marked up with a pencil. Some secretaries put a mark only under references to enclosures.

Writing answers without directions

Never hesitate to use your own ability to write letters. Try this out on a few letters first and gradually increase the number as you become accustomed to the work. No businessman should be compelled to dictate a letter which you can answer. Requests for information usually make an easy starting point. On her second day in the office, one girl surprised her employer with half a dozen replies attached to the morning's mail by ten o'clock. The secretary had looked in the files, observed the form used on similar correspondence, and written the letters from data which she had been able to procure. The employer was much amused at first, but some of the letters did not have to be changed. After an explanation of why certain letters had to be rewritten, the girl was able to write more and better letters each morning. This ability to handle correspondence independently usually distinguishes a secretary from a stenographer.

Handling confidential mail

Be especially careful not to open mail marked *personal* or *confidential*. It is usually wise to segregate these specially directed letters as you hastily go through the morning mail. The practice of mailing advertising and begging letters with confidential or personal notations on them has led many businessmen to entrust the opening of personally marked mail to their secretaries. Even with permission to open confidential letters, however, it is courteous to err on the side of caution. If you have opened a letter which you know your employer would rather you did not read, close it up again at once. You would not relish having your employer read a personal letter which might come to the office for you; as a matter of honor, therefore, you should accord him the same courtesy. Prying tendencies in a secretary destroy the confidence of an employer who has been accustomed to respect for his personal property. You cannot afford to do anything which will shake your employer's confidence in your discretion and integrity.

Mail pickup and delivery

In many offices triple-decker trays of wood or metal are used for mail-delivery and pickup purposes. The bottom shelf receives carbon copies and matter that is to be taken to the general files; the second division receives outgoing mail and the top incoming deliveries. This arrangement sorts mail so that messengers can quickly handle each type on regular trips. If you are using such a container, turn correspondence for the files face downward, to conceal it from the public gaze.

Many executives use a desk pad very much like a leather-bound tablet to hold mail. Different sections of the pad are marked to show their contents. In a section of this folder designated *Current Mail,* you will put the morning mail which you are bringing to your employer's attention. If no such file is available, place the mail in a manila folder. Mail placed openly on your employer's desk invites inspection by anyone who happens to enter his office.

Outgoing mail

Note three things carefully before putting an outgoing letter into its envelope:

1. That the signature is appended.
2. That all enclosures are included.
3. That the inside address corresponds with that on the envelope.

The necessity for checking these points would seem to be self-evident, but few secretaries have learned the essential value of this final-check system in mailing every letter. Much mail goes astray because of carelessness in this respect. A surprisingly large number of letters go into the mail without signatures.

Everyone has heard of instances such as that of the old maid who wrote to a widower friend and to her sister on the same day. In each letter she used the salutation *Dearest*. In one she requested that a bottle of hair dye be purchased so that she would get it the following day. The next night the widower appeared with the hair dye, much to the lady's discomfiture. This was easily patched up, but nothing she could do was effective in muzzling her several nephews, who delighted in the contents of the letter their mother received. This is amusing, but grave errors can be made by the secretary who does not make it a practice to compare addresses. Just because you put the flap of each envelope over the top of its letter as you typed it is no reason to feel assured that it is still there after your employer has signed the mail. One often wonders how some men can get a pile of mail into the mess in which it comes back from their desks.

Be sure that each letter is correctly folded and supplied with sufficient postage before it is put in the outgoing section of the file basket, if this work is not done in a mail department. If the contents are valuable or confidential, it is always advisable to see that a letter is securely sealed.

Never hand carbon copies to your employer, but neither should you file them until the letters have been mailed, because if changes are made in letters, they must be added to the carbon as well as to the original. Also, an unfiled carbon can easily be destroyed if the letter is not sent.

Items accompanying correspondence

Items of little weight should be sent together with a letter in the original envelope. These enclosures should be attached to the upper left-hand corner of the letter. A small clip is best for this purpose, because it does not tear the paper. Enclosures that are to remain attached to a letter in the addressee's files should be fastened by some form of permanent stapling rather than by a removable clip. A small item such as a check may be placed on the face of the letterhead, but anything large enough to interfere with the reading of the letter should be attached to the reverse side.

Heavy items should not be enclosed in a letter but should be sent in a separate package. This second package, if it can be sent under a different rating, often saves postage. If you say you are sending something "under separate cover," be sure that you do so the same day. It is most annoying for a correspondent to have to hold a letter several days before receiving the companion package. Notations of packages being sent under separate cover should always be put on a tickler memorandum pad at the time you write the letter. You thus make sure that the mailing of an accompanying package will not escape your attention. A first-class letter may be attached to a package which goes at a different rate, but it should be clearly marked, "This Envelope Contains a Letter," because many persons who open packages throw the wrapping away with the letter attached.

If coins are sent through the mail, they should be enclosed in a coin card, which holds the metal pieces near the bottom of the envelope so that they will not interfere with the stamping machines in the post office. Small remittances should usually be made in stamps.

Addressing envelopes

Shadowing on cards and envelopes comes from improperly securing the writing surface. It is imperative to see that both sides of the card are fastened to the typewriter platen by means of paper fingers or an envelope guide, depending upon the machine used.

Usually no part of letter writing is more poorly executed than the addressing of an envelope. An address is often simply thrown at the face of the envelope, with no thought of artistic arrangement. Perhaps the writer thinks the envelope will be destroyed before anyone of importance sees it! Begin to write the address just below the middle of the envelope, centering the first line. Indent other lines five or ten spaces, according to the relative length of each line. Of course, placement will depend to some extent upon the address. Write in full the name of the state, and the words *street, avenue,* or *company.* Spacing and arrangement should correspond to the inside address of a letter.

If the inside address is in block style, the envelope address should conform.

While artistry is desirable in typing addresses, correctness is absolutely essential. Striking a wrong figure may make it impossible to effect delivery of a letter, thereby wasting time until the letter is returned. On one occasion, a very important letter was typed beautifully, but the secretary typed the street number as 1160 instead of 1060. This mistake caused five days' delay in the delivery of the letter.

One cannot take too great care in typing envelope addresses. Not only does an incorrectly written name incur difficulty in delivery, but it frequently offends the person receiving it. The natural reaction is to feel that a firm capable of such carelessness would not be careful about business matters.

The *care of* or *attention* line should be placed in the lower left-hand corner, unless an address is so short that it can form the second line of the main address. When the notation *personal* or *confidential* is used it should be typed and underscored at the left-hand side of the envelope, about three single spaces above the first line of the address. A space between the letters of these words will bring them out clearly. In cases where extreme caution is called for, some secretaries write these words in longhand to attract the attention of the person opening the mail. If the letter is to go special delivery, the words are placed to the right of, and approximately three spaces above, the first line of the address.

Window envelopes are often used for statements and certain kinds of routine mail. Transparent windows make it unnecessary to address an envelope and preclude all possibility of sending bills to the wrong addressee. However, bills or letters for window envelopes are generally poorly folded; in fact, one sometimes wonders how secretaries can fold letters into so many odd shapes. Contrary to the usual method for folding letters, an inside address must be folded back to be seen through a window envelope. The contents should fit into the envelope snugly, in order to prevent the address from being moved to a position in which it cannot be read easily. This necessitates finding a uniform place for typing the address on a letter or statement.

In order to assist postal employees, confine your mail as nearly as possible to number six and number ten envelopes. Odd-sized letters make the working of automatic canceling machines slower. Even the slightest delay is important, as some of these machines are geared to stamp from ten to twenty thousand letters an hour. Avoid including hard objects such as money, samples, and buttons as they jam canceling machines.

Packages should have labels pasted on them, or they should be addressed in handwriting commensurate with the size of the package. Write a return address on the package unless it is printed on the label.

Using postal cards

Enclose a self-addressed postal card in a letter when you want a brief return message that is not confidential. The card can be marked, signed and mailed with practically no effort, and therefore is an excellent method of securing replies.

Machines are taking over

Not so long ago a mailing of any size or the collating of a multi-page report disrupted the entire office staff. Everyone had to pitch in, either spreading papers around on every flat bit of space available and then picking them up again in numerical order, or folding letters, stuffing envelopes, and sealing and stamping the mailing.

Modern machines do all that work. They collate, fold, stuff envelopes, seal and stamp. If bulk mailings and bulky reports are common in your business, your employer will be interested in learning about machines that prevent high-salary employees from spending time on this type of work.

If the times when your office undertakes a huge mailing are infrequent, you would be well advised to call for an estimate from one of the "Letter" and "Mailing" services listed in the classified telephone directory. These firms will do the job at a flat fee, sending the letter either to your mailing list or to their own. A charge is made in the latter instance.

Redemption of postage

Government stamped envelopes, even when spoiled by mistakes in the address, can be redeemed at the post office for the full amount of the postage.

Postal cards which are not used also may be redeemed, the rate being three-fourths of the original value.

Stamp payments which are received through the mail in a torn or ruined condition can usually be exchanged. Unless they are damaged however, there is no refund on stamps.

Mailing lists and address books

In a small office, where the mailing procedure is fairly simple, an indexed address book should be kept. If possible, such a book should also contain the telephone number of each correspondent. Christmas card and other special lists may be put in the back of this book. In large offices a card index may be preferred.

Complicated mailing problems that may arise, for example, when a great deal of advertising is to be sent out, make it necessary to compile mailing lists. These indexes should be made up very carefully, because postage can be wasted in following a poor list. Special lists are frequently drawn from individual sources, but companies found in the classified telephone directories under "Mailing Lists" construct or supply general compilations for different trades. Stencils are usually made for an active mailing list composed of regular customers or subscribers.

A permanent mailing list can degenerate into one of the most useless things in the office if it is not periodically revised. You can help in effecting a perpetual revision by bringing changes to the attention of the person supervising such a list. A man informed the vice-president of a publishing company that he had moved and wanted all future circulars sent to the new address. Six months afterward mail was still being sent to his old place of business; the publishing executive's secretary had neglected to notify the proper department.

The best way to change your own address on any mailing list is to tear the stenciled address from the wrapper and return it to the company with the new address correctly typed below the old one. The number will enable a clerk to locate its old stencil quickly and replace it with a new one. If mail becomes annoying, it is wise to request that your name be removed from the mailing list of the company. When you receive undesirable mail, such as that containing small articles for which a monetary return is expected, you may either write the word *Refused* on the envelope and return it to the post office or throw it away. You are not required to purchase the article, or even to return it, if you do not wish to do so.

Mail schedules

It is said that over seventy-five per cent of the mail in the United States is deposited after four o'clock. If this is true, mail deposited earlier in the day should receive better attention. In order to help avoid congestion, try to mail as many letters as possible at noon or during the day.

One may effect quick delivery by becoming familiar with the schedules of trains, planes, and ships carrying mail, and by posting important letters in time for the service desired. Notice of the arrival and departure of mail ships is published in the daily papers. Speed in dispatch to a boat may be effected by typing on the envelope such an inscription as VIA SS AMERICA.

Kinds of mail

Mail is classified according to type, weight, and destination. The ounce is used as a unit of measure, weights fractionally over an ounce being charged as an extra ounce. Weigh one of your envelopes with a number of your letterheads, so that thereafter you can determine the postage charge by counting the number of sheets. Enclosures will make it necessary to adjust estimates.

Unless you have a mailing department, you must get specific and current information from your post office; but you should have a general idea of the types of mail in common use.

First class

This classification covers all written or typewritten matter. Such mail may be sent anywhere in the United States or its territories. Any of the reproduced forms of imitating handwriting or typewriting are included in this classification. (If twenty or more identical copies of the same reproduced matter are enclosed in one package, they may be entered as third-class matter.) All sealed mail is considered first class. Special delivery stamps may be put on first-class mail. These extra stamps insure prompt delivery at destination, even though no regular delivery is scheduled at the time of receipt.

Second class

This classification covers newspapers and periodicals which have been registered with the Postal Department. Publishers and those sending out periodical literature obtain permission to use this type of mail. Charges vary according to distance and weight.

Third class

Any unsealed material not designated second class is included in this division. Weight limit is *up to* sixteen ounces.

Parcel post (Fourth class mail)

Practically all mail weighing over a pound may be sent by parcel post to points within the United States. Zones are used in computing the destination charge. Rulings enlarging the size of packages, which may be sent by this system are frequently made and the use of parcel post is constantly widening. All packages should be securely wrapped and labeled. A sealed package will be accepted, providing it bears the inscription that the package may be opened for postal inspection. Parcels sent *special handling* will receive the same prompt delivery as first-class mail.

Air mail

Special stamps are provided for air mail, but the same amount in regular stamps will suffice if the words *Via Air Mail* are typed or stamped on a letter or package. Air mail envelopes and stickers may be purchased from any stationery supplier. Air mail may not exceed 70 pounds or 100 inches in length and girth combined.

Registered mail

Important and valuable mail may be *registered* as an additional safeguard. In sending a registered letter—such as notice of an overdue account—to a person who will not acknowledge your letters, it is customary to request a delivery receipt. The letter will not then be released until it is given to the person or his agent; the signed receipt will be returned to you. If you have reason to think that an agent is not giving your letters to the addressee, you may request that a personal receipt be returned. A letter will not then be released until it can be delivered to the person himself. Of course, there is an additional charge for this service. Registered mail may be sent C.O.D. Air mail may be registered.

Insured mail

Valuable third- or fourth-class mail, which cannot be registered, should be *insured*. Insured mail is sent with the understanding that forwarding or return postage is guaranteed by the sender. Return receipt may be had for an extra fee.

Certified mail

Proof of mailing of a first-class letter with no intrinsic value is supplied by *certified mail*. Cheaper than registered mail, it is handled like first-class mail and there is no indemnity. A return receipt can be had for an extra fee.

Cash on delivery mail

Materials which are not paid for may be sent through the mail and the post office will collect the amount—up to $200—plus postage and the C.O.D. fee. The actual amount collected is forwarded to the sender in the form of a money order. The sender must guarantee return and forwarding postage. For additional fees, C.O.D. mail may be sent special delivery or special handling or by air.

Foreign mail

Postage on mail directed to a foreign country varies with the country to which it is being sent and should be weighed at the post office. There are eight types of international mail: Letters and letter packages, post cards, printed matter, samples, commercial paper, small packets, parcel post, and eight-ounce merchandise packages. Consult with post office authorities before sending a package abroad.

Separating the mail

In sending out foreign mail, air mail, or special delivery letters, it is wise to separate such mail from the regular mail at once, in order not to forget the special postage. Letters of more than one or two pages should also be kept in this special pile to facilitate weighing.

Money orders

Money may be sent anywhere in this country and to foreign countries by purchasing a money order at a post office. If the amount is over one hundred dollars, more than one money order must be purchased. Money orders can be cashed at any post office upon identification of the addressee. Money order receipts are easy to locate if stapled to the carbon copy of the letter of transmittal.

Tracing mail

Receipts for money orders and mail should be preserved at least until delivery is acknowledged by the addressee. In case of non-delivery, ask the post office to trace the package or letter. You will be given a blank upon which to record data found on this receipt and other necessary information for identification of the lost piece of mail. Regular first-class mail is not often traced, but postal authorities will attempt to locate a letter, if its loss is reported to them.

Letters may be returned to the sender before they are delivered to the addressee, if for any reason it may be desirable to recall them. For instance, prices may have advanced so much that a quotation is too low, or some serious error may have been discovered in the letter it-self. A telegram must reach the post office at the place of destination in time to intercept delivery. Return instructions are supplied through your own postmaster. The sender who wishes undeliverable mail re-turned to him, must endorse it *Return Requested*.

Other ways to send things

In addition to parcel post, shipments can be made by rail or air express, rail freight, or water.

REA Express will ship anything anywhere by rail or by air, and in addition supplies over forty other services, such as making bank de-posits, paying taxes, and recording deeds.

They pick up and deliver packages and luggage upon request. Save your receipt until delivery is acknowledged. Shipping charges may be prepaid by the shipper or collected from the consignee and C.O.D. service is available. Supplied with proper written instructions and funds, REA Express will purchase articles in distant cities and bring them back to you, and will even redeem pledges at pawn shops.

Air express

By means of air express you can get close to even the most remote outpost of civilization in the world. The classified directory lists the many air lines handling this service.

A consignee must sign for each express package at the time of delivery. Payments for C.O.D. shipments are made to the express company's agent, who delivers the package.

Shipping by freight

Railway freight is used for sending bulky packages or for material upon which immediate delivery is not urgent. Bills of lading are usually made out at the time of delivery of goods to a transportation company, though a temporary receipt may be issued for various parts of a shipment. A bill of lading will later be made out to cover all of the items for which you present receipts. A pick-up and delivery service is available to users.

Freight charges may be paid at the source, but the customary procedure is to have the receiver pay at the time he receives the goods. An arrival notice is sent to the consignee the day the freight reaches its destination. You will have to be careful to bring these notices to the attention of the proper person in your office, because the time for claiming freight is usually limited. If freight cannot be unloaded within the customary two days, or whatever time is specified on the arrival notice, a demurrage charge will be made for storing in warehouses or for holding cars.

Under special conditions, an extension of time may be granted for removing freight. For instance, a builder has ordered a carload of lime; a week of rainy weather makes it impossible to unload this material because water would spoil it. The consignee therefore applies for an extension.

Delivery to and from a transportation company is not made by the railroad companies, all charges for hauling being paid and arranged for by the consignor and the consignee at their respective ends of the route. Cars must be ordered from the railway office in anticipation of a shipment of carload lots.

Water shipments

Shipping by water is similar to railway freight shipping, except that the *bill of lading* is called a *wharf receipt*. The usual time for removing goods is five days from the arrival of a ship. A manifest must be filed with the shipping company for all goods sent to a foreign country.

Shipping documents and correspondence

As a secretary, you will not often be required to assist in the physical handling of express or freight packages, but it pays to have a working knowledge of receipts, bills of lading, and manifests; how to write correspondence regarding tracers, notices, extensions, listings of losses, and various other details.

Be especially careful in typing references to one of these numbered transportation documents. If you want quick service, you must be sure that references are correctly and clearly stated. The number on the bill of lading for a ton of hay may be almost like that on a bushel of walnuts, but one incorrect figure may cause considerable trouble in locating the shipment which you have wrongly designated. Be sure the destination, the date, the consignee, and the consignor are included, so that identification can be made easily.

BOOKS THAT HELP IN LEARNING TO HANDLE OFFICE MAIL

Leonard's Guide (Freight, Express, Parcel Post Rates and Routing), G. R. Leonard and Co., Inc., New York–Chicago

Postal Manual; The Directory of Post Offices; Domestic Postage Rates and Fees; How to Prepare Second- and Third-Class Mailings; Superintendent of Documents, Government Printing Office, Washington, D.C.

Chapter 3

Filing

You must hack through much deposit ere you know for
sure who was it came to burial with such honor in the Files.
—RUDYARD KIPLING

Importance of filing

A person who can file a letter and find it when it is wanted has one
of the indispensable qualifications of a good secretary. If you cannot
produce a paper promptly when it is requested, you lose your employer's confidence. Good will, which may have been created by
painstaking work in other directions, is sacrificed through a single
misstep in filing.

Regardless of how extensive or how elementary your filing system
may be, you must have two basic qualifications: accuracy and a general knowledge of the principles of filing. Remember that the adjective
accurate is not one which can be compared. You cannot be *accurate,
more accurate, most accurate;* you are either *accurate* or *inaccurate.*

Developing accuracy

Because filing cannot be checked for accuracy, as can bookkeeping
or typewriting, you will have to do it more carefully than any other ·
part of your office work. Some secretaries make a practice of looking
at a file, determining the approximate position of a folder, and then,
while gazing in another direction, inserting a letter. Such momentary
carelessness results in time-consuming hunts through adjacent folders
if a letter cannot be found in its proper place. However, these errors
are really not so serious as those caused by a cursory glance at a name

or filing title. A firm may be listed in your files as W. E. Kelly & Company. Your employer, who knows Mr. Kelly, may unconsciously dictate one letter to Wade Kelly & Company. If you are not watchful in filing, this may be filed under *W*, for Wade, Kelly & Company. You will never know you have made a mistake until the letter is requested. A complete search of the files is impossible, so the letter will be given up for lost until you some day find the letter while filing something else in the general correspondence folder for W's.

Filing is one secretarial duty for which you can sit down and calmly plan the best method of operation. (Of course, sitting down to work out the problem refers only to the original filing of a paper and not to locating one which has already been filed.) Never file anything until you are so well acquainted with its classification that you can find it again without hesitancy. If a file is already in operation, go through it and note the disposition that has been made of similar papers. Just because you are in a hurry to get rid of a certain letter is no reason for misfiling it. Keep in mind that the time spent in *filing* is gained in *finding* what you need quickly.

Summed up in three words, *filing and finding* are the basis of efficient operation in this part of secretarial work. One without the other is useless.

Principles of filing

To get the most out of your filing system, it is absolutely necessary that you understand the underlying principles upon which various filing systems are built. Rarely is a single type used alone; rather, most files are built upon a combination of principles. While it is important that you learn filing principles for the sake of correctly placing papers, it is more important that you apply these principles so as to find a document when it is needed. Some inefficient people can expound filing principles well, but are so careless in applying them that their knowledge is useless.

Never get the idea that filing is extremely difficult; the principles underlying filing are easy to understand if they are studied in their simple form and with a constant view to their utilitarian purposes.

Nevertheless, the necessity for constant vigilance in following any filing system does make its operation an ever-present burden.

Chronological filing

The simplest form of all filing systems is based on time sequence. A purely chronological file is often used for personal correspondence and bills. Each letter is put in the folder as it arrives, those coming the first of the month being placed at the bottom and those of each succeeding day on top. When a month is ended, the folder may either be destroyed or put away to be referred to if the occasion arises. This type of file has the advantage of calling attention to correspondents who have been neglected for a long time.

Filing in chronological form is very simple; finding what has been filed is more difficult. If you do not remember the exact day on which a letter came, you may be compelled to search through any number of letters before the one you are looking for is uncovered. For this reason, the system must be supplemented by some other if the material handled becomes bulky. However, the chronological principle is carried through as part of almost all other filing systems.

Alphabetical filing

By far the most widely used form of filing is that built upon some alphabetical division of material to be filed. The simplest form is that in which the names of correspondents are arranged in alphabetical order. Letters received from or sent to people whose names begin with *A* are placed just behind a guide marked *A*, and further classifications and guides are provided for the other letters of the alphabet. Certain little-used letters, such as *X*, *Y*, and *Z*, may be combined under one guide. If a straight alphabetical file becomes burdensome, subdivisions can be made by adding second, third, and even fourth letters to the respective initial guides. For example, one guide may be *Braa*, the following *Brag*, and the third *Bran*. Correspondence with a person named *Brace* would be placed back of the first guide, *Bramley* back of the second, and *Brandon* back of the third. Scientifically worked out subdivisions of the alphabet can be procured from any stationer. These printed tabs are usually much more satisfactory than trying to make a division of your own.

Difficulty in alphabetizing

Alphabetic filing appears very easy on the surface, but give an average secretary two hundred letters to file under one letter of the alphabet and the results will be astonishing. An experiment with fifty-four students in a large high school revealed that only one student could arrange the letters correctly. Files were returned to some individuals as many as fourteen times before they could locate their errors. If this was true of high-school students, one can only guess at the condition of the files in offices where employees are not subject to systematic checking and where many who use the files have not had the advantage of a good filing course. Under such conditions one should not be surprised that correspondence cannot be located readily; probably it is a miracle that it can be found at all.

Spend enough time on alphabetizing to be able to recognize instantly a name that is out of order. The degree to which this ability can be attained was illustrated recently by a little incident aboard a transatlantic liner taking a group of tourists abroad. Shortly after leaving port, the members of the tour each received a passenger list. An hour later, a cablegram was received for a man named *Zucker*. When consulted, the conductor of the tour glanced quickly at his list and said: "We have no one by that name." His secretary brought to his attention the fact that this passenger was listed but in the wrong place. She had noticed that *Zupke* appeared before *Zucker*. "As those were the only names not in proper sequence," she told her employer, "they stood out from the rest." Would you, as a secretary, have detected such an error?

Rules for alphabetizing

If you are in doubt as to the placing of a name, consult a telephone directory. Compilers of these directories have spent much time in perfecting an alphabetic list which you can safely follow as an authority. However, you will be able to improve your own filing ability if you observe the following guides for alphabetic filing:

1. The first letter is not enough to use in filing. Classification should be carried through to the second, third, and succeeding letters of a subject title. The capital letters in the following illustration indicate which letter determines filing position.

> AarEn
> AarOns
> AaronsEn
> AaronsOn
> AbrahAms
> AbrahDo

2. Always file general correspondence under the surname. When indexing names, write the surname, followed by a comma, and then write the given names or initials in order.

> Adams, Oliver G.

3. When the same surname is common to several people, the given name will form the basis for filing.

> Adams, BLanche E.
> Adams, BOris E.
> Adams, BRandon D.

4. When a name is carried through several generations, the one who first bore the name should appear before the rest.

> Harris, Philip R., Sr.
> Harris, Philip R., Jr.
> Harris, Philip R., 3rd.

5. When initials are used in some cases and given names in others, the initials should be placed first in the order determined by the second initial. Given names should then follow in their proper order, as indicated by the middle initial.

> Baker, G. D.
> Baker, G. E.
> Baker, G. T.
> Baker, George A.

> Baker, George M.
> Baker, Grace

6. Such designations as *company, hotel, corporation,* and *school* are filed as though they were part of a name.

> James Apartment, The
> James, Bernard
> James & Company
> James Corporation, The
> James, F. W.
> James Hotel

7. Prefix syllables, such as *la, de, di, van, von, O', Mac, Mc,* and others, should be included with surnames and not treated as initials.

> Davis, James
> de Lima, J. D.
> di Gierge, M. B.
> du Pont, A. I.
>
> Macarow, Prentice
> MacArthur, Phillip
> McArthur, Phillip
>
> Oteale, John
> O'Tool, James

8. When the entire name is used to designate a building or an institution, index it as a unit.

> Alexander Hamilton Institute (*not* Hamilton,
>   Alexander, Institute)
> Joseph Ratti Hospital
> Laura Spellman Hall
> Robert E. Lee Memorial

9. Material filed under each name in an alphabetic system should be arranged in chronological order, with the latest date on top, because recent correspondence is most likely to be used. It is a nuisance to have to hunt through twenty-five letters to find one that might have been found quickly had the files been arranged with respect to time sequence.

> Adams, Henry
> January 15, 1940
> January 7, 1940

April 23, 1939
February 7, 1939

Put correspondence of most recent dates at the front of a file folder. For this reason a letter should not be inserted in a file drawer until the folder has been taken from the file and opened far enough so that dates can be seen clearly.

Subject filing

The subject of certain correspondence is more important than the name of the correspondent. In such cases a *subject file* can be used to advantage. Subjects are also often interspersed among names in a straight alphabetic file; or subject folders can be intermingled with name folders in a single file; in fact, the user of a file seldom stops to think whether he is filing by subject or by name. However, a mixture of both systems leaves the way open to many mistakes. The head of a large secretarial school says that she cannot get girls to file under the subject. If she directs a memorandum to *E. H. Blake, head of the Psychology Department,* the secretary will open up a new folder for *Blake, E. H.,* instead of filing the memorandum under *Psychology Department.*

Knowledge of business essential

A strict subject file is less commonly used but no less important to understand. You cannot construct a subject file unless you are thoroughly familiar with the material which is to be filed. For example, a young woman working for a dress manufacturer who is collecting information on women's garments would probably have little difficulty in handling a subject file in her work; she would not file a magazine article on slipper buckles under *Hats.* On the other hand, it takes an experienced person to manipulate a legal or library subject file. In the book title, *Trusts, Pools, and Combinations,* the word *trust* denotes combinations prohibited by Federal antitrust laws. A professor looking for this book in a library could not find it on the proper shelf. Then it occurred to him that it might have been placed among books on trust companies and banks. Sure enough, it was there that he found it. Similar misplacements are made by many secretaries, who file before they think.

Changing the basis of classification

Great care will have to be taken in shifting the basis of subject classification in compiling a subject file, for only by careful and intelligent handling will you secure logical headings and prevent duplication and confusion of subjects. A subject should be sufficiently inclusive to embrace all material desired, but it should be equally exclusive in order not to include extraneous matter.

In keeping a subject file for mailing purposes, the danger of duplication must always be borne in mind, not only to prevent waste of postage but also to avoid incurring the scorn of the man who receives five letters telling him "this offer is being made only to a selected few."

Subdivisions of a subject

When a subject file becomes bulky, its main topics must be broken down. Subtopics are frequently arranged in alphabetical order. One of the common files in an office is that of "Insurance." It is quite impossible to refer to a policy or letter readily if all material is kept in one folder. New folders will probably be made to cover the general groupings of insurance used in an office somewhat as follows:

> Insurance, Accident
> Insurance, Automobile
> Insurance, Burglary
> Insurance, Casualty
> Insurance, Fire
> Insurance, Group
> Insurance, Registered Mail

If policies make the folders too bulky to handle, a double division of the subject of insurance may be made, so that the front section of folders may be used for correspondence and the back section for policies. Each section will include a folder for the various headings grouped under insurance.

The subject index

Very often several subjects may be discussed in a single piece of correspondence to be filed, so that it becomes necessary to make a subject index on three-by-five-inch index cards. The subject treated should be typed on a card, together with directions for locating the proper folder. Some companies often add a brief digest of the contents of the correspondence in question. The following arrangement might be applied to cards made out for a policy covering a group of officers in an organization:

GROUP INSURANCE

John Hancock Insurance Policy
#1497235   9/14/60
Covering Class One officers.

JOHN HANCOCK INSURANCE COMPANY

Policy #1497235   9/14/60
Group insurance covering
Class One officers.

OFFICERS' INSURANCE

John Hancock Insurance Policy
#1497235   9/14/60
Group policy covering Class One.

The three typed cards are put into an index box in order to make it easy to find material located in a file.

Time element in operation of indexed files

As a secretary, you will generally find your time at a premium. Consequently, your greatest problem in maintaining a subject file will be the ever-present danger that, in the rush of other work, a card index may be slighted. Only a full realization of the hopeless muddle that will result if entries on cards are deficient can save you from inefficiently operating an extensive subject file. For this reason, be sure, before installing such a system, that its merits far outweigh the difficulties you may encounter. A filing department—the main function of which is to keep correspondence—is much better able to supervise a complicated filing system properly than is a busy secretary whose many other duties encroach upon filing time.

Numerical filing

When a number is assigned to each paper, there is little excuse for disorder in files. Forms on which numbers are printed are easy to arrange. When these numbers must be entered by hand, extra care should be taken to write the figures correctly and legibly. Do not make the mistake, for example, of copying *731* for *713*.

Invoices, checks, orders, and similar instruments are commonly filed numerically. These documents are so important that the chance of error must be reduced to a minimum. When you refer to anything in a numerical file, check the numbers carefully. The slightest deviation in copying a number may necessitate hours of work in locating a paper. The only other key is usually the date, which may mean that a thousand orders will have to be gone over before the right paper on which a wrong number was written is turned up. Accuracy is especially important in writing letters that refer to an invoice number of another firm. Lack of accuracy in checking your figures may cause much inconvenience to your correspondent.

A numerical arrangement may be used to simplify a subject file. For example, your employer may be assigned the task of interviewing prospective employees. Suppose the only positions for which applications are received are for salesclerks, bookkeepers, and shipping clerks, and that in each case the applicants are to be classified on the basis of experience or lack of experience. You might set up an index for the applications received as follows:

      1. Salesclerks
          a. Experienced
          b. Inexperienced

   2. Bookkeepers
      a. Experienced
      b. Inexperienced
   3. Shipping clerks
      a. Experienced
      b. Inexperienced

If the index number for applications were *600,* the individual classification number would follow. Thus an application from an inexperienced bookkeeper would be filed *600-2b.* The number *600* indicates that the form is an application for a position; *2b* indicates that the applicant is an inexperienced bookkeeper.

The application would be placed in the folder containing all forms *600-2b,* in its proper alphabetical order. Time sequence might be provided for by starting new files monthly, quarterly, semiannually, or yearly.

The Dewey system

The Dewey classification, prepared by Melvil Dewey and used extensively by libraries, divides the entire field of human knowledge into nine groups, with a tenth group covering encyclopedias, periodicals, and works of too general a character to be placed in any of the other nine divisions. This system uses a combination of subject and numerical indexing.

The ten groups are:

000 General works	500 Natural science
100 Philosophy	600 Useful arts
200 Religion	700 Fine arts
300 Sociology	800 Literature
400 Philology	900 History

Useful arts, *600,* may be further divided into nine parts:

600 Useful arts	650 Communication, commerce
610 Medicine	660 Chemical technology
620 Engineering	670 Manufactures
630 Agriculture	680 Mechanical trades
640 Domestic economy	690 Building

If *Engineering, 620* (or any one of the other divisions), were taken, it, too, might be broken down into nine subdivisions:

620 Engineering
621 Mechanical engineering
622 Mining engineering

623 Military and naval engineering

624 Bridges and roofs

625 Railroad and road engineering
626 Canal engineering
627 River, harbor, and general hydraulic engineering
628 Sanitary engineering—water works
629 Other branches of engineering

The decimal system, as the Dewey system is sometimes called, is generally maintained by an extensive filing department, and the secretary is seldom called upon to install one. However, if you are familiar with the general scheme as outlined above, you may make intelligent use of a library.[1]

Geographical filing

When a firm's business is divided into territories, some form of geographic filing is usually advisable in order that each division may be clearly identified. The basis of classification may be branch office territories, sections covered by different salesmen and distributing agents, or political units—such as states, counties, towns, or wards. Under these broad geographic headings, the supplementary arrangement may be alphabetic, topical, chronological, numerical, or, as is frequently the case, a combination of all or several of these principles.

Suppose you are keeping a customers' credit file from which you approve for shipment orders sent in by salesmen. If all names in the Philadelphia territory are in one division and those belonging to Detroit territory in another, locating a name will be comparatively easy. Not only will the files be less unwieldy but, because of their setup, several people will be enabled to work at them simultaneously.

[1] Books describing the Melvil Dewey system may be obtained at most public libraries. The Library of Congress has worked out a system of this kind for indexing the unlimited variety of books submitted for copyright which is commonly called the L.C. system. A descriptive pamphlet can be procured from the Superintendent of Documents, Washington, D.C., for a small fee.

Special types of files

The foregoing review of the principles upon which filing systems are built should aid you in applying the fundamentals of filing. Next, it will be advisable to consider some of the commonly used files of special types which you, as a secretary, may wish to adapt to particular work in your office.

The tickler file

Tickler files are the mainspring of efficiency in any office. They may take the form of a simple calendar index, a card file, or a chronological folder file. Any of these forms will serve to bring a matter to your mind. Memory is a wonderful thing, yet it must not be trusted too far. A girl became secretary to a man who prided himself on his memory. She made a shorthand note of everything he told her. For the first few days he was annoyed and asked her to "remember some things." Laughingly, she replied: "I shall, when I know something to remember." During the next week she reminded him of a promise to get some data for another officer, of an important dinner engagement, and of a new fund drive board meeting—all things that he had forgotten. Within a month he had learned to depend upon her shorthand notations to such an extent that, when he was not certain she had heard an appointment, he would ask: "Will you make a note of that for me, Miss Smith?" Your value will increase directly in proportion to your ability to make yourself a human tickler file.

The calendar pad

In many offices a calendar pad is all that is needed to keep full and accurate records of matters to be attended to. Often these daily memorandum sheets are divided into hourly periods. As each item is completed, draw a line through the notation, and do not discard a sheet with uncancelled items. In this way you can tell when you have taken care of all matters. Transfer a notation to the next day's work if advisable.

Recurrent items such as lodge dues, rent, insurance premiums, taxes, and anniversaries should be placed on the calendar for the entire year. If you do not have time to finish the yearly schedule at one time, make a note on the last entry to indicate that the notations have not been completed. In this way you will guard against forgetting to list some important date.

The card index

A card index tickler usually has a dated guide, consisting of thirty-one numbers, which divides a month's notations. As each day's work is finished, the guide for that date is placed at the back of the box in order to provide for that same date the following month. A small calendar sheet for both the current and the following months may be pasted in the cover of the box, so that a glance may confirm each date, thereby eliminating guessing at the dates upon which certain days of that week fall. At the beginning of each month, go through the file and remove the guides of all dates falling on Sundays and holidays. Placing these in the back of the file precludes the possibility of scheduling work for dates when the office is closed.

As you find that certain matters are to be taken up at some future date, make out a card similar to the following for each one:

4/20
Shall probably hear from James Smith today regarding acceptance of our offer. Write him if no word by 5/1.

As each task is completed, cancel the card. If the card directing attention to James Smith's acceptance has not been removed at the end of the day, transfer it to the next day's business. Repeat this operation until May 1, when you will see to it that a letter is sent to Mr. Smith. Between April 20 and May 1, however, you will have been constantly reminded to be on the alert for the receipt of the acceptance.

The chronological folder file

The calendar pad and the card file are merely indexes; they do not provide space for storing the materials necessary for carrying out their daily instructions. For this reason, some firms make extensive use of the dated folder file, sometimes called the "up file," which has the advantage of being large enough to include necessary papers.

As the name indicates, this file contains material which must be brought up for the attention of the executive on the day specified. For example, each bill, as it arrives, is put into the dated folder to insure payment in time to take cash discounts. Letters which need future attention are filed under the date when the matter is to come up again. The secretary removes the current folder from the cabinet upon her employer's arrival each morning, in order to go over the business for the day.

Some firms file an extra carbon copy of all correspondence to which answers are anticipated. The date when a reply can be reasonably expected is used for the first date under which the copy of the letter is filed. The correspondence is transferred to the next date if the reply is delayed, and a follow-up may be written if any undue length of time lapses.

The folder system is very helpful where instructions concerning a particular matter are given to various persons in the concern. In such cases, you should make two copies of the instructions, one to be sent to the subordinate who is to put them into effect and the other to be placed in an "up file" until the day when they are to be carried out. Thus the executive is reminded to make inquiries at that time as to whether the job has been completed. If he finds that the work has not been finished, he can make a notation of the cause of the delay and the time for which the work has been promised. The instructions can then be refiled and followed up again on a future date.

Officials who pay the firm's bills find that a folder system enables them to write checks covering payments which fall due during a period when they expect to be away from the office. Attach each check to the invoice and put the folder back in the safe. When the day arrives for payment, all you have to do is mail these checks. A folder tickler is especially valuable in real-estate offices, where rent, insurance, taxes, and other important items need prompt attention. Follow-up files containing checks and similar valuable instruments should be kept in a vault.

Odd moments may be utilized in addressing envelopes for the

checks, in writing letters of transmittal, and in otherwise anticipating work which may confront you on a busy day. A tickler file is an ideal place for storing such completed work until it is needed.

The docket file

A concentrated form of subject filing commonly used in certain types of business, but which is often not generally understood, is a docket file. Each letter or instrument, as it comes in, is placed in its subject folder in chronological order and bound. Papers arranged in the form of a tablet can be inspected without danger of loss through any one leaf becoming loose. When the subject is completed, the docket is closed. Before the packet is placed in the "completed business" section of a file, an inscription, of which the illustration below is typical, is placed on its side.

GREENWOOD ELEVATOR COMPANY,
116 Bank Street,
New York City

Equipment installed in

Curtis Building

1817 East Street,

Syracuse, N.Y.

Contract awarded April 18, 19—
Final inspection January 7, 19—
Fire number C-1843

Docket filing is used extensively in law offices, where it is desirable to have all papers on a given case neatly assembled. Contractors often use a double docket folder for keeping records of building operations—one side for legal papers, such as the original contract and agreements for subletting parts of the contract, and the other side for correspondence, bills, and other papers. When the building is completed, the docket is closed and filed until the firm is no longer legally liable for any of the work.

Investment banking houses use docket files in their purchasing departments for recording matters relative to security issues which they are sponsoring and in their syndicate departments for keeping data on particular syndicate operations.

The overlapping envelope file

A visible index of the contents of envelopes may be made by using some form of the overlapping envelope file. Each envelope is placed in a frame which forces the top edge just a little above that of the envelope below it. This makes it possible to write the name or index on the visible space. The contents of such a file is usually arranged alphabetically or numerically. In typing the inscription at the top of an envelope, begin each name an equal number of spaces from the edge, so that the list will appear straight when envelopes are inserted under one another. A saw-toothed right-hand margin makes the finding of a particular envelope difficult.

The holder is sometimes a steel frame with grooves in which the envelopes are inserted. The upright type of file is valuable in payroll and registration offices but is often unsightly in a private office, where the flat or tablet holder can be used to better advantage. A similar file may be used for cards, hundreds of cards being attached to an upright file with several wings, or in a book file with a number of leaves.

The clipping file

A clipping file is usually constructed on a subject basis, though sometimes classification is left entirely to a comprehensive index. Either a loose-leaf or bound book may be used, the size of which will depend upon the volume of clippings it is estimated will accumulate. In some cases, clippings are posted on loose sheets to be placed in a folder. In any event, do not paste clippings as you would pictures in a photograph album, for this method takes up needless space. The entire article need not be seen at a glance, as is the case when looking at a photograph. Paste only the top edge of the clipping, so that the second column can be inserted underneath. The left edge of the second clipping should be pasted to the left edge of the page. The next clipping can be similarly attached about an inch to the right and under the first clipping. This overlapping makes it possible to attach an incredible number of items on a single page.

Clipping agencies will comb thoroughly through current literature for articles on any designated subject. These bureaus will be found listed in a classified telephone directory under "Press Clipping Bureaus."

While the clipping bureau service is valuable in making a thorough survey of current news on any one subject, a variety of interests will necessitate finding your own material. You can best do this by going through the papers with a colored pencil in hand and marking the articles you plan to save. Write the *name of the publication* and the *date of issue* across the top of each article. After reading and labeling the articles, you can quickly cut out the marked items. This method enables you to choose between two articles appearing on opposite sides of a paper. If you clip the first article before you have read the second, you may miss the latter altogether, even though that may be the more important of the two. If you want both items, get another copy of the paper. Back numbers of a paper or magazine may be purchased—at an extra charge—by sending for them to the publishers.

Indexing and cross-indexing

The index to any type of file may be in the form either of guides on the files themselves or a separate listing on cards. It should contain all the information necessary to locate given material. Place similar information in a uniform position in the index. Typewritten inscriptions are usually preferable, because handwriting lacks uniformity.

If you are indexing magazine articles, you will probably use the following arrangement:

1. Your classification.
2. Name of the article.
3. Name of the author.
4. Name of the publication.
5. Date.

6. A notation as to value, contents, and so forth. (This item may be omitted when its contents are connoted by the title of the article.)

7. Where the article is to be found. (If it is to be found under the classification indicated in item one, number seven is omitted.)

Cross-indexing is a part of filing that is usually neglected. If a letter is being filed under "Instructions," probably another memorandum card should be filed under "Accounting Department" and still another under "James Grant," the accountant to whom the instructions are addressed. Of course, this involves making three cards, but it will help you find an elusive letter or memorandum when you have forgotten the heading under which it was filed.

Codes are extensively used in indexes, especially in numerical and subject files. Beware of misinterpreting the code when you assign a symbol.

Suggestions for keeping files in order

If filing is to be an important part of your work, you will probably wish to make a thorough study of the subject. The breadth of the field is indicated by the great number of books devoted exclusively to its study and by the fact that one examination on filing lasted nine hours.

Become familiar with some of the commercial indexes if you are keeping trade information. People who compile these indexes spend much time in determining the best titles for your particular trade. Your work can be improved and simplified by comparing subject titles you are using with those used in these printed indexes and by adapting such good features as you may find.

Use a stapling machine to fasten papers together. Clips will make your files bulky and pins are likely to prick your fingers. The staple should be attached at the upper left-hand corner of a letter, the accepted place for fastening papers together.

Subject classifications written for filing purposes should appear in the upper right-hand corner of a letter, so that they can be seen when glancing at the date. Some letterheads have a place expressly provided for typing the subject; many firms insist that it be typed on the line below the salutation. Even though the title is not indicated on the original letter, it should be placed on all carbon copies. When a title on an incoming letter does not correspond with your file heading, be sure to write in your own classification.

A colored pencil mark underscoring the filing index—whether the address, typewritten subject, firm name in the letterhead, or signature of the letter—will help you when you are ready to file if the subject is not specially written under the date. This underscoring at the time of the original reading or filing will make it unnecessary to reread any letter which you may have occasion to refile.

If you keep a card index to your subject file, always indicate when the subject was opened up. Then you will not have to go back over files made inactive before the new subject was added.

Copies of letters are a help

Make several copies of a letter if you cannot determine offhand exactly under which heading it should be filed. Some letters should be cross-filed under several headings. In this way you will be able to locate copies when they are requested.

If you feel that making extra copies entails too much work, you can save time by writing the address on a sheet and indicating the heading under which you have filed the letter. File this sheet in the folder for which you have no copy of the letter.

Use of colored cards and clips

Colors are used extensively to indicate which customers are prospects for special lines. Certainly it would be futile for an electric supply company to send circulars on washing machines to a woman living in a hotel apartment. By putting prospects for radios on pink cards and prospects for washing machines on yellow ones, for example, the sales department can sort cards quickly when a special sales effort on any one item is to be launched.

Colored cards and clips are often used to call attention to special information. The color is in the nature of a code and has the advantage of being understood only by those using the data. A red card in a box of white ones will clearly indicate that a customer is a questionable credit risk, without necessitating any derogatory comment in writing.

Removable signals may be used to indicate when a customer's account is past due. These signals may be paper pasters or movable clips, which can readily be changed in position or replaced by a signal of another color.

If customers are to be circularized on several matters, duplicate their names on cards of several different colors. Highly efficient systems operated with perforated cards make selection almost automatic. A patented selector goes through and picks out all cards through which a hole has been punched in a position to indicate a prospect, say, for a washing machine. With these machines only one card is needed for a prospective customer of a number of products, because perforations may be made in different positions on the card to indicate various products. This principle may be used in smaller systems, but naturally hand selection is slower.

Handling odd-sized reports

If odd-sized reports are sent to you, it may be necessary to fold them to fit an ordinary filing cabinet or book binder. Do not go to the expense of having a special binder made for such reports unless you are sure they will be continued over a long period of time. When such unstandardized reports arrive, inform your employer that they do not fit into the standard filing equipment. Possibly they may be changed to standard size, or, if it becomes necessary to route them to a number of departments, he may recommend photostating, which permits the making of copies of standard size regardless of the size of the original.

Protecting your files against borrowers

Protect yourself by making careful notations when someone takes a folder or a letter from your file. If you ask a man some such indefinite question as, "Did you take our purchase folder?" the answer will probably be a defensive "No." If, on the other hand, you tactfully ask, "Are you through with the purchase folder you borrowed from our files last Friday?" an individual will usually make every effort to think what he did with that folder.

Letter hunting is a costly sport. Responsibility for taking a letter from a file should always be fixed upon a particular person. The accompanying form (see Fig. 1) is a written instruction to a file clerk to get a certain letter and send it to an individual who accepts responsibility for it. Later the clerk will not have to spend hours searching for that letter, because his record will show who now has it. As a secretary, you may keep a very small file, and requests for your material may be too infrequent to warrant having a printed card system. However, it is advisable to keep on hand in the front of your file a few typed cards

LETTER TAKEN FROM FILES To File Clerk: Date——19—	Please get ☐ a letter from ☐ copy of letter to	Name ——————— Company ——————— Address ——————— Dated ——————— Other Identification ——— ——————— ——————— ———————

Send it to ————————————
Department ————————————

NOTICE TO FILE CLERK

This form must be put in the file in place of the correspondence requested,
When correspondence is returned, remove this form.

Requested by ————————————
Department ————————————
Handled by ——————————Date————
File Clerk

Figure 1. Notice to File Clerk

that may be filled in easily. Without some guide, you will omit necessary information when you hurriedly make a memorandum of the fact that someone is taking part of your correspondence.

If a man gets a letter to which is clipped a notation that the letter is to be returned to you, he is not likely to forget where it came from. At the same time, clip another card to your folder to indicate the disposition of its contents. Many secretaries prefer letter-sized sheets for recording missing correspondence, because the card may slip down in the folder where it cannot easily be seen.

A time allowance for borrowers is usually a very effective way of speeding up the return of papers. By asking a person when he will be able to return a file, you impress upon him his responsibility in caring for the material. If you appear with a written record that a certain file was to have been returned yesterday, the offender, realizing that you are supervising your files systematically, will probably try to return future material promptly.

The location of correspondence permanently removed from a folder should be carefully noted on the folder.

Physical care of contents of files

Close the drawers of your files when you are not using them. Even efficient secretaries have the annoying habit of pushing drawers only partly shut. Aside from the danger of personal injury from walking into protruding corners, nothing makes an office look more untidy than several partly open drawers.

Lock the files when you leave for the day. After some material has been unceremoniously removed from them, you will probably learn this duty from bitter experience.

Watch to see that the edges of papers do not prevent the locks of your file from catching. One secretary always locked her files, but two drawers could be easily opened. She was unaware of this until information that could have come only from her confidential records leaked out. Investigation proved that a janitor had known the drawers didn't close. Instead of reporting this, he had complained about it one evening to an employee who was working overtime. This employee couldn't resist the temptation to go through the files and then to spread the information he had come upon.

In another instance a secretary repeatedly failed to lock her files, even though she was told countless times that she had to protect certain papers that were kept there. One night these important documents were removed from the files and no trace of them—or the robber— could be found. Despite the secretary's protestations that she had locked the file the night of the robbery, her integrity was questioned and not long afterwards the firm dispensed with her services. Do you need such a costly lesson?

Think before revising

Secretaries often attempt to revise a file about which they know nothing. This revision is a hazardous proceeding that will probably cost your firm money, if it does not cost you your position. Folders should never be started indiscriminately without due consideration for their usefulness. A great many folders is no guarantee that anything can be found in the files; quite to the contrary, an experienced worker views them with distrust. As one veteran secretary told the author: "I have learned to pray before I make up a new subject heading. When I first started out, I made a folder for everything and I could find nothing." Certainly a period of meditation will help you to reduce the number of topics by working out various combinations. Be careful to avoid duplications; G. C. Smith, George C. Smith, and Smith & Company may all be the same party. Make a cross reference where a letter is written to an individual in a firm, but file under the firm name unless the correspondence is of such a nature that the individual, rather than the firm, is clearly the important factor.

Use of suspense folder

All too often correspondence is stored in drawers, only to be forgotten. Your desk shouldn't conceal matters requiring attention. Many a secretary has placed a letter in her desk, because she had no regular place for pending matters, and then forgotten about it completely until the matter was brought to her attention with a jolt. It is hard indeed to convince an angry employer that you did not wilfully conceal a paper that is eventually brought to light. The usual attitude toward this type of slipup was rather harshly, though forcefully, impressed upon a young secretary in these words, "Hades is paved with good *intentions;* it's *attention* we want around here!"

A suspense folder placed in the front of your file makes an excellent place to store letters which you are temporarily unable to file. While problems raised by the receipt of a letter are current, the letter will often be needed for reference. A suspense folder should never become a "catch-all" for matter which you do not know how to file. It should be used only until you have time to get around to filing the mail. Above all, it should not be used in place of a chronological pending, or tickler, file.

Employers themselves are prone to put letters in their desks and then forget all about them. When this correspondence is needed, you may be put to much discomfort trying to unearth something you never had. Try to insist upon receiving all papers, but if this is impossible, maintain diligent watchfulness to detect the stowing away of papers you will be expected to have.

Disposing of inactive matter

The disposition of material into inactive files always raises two questions which you should study carefully:

1. When shall I consider material inactive?
2. What shall I throw away?

Little deviation from a strict periodic transfer of regular files is usually considered most effective. However, continuous transfer systems, based upon a specified limit of time for names to be kept in a file, are easily operated. Continuous transfer is especially effective in keeping a mailing list file, names being discarded when there has been no transaction with a firm over a period of time. If all mailing lists were subjected to such a systematic transfer rule, letters would not be sent to people many years after their death. Discarded lists form an excellent basis for a follow-up campaign by a department which may be interested in ascertaining reasons for discontinuance of trade relations with a house.

Conservation of valuable records

Because space in most offices is valuable, all records cannot be kept indefinitely. However, do not blithely go about tearing up everything in the files, as is often done at the end of a six-month period. Never ship away, burn, or otherwise indiscriminately dispose even of inactive files. Usually files of a completed period can be systematically arranged in an inactive file for a certain length of time. You will need much experience with a business to know what to discard. Use spare moments in this selection process. After much material has been destroyed, carefully pack and label the more important matter, so that future reference may be made to it if necessary. This system will save searchers much time and annoyance at a time when nerves are usually on edge. You cannot always keep your files in order if a number of people have access to them, but have them in order, chronologically and alphabetically before packing them away. In most states, suits for collections cannot be brought after seven years. Litigation files should be carried for this length of time at least.

Microfilming

Microfilming of records is a standard procedure in many offices. The material is photographed on 35 mm film, which can then be stored or filed in a small space. The film can be run off and the documents shown on a viewer whenever anyone wishes to look at them. Most newspapers use this method of filing, making copies of each edition. Banks and other businesses, which would otherwise accumulate enormous quantities of valuable data for which they would have to find safe, fireproof filing space, find microfilming a useful and compact method of filing.

Care and cleaning of files

You can seldom give your files a complete, old-fashioned house-cleaning, but you should be constantly putting them in order. Start at the beginning in some of your spare moments, rearranging a folder at a time. Put a marker in a conspicuous position, so that you can quickly resume the work. You will be surprised to find that you can complete the task without the disorder which usually accompanies efforts at housecleaning.

Provide reinforcements for the punched holes in book fillers. Go over book files periodically to reinforce leaves that have been torn out and to provide new folders for those which have become damaged through constant or careless use.

Do not throw things into a file. Avoid overcrowding. Make frequent use of the expansion devices on your file. At the same time, do not overtax its capacity. When a file can no longer be enlarged, remove some of the material. A file that is choked with papers is difficult to handle and its contents are in danger of being torn.

Uneven growth of correspondence causes some folders to fill up much more quickly than others. A crowded folder should not always be transferred to an inactive file, even though some subdivision of its contents is necessary. Keep the older material active by placing it in a second folder behind the current folder. Plainly indicate both opening and closing dates on the folder of the older material and the opening date on that of the newer material.

Filing in a typical office

Besides the centralized correspondence file maintained in most offices, you may have a private office file, various card indexes, book files, and other catalogued lists under your personal supervision. Even the least of these may be your undoing if you are not careful at all times. Remember that, even as with Caesar, "the evil that men do lives after them; the good is oft interred with their bones." No matter how excellent a secretary you may be, your employer will be impatient and curt, and entirely forgetful of your manifold good qualities, if you cannot produce a document when he wants it. Keep files strictly up to date, for you never know the hour or the minute when something will be needed.

BOOKS THAT WILL HELP IN FILING

Using Books and Libraries, Ella V. Aldrich. Prentice-Hall, Inc., Englewood Cliffs, N.J.

File It Right, National Education Association, Educational Secretaries Department, New York

Progressive Filing, McGraw-Hill Book Company, New York

Filing and Finding, Selden, Straub & Porter, Prentice-Hall, Inc., Englewood Cliffs, N.J.

Chapter 4

Office Printing and Purchasing

In every enterprise, consider where you would come out.
—PUBLILIUS SYRUS

You and office machines

There are machines to do just about everything in an office except put a fresh rose on your employer's desk. Although it doesn't seem likely that robots will replace first-rate secretaries, there are many ways in which machinery can increase a secretary's efficiency and cut down on time wasted doing repetitious chores.

Of course, it is as easy to go overboard on the purchase of machines for your office as on gadgets for your kitchen. Before you urge your employer to buy such and such a machine because it will save time and money, be certain of two things: (1) you will use it often enough to warrant the expense, and (2) its use will cut down appreciably on the cost of extra or outside help.

Material to be duplicated

Many types of office work can be duplicated by mechanical processes other than typing. Not only do these methods assure uniformity when making many copies of notices of meetings, instructions, form and sales letters, news letters, and similar kinds of typewritten work, but usually economies are effected.

When preparing material for reproduction, be more than ordinarily careful to detect all errors. Check the typewriting, spelling, and division of words at the end of lines. Copy for any type of duplicated work should be so carefully prepared before it is submitted that any

68

good copyist will have practically no reason for making errors. Occasionally, however, things do happen that must be corrected before the run is made. A stencil cutter may type a table for a race and, in one heading write, "Number of Hards Run," for "Number of Yards Run." Such an error is so obviously wrong that probably few readers will take more than passing notice of it, and you will have to decide whether it is desirable to lose time and money in having the correction made. However, some errors kill the whole purpose of a duplicated mailing. Be particularly careful to check dates and titles, which are easily neglected in a hurried reading. For example, a few years ago the very poetic title, "Follow the Star," appeared as, "Follow the Rats."

Stencil duplicating

When typing material that is to be stencil duplicated, give time and thought to preparing it exactly as it will appear on the finished copies. Even if you cut the stencil yourself, you will be unwise to risk working from a rough draft or from material on which much extemporaneous editing has to be done.

Because exact measurements are important in turning out acceptable stencils, a good secretary can save time and expense by preparing the stencil herself and sending it out to be run off. Of course that effort presupposes that the secretary has available a machine with sharp, clean type. If you have your own duplicator, see that placement of work on the proof sheet is as you originally planned; if not, make the necessary adjustments before the run is made.

Changes on a stencil are hard to make after it has been removed from the typewriter. If the duplicator machine has been run to take off a proof and an error has been found, a new stencil usually has to be cut if changes are indicated. The inked copy cannot be inserted in the typewriter again (at least until it has been thoroughly blotted and dried); practically all corrections possible are those that can be made with a stylus or by blocking out undesired portions of the writing with correction fluid.

There is an electronic method of making stencils from original copy that does away with typing the stencil, thus eliminating a step in which errors can occur.

Photo-offset duplicators

This form of duplicating is far more versatile than stencil duplicating. In addition to reproducing material typed, written, printed or drawn, it is an inexpensive way to reproduce charts and photographs not possible to reproduce on a stencil duplicator. From a master sheet, a metal plate is made that can be used for thousands of copies and then cleaned and stored until additional runs are needed. The advantage of this process is that from odd-sized material, copies may be produced in sizes that will fit into a regular binder. Master plates made of paper can be used in the same machine, but will reproduce copy in only one size.

The material can be reproduced in black and white or color. This process permits instant transparencies to be made and, with overhead projectors, used to illustrate speeches, reports and presentations.

Typing original copy for offsetting demands expert skill. Erasures should not be made, but corrections that are absolutely necessary can be made with a safety razor blade. Be especially careful not to get smudges or finger marks on the original paper, because any mark will photograph and appear on all of the copies.

Spirit duplicating

This method of duplicating provides a practical and inexpensive method of reproducing several hundred copies of anything written, typed or drawn on a master. Copies can be made in black and white or color.

Multigraphing

The usual multigraphed copy is produced from type which is set much like that for printed matter. The copies look almost like typewritten work and, if the weight of inking on your typewriter ribbon matches the inking on the multigraph ribbon, addresses and other data may be so carefully inserted that only an expert can detect that the processed letter is not typewritten. Multigraphing is generally more expensive than stencil or offset methods of duplicating, but you will usually be wise to choose multigraphing for making realistic copies of letters because of the similarity of the reproduction to actual typing.

Corrections on multigraph proofs are rather easily made. The type is merely changed in the incorrect spot. For this reason, one does not need to hesitate so much about slightly editing multigraphed proof. However, bear in mind that any correction must involve practically the same amount of space as was originally used. If the inserted part is longer or shorter than the space used for deleted matter, an entire paragraph may have to be reset. Writers who understand multigraphing try to use as many short paragraphs as possible in preparing their original copy, in order that hand setting of long paragraphs may be avoided if corrections are necessary.

Photographic copying

Photographic copying of papers and even books is available to every office through a variety of machines. These copying machines also reproduce labels and paper offset plates. When it is necessary to reduce or enlarge copy, or to reproduce difficult subjects, such as photographs, multi-tone charts, and so on, it is advisable to have the work done by a photostat company.

Varityping and automatic typewriters

The varityper, a form of typewriter has interchangeable type fonts which enable you to approximate the appearance of printed material at lower cost.

Automatic typewriters permit copying of form letters of different kinds. A tape or master record of an original letter is made first and then approximately 250 letters can be produced.

Addressing from plates

Addresses and other forms of typing which must be printed repeatedly can be transferred to plates of metal, paper or plastic. These are filed when not in use. They are used for mailing lists, magazine and newspaper subscription lists, credit and identification cards, statements and similar matter.

The secretary as housekeeper

A secretary is the office housekeeper in the true sense of that word. Though you are not expected to do heavy cleaning, you will be expected to maintain an orderly place in which to work. It is said that men are better housekeepers than women because they get the needed supplies and devices for doing work well. Most offices are not niggardly about buying necessary supplies, so suggest little things which will aid in making the place more livable. A dusting mitt or a piece of clean cheesecloth is much more appropriate for emergency use in the presence of a caller than a piece of worn-out underwear brought from home, even though the latter may make a better dust cloth. False economy is neither sensible nor desirable.

Ordering supplies

An inefficient housekeeper rushes to a delicatessen upon the arrival of unexpected guests, when household efficiency demands that a good hostess have on her shelves and in her freezer a supply from which she can prepare a carefully planned "quick menu." Likewise, business efficiency demands that you check over your supplies, so that you won't be compelled to make purchases or send to the supply room at odd times during the day. Keep a requisition sheet where you can constantly add items to it. In a large office, hand your order to a supply clerk at night, so that the supplies may be delivered early in the morning.

Make yourself responsible for the ordering of all supplies, whether this duty must be undertaken on your own initiative or through your employer. In making purchases over a period of time, make a memo-randum of what you have ordered. If placed on your employer's desk, this memo will keep him informed of what is being done. However, there are two sides to this procedure which must be considered. Your employer may not want to be bothered with details, and, if you ask his permission to order things which you should be perfectly well able to get by yourself, undue discussion of the matter may annoy him. A memorandum usually enables him to cancel orders of which he does not approve. Even seemingly safe purchases are sometimes unfortu-nate. One secretary handed her employer a two years' supply of en-graved name cards just an hour before it was publicly announced that his title had been changed by the directors of the organization. The promotion was no surprise to the man himself, but the outburst of disgust that he emitted upon receiving the cards was at least one rea-son why the secretary might have regretted his advancement. Mergers, consolidations, bankruptcy, and change of firm name often make perfectly well-intentioned ordering of supplies undesirable.

Until you are perfectly sure of the absolute bounds of your author-ity, it is well to err on the side of caution. It is well to remember that some employers are not capable of totally releasing their hold on even minor details. When they are busy, their secretaries may do much to relieve them and will be censured if they do not do so; but in an idle moment, these men are prone to revert to their former habits and will reassume duties they have not been performing for some time. Unex-pected reversions of this type are frequently most exasperating to an efficient secretary.

For example, one secretary had been ordering supplies in her office for years without instruction. No thought of overstepping her author-ity entered her mind when, after the yearly budget had been made up, she placed an order for the year's supply of fifty thousand envelopes. Much to her discomfiture, another fifty thousand envelopes arrived just a few days after her order had been delivered. Her employer, hav-ing been experiencing a lull in business, had gone out and ordered the supplies himself. Worry about the consequences of her action led her to consult a secretarial group that evening, in the hope of finding a way out of her dilemma. Of course, no set procedure which would work in every case could be prescribed. The fiery little secretary who advised the young woman to "go in and *jump* him before he gets a chance to *jump* you" probably did know the *right* course of action. Whether such a procedure would be advisable in most cases is debatable. Forest and prairie fires are often controlled by building up a backfire of sufficient proportions to stop the progress of the blaze, but the fire of men's tempers is not always counteracted in the same manner, especially not if a man knows he has been in error but does not want to admit it. Decide whether *rightness* will seem so important to you in case you are compelled to seek another position.

Verifying receipts of materials

A great number of secretaries are extremely careless in verifying the receipt of supplies. Check materials against the requisition or the bill as you unpack them. Listings of omitted items should be clearly deleted from a bill, and notations of items which are defective, broken, or of inferior quality should be perfectly clear. Every bill should be checked at least once to confirm receipt of goods as listed. If prices are given, these should be checked with the original quotations. Extensions and additions should be verified. Sign your name to the checking you have done. Systematic attention to this duty will save your firm much money in the course of a year.

Reliable firms usually make good on any articles found to be broken or defective. However, if credit is to be given, a wholesale house usually demands that an article be returned or shown to the salesman, even though it is too damaged or defective for future use. You will enable the seller to recover loss from the manufacturer or trace down insecure packing if you carefully preserve such goods. For this reason, when notifying a company of defective goods, always refer to the number or name on the packing slip, if one can be found in or on the package.

Verify the contents of a package before signing a receipt if verification is at all practicable. However, a delivery man cannot always be kept waiting until you have taken all supplies from the box and examined them. Nevertheless, watch to see that you are not signing a bill which says, "Goods received and found to be satisfactory" unless you have thoroughly examined the goods. Some secretaries write on bills, "Received but not examined." A rubber stamp may be used for putting this inscription above your name.

Quantity ordering

Use good judgment in the quantity of supplies you order. Paper usually shows a slight yellowing with age. A large supply of letter-heads or printed office forms in your cabinet will prove very wasteful if another form is adopted. One secretary got a bargain on typewriter ribbons, so bought a supply which she thought would last the office for five years. Before that time, the ribbons had dried out to the point where they would not stand up under more than two days' hard usage. No one can control the change of a telephone number; hence forms on which a telephone number appears may become obsolete when a telephone company decides to change the number of a firm or the exchange.

Purchasing responsibility

In buying for the office or for your employer, use judgment in se-lecting things that will serve the purpose well. Do not be afraid to spend money if you think your employer would want high-quality merchandise, yet do not use your unlimited buying privilege to throw economy to the winds. Learn to buy goods because they suit the needs of your office, not because you like the salesman of a particular company. Personal preference, though always present, is easily dis-cernible if quality and prices do not measure up to the standards set by competing firms. Tips, concessions, and favors that influence your choice are not worth the price you will pay in loss of confidence.

You will probably be called upon to purchase personal or family articles for a busy employer. A man who does not have a home, or one whose wife's shopping time is limited by illness or by family cares, often finds a secretary's help invaluable. Develop judgment and ability as the office and personal purchasing agent of your employer.

System and forethought in buying

Though the spontaneous buying of gifts for one's family and friends and in observance of special occasions is fine in principle, a wise businessman arranges a system whereby he cannot overlook such matters. Keep a calendar of birthdays, anniversaries, holidays, and special events which your employer wishes to remember, so that you can remind him of their approach.

He may become so involved that he will neglect to buy a gift for Mother's Day, mail a remembrance on Father's Day, or get that all-important present for his wife on their wedding anniversary. To the one slighted, it will seem inexcusably thoughtless for him to have forgotten such an important event, but you who live through a busy office day will know how difficult it often is to remember any personal matter that is not forced upon one's attention. Even though an employer's memory has proved perfectly good, he may often be prevented from getting away in time to make a purchase. Help him to remember early enough either to get the gift himself or allow you to make the purchase for him. In mailing or sending gifts, always see that price tags are removed.

Keep on hand a supply of conservative cards of condolence and congratulations. The businessman who sends these cards to business acquaintances or associates experiencing some of life's joys or sorrows shows a thoughtfulness which marks him among men. Little remembrances are very much appreciated, even though the event may not call for a personal letter from a busy executive. You can often apprise your employer of a death or promotion notice which appeared in the papers. Office employees generally feel more disposed to confide in you than in your employer. An executive who sends a card to an office boy who is graduating from night school or to a clerk who has lost his mother succeeds, not only in surprising the employee, but usually in winning his undying devotion.

Care of supplies

Most secretaries make the mistake of putting too many supplies in a desk. To unload an entire box of envelopes or a package of letterheads in a desk drawer is destructive to both supplies and desk. The edges of paper become torn or wrinkled, and the drawer is strained because it is too full to be worked smoothly. A reserve cabinet or drawer is always a good outlet, but if you have no storage space, try to avoid crowding by getting another secretary to take part of the contents of the box. Do not let your employer's supply of name cards and personal stationery become completely exhausted before ordering a new supply, because engraving sometimes requires time.

Arrange correspondence materials in your desk so that copies are readily accessible in the order in which they are generally used. Try to keep everything in its place. Be especially careful to keep carbon paper in a folder where it will not become creased or rub off on other materials. To have to search for an article may not always be evidence of the fact that your desk is not in order, but it does indicate that you have not thoroughly learned where things are. If you give a little thought to working out a satisfactory arrangement of your desk, you will not be so likely to forget where to put your materials.

Ability to advise and suggest

Most employers welcome suggestions in buying equipment or making a change of system. Sometimes letterheads which are carried over long periods of time are chosen with little thought. If you show an interest in the office stationery, changes may be made which will place the office on a higher plane. Paper of a white or neutral shade is most frequently chosen for business use. Letterheads with gaudy pictures on them may be replaced by ones bearing only a neat trademark and the name and address of the concern. Envelopes should be opaque, so that contents cannot be read, and of the same quality as the letterhead you use. Two sizes are usually sufficient for general correspondence.

Acquaintance with standard supplies

You can be of great help in ordering supplies if you know something about standard materials. If you ask for a book binder 17½ ×

29¾ inches, it will often be made up for you without question. You are expected to exercise judgment, and the buyer shows his confidence in your ability by not questioning your requisition. Do you know enough about supplies to justify such confidence? Talk to salesmen, go to business shows, and look through office equipment catalogues to inform yourself on this part of your work.

Standardization of filing equipment makes it advisable, from the standpoint of economy, to confine all forms as nearly as possible to the letter size (8½ × 11 inches) and the library card size (3 × 5 inches). Other standard sizes (taken from a table prepared by the Hammermill Paper Company) which may be cut without waste are indicated on page 79. Special sizes are expensive and usually soon outlive their usefulness.

In ordering printed forms a secretary can be especially helpful in seeing that the alignment is adjusted for a typewriter. Considerable time is lost because forms are so poorly planned that each line necessitates adjustment by use of the variable line spacer.

Study of individual office needs

Accustom yourself to the materials used in your particular office in order to superintend their ordering and care. However, do not allow yourself to continue items over a long period of time merely because they have been traditionally used there. Your business is a growing and expanding organization, so your equipment must be molded to fit its changing needs. Be alert to detect the need for improvements. An inventor is one who sees possibilities that are not observed by those who are completely absorbed in the everyday operation of a machine.

Do not be afraid to make suggestions, tactfully, for the betterment of your office. A machine sorts with automatic precision, but the wide-awake secretary, by getting a mental vision of the needs of an organization, adds to this machinelike precision the results of thinking. Again, it is suggested that you study office equipment catalogues in order to sharpen your perception and clear your vision sufficiently to weigh impartially and accurately the merits and deficiencies of your office equipment.

STANDARD FORM SIZES

The form sizes listed below meet practically any need.   Each cuts without waste from standard sizes used by all printers.

Size of Form	Cuts Without Waste from Standard Sheet Measuring:	Number Obtained from Single Standard Size Sheet	Number of Single Forms Obtained from One Ream (500 sheets) of Paper
2¾ × 4¼	17 × 22	32	16M
2¾ × 8½	17 × 22	16	8M
3½ × 4¼	17 × 28	32	16M
3½ × 8½	17 × 28	16	8M
3½ × 17	17 × 28	8	4M
4¼ × 5½	17 × 22	16	8M
4¼ × 7	17 × 28	16	8M
4¼ × 11	17 × 22	8	4M
4¼ × 14	17 × 28	8	4M
4¼ × 28	17 × 28	4	2M
5½ × 8½	17 × 22	8	4M
5½ × 17	17 × 22	4	2M
7 × 8½	17 × 28	8	4M
7 × 17	17 × 28	4	2M
8½ × 22	17 × 22	2	1M
8½ × 28	17 × 28	2	1M
11 × 17	17 × 22	2	1M
14 × 17	17 × 28	2	1M

Sizes 8½ × 11 and 8½ × 14 are available in single sheets,
so that no cutting is necessary.

Bond and ledger papers are usually promptly obtainable in:
17 × 22, 17 × 28, 19 × 24, 22 × 34, 28 × 34, 24 × 38.

Hammermill Paper Company, Erie, Pa.

Figure 2. Standard Form Sizes

BOOKS ON OFFICE MANAGEMENT

Office Organization and Management, Harry L. Wylie and Robert P. Brecht, Prentice-Hall, Inc., Englewood Cliffs, N.J.

Office Management, Charles B. Hicks and Irene Place, Allyn and Bacon, New York

Purchasing: Principles and Applications (3rd ed.) Heinritz, Prentice-Hall, Inc., Englewood Cliffs, N.J.

Chapter 5

The Reception of Office Callers

> Good manners is the art of making those people easy
> with whom we converse. Whoever makes the fewest people
> uneasy is the best bred in the company.
>
> —SWIFT

The office caller

A person who calls at your office has a reason for doing so which
seems important to him. Unfortunately, many business offices have
habitually put up such a "barbed wire" fence of resistance against
intrusion that many visitors approach the reception desk in a defensive frame of mind. Some will persist until they get what they
want; a few will report rudeness; but the majority will go elsewhere.
The success of any business depends both on friends that *are made*
and enemies that *are not made,* for business cannot be divorced from
friendship.

Courteous consideration for all

Everyone likes to be made to feel that he is important. What a delight to see a visitor's face light up when he is satisfied that you have
given him a square deal! Contrast this with the expression on the face
of a man whose arrival is heralded by a receptionist telephoning the
man he wishes to see and saying: "The First National representative is
here. You don't want to see him, do you?" Even a cordial reception
from an officer cannot erase effects of such a negative attitude on the
part of an employee. Your first duty is to see that each caller gets a
courteous and fair hearing. Even those reputed "office pests"—sales-

men—are self-respecting, hard-working individuals who should receive just treatment. (If you do not believe selling is hard work, go out and earn your living that way for a month.)

A merchant in a large town always gave salesmen ungrudging attention. He hastily put aside other work and listened pleasantly to their story. He told them frankly if he wanted their product and just as frankly if he did not. All representatives departed quickly because he impressed upon them the value which he placed upon a salesman's time. This considerate attitude appealed to the men so much that the merchant became known as "a shrewd buyer but a prince among men." When special purchases were available, the salesmen made sure he got first choice. Other large buyers were slighted whenever possible because representatives remembered that they had previously been treated as impostors.

The receptionist reflects management

Office managers complain that they find it impossible to hire people to receive callers efficiently. This situation seems to be another evidence of the axiom, "It is easy to make a perfect machine, but it is hard to find a perfect man to run it." Serious thought must be given to the problem of filling the positions of reception clerks if an office would be outstandingly successful. The grade of mentality which is drawn for this job in many offices is a strong indictment of the management of the concern.

A woman who lives abroad stopped at a Wall Street office while on a visit to New York to see a young man who had lived in her home as a boy. The girl at the desk ceased chewing gum long enough to say, "Mr. Patterson is not in." When the caller suggested that she wait for his return, the receptionist said ungraciously, "If you want to, but I don't know when he'll be back." The woman scribbled the name of her hotel on a visiting card and left it for her friend. The young broker located the woman at her hotel and showed so plainly that he was sincerely flattered by this evidence of her continued interest in him that she could not refrain from informing him how uncertain of his welcome the reception clerk's remark had made her feel. He was so annoyed to hear of this that he had the receptionist fired.

Qualities of a good receptionist

Skill in dealing with people is often lacking in businessmen and women—whether executives, secretaries, or office boys. To anyone who enjoys studying human nature, this talent would seem easy to gain. A person who excels in the ability to meet people well is always alert and polite, tactful and tolerant. He knows business principles in general and the policies of his own particular organization. A thorough acquaintance with the set-up of the office and the duties of the officers and department heads is essential. It is a progressive office that puts at its information desk a retired man who has been successful in business. The mellowing influence of age will enable him to form sound judgments based on years of experience. His knowledge of business will have impressed upon him the importance of courteous and intelligent understanding of the wants of others. On the other hand, many very young people are so interested in pleasing others that they deliberately formulate plans for cultivating good will. Youth's flexible attitude of mind sometimes gives them an advantage over the older generation.

Meeting your employer's guests

Even though an office is large enough to maintain a reception clerk, you as a secretary will have to meet people who ask for your employer. In developing a proper background for this work, you should realize that "lack of understanding, which is a form of ignorance, is the cause of discourtesy." For this reason any information which you may be able to obtain about the person who is calling upon your employer will be helpful to you.

Treating everyone alike

In the business world, you are sure to meet individuals of many different types. Cultivate a kindly interest in people of all ages and conditions. Naturally, we all respond more graciously to attractive, friendly people. But try very hard to be as pleasant to those who are not quite so prepossessing, who may even seem to have a chip on their shoulders, or to be unduly hard to please. Don't react in kind. Treat everyone the same—the unknowns and the famed—being courteous and helpful to everyone you meet.

Keeping track of your employer

You should know where your employer is and when he is expected back. This requirement is a bone of contention between many secretaries and their employers. Even the man who wrote a very severe reprimand to all executives and office secretaries, because the officers' whereabouts often were unknown when telephone calls came for them, would never let his own busy secretary know where he was going. His neglect forced her to run miles trying to locate him. Employers usually know what a help this information is, but are extremely careless about keeping their secretaries up to date. Every so often you will have to do much guessing and jumping to conclusions when you want to locate your employer. Be careful about turning away an unsatisfied caller when you just *guess* that your employer is not in the building.

Appointment calls

You will keep an appointment calendar for your employer to enable him to be prepared to receive a caller with an appointment. Because these engagements are prearranged to save time, a guest should be received promptly at the appointed hour. Keep your employer reminded of all such engagements. As soon as you find that your employer cannot keep an appointment, make every effort to postpone or cancel it before the person comes to your office. This courtesy will be appreciated. Often you will make appointments for your employer, but they should be confirmed as early as possible.

Preparation of office for caller's reception

When the reception clerk announces a caller, you can generally determine what course of action to pursue. If the caller is to be brought into the private office, see that the room is in order before you go out to meet him or before he is escorted in by an attendant. Be vigilant in seeing that papers on your employer's desk are in folders or removed, so that his visitor may not be tempted to read them. The customer who left Mr. Brown's office to spread the report that, "Jones must have a miserable secretary now; I saw a letter from him on Brown's desk today with five ink corrections on it," was also unconsciously criticizing Mr. Brown's secretary. (He probably did not stop to think that his friend Mr. Jones was equally "miserable" not to have made those corrections in pencil so that his secretary could have corrected them on the typewriter.) Protect yourself and your correspondents from such thoughtless criticism.

A gracious greeting

Give a personal greeting whenever possible. Even people whose sole pride is their humility are secretly flattered when you remember them. Treat everyone as though he were worthy of your best attention. Use individual treatment for each customer, but make it uniformly polite. Always talk directly to the person, not around him.

Insist on getting the name and business of every caller. Impostors have made the "blind call" so unpopular that you can safely make a rule of admitting no one who is not frank in his approach. Cultivate your memory of names and faces. That this faculty can be developed quite apart from a good memory for other details was demonstrated by a man who could name and classify fifty persons upon being introduced to them once. After giving his course in memorization at a college for a week, he forgot the number of the lecture room and got lost, much to the delight of the students, who had difficulty in remembering five names correctly.

Contagiousness of optimism

Others reflect your spirit of optimism, but a gloomy mood is equally catching. Never underestimate the value of a joyous outlook on life, but do not make the mistake of smiling all the time. Business is a serious matter and should not be treated lightly. A permanent grin is annoying because it is expressionless. A forced smile is so insincere that visitors often get the impression that you are laughing at them. "American women are the efficiency experts of charm. . . . I am a little weary of being exposed to charm," was part of a criticism leveled at us by J. B. Priestley. Although few will agree with this English novelist, a great many people would rather have a reception clerk or a secretary swear at them than be compelled to witness the agony caused these office employees by having to be perfunctorily pleasant. Force yourself to think pleasant thoughts, so you will not have to veil ill feeling. "Every thought bears fruit of its own kind." Feel pleasant and take joy in the response which others give to your greeting. A nervous frenzy leaves a feeling of exhaustion, so you must strive to be studiedly controlled in meeting others. Your greeting, however, should have enough enthusiasm not to give the caller a feeling that he is being "frozen out."

Acting for the employer

Many office callers will be amply cared for by you without aid from your employer. The extent to which you can assist will depend upon your knowledge of the business. The secret of success in this work is your ability to see things from your employer's angle—not to do what *you* would like to do, but what *your employer* would want you to do. Do not take too literally the admonition to be natural and frank, but you must retain honesty. Do not tell a caller "Mr. Brown is not in" just because he cannot receive the caller personally. The prevalent lack of faith in office employees is increased by such procedure. Employers who are so unfair as to oblige their secretaries to tell falsehoods have a way of thoughtlessly appearing while the secretary is engaged in trying to convince the caller of their absence. There is no objection to telling a caller: "Mr. Brown is completely tied up this morning, but I shall be glad to try to help you."

Handling a displeased caller

No one can please everybody all the time, so do not become too concerned if some callers are unreasonably displeased by your treatment of them. Keep calm and the other's anger will be likely to subside. "The customer is always right" is a fallacy. All he deserves is a square deal, courteously given. Abraham Lincoln, in refusing to grant a favor to a friend, wrote, "I should have been glad to do anything for you, consistent with justice and proper courtesy toward the others." This should be your attitude toward callers. Rash promises are childish and unrealistic. Callers should leave with a feeling that your denial of their demands had a firm basis and was not caused by a lack of desire to help.

Making a digest of calls

Keep a complete record of calls you have handled for your employer during the day. If you have not discussed these matters with him during a lull in the office day, or given him a written digest to look over, he will often be embarrassed to find that he knows nothing about a matter which you have handled for him. Strict adherence to this report plan will do much to dispel any feeling of doubt he may have about letting you handle calls.

Granting an interview

No visitor should be granted an interview unless he is to be cordially treated. Simply to tolerate people is inexcusable. The dean of a certain large school always lets you know how busy he is before he starts to talk. He then refers to the matter again several times during the conversation, even though you may have called at his request. He detains all callers too long because, like the minister who wastes half of his service time telling the congregation that "time will not permit," he does not use his time to good advantage. Some executives have this way of trying to make people feel their importance. The visitors' discomfort is further increased by being compelled to face a framed admonition above his desk, "No loitering." Can you imagine such a man getting any help from callers who are constantly kept in such a state of mental perturbation?

Your employer may be relieved of having to force the early departure of a caller if you thoughtfully limit the time by wording your sentence intelligently when you grant the interview. "Mr. Brown has an appointment in ten minutes, but he will see you now" will warn a caller not to overstay his time.

Keeping a line of callers moving

Many business houses have gone to the other extreme in extending interview privileges to all who request them. They work on the theory that the servant of the people must be readily accessible to them. The president of a large bank has a line of fifteen or twenty waiting to see him much of the day, but he insists on obliging anyone who expresses a wish to see him personally. The line is kept moving swiftly by well-trained secretaries and assistants. This bank president has a happy faculty for talking to everyone in a leisurely manner and makes callers feel that he is granting them a favor by quickly turning their business over to a competent assistant. His subordinates have cultivated a grace in deftly taking over these matters, with the result that no one feels that his case has been delegated to an inferior. Each caller is quickly invited to another room so that the next in line may take his place at the president's desk.

Ushering in a caller

In bringing a visitor into an office, walk beside him or a little ahead of him, with head slightly turned in his direction. Quick, staccato movements instead of easy graceful ones indicate a lack of self-control. Stumbling, dropping things, and stepping on or running into objects are due to lack of poise, but as everyone is occasionally subject to such accidents, do not become extremely embarrassed if you prove to have this quite human failing. Quietly pass off any mishap of this kind without making excuses for yourself, but stop to calm yourself when you start to blunder around in an awkward manner. If the caller helps you "pick up the broken pieces," accept the courtesy with a "Thank you," which neither places too much emphasis on the act nor ignores the help. Make the caller believe you expected the courtesy by acknowledging it naturally. Profuse gratitude might give him the impression that he is the first gentleman you ever met.

Making the introduction

As you approach your employer's desk, step aside so as not to stand between him and his caller. You are not called upon to make either a formal or an informal introduction; you are performing the function of a butler, and should merely announce the guest by name. Your voice should be directed toward your employer because he must hear the name. (You will have carefully given his name to the visitor before you came in.) When your employer is busy, you may attract his attention by saying, "Mr. Brown," if a period of silent waiting does not cause him to look up. As soon as you have secured recognition, say, "Mr. Jones." The employer will then rise and remain standing until his guest has been seated—two men usually are seated simultaneously.

Rules of social conduct

Although a wide divergence of opinion exists as to the extent to which social amenities may be practiced in a business office, it is safe to say few companies are in danger of erring on the side of politeness. Most men remove their hats in a building or in a private elevator, but other courtesies equally pleasant are often neglected. Good manners are the result of thoughtfully adapting yourself to your surroundings. For this reason, what might be proper at a formal function is out of place in an office, but you are never free from an obligation to follow the rules of business etiquette.

When you are present at an interview

While a caller is engaged in conversation with your employer, your duty will be to efface yourself from their consciousness, even though you remain in the office to give assistance. Keep busy, even if you have to pretend you are working (a dilemma seldom encountered in an active office).

Interrupting an interview

Relieve the host of all needless interruptions during an interview. If it is absolutely necessary to talk to your employer, ask, "May I interrupt?" He can then excuse himself from his caller. You should never direct any comment to the visitor when you interrupt. The best method of communicating a telephone call or some urgent matter is by writing a note which you can lay on your employer's desk. He may be able to nod his answer or he can ask the caller to excuse him while he instructs you. Usually it is not wise to discuss a matter so that a caller can hear, and it is impolite to speak in a whisper. A note, therefore, is an aid in avoiding embarrassment.

Assisting during an interview

Quickly procure any information and data requested by your employer. By anticipating such needs as correspondence, contracts, and other materials, you will make it unnecessary for your employer to direct the caller's attention away from the interview by asking for them. Some employers like to have you unobtrusively take notes on the conversation. Although this is not necessary in most instances, an engagement overheard or figures jotted down are sometimes of inestimable help.

The secretary who knows the work can frequently substitute for her employer without causing a break. The extent to which you can assume this responsibility depends upon the trust your employer places in your ability. The principle of cooperation is the ultimate salvation of an employer.

Watching appointments

Always inform your employer of an appointment, even though he has a guest. Work out a probable course of action and then place a note on his desk. "I am telephoning Mr. Jones that you will not be there for twenty minutes," may enable your employer to signify his approval with a nod.

If you hear a guest say that he has to be at Mr. Jones's office at a certain time, watch this appointment for him. Should the time approach before he has finished with Mr. Brown, place a note on Mr. Brown's desk asking if Mr. Smith would like you to call Mr. Jones's office to let him know he will be late.

Making a graceful exit

If you are included in the conference, rise when the caller leaves. Guests should usually be accompanied to the door or elevator. If your employer does not wish to perform this courtesy, you should be alert either to do it yourself or to summon a page to conduct the caller from the office. In a small office or in the case of callers who are acquainted with the office through frequent visits, this procedure can be considered superfluous, but any stranger feels like an intruder if compelled to wander around a place with which he is not acquainted. Most people do not have a keen sense of direction and are extremely embarrassed if they break into a conference room or a broom closet while searching for an exit.

An unavoidable wait

If your executive has had to leave the office, tell a caller frankly when he will be back and make another appointment if uncertain of the time of his return. Do not insist that the caller wait; you can assure him of your employer's regret at his absence, but permit him to exercise his own choice easily. You must try to develop your perceptive powers until you can discern what others want to do.

If a caller must wait, "counting time is not so important as making time count." Although it is not usually within your sphere to discuss the business at hand before your employer's arrival, you may be able to detect enough during the wait to have papers and data ready when your employer is ready to talk .

Observing callers' interests

Visitors usually look around your office to learn about your employer through his surroundings. When a caller comments on your pleasant office, do not be afraid to agree. It is much better to say, "Yes, we think it is nice; did you notice that lovely view of the Empire State Building over there?" than to make some derogatory remark such as, "It would be, if those tenement families didn't hang their wash out down there."

One firm has on the walls of its offices beautiful pictures sent in by its South American branch. A new secretary was asked five times what they were. Each time she replied, "I haven't any idea." The next girl searched out someone who had worked in the South American branch and discovered such an interesting story that many visitors were sorry when the employer interrupted them by entering before she had finished her tale.

Smoothing out difficulties

A stranger is not familiar with all the rules of your office. Whenever you can, help him unobtrusively, try to prevent any error he may make, but never get excited when you cannot. This ability to smooth over errors is a grace which is cultivated by few. So much emphasis is put on avoiding errors that we forget to develop the greater self-control required to ignore them. Although you must not excuse your own errors on the basis of heredity, environment, and training, you must make allowance for these handicaps in others. Try to make those who commit social errors feel at ease. The following illustration shows how a mistake may be glossed over:

A wealthy family hired a New York traffic policeman to direct people at a fashionable wedding in a small New Jersey church. Just as the bride and her father arrived late at the church, there was a torrential downpour. In the dash from the car to church, the bride's bouquet was handed to the policeman. In the excitement of getting the wedding started, the bouquet was forgotten and the bride and her father started down the aisle without it. They were all the way to the altar when a few snickers from the guests alerted them to the fact that something unusual was going on. The bride turned her head, and there was the policeman right behind her carrying her bridal bouquet. After handing it to her, he retreated to the back of the church in military fashion, with the bridal couple and their families smiling in friendly commendation of him. No one reacted angrily, and there was no scene.

The family has had several years of pleasant bantering about the bridegroom's having married the bride to rescue her from the clutches of the law, but the big traffic cop probably does not yet know that he committed a social error in following the bride down the aisle. Reared in a courteous atmosphere, the bride even asked the photographer to include "the bearer of my bouquet" in one of the wedding pictures taken on the steps of the church.

Conversation checkup

A doctor found his patients leaving him because his secretary annoyed them by asking impertinent and irrelevant questions when she was not giving them lurid details of her five operations. He had people report subjects which his next secretary discussed in order that his former experience might not be repeated. Would your conversation bear such a checkup?

While the caller is compelled to wait, you must never force a conversation on him if you suspect that he is an unwilling listener. However, the majority of people like to talk and will appreciate any attention you have time to give them. Avoid topics of age, price, clothes, salary, business secrets, scandal, disease, gossip, and personalities. Do not criticize a rival house or its products. The question is then asked, "About what shall we talk to callers?" A safe rule to follow is to talk on subjects in which the caller shows an interest. The extent to which you can participate will be largely determined by your background. Strive to learn about music, drama, current events, different sections of the world, books, sports, and nature. A secretary to an engineer took a college course in opera because she knew nothing about music. A few months later she came home one night and exclaimed: "I'm repaid for all the hard work I did last winter. Those men were discussing opera today and I knew what they were talking about. Why, I was even able to contribute my two cents' worth to their discussion by furnishing some dates!" On the other hand, a candid confession of ignorance is better than proceeding blindly. By evincing an interest, you may lead the visitor to inform you about a subject.

Asking and answering questions

Recently a woman heard something about which she had wondered for forty years. Gleefully she exclaimed: "Mother was right! If you don't ask questions, you will keep alert enough to find out everything in time." This excellent rule is worth keeping in mind when asking questions, although in business many things must be ascertained sooner than "in due course." However, unless you have a very definite reason why you should know a thing, hesitate before questioning a caller. Most questions reveal lack of self-control rather than wholesome curiosity.

When it comes to answering questions, one can be perfectly courteous and yet refuse to answer any. An executive, arriving to accompany an official of a rival concern to lunch, took advantage of his luncheon guest's absence from the room to ask the man's secretary whether her firm was taking over another house. Conjecture had been rife among people in the trade, and he thought he would surprise this young girl into revealing the secret through her embarrassment. Looking directly at him and assuming a confidential tone, she said: "These rumors are becoming interesting, aren't they? Of course, one can't be so curious as to ask direct questions!" The man was not quite sure whether she had noticed that he had asked a question or whether she was flattered that he would discuss the matter with her. He did not confirm his suspicion that her organization was the one involved. Her employer lost much respect for the executive who resorted to such means of eliciting information, but highly commended his secretary's discretion.

Etiquette in business

In business you cannot devote all of your time to being agreeable, but time so spent pays high dividends. Business houses demand courtesy in their employees because they are trying to build up a profitable business. As an essential text in learning to be an office hostess, obtain a good book on modern etiquette. Surely no one should allow this part of his education to be left to the hit-or-miss theory that he can pick up all points he will need. That method puts a burden on the powers of perception which is not assumed in any other field of learning. Most modern treatises will sum up the subject in such an admirable way as to include points overlooked, even in a thorough training. This study of etiquette will not be a whitewash to cover up your defects, for good manners cannot be divorced from character; however, it will help you to attain a finish which will bring out the good points of your character.

Modern attitude toward social rules

Young people are reticent about asking questions on matters of etiquette. They are sensitive about making their ignorance known, but they are most happy to do things correctly. An experiment at a college, where a big hotel banquet was never well attended, revealed the fallacy of an insinuation that the young generation does not care about its manners. A teacher, suspecting that poor attendance was due to lack of knowledge of how to appear, quietly distributed mimeographed instructions on hotel etiquette. Only one student out of over three hundred missed the banquet that year, and they all appeared looking their best. Because every stiff and stilted person has been dubbed "a follower of Emily Post," young people are led to distrust the benefits to be derived from reading the books on etiquette.

Developing ease in manners

Most people who try to acquire social grace by rule wear their efforts like a mask, evident to all except themselves, or exercise their newly learned courtesies at unappropriate times. A man who became an official of his company at middle age learned that a gentleman stood up whenever a lady entered the room. Laudable as was his desire to polish his manners, he made others extremely uncomfortable by the way in which he carried out this courtesy. Every time a secretary entered his office or one in which he was at a meeting, he would leap to his feet. If there were other men in the office they would become embarrassed and uneasy, not knowing whether to follow suit or ignore him. The secretaries were so unnerved, they hated to go near him. This was a case of following a pleasant courtesy to the point of absurdity.

Dressing the part

Practically all treatises on meeting callers lay the greatest emphasis on dress; in fact, there has been such an overemphasis on dress that one should forgive the innocent young secretary if she does not realize that it takes more than clothes to handle an office call well.

If you are really interested in what to wear, pick up any current newspaper or magazine, or walk into any department store to find "just the clothes to make you a business success." One should not minimize the value of these worthy attempts to raise the standards of dress. As long as women scramble articles of evening, sports, afternoon, and street attire (even in clashing colors) to make up one office costume, we cannot believe good dress will ever be learned by perception any more than etiquette has been. However, while the modern businesswoman is being made the butt of good hints directed at mankind in general, we would warn *both employer and secretary* not to lose sight of far more important qualifications for meeting people.

Avoiding clothes consciousness

A prominent actress, when questioned about her stunning appearance, said: "I buy clothes, I wear them, and I forget them. That is all there is to it." Similarly, you should be able to dismiss clothes from your mind when you meet a caller. Thoughts on dress should always be strictly confined to your home and dressing room. You would probably not have received your position if your attire had not passed certain standards. If you are not maintaining that standard, your employer is at fault if he lacks courage to draw your attention to the fact. A true compliment to a businesswoman was the remark made by a nationally known architect to a contractor: "Your secretary is the only girl I have ever known whose mind was on business to such an extent that she was not patting her hair or making other gestures which draw attention to personal adornment."

Attitude toward compliments

Personal compliments, though seldom evidencing good taste, should be accepted in the spirit in which they are given. If a visitor happens to mention your clothes, thank him naturally, because he evidently thought you would enjoy the comment or he would not have volunteered it. You would be discourteous not to acknowledge his effort to please. Never belittle the speaker's judgments of dress by saying, "Oh, this is a cheap old thing!" Learn to change the subject as quickly as possible without letting the person know that he has caused you embarrassment. If these irrelevant compliments become frequent, analyze the reason. You will usually find that you have not been able to forget yourself and are giving an impression of showing off and attracting attention to your clothes.

Creating an atmosphere of welcome

Do not apologize for disorder in your office. An office caller is intelligent enough not to expect you to put away your work to entertain him. He will not be disturbed to find your desk piled high with things which indicate that he has stepped into a busy office. If things are in the way, remove them with as little commotion as possible. Most people are incapable of refraining from long and tiresome explanations which serve no purpose.

The fussy mother who accused her young daughter of "having no shame at all" nearly ruined an excellent hostess. If an early guest caught this girl in the midst of preparations for the evening, she made no excuses. After a cordial greeting, she would ask him to do some chore while she proceeded with the work he had interrupted. Instead of making the visitor feel that he had committed a *faux pas* by appearing so early, she made him feel that he had arrived just in time to help her. This uncommon understanding of true hospitality has helped her husband in his career as an attorney. Any of his clients can come to his home at a most inconvenient hour and be assured of a sincere welcome.

Respecting property of others

Do not touch the property of another. If some of it is in your way, politely ask the offender to move it. A visitor becomes very much disturbed if you pick up packages which may contain personal or confidential data. One young secretary has a most annoying habit of looking over the shoulder of a caller and reading any letter or document which may be exposed. She never seems to realize that she is making others uncomfortable.

The body of another person should certainly be regarded as his own property. Patting people on the back, tickling them under the chin, linking arms with them, and similar intimacies are obnoxious to most people, although they may tolerate these acts rather than offend. Do not intentionally touch another person in a business office, but whenever you accidentally do so, be careful not to move away so obviously as to give the individual the impression that he is personally repulsive to you.

Personal indulgences

Gum-chewing, smoking, and drinking are habits upon which public opinion has been pretty clearly crystallized. Whatever your convictions may be on these subjects, while you are on duty you must refrain from any possibility of offending others. If you refuse to indulge, do so in such a way as to cause no embarrassment to the one offering you the treat. Because gum-chewing and smoking interfere with clear enunciation, you cannot talk to a guest intelligibly if your mouth is thus engaged. One secretary heard an executive say, "Smoking is just an evidence of lack of poise." Because she was a smoker, that seemingly extravagant statement made her watch this conservative man's guests. She became convinced that if a man would be forceful in dealing with a customer, he should refrain from smoking when he went out to greet him.

Business, especially secretarial work, which is based so largely upon the powers of observation, demands clear thinking. Enough foolish deals are made by representatives whose minds are beclouded by liquor without your adding to the list. A secretary who must keep her employer in partial seclusion while others handle his work after a business luncheon will need no admonition on this point; but the average secretary, having no such horrible example, is sometimes careless in accepting a lunch hour cocktail.

Treatment of an office visitor

When a guest is at your office for any length of time, put the office facilities at his disposal. You may be able to aid him in making telephone calls and appointments, procuring railroad and theatre tickets, making hotel reservations, and taking care of his mail and dictation. Acceptance of tips, gifts, and entertainment for these services should usually be avoided. However, if a service has been outstanding, the guest may feel happier in giving you some impersonal return for the time you have spent. The idea of working for a tip is undemocratic, but sometimes a visitor is not inclined to accept unlimited service from a secretary who rigidly refuses all tokens of appreciation. Flowers, candy, theatre tickets, and other impersonal gifts which you receive from a pleased visitor should be enjoyed, and a note of appreciation dispatched to the sender. However, you must be careful not to embarrass an office guest by placing him in a position where he feels obliged to make some return for it.

When a guest is to stay for luncheon, you may make table reservations at some dining room. If a number of guests are invited for a conference, it is usually important that they be seated so that the discussion can proceed during the meal. Confusion will be avoided if you make out place cards. After the seating arrangement has been approved by your employer, send the cards to the head waiter.

It's the little things that count

The person who is willing to serve usually has ideas or he would not see the little things to do. Think of the little things and the big things, for no person can put the right degree of emphasis on each of life's efforts! Emphasis in secretarial teaching is put on outstanding duties, but it is the little services which make a caller aware of your intelligence and thoughtfulness.

BOOKS THAT WILL HELP YOU TO MEET PEOPLE

Psychology Applied to Life and Work (3rd ed.) Harry Walker Hepner, Prentice-Hall, Inc., Englewood Cliffs, N.J.

How to Have Model Beauty, Poise and Personality, John Robert Powers, Prentice-Hall, Inc., Englewood Cliffs, N.J.

Eleanore King's Guide to Glamour, Prentice-Hall, Inc., Englewood Cliffs, N.J.

How to Have Confidence and Power in Dealing With People, Les Giblin, Prentice-Hall, Inc., Englewood Cliffs, N.J.

The Art and Skill of Getting Along With People, Sylvanus M. Duvall, Prentice-Hall, Inc., Englewood Cliffs, N.J.

Business Behavior, Bell and Abrams, South Western Publishing Co., Cincinnati, Ohio

Emily Post's Etiquette (9th ed.), Funk & Wagnalls, New York

Vogue's Book of Etiquette, Mildred Fenwick, Simon and Schuster, New York

Chapter 6

Telephone Technique

A vast expenditure of human voice.
—ARISTOPHANES

No feature of your work will be more important than the efficient handling of the telephone. If you can master this art, you will become a real asset to your employer. Telephone problems demand an immediate and correct response. You cannot concentrate on them and solve them in a leisurely manner. If you make an error, there is usually no way of rectifying it. For this reason you must give much thought to the general technique of handling calls in order to have a well-defined idea of the ways in which various demands are met. When faced with a particular problem, bring all of this stored-up knowledge to bear upon it.

Courtesy heads the list

A condensed résumé of hints on telephone courtesy in various booklets published by the telephone companies covers the following points:

1. *Speak clearly.* Over the telephone, your entire message must be trusted to your voice. Your pleasure, your cordiality, your sincerity must be expressed, not by your eyes or smile, but by the quality of your enunciation, by a cheeriness in your greeting—by the rising inflection which you give to your sentences.

2. *Pay close attention.* In speaking over the telephone, you must give a customer scrupulous, courteous attention. There is no reason for listening to his conversation with half your mind and entering

figures with the other half. Your voice reflects your attentiveness; a lack of interest is easily detected.

3. *Be concise and courteous.* A good telephone salesman makes his point in a few sentences. Try to shorten your telephone conversations, not by leaving unsaid something that is of real importance, but by saying it in as few words as possible. Let your tone be both cordial and sincere.

4. *Answer promptly.* Promptness indicates alertness. Readiness with which a telephone call is answered shows pretty accurately the quality of service an organization may be expected to give.

Developing a consciousness of what others want

When you cannot see the person with whom you are speaking, it is easy to forget that he probably had some definite reason for calling. Keep keenly alert to comprehend just how you can be of service to him. A large organization sent the following circular to its secretaries:

When you are handling an incoming telephone call for an officer, in his absence, bear in mind the following points:

1. The customer, disappointed at not reaching the officer directly, wants only one of three things:

   a. To be called back.
   b. To leave a message.
   c. To know definitely where or when he can reach the officer.

2. This being the case, you should avoid particularly the hackneyed phrases, "Mr. Blank is in conference," and "Who is calling?" and reply instead somewhat as follows:

   "Mr. Blank is in a meeting until about 11:30. May I ask him to call you back?" or "Mr. Blank is out, but is expected back in about an hour. Do you wish to leave a message for him?"

3. In order to have this information when you need it, you will have to be on the watch for your officer's leaving his desk, and

if he forgets to tell you where he is to be located, remind him that you are expected to know.

The above instructions are valuable in taking care of a call, but they do not render any service in accomplishing the thing for which the person called. If you are a real secretary, you will know the business of the office so well that you can take care of many calls without making it necessary for your employer to handle them personally. Instead of saying, "May I ask him to call you?" say, "I wonder whether I could help you; Mr. Blank will not be back for an hour." The man thinks he wants only the officer, but it is entirely possible that someone else can give him the information he wants, or get it for him. Suppose the man tells you he wants to inquire whether the XYZ Railway 5% Bonds have been called. You may be able to inform him that they will be redeemed on March 15 at the main branch of your bank. If you are not sure that your firm is giving out this information, you may say, "I'll find out in a moment." This will free you so you can ask someone in authority.

Never let yourself get to a point where you "dispose" of telephone calls. You must always keep in mind the ideal of service, for this is the secret of a successful telephone technique. An inexperienced girl, picking up a call, was told that Mr. B. wanted to speak to Mr. M. Her reply, "He's not here," and her careless tone of voice closed the call. In the same careless tone, she added, "If it's anything urgent, we can call him in Boston." Her attitude had by this time annoyed the caller, a very important man, for he asked her to put someone else on the telephone. Her lack of effort, coupled with her ungraciousness, made her intolerable. Fortunately, most secretaries do not lack a desire to help; their most grievous errors are due to thoughtlessness.

Extent to which you may save your employer's time

Every successful man is subjected to the wiles of salesmen and others who would occupy all of his time if they were allowed to do so. As most large offices do not permit solicitation during office hours, the information clerk or receptionist will insist that any visitor tell his business before he is announced to an executive. This system precludes the possibility of many such interruptions; but, as the telephone has no "watchdog," you will be expected to perform this function.

Many executives answer their own calls when they are free to do so, but many others prefer that each telephone call be announced. Although you will be expected to follow the policy of the firm, it is generally conceded that if you say, "Mr. Jones is on the telephone," your employer can begin his conversation with a much more personal note.

Many people are sensitive about being bluntly asked, "Who is this?" So much has been written about that form of question that the secretary who uses it is branded as ignorant of the rules of the profession. Courteously inquire, "May I tell Mr. Brown who is calling?" or, if your executive is not in, "May I ask who is calling?"

If a man wishes to answer his own telephone there is no reason why he should not. In fact, the trend is now toward this method of receiving calls. However, young men and those not firmly established in their positions often delight in the trivial ostentation of having a secretary announce their calls. If their callers are impressed, this procedure is possibly a matter of good business. However, many customers and clients today look on this as an annoying practice and one that wastes valuable time for all concerned. In either event, you should be quick to sense the preference of your employer and accede to his wishes.

Although it is desirable to save your employer, you must always be careful that you do not become too zealous in protecting his time. Do not waste the time of the person who is calling by asking useless questions. The realization that your employer is a busy man sometimes dims your perception of the fact that the caller may be equally busy. A certain Wall Street secretary has made herself very unpopular by never connecting anyone with her employer (either on incoming or outgoing calls) until she hears the voice of the other man. If you wish to be helpful, it is usually possible for two secretaries to hold the wire until both men are ready to talk. Etiquette demands that your employer be ready to speak before you put in the call, but sometimes he is interrupted before you reach the other person and finds it difficult to make an immediate response. People are generally tolerant of these delays, unless they are known to be habitual.

Ways of getting names and information over the telephone

So much emphasis has been put on brevity that many secretaries try to reduce their conversation to telegraphic curtness. Take time enough to get essential data. Nothing is more exasperating than to find that a call is lost because someone has failed to obtain sufficient information. In every call a minimum of two things must be taken down correctly—first, the name, and second, the telephone number. If you do not assure yourself on these two points, your services are of little value. Do not be too sure that you know a certain voice and so neglect to check the name. Often two people have voices very much alike. If your employer telephones one of them and finds that he was not the person who called, it may be impossible to locate the man who did call. To avoid confusion say: "May I ask him to call you as soon as he comes in? This is Mr. Jones, is it not? . . . And your number is? . . . Thank you, Mr. Jones." Since a man may not be in his own office when he calls, get his number and extension.

In receiving names, it is often necessary to have them spelled in full. You may mistake the spelling—and nearly always the initials—if you do not check carefully by saying, "M as in Mary, L as in Lawrence." In confirming messages, some secretaries make use of the following letter code: A as in Adams; B as in Boston; C as in Chicago; D as in Denver; E as in Edward; F as in Frank; G as in George; H as in Henry; I as in Ida; J as in John; K as in King; L as in Lincoln; M as in Mary; N as in New York; O as in Ocean; P as in Peter; Q as in Queen; R as in Robert; S as in Sugar; T as in Thomas; U as in Union; V as in Victor; W as in William; X as in X-Ray; Y as in Young; Z as in Zero. This is an excellent method by which to attain speed, for it is possible to repeat letters with great rapidity if you have learned the code. True, a message is made much more individual if you can insert some word which is of timely interest. For example, you might say to a baseball fan, "D as in Dodgers," or for a person who has been following current events, you might say, "N as in Neutrality." You must, however, be sure that the interests you stress are those of a listener and not your own. Above all things, never try to confuse another person by flaunting your superior knowledge. One businessman, in repeating a message to a girl with very limited educational background, was heard to say: "P as in Psychology; A as in Aklavik." The girl might not have known much, but she did know that he was being unpleasant.

Numbers may be checked by repeating them. Be sure to get numbers correctly, and write them down before you repeat them. If this is done, you can read the numbers from your own writing, thus avoiding the danger of transposition caused by noting them down later.

How to handle a volume of telephone business

When the bulk of the business of a concern is transacted by telephone, it is necessary to learn how to handle these calls in such a manner as to keep the lines free for incoming calls. You may have three or four wires coming into a small office. Often these lines are so connected that a call on any line can be picked up on any telephone. Do not keep anyone waiting unnecessarily. Get the number and call him back. This practice will free your lines for other business.

Make calls concise. You can often terminate a call by careful wording. However, this requires tact, for you must not leave a customer with the feeling that he has been shut off.

Cultivation of voice develops telephone personality

Nothing is more essential to good telephone work than a well-modulated voice. The majority of secretaries have taken little time

EVERY DAY—*Your Telephone Voice*

When you answer your telephone, does your voice do you justice?

Does it do the office justice?

At your desk or at the counter you are gracious, friendly, and tactful. You are face to face with your customer, and your personality is seen as well as heard. Each of you sees the other's smile and his sympathetic changes of expression.

But on the telephone your *voice* has to do all this.

It has to carry your personality over the wire, so that your customer may hear the smile he cannot see.

You should be as particular with your telephoning voice as you are with your personal appearance. Every time you use the telephone it is your company that is talking, and you have the opportunity to make or lose a friendship that may be very valuable to the organization.

Listen to yourself once in a while, and see if your telephone "appearance" is all that it should be. Only when it is low, clear, distinct, and well modulated can your voice do you justice.

It is easy to let down a bit sometimes, and give an impression of indifference that your customer may be quick to detect.

Clear, cheerful speaking on all your telephone lines is bound to make friends for the company.

KEEP THIS BEFORE YOU
till YOU *are satisfied with your telephone manners*

to train their voices, having been too busy learning the "silent art"— shorthand. It is well to devote some thought to voice culture. Most defects in voices are the result of some form of improper placement which could be corrected by instruction. A lisp is a serious handicap to telephone work, but it can be overcome by special instruction. However, do not become discouraged if your voice does not pass a broadcasting test. One of the most beloved men in Wall Street has a voice that is high-pitched, unmelodious, and otherwise distracting in tone; yet his desire to help others makes everyone happy to talk with him.

A reminder on your desk, like the foregoing one, will help you to develop a consciousness of the value of a pleasing telephone voice, even though you may lack much in tone quality.

Making use of directories

The directories put out by the telephone companies are handbooks with which you must become familiar. Make the utmost use of them by studying the tables of rates and general instructions in the front of the book. The classified directory, which often enables you to locate a business when the name is not known to you, is a source of information which most secretaries bury in an unused drawer.

A man said to a woman caller, "I wanted to call you, but I did not know where to reach you." She replied, "You must have a very inefficient secretary; the name is listed in the telephone directory." That criticism of the secretary was justified but should have applied equally to the employer. Many people do not exhaust the possibilities of securing information from a telephone directory. When any question of location comes up, be sure that you consult the directory to verify your answers.

Make up a "frequent call" index. Many large organizations issue an internal directory which gives the extension numbers of their officers and departments. Space is usually provided in these books for inserting other numbers frequently called. Stationery stores carry a number of helpful gadgets for listing the telephone numbers you call most frequently. Telephone companies usually furnish, without charge, booklets for listing the numbers you call most often.

Cooperating with operators

When you want to reach the switchboard operator move the hook slowly up and down. A quick depression of the hook does not flash a light on the switchboard.

Should a switchboard operator connect you with the wrong person, never be discourteous to the person answering the call. He really has more reason for impatience than you have. Do not reveal a petty nature by complaining to the caller if your own operator has put a wrong call on your telephone. One businesswoman has much trouble with her calls because another officer of the company has the same name. She impresses callers with the dignity of her organization by calmly saying, "I am sorry, you have Miss Smith's line, but I will have you transferred to Mr. Smith." Even though she is often annoyed, she controls herself so that she always displays courtesy in telling the company operator when a call is not meant for her.

Telephone companies provide operators to give assistance when you need it. In very small places all types of requests may be handled by the operator who first answers your call. This is not so in the large cities, where there are several kinds of operators. In most cities, for instance, you dial the special number for "Information" to obtain a number not listed in the directory. If you want to report a telephone out of order, you call the number listed for "Repair Service." These numbers appear in the front of your phone book. In dialing "Operator" for all of your needs, you are wasting your own and the girl's time, even though she will always tell you how to call these special operators.

Recording telephone calls

Do not trust your memory on telephone messages. Have a pad and pencil in a position where it is always readily accessible for taking down information as it is given. Some organizations have a specially printed form for telephone messages. When an executive returns and finds a notice on his desk similar to the form shown on page 109 he can confirm the engagement. If the appointment is satisfactory, nothing more will have to be done, but if he has made other arrangements, it will be necessary to call Mr. Jones. This call will be facilitated by the data he has in front of him. Even if you are not supplied with such pads, it will be well to keep the same points in mind as a guide in making notations on calls.

Some executives have a calendar on their desk for recording all memoranda; others prefer to have telephone calls recorded on a slip of paper which can be destroyed when the call is completed. Care must be taken to place these loose memoranda in a conspicuous place, always weighting them so that a gust of wind won't take them off the desk before the executive returns.

Proper use of the hold key[1]

Use of hold keys on a telephone is often not understood by secretaries. By pressing these keys, a call may be held or another one made simultaneously. This arrangement is advantageous when it is necessary to make another call to secure information with which to answer the first call. When holding a call, you must not forget to pick it up again; you may easily become so engrossed in other work as to

---

[1] Suggestions for special arrangements of telephones and hold keys are made by telephone company officials upon request, so do not hesitate to have a representative of the telephone company study the secretarial problems peculiar to your office.

```
┌─────────────────────────────────────────────────────┐
│              TELEPHONE  CALLS                         │
│   Mr. _____Brown_____     │
│     Called by __F. E. Jones_____     │
│     Firm_____First National Bank_____     │
│     Telephone number __Main 459_____     │
│     Extension number ____23_____     │
│     Time____2:30_____     │
│     Message: _____I made a luncheon engagement for    │
│     Friday at 12:30   Mr. Jones will meet you here.    │
│     Call received by _____M. J. Smith_____     │
│                                                       │
└─────────────────────────────────────────────────────┘
```

Figure 3. Telephone Calls

neglect to draw your employer's attention to a waiting call. The safest method is to put a memorandum on his desk to the effect that Mr. Philips is waiting for him on another line. This procedure has two advantages—first, you are relieved of the responsibility of notifying him again; and second, he may make an effort to terminate the other conversation if he knows someone is waiting.

A courteous lifting of the receiver and some such remark as, "This seems to be a long conversation, but I'm sure Mr. Brown will be with you in a minute," makes the wait much more pleasant for the one who is holding a wire. Nothing can be more bewildering than to hold a receiver and not know whether your call is receiving attention or not. Time goes much more slowly for one waiting for it to pass than it does for one who is busy. You must be aware of this and bridge any awkward wait in the most helpful way possible. Sometimes you can ascertain enough about the call to have needed data ready when your employer is free to talk. However, it is usually bad taste to force your conversation on someone who does not wish to talk with you. Some men take such opportunities for banter, yet they usually lose some of their respect for the efficiency of an office if you enter into an extended personal conversation. On the other hand, you should never give offense by "putting him in his place" sharply. A pleasant and intelligent, though busy, manner is best suited to your position.

When you have more than one extension

Where several lines can be picked up on one receiver, great care must be taken not to interfere with a person talking on one of them. If you do not have lights on the telephone or desk to signal what lines are in use, listen before you answer a call, in order not to interrupt a conversation that is in progress. Study your bells and distinguish between them before answering.

If you are stationed in a room separate from that of your employer, the telephone need not ring in the executive's office. A private signal will summon him when it is advisable that he handle any call personally. However, because an executive can usually call outside direct, avoid any danger of breaking into his conversations through picking up the extension in your office hastily.

Many men appreciate a secretary's remaining on the line to take down information and figures, but this should be done only at your executive's specific request.

Using a dial telephone

A dial telephone acts with mathematical precision. First, listen for the "dial tone" before starting to dial. When ready, dial correctly; the fact that you are thinking 2887 clearly will not place the call. You must dial each number slowly until the finger touches the stop. Give the dial time to return to its normal position after each turn; don't force it back.

When you reach a wrong number, be sure to report to the operator promptly when charges are involved. This precaution is necessary because, if a number dialed in error is answered, the telephone company's call-recording mechanism will, of course, register it. When you dial a number again, another call will be charged unless you have notified the operator to cancel the first charge. (Of course, you should not make the telephone company responsible for errors you make through carelessness in dialing.)

For telephone purposes the United States and Canada have been divided into over 100 areas each with its own 3-digit code. If you have Direct Distance Dialing you can reach a point in another area by dialing the area code before the telephone number. If you place your calls with an operator, give her the area code and the number. When you call someone in your own area, no code is needed. Direct Distance Dialing makes it possible to dial the Information Operator in many places, without charge, by dialing the proper area code and 555-1212.

A new system of telephone numbers (known as ANC, All-Number Calling is gradually being introduced throughout the country. You will therefore see telephone numbers like 829-9970. In these instances, you dial all seven numbers or give them to the operator. If there is an area code, dial it before you dial the seven numerals, or give it to the operator along with the number.

Keep personal calls to a minimum

Most businessmen give their secretaries the privilege of using an office telephone for their private calls. They realize that you are kept in all day and must occasionally arrange personal affairs by telephone. However, abuse of this courtesy has caused some organizations to make rules restricting personal calls.

Your friends probably won't call you often enough to become annoying, but they cannot see when you are busy and often call at an inopportune moment. They should realize your time is not your own when employed by another, so do not hesitate to inform them that you are busy and must cut the conversation short. Usually a message can be condensed into a few words. When you are busy taking dictation, somebody else can usually take the message or the number so that you can call back. Above all, it is fatal to give your employer the idea that you are giving personal calls precedence over business.

Although it is advisable to put in personal calls when your employer is absent so that you will be free to help him when he returns, do not hide the fact that you are making them by hanging up when you hear his step in the hall. An impression of stealthiness is so offensive that you must be careful to terminate calls in an open manner.

Don'ts for telephone use

1. *Don't scream.*   A loud voice does not travel smoothly over the wires; a well-modulated tone will make a much clearer impression on the electrical mechanism. Also be considerate enough to remember that, even though your business may not be a secret, few are interested in what you are saying. Loud speaking is often most annoying to your colleagues.

2. *Don't talk with the transmitter away from the mouth.*   It is easy to talk at the desk or in the direction of the note you are making instead of speaking directly into the transmitter. The rule is: Speak distinctly in a normal tone of voice, with the lips about one-half inch away from the mouth piece.

3. *Don't say, "Hello."*   This is a meaningless answer. If you say, "Mr. Brown's office, Miss Smith speaking," the one who is calling will not have to ask any questions and can save time by immediately delivering his message.

4. *Don't guess at who is calling.*   Phrase your conversation so that you can make sure of the identity of the speaker.

5. *Don't give out information indiscriminately.*   Always consult others, unless you are perfectly certain that your firm would wish the caller to receive the requested information.

6. *Don't slam the receiver back on the hook or dòwn on the desk.*   Untold annoyance and discomfort are often caused by this thoughtless habit of people who would never think of closing a door in a caller's face with a deafening bang.

7. *Don't neglect to accord your employer the courtesy of a title.*   The secretary who says, "Brown is out," has not only failed to uphold the dignity of the office, but has shown a lack of good breeding.

8. *Don't transfer a call without asking permission to do so.*   Anyone resents being racketed around like a tennis ball. Either get someone to pick up the call or, if you are sure another department can complete the call, ask the permission of the person calling to make the transfer.

9. *Don't neglect to cover the mouthpiece or press the hold key when holding a call.*   A listener is usually much embarrassed to hear a complete discussion of his request, especially if a comment happens to be uncomplimentary. You cannot always guard against impolite remarks, but you can be careful to spare a caller the pain of hearing them. If you wish to talk to someone in the office while on the telephone, press the hold key or cover the mouthpiece and the earpiece. (The earpiece can also pick up sound.)

10. *Don't keep people waiting.*   Be sure you are ready to talk before putting in a call. The "wait-a-minute" command is especially irritating to a person who has been called away from his work to answer your ring.

Examples of poor telephone habits

A study of the foregoing "Don'ts" would enable any experienced worker to go on indefinitely giving illustrations in which good telephone usage has been violated. However, a few concrete examples are given in the hope that they may serve to emphasize particularly annoying practices which have grown up in a large number of companies.

Loud speaking.   Secretaries who speak above an audible tone are not the only persons at fault. One officer shouts so loudly that he really needs no phone to communicate with local points—his voice, if directed out the window, would carry for several blocks. Although his office conversation is not loud, those who work with him have to become accustomed to his loud telephone calls. Strangers are much distracted by them. One important customer decided not to wait for the executive in an adjoining office. Upon departing, he confided to the secretary, "That noisy fellow would have me insane if I waited here half an hour."

Lack of discretion.   Many secretaries do not realize that within an organization there are trade secrets which must be guarded jealously. It is hard to realize, upon coming from the friendly atmosphere of a home, that there are people who will stop at nothing to get information that will further their own interests. In one instance a competitor was anxious to know whether a certain wholesale house was selling to one of its customers. A salesman, waiting until the sales manager of the rival house went to lunch, called his secretary and calmly asked the amount of the sales to Jones & Company for the month. Assuming that the voice came from someone in her own organization, the girl checked the files and gave the salesman the figure without question.

Shifting of calls. Secretaries often cannot answer questions, but they must be sure that in shifting the call they are not starting a chain of transfers, which becomes a growing annoyance in dealing with highly departmentalized offices. A customer called a department store and was connected with first one person and then another. Each time he told his story, he was transferred to someone else. Upon reaching a fifth person, he refused to repeat his complaint until assured that he would not be switched to someone else. A young clerk listened carefully, took the message, and then said: "This is Miss Lee speaking. My extension in 818. I will have this error checked at once and Mr. Smith will call you back in fifteen minutes. I am sorry you have had so much difficulty. Will you call me back in half an hour if everything isn't satisfactorily adjusted?" This girl knew absolutely nothing about the matter, but realized the impression repeated shifting of responsibility was giving the customer. Few people will deliberately slight a person when he is present, but they have no hesitancy in seeking the easiest way out of a telephone call.

Inability to relate a call to business. Many secretaries do not realize that proper handling of a telephone call often has a money value. One noon hour a stenographer for a firm of building contractors received a call from a stranger who asked her where a mortar mixing machine was wanted. The man said he had taken it to one building as instructed and found it was not needed there. The girl said she had no idea where it belonged and that the man who would know was out to lunch. The secretary to the president knew that the charge for these machines was about seven dollars an hour, so she rescued the call. After taking the number of the booth telephone, she carefully instructed the man to stay where he was until she called him back. By telephoning to several of the firm's twenty-eight contracting jobs, she located the building where they were waiting for the mixer. In ten minutes the man waiting at the booth had been recalled and proper instructions issued. Money was saved for the firm by the secretary's intelligent thinking. Is it any wonder that one of New York's largest contractors commented to her employer that she was the only woman he would trust to handle a business deal?

Keeping others waiting.   Many secretaries are blamed for keeping people waiting when really the fault lies with an employer who has no regard for the time of others. It is easy for secretaries to criticize this fault in a superior, but they are often equally guilty. One firm was constantly getting credit information from its bank, the secretary taking down the report in shorthand. Such scrupulous care was always taken to cause these credit men little trouble that nothing was too great a demand from this firm. A short time after a new secretary had replaced the thoughtful one, an officer of the bank called all the credit men to his office, saying, "I cannot understand this; there is now nothing but trouble with the firm where formerly we had nothing but praise." It was explained that the new secretary would call the credit department and then say, "Wait a minute." Sometimes she would keep a busy man waiting as long as eight minutes before she picked up the call again. Then she would be unable to take the report down correctly and had been known to call back three times to have figures repeated. Each time the credit man had to send to the files for the folder, and frequently by the time he had the information the secretary had picked up another call and was expecting him to wait until she finished. Even courteous explanations failed to make her change her tactics in dealing with a free service department.

Telephone answering services

Offices established to take care of telephone calls in the absence of a secretary may be found listed in any classified telephone directory under Telephone Answering Services. A small fee is charged for the service. Business and professional men often employ such a service to supplement their regular office force. In the case of a physician, it is imperative that calls be taken care of at all hours of the day and night, but usually there is not work enough to warrant hiring more than one office secretary. To provide him with 24-hour telephone coverage, a connection may be made with a telephone answering service, which will take his calls when the secretary is not in the office. Temporary service may be secured for such periods as vacations of the regular secretary.

If this service has been retained to relieve you, the secretary, do not forget to notify it when you leave the office. In allowing the service to make appointments, be sure that it has a correct copy of the office calendar for the next few days. See that you instruct it as to where your employer can be reached in case of an emergency call. When connected direct with your office, the answering service may pick up a call if you are slow in answering. Do not break in on the conversation, for the caller will not know that the call is not being answered in your office. If it is absolutely necessary to make a correction, use special tact in interrupting.

Intercommunication systems

These devices permit a direct connection between individuals or two or more people who communicate frequently. The communication may be one-way or two-way. A key is depressed or a switch turned to make the connection. So varied are the features and uses of intercom systems that it is best to discuss your requirements with representatives of the different manufacturers.

Some of the advantages of such a system are that: (1) the switchboard is relieved of handling a volume of interoffice calls, (2) no dialing is required, (3) one can get necessary data or information over it while talking to a client or a customer on the telephone, and (4) it saves the time of executives, who can confer with each other without leaving their desks.

An intercommunication system is particularly necessary when an executive prefers to turn off the telephone bell in his office. His secretary then is expected to take complete charge of telephone calls and to announce by way of the intercom only those that require his attention.

Be especially careful, when communicating with anyone over this device, not to place the telephone receiver on the desk in such a position that it will pick up sounds from the intercommunication system. Some systems allow for the microphone in the unit to be turned off and a handset substituted when privacy is needed.

Types of telephone service

Telephone facilities have been developed in this country to a point where there is a form of service to fit almost every need. Make an intelligent study of these services, so that you will be able to use each most economically and efficiently. Telephone companies are happy to cooperate with you in working out your individual problems.

Person-to-person calls

A person-to-person call is the more expensive of the regular types of out-of-town calls. For example, you put in a call for the Girard Metal Works, Philadelphia, and ask to speak to Mr. Howard Worthington. When the long distance operator calls the Girard Metal Works, she gets Mr. Worthington to the telephone before she notifies you that your call is ready. You are then free to begin talking at once, charges being made from the time the conversation begins. If Mr. Worthington is not there, a small report charge may be made. However, if you instruct the operator to try again a little later and she succeeds in reaching him, you pay only for the call. Person rates are charged on all calls placed to a specific person, room, or extension number.

Station-to-station calls

A station-to-station call is cheaper than a person-to-person call and is usually handled more quickly. You give the number you want in a distant city, agreeing to talk to anyone who answers the telephone.

If the operator asks you if you want to speak with some particular person and you give a name, you have made a person-to-person call of your station-to-station call and, accordingly, will be charged more.

Judgment in placing a call

The desirability of a particular type of call can be decided upon only by knowing both your employer's wants and the circumstances surrounding the person called. Remember that in a station-to-station call, you are charged from the time the telephone is answered. An electrician asked his secretary to place a call for Mr. Smith of the Gray Electric Company in a distant city. The young woman called the telephone number engraved on the stationery of the Gray Company. Because the call had been executed on a station-to-station basis, the charges began as soon as the Gray operator answered. After much waiting, Mr. Smith was located. In the meantime the charges had mounted to $5.20, whereas a person-to-person call would have cost only $3.35. Had the secretary known her business, she would have been aware of the risk in making a station-to-station call to a busy executive in a large organization.

If you know the person desired will answer his own telephone number, or if you have previously arranged to talk to a person at a certain hour, or if anyone who answers the telephone can take care of your request, it is advisable to take advantage of cheaper rates. When you receive a reply that Mr. Smith is at his desk waiting to talk to your employer, it is safe to place a call on a station-to-station basis.

If the line is disconnected

If you are disconnected during your conversation, hang up immediately if the other party called you originally. However, if you placed the call originally, signal the operator, tell her you were disconnected and give her the number of the other party. She will then reestablish the connection.

Night and Sunday rates

Reduced rates to most points in the United States and Canada are in effect from six o'clock P.M. to four-thirty o'clock A.M., all day Sunday, and on many holidays, such as Christmas. They also are in effect to foreign countries, but at varying hours. Check with the rate operator as to what hour the lowered rate begins in the country you wish to call. These rates apply both to station-to-station and person-to-person calls. In some businesses great savings are being effected by making use of night rates for long distance calls to salesmen and branch offices. Each man can be ready to talk when he is free from distractions of a busy day by making arrangements for the call beforehand.

Appointment calls

In placing a person-to-person call, you may specify a certain time that you will talk with a person. The telephone operator will endeavor to put the call through at the exact time. The charge is the same as for a person-to-person call.

Messenger calls

If an individual with whom you wish to speak does not have telephone service, a messenger will be sent to call him to the telephone. The charge made by the messenger (often a telegraph messenger) will be added to the charge for the telephone call, and is made whether or not the call is completed.

Conference telephone service

By means of conference telephone service three or more persons in the same city or in different cities can confer with one another by telephone just as though they were all seated around the same table. Each can hear and be heard by the others. The secretary may arrange a telephone conference by telling the operator she wishes to make a conference call.

Collect calls

The recipient of a call may be charged for it if he agrees to accept the call at the request of the caller, or if he requests that the charge be reversed. You should understand thoroughly how to handle calls in which charges are reversed. In some businesses customers have a habit of calling up on any pretext and reversing the charges. The cost of such calls sometimes makes their patronage unprofitable.

Some businesses advertise that their customers may call collect, or they use a service which automatically makes incoming calls "collect" calls. Many firms ask their salesman to reverse charges on all calls made to the home office. The salesman putting in a call will request that charges be reversed. When the telephone operator passes the call to you, she asks whether you will accept the call. Be sure that your employer would want to pay for the call before you accept it.

When a businessman feels that the necessity for the expense of a telephone call was the responsibility of his firm, he may, when the call is finished, ask you to tell the operator to reverse the charges. Suppose a farmer, failing to get repairs for his plow, calls the hardware store to ascertain the reason for this delay. If non-delivery was due to negligence at the store, it would probably be good business for the storekeeper to insist on paying for the call. The operator should be signaled and instructed accordingly, as soon as the call is finished.

Some private businessmen ask their secretaries to reverse charges on all family calls. For instance, when son calls from college, father pays. It is important that you be alert to carry out such arrangements.

Initial period rates

Charges for local telephone calls are usually based on an initial period—most frequently of four minutes. For long distance calls, the initial period is three minutes. Lists of important places, with the initial charge made to each, are published in many directories. They also usually include information concerning government taxes applying to such out-of-town calls. Offices which do not have a booth telephone for the convenience of visitors sometimes depend on the secretary to make collections from those who use an office telephone for other than local calls. When the call is placed, ask the operator to let you know the charge, and she will do so after the call is finished.

International and mobile telephone service

From your telephone you can be connected with millions of telephones in Alaska, Hawaii, Canada, Central and South America, Europe, Africa, Asia, and Australia; in fact, practically anywhere in the world. With the increase in international business, a secretary will not find it uncommon to be called upon to put in calls to foreign firms. Long distance operators are highly efficient and very helpful, but only complete and definite information enables them to place a call in a minimum of time. To make your call, tell the operator you wish to place an overseas call and give her the name of the country you are calling.

Telephone calls can be made to ships and boats, automobiles, trucks, and trains equipped for mobile telephone exchange service. Ask the operator for the mobile service operator or the marine operator.

Private switchboards

In smaller offices secretaries are frequently required to operate a switchboard. In fact this has become so common a requirement either for steady or relief work that some business schools have had switchboards installed in their school office in order to give secretarial students this training. Three main types of telephone boards are in common use—those where a plug is employed, those where a key is on the board itself, and those which are called consoles and are operated by buttons. Telephone companies maintain instructors for teaching the technical operation of any type of switchboard which you may be called upon to use. Avail yourself of this service; do not be content to absorb your knowledge from a girl who has probably had little or no instruction herself. You will need to know the best practices in mechanical operation so that you will be free to concentrate on caring for calls efficiently.

Do not feel that telephone switchboard operation is beneath the dignity of a secretary. You will probably find that many calls will tax even a good secretary's ability. If all offices tested the business background rather than the voices of their operators, they would save money and customers through not having inquiries met with a silvery-voiced "I haven't the least idea." Who is more admirably trained to handle a business call than the secretary with a broad knowledge of English, office organization and management, business psychology and procedure, and trade terms, coupled with an ability to record messages speedily by means of shorthand? The question is usually not whether you are too big for the job, but whether you are big enough.

TELEPHONE HELPS

Telephone directories (instructions in front).
Classified directories (helpful groupings).
Telephone companies distribute pamphlets from time to time which will aid you in developing your telephone personality and in using equipment more efficiently. They also offer telephone technique training programs.

Chapter 7

Telegraphic Communication

Across the wires the electric message came . . .
—ALFRED AUSTIN

Mankind's efforts to communicate

Smoke signals, relay runners, carrier pigeons, the Pony Express—all were used as means of communication between men in one place and men in another. It was not until the 13th Century that thought was directed to the use of electricity for sending messages through space. The man whose concept this was ended up in prison for dealing in black magic, and it was four hundred years before the first electricity-producing machine was made. By the 18th Century electricity had been sent through 800 feet of wire, and man was well on the way to overcoming the handicaps of time and space in his search for rapid communication.

The invention of a telegraph system was inevitable, but the steps in that direction were slow and halting. It was with awe and wonder that America's first telegraph line (between Washington, D.C. and Baltimore) was inaugurated. The initial message was sent in the code devised by the inventor of the first practical telegraph system, Samuel F. B. Morse.

Today communication is carried on with high-speed automatic transmission systems, radio beams, and facsimile telegraphy. No longer does distance impose limits on communication. Western Union Research and Engineering Department predicts that in the not-too-distant future new electronic developments will cause the world to "shrink to a split second in size."

123

Methods of sending wires

All wires, whether telegrams or international communications may be filed at the same office. You may file messages personally at the nearest telegraph office or dictate them over the telephone. Some offices have call boxes connected directly with the telegraph office, and a turn of the handle will bring a messenger to your office within a few minutes to pick up your wire.

However, the majority of telegrams are transmitted by means of facsimile or teleprinter machines in business offices. Facsimile machines permit direct connections with the nearest telegraph center. Telegrams may be sent and received over it instantly in "picture" form at the press of a button. A tiny electronic eye reads the telegram and flashes a replica of it to the nearest telegraph office. The same machine receives messages in as swift and simple a manner. A teleprinter is a printing telegraph machine with a keyboard resembling that of an ordinary typewriter. It is connected by direct wire to a telegraph office and is used for receiving messages, as well as sending them.

The time element must be considered

Think of the time of day when you send a telegram. Differences in time in various regions of the country will help you decide whether to send a fast or a delayed message. For instance, at the close of day for businesses on the Atlantic Coast, there is still an hour to go at points in the Central Time Zone, such as Chicago, St. Louis or Dallas; two hours to go at points in the Mountain Time Zone, such as Denver or Albuquerque; three hours to go at points in the Pacific Time Zone, such as Reno, Seattle or Los Angeles. Of course this works in reverse from the Central, Mountain and Pacific Time Zones to the Atlantic Time Zone. Supposing, though, that there is a time difference to your advantage. This would mean that your employer could send a fast telegram and close a deal or confirm an order before leaving for home. On the other hand, if the Time Zone you are in means that your office is open later than the one you want to get in touch with, he could send an economical night letter.

Fast telegrams provide the speediest service. Fifteen words can be sent at the minimum rate. Each word over the minimum adds an additional low charge. The address and signature are carried without charge.

Day letter service is best for longer messages that can be sent a little less speedily and at lower rates and still serve their purpose. In general, the cost of a 50-word day letter is the same as that of a 25-word fast telegram. When what would normally be a day letter is sent to a business house so late that its delivery during regular business hours is doubtful, use the fast service.

Night letter service is an economical overnight method of sending a message. There is a 2 A.M. deadline for messages to be delivered the next morning. The basic charge for a night letter is for 50 words. Additional words are charged for in groups of 5 words. Lengthy, complex business proposals, reports, and so on can be sent in this way.

Delivery of wires to local points

Messages are usually delivered to local points through regular messenger service. However, telegraph companies often telephone messages in order to expedite service. Although the telephone hastens delivery and is often very satisfactory, you frequently will want a copy of the message for your files. Ask that the message also be delivered by messenger or by mail, if a file copy seems desirable. Copies of telephoned messages may be called for at the telegraph office if it is found that they are needed later.

Sending messages to distant points

Messages are usually telephoned to places beyond the limits of local messenger service, although they may be mailed if no telephone is listed. For this reason include in the address the name of a telephone subscriber in whose care the message may be delivered. In remote sections of the country, a special charge may be made for telephone delivery. For instance, if your employer is on a hunting trip, you may want to reach him though he is far from a telegraph office. Your message can be sent to the telegraph station nearest his location, and you will be informed of the amount of any telephone toll charge necessary to relay the message to him. If you do not wish to pay the telephone charge, your message will be dispatched in the next mail delivery to the hunting lodge. Of course, special telegraph messenger service will be provided to any point if the expense seems warranted.

How to write a telegram

If your office does not have a facsimile or teleprinter service, type the messages you send in order to avoid the danger of misinterpretation by the operator who reads it.

Telegraph blanks are available at any branch office of the telegraph or cable companies. Mark the class of service you want in the box at the upper left-hand corner of the telegraph blank. Point of origin and date should be put at the upper right side. The name and address (for which no charge is made) should be as complete as possible. When sending a telegram to a passenger on a train, airplane or bus, give complete details. For instance, if the message is being sent to an airport for delivery to a passenger on an airplane, include the name of the airline, the flight number, and time of arrival if possible.

Whether the telegram is being sent *Paid* or *Collect* should be written under the service classification. If it is to be charged, write the name of the account in the space provided.

Word a message concisely, but not to the point where it is not clear. Don't divide words at the end of a line.

Figuring out the charges

Punctuation is free and is no longer written out as a word. Messages may be written in paragraph form. Combinations of two or more dictionary words are counted according to the number of words used. Abbreviations are counted at the rate of one word for each five letters. Proper names in any language are counted according to the number of separate words in the name, such as New York City, which counts as three words. No charge is made for one signature.

Confirming wire messages

Make at least one carbon copy of each wire for your files. A second carbon copy is sometimes mailed to the person to whom the wire is directed. This confirmation checks any error in transmission.

Usually a letter is written in which the contents of the wire are blocked in the center of the sheet. Suppose a brokerage house received an order from a customer and action on the order is confirmed by wire immediately. You will probably be expected to send a letter confirming the wire as follows:

March 21, 19—

Mrs. R. M. George,
   875 Ridge Avenue,
      Milford, New York
Dear Madam:

PURCHASED FOR YOUR ACCOUNT

ONE HUNDRED WESTINGHOUSE AT FORTY

Confirming the above telegraphic message which was sent you yesterday, we have purchased for your account:
100 Shares Westinghouse Electric Common @ 40
This stock will be delivered to our safekeeping department, where it will be held pending your instructions. Attached is a statement of your account.

Thank you for this business.

Very truly yours,

SMITH & BENNETT
By . . . .

Sending international messages

International cable and radio messages differ from domestic telegrams in that registered code addresses may be used and code words are permitted in the full-rate classification. Write these messages as you would a domestic telegram. Senders are responsible for incorrect or insufficient addresses. Check carefully before sending an international message. There is a charge for correcting or adding to addresses so that delivery can be made.

Full-rate cablegrams. This is the standard fast service for messages in plain language or in code or cipher or in a combination of plain language and secret language. There is a minimum charge for seven words.

The letter telegram. This service is for messages in plain language only. The charge is one-half of the per word rates applicable to full-rate messages, and the minimum charge is for twenty-two words. This is an overnight service. Delivery is usually made the day after the message is filed, but in certain Far East countries delivery cannot be made until two days after filing. Letter telegram messages are designated by the letters LT which should be placed before the address and are counted and charged for as one word. Secret language may not be used in letter telegrams, but registered code addresses are permissible in the address or signature.

Shore-to-ship messages. This service permits communication with ships at sea in all parts of the world. Only full-rate messages may be sent.

Writing international messages

Write these messages as you would a domestic telegram. Code addresses may be used to save charges, and the use of secret language is permitted in the full-rate classification. Each word in the address, text and signature is counted and charged for. Each plain language (dictionary) word used in either full-rate or letter/telegram messages is counted at the rate of fifteen, or fraction of fifteen, letters to the word. Figures are counted at the rate of five, or fraction of five, figures to the word. Punctuation marks are counted and charged for as one word each in international messages, except when they appear in a group of figures or letters. Each then counts as one figure or one letter, not as a separate word. Secret language, consisting of non-dictionary words, can be sent full-rate only and is counted at the rate of five, or fraction of five, characters to the word.

Use of codes

Code words are used either to reduce costs or to insure secret transmission of the message. Both sender and receiver must have the code, or it is useless to send the message in that way. Secretaries who use a code in much of their work are not always mindful of this point. Code words are now allowed in all domestic messages; until recent years they were restricted to certain types of service.

Code words and regular words may be used in the same full-rate message. For example, a travel department might send the following telegram to its main office: SOLO SEVENTEEN NEW YORK PITTSBURGH JULY TENTH DAVIDSON. Translated this would mean, "Kindly reserve a lower berth on Train No. 17 from New York to Pittsburgh on July 10 in the name of Davidson." Because the requesting office would probably want to give Mr. Davidson a copy of the wire confirming the message, the New York branch would not send the message back in code but would wire: RESERVED FOR DAVIDSON UPPER SEVEN CAR ELEVEN TRAIN SEVENTEEN NEW YORK TO PITTSBURGH FRIDAY JULY TENTH. Notice how the number of words is not limited in the reply because every contingency must be covered. It would be unsafe simply to wire back: OK.

Extensive commercial codes, such as Acme, Bentley, ABC, Lieber, and others, are also published. In some of these codes, as many as one hundred thousand selected phrases are coded in words of five letters each. Sums of money are so arranged as to have at least three different letters. These differences make it impossible to mix sums by striking one letter incorrectly; three letters could scarcely ever be inadvertently changed in sending a message. Special supplements, such as the Wool Supplement, can be secured. These supplements make the prepared codes easily adaptable to any branch of commercial work.

Private codes. Codes are made up for the use of individuals or firms, and are usually employed only when it is desirable to keep the contents of wires strictly confidential. Contents of a message written in a commercial code could not be concealed if the reader were very eager to learn its meaning, for the message could easily be translated by referring to a copy of the code. For this reason commercial codes are used only for expediency or to obscure a message so that the casual observer will not know its importance. Secret codes are the only means of gaining absolute privacy. If you have access to one of the keys to a secret code, keep it safely locked when it is not in use. Even if you are not admitted to the inner circle of office secrets, when you receive a message which means nothing to you, be awake to the fact that it may be a code message. One secretary took a position in which one of her duties was to record sales of a syndicate issue. She received this message from one of the salesmen: SOLD FIRST 10M GUAR- ANTEED FIVES HAPPY. She sat there for a while and then said, "No wonder he's happy. His commission will be good." Some code words are invented to test the transmission of a wire, and *happy* was the code word by which the teletype operator checked the figure 10M.

In taking dictation of a message in secret code, you will have to be more than ordinarily careful not to get any of the words or letters confused. This is one occasion where it is best for you to obey in- structions blindly, without too much curiosity as to meaning. You will probably find yourself much less involved if you remain content to be ignorant of a secret message, for you will know nothing which you might divulge inadvertently.

Keys to a code. For the effective use of a code a well-organized key is necessary. Usually this key is arranged in two parts: the first is a dictionary-like grouping of words and phrases so they can be easily found in coding a message for sending; the second is an alphabetical arrangement of the code words themselves so that they can be readily translated in decoding a message. In the first section the code word appears after the phrase or word for which it is a symbol; in the second section the translation appears after the code word.

Decoding. You may be called upon to decode a message. See that you do not leave scraps of paper from this decoding around which might give away the key to any part of the code.

Suppose a cable you receive contained only one word in the main message—LOHAUNMEET. You have been informed that the Bentley Code is being used in your office. Turn to the second section of the code book which will have been provided for your use. First, divide the message into two words of five letters each and then look up each word. These would be found to have the following translation:

LOHAU—market firm with upward tendency

NMEET—telegraph best offer you can make

The decoded message should usually be typed on the bottom of the original wire.

If you cannot find a word after looking carefully for it, send the cable back for verification. Do not attempt to change anything, because you have no way of telling what letter has been changed. Secretaries, being accustomed to filling in words from context in transcribing shorthand notes, often make the mistake of guessing at what is meant in a cable. Some very good secretaries have caused their firms serious losses because they have shown too great ingenuity in making a plausible translation of an incorrect message.

Decoding companies. Warning has been given you to ascertain the code being used by the recipient of your wire before you send it, but some of your communicants will not be so careful. Suppose you are using the Bentley Code exclusively, and some foreign house gets mixed up and sends a message to you in the ABC Code; what are you to do? If you can identify the code, you may be able to procure a key; but, if not, special companies will decode a message for a nominal fee. These companies may be found in a classified telephone directory under the heading "Codes."

Western Union Telex service

One of the most popular communications methods today is Western Union's rapidly expanding Telex service, the direct-dial customer-to-customer teleprinter exchange service. Already in use nationally, Telex provides almost instantaneous direct connections, at the turn of a dial, among all subscribers in the United States, over 100 points in Mexico and Canada, and 67 overseas countries. After dialing the number of the distant subscriber, the employee in a business office presses a "Who are you?" key and an automatic "answer-back" feature confirms the connection, assuring instantly that the connection has been made with the desired customer and that transmission—even when no one is in the distant office—is being received.

Teletypewriter service

Many large business houses subscribe to teletypewriter wire services, either private or public, as a means of transmitting and receiving messages. A fast and accurate means of communication, teletypewriters of various kinds permit written conversations between businesses and their customers or branch offices.

The teletypewriter has a keyboard like that of an ordinary typewriter. Seated at it, the operator can ask and answer questions, give and receive information. The words the operator types will appear on all the machines with which her office is connected.

Private wire services

Private wire service is leased from the commercial telegraph and telephone companies for the exclusive use of a concern. The cost of leased wires is based on mileage, plus certain equipment charges, depending on how many offices are on the circuit. For example, a wire from New York to Washington may be leased on a mileage charge, but if Philadelphia and Baltimore offices were to be included on this wire, extra charges for each city would be made.

Most private wire systems today are used for data processing as well as for administrative communications. The telegraph equipment and circuits are combined with modern business machines and perform such functions as controlling manufacturing processes, and speeding the processing of bills, sales, inventory, payroll, production, and shipping in a company with offices many miles apart.

Thousands of large companies, organizations, and Government offices lease private wire systems. Sometimes several firms band together in installing a private wire system. Large banks all over the country are linked in this way, as are branch offices of airlines, brokerage houses, and so on.

Two-way overseas transmission is also available to firms having extensive foreign transactions.

Facsimile process

Private and public facsimile telegraph systems are available for accurate transmission of letters, orders, requisitions, drawings—every kind of document—with the utmost speed. One of the latest models reproduces a standard 8½ x 11 inch document in less than three minutes and can send 300 typed words a minute. Some facsimile systems are also used between railroad stations for sending duplicates of tickets.

Leased wire systems of communication have made tremendous strides in recent years. A businessman, in a recent speech before a trade convention, predicted that correspondence by mail would in a few years be completely displaced by machine-transmitted letters. This may be an ambitious assertion, but correspondence between branch offices has already been reduced to a minimum through teletypewriting and facsimile services. No delay is necessary to ascertain what the other fellow is going to do; his answer may be received within a few minutes. A whole transaction is completed and forgotten before a letter could be mailed. Also, instructions may be broadcast by wire to all branch offices simultaneously instead of by a special letter to each.

Special services available

In recent years the telegraph company has added many services to the basic one of transmitting messages. Indeed, few business people are aware of all the help the company is capable of rendering. An outline of some of these special services may acquaint you with the demands you can properly make on the telegraph company.

Transfer of funds

You can send money orders wherever there is a telegraph or cable office. The addressee goes to the telegraph office nearest to him to collect the money. This service is also available nights, Sundays, and holidays, when it is impossible to get money from banks. If immediate transmission of funds is not necessary, American Express money orders, which are less expensive, can be purchased at telegraph offices.

Two types of instructions may be given in sending money by wire. The "vigilant" order calls for identification of the receiver of the money by a third person known to both the receiver and a representative of the telegraph company. The "caution" order is used when positive identification is impossible, although a representative of the telegraph company exercises all possible caution in paying out the money. In filing a caution order, it is customary to give an answer to some question which would be known only to the person whom you want to receive the money. For example, "Mother-in-law's first name is Jennie" might be included in the instructions to the telegraph company. When the representative at the paying station is asking for personal cards and letters, and other types of identification held by the receiver, he will look up and ask, "What is your mother-in-law's first name?" If the receiver answers "Jennie," he is considered identified. Vigilant orders should be sent whenever possible, but sometimes money must be paid to a representative who is in a place where he cannot be identified by a third person.

Gift orders and shopping service

Attractive gift orders may be sent by telegraph. They may be cashed or used anywhere by the recipient for the purchase of a gift.

Through the shopping service, flowers, candy, gifts of all kinds can be sent by wire and delivered on the same day to persons in distant cities. You tell the telegraph office the type of gift you want purchased and the amount you wish to pay. The telegraph company purchases the gift in the destination city and delivers it.

Messenger and errand services

A complete line of messenger and errand services is available through telegraph offices. They will see to the pickup and delivery of envelopes, documents, blueprints, briefs, news copy and press releases; advertising cuts, mats, proofs and drawings; biologicals, pharmaceuticals, and other professional materials. They will pick up forgotten articles at home or the office, garments from the tailor, books from the library, and take prescriptions to a pharmacist.

Market and opinion survey service

Telegraph offices make local, sectional and nationwide surveys in thousands of communities in every section of the country. Through telephone interviews or by messenger delivery and pickup of questionnaires, data is gathered in regard to consumer opinions, buying habits, and radio and TV audience reactions. This service also checks retailer advertising displays, makes traffic counts, and brings dealer or reader lists up to date.

Among the other services offered by telegraph offices are hotel-motel reservations, weather reports and forecasts, collection of installment payments, advertising distribution, delivery of air cargo of limited weight, and commercial news.

Chapter 8

The Business Trip

When I was at home I was in a better place; but travellers must be content.

—SHAKESPEARE

Many businessmen travel over the country in the interest of their concerns. Large corporations with branch offices and the close affiliations of business activities today make it increasingly probable that every businessman will travel to some extent. Even week-end and vacation trips are often so closely combined with business that they have a commercial value. In the rush of modern business it is usually necessary to delegate many of the details of travel to someone not involved in the preparation for leaving. Of course a secretary will take the burden of this responsibility for her executive.

Planning the trip

If your employer goes away periodically, he can show you from experience what to plan; but if a trip is only an occasional break in his office routine, he will not have clearly defined ideas on the subject. You should prepare yourself to render even more assistance than the employer demands; this will enable you to be of inestimable help in anticipating and preparing for his needs.

Your own experience in traveling will not always be a help in making arrangements, if others have attended to the details of your personal trips. Many widely-traveled secretaries are perfectly useless in planning a business trip, for they have not learned that work and intelligence were required to procure the services which they enjoyed.

Imagination and an enthusiasm for making others comfortable will cause you to seek information which will enable you to plan a trip well.

Ways and means of travel

In choosing a mode of travel, remember that your employer is traveling at the company's expense. He is being sent on a mission because his firm believes him capable of transacting its business. See that he is made so comfortable that he will be fresh and fit to do his work ably. Long, hard rides, with uncomfortable accommodations and little time to clean up after the trip, make the representative of a company incapable of giving his best to the work at hand. However, expense accounts are often limited, so you must know how to get the best accommodations for the money allowed, unless your employer wishes to supplement the firm allowance with personal funds.

Know something about the different modes of travel. Learn to read maps and to take advantage of travel services. Transportation companies would seek you if they knew you were interested in travel; therefore, you should not hesitate to take advantage of their information facilities. Travel agencies will arrange all details of any trip for you, but even they cannot give you the best service unless you have well-defined ideas of what you want. For this reason you will need to get a clear concept of the scope and purpose of each trip.

Train service

If a trip is to be taken by rail, consult the consolidated ticket office or the railway office of the line on which the trip will be taken. The *Official Railway Guide,* published by the Railway Equipment and Publication Company, 424 West 33 Street, New York 1, New York, will give you much information which will prepare you to talk intelligently with railway people. If you are not familiar with timetables, study one through from cover to cover. Take particular note of methods of indicating chair, sleeper, and dining car service, as well as holiday and Sunday exceptions. When you have studied one large timetable thoroughly, you will be much better able to make quick and intelligent use of another. Never wait until you are called upon to plan a trip before making the acquaintance of railway literature. Keep timetables of commonly used routes on hand in your office, so that you can refer to them quickly when your employer or a visitor desires information or train schedules.

Train accommodations

Choose trains which make good connections and are equipped with chair cars for a day ride and sleeping cars for an all-night trip. An upper berth is cheaper than a lower berth, but is usually considered less desirable. Other Pullman accommodations include drawing rooms, compartments, bedrooms and roomettes, all of which have private toilet facilities.

Dining cars are not attached to all trains, and even when carried part of the way, they are often detached soon after regular meal hours. Because it is often desirable to while away a tedious train journey by eating, always include the hours during which dining car service is provided when making up the itinerary of a trip.

Notifying others of arrival

Do not be afraid to ask questions at railway offices. Be careful to have standard or daylight saving time clearly specified during the summer, although railways usually give out only standard time. Be especially careful to ascertain at what stations trains stop, because you will need this information in making confirmations. A businessman going to Boston asked his secretary to notify the branch manager to meet him. She merely wired: MEET TRAIN SEVEN FIFTEEN TONIGHT. The branch manager, not thinking to inquire what train arrived at that hour, went to the Back Bay station, which was near his home. The fact that the branch manager should have found out where the train arrived did not clear the secretary of a charge of carelessness. Because errors and misunderstandings do occur easily, you must assure yourself on each point so you can confirm everything, even to the extent of erring on the side of safety. Although you have made intelligent use of such published data as timetables, consult the railway information service to confirm that recent changes have not been made in train schedules.

Air service

Most passengers on American airways are businessmen. Travel by air is a quick and comfortable way of covering distances.

The principal annoyance to air travelers is the time it takes to reach airports outside of the larger cities. In some cases, the time it takes to drive to one's home or the office is longer than the time spent in the air. A theatrical agent who was in Bermuda on business returned to New York International Airport by jet in one and a half hours. The trip to his home in New Jersey by automobile took two hours. However, methods of quick commuting are being constantly devised to make air fields more accessible to business centers. The most helpful so far has been the establishment in major cities throughout America and Europe of helicopter taxi service between airports and to and from airports and downtown business areas. Your airline or travel agent can tell you in what cities this service is available.

Businessmen who are able to do so are wise in patronizing the bus or limousine service the airlines provide between some central point in each city and outlying airports. Planes will not leave until their own buses or cars arrive, but they do not wait for passengers who choose other means of reaching the field. With traffic conditions as they are, the traveler who drives himself or has someone drive him to the airport is under considerable strain wondering whether he'll get there before the plane takes off.

The airlines are glad to provide information on their scheduled flights. An excellent source of airline information is the Official Airline Guide, published by American Aviation Publications, Inc., 139 N. Clark Street, Chicago, Ill. In purchasing tickets and making reservations by telephone, specify clearly where you want to pick up the tickets. Unless you have an air travel credit card, find out how soon payment must be made before reservations are canceled, and check the times and places from which the planes and limousines start.

Reconfirming flight reservations

Plane reservations must be reconfirmed at each point of departure except the initial one. Check with the airline office at least six hours before flight time for domestic flights and twenty-four hours before an international flight is scheduled to leave.

Bus service

Private bus companies have regular service between most cities and on transcontinental routes. These buses often run at hours when it is impossible to get train or car service, thereby supplementing passenger service between many cities and towns.

Bus travel is usually quick, cheap, and conveniently accessible. Short trips are generally pleasant, but it must be remembered that buses do not have space to provide many facilities for a traveler's comfort on a long trip. A businessman will need to have ample time for rest after a long bus ride. Tickets cover transportation and hand luggage, and can usually be purchased at considerable reduction for a round trip. Meals may be purchased by a traveler at regular stops on the route.

Steamship service

Most steamship lines have agents or branches located in large cities. These agencies can be found in a classified directory or in the daily papers, or reference may be made to the Official Steamship and Airways Guide, published by Transportation Guides, Inc., 5 East 40 Street, New York 16, New York.

If your employer has been abroad before, his record will be on file, so you can renew his old passport by presenting it accompanied by a recent photograph. A passport is good without renewal for two years from date of issue. A person who has not been abroad will have to show a birth certificate, naturalization papers, or an affidavit evidencing citizenship. If reservations are made through a travel agency, getting together the foregoing data is all that will be required, but if arrangements are being made direct, a notarized form together with passport pictures must be forwarded to The Passport Department, Sub-Treasury Building, New York City, in ample time to secure passports and make any corrections necessary. Visas, which vary in price, must be secured from the consuls of the different countries which are to be visited.

Automobile travel

Although most business travel is done by means of commercially operated vehicles, many men prefer to use their own automobiles in these days of good roads. Although this method of travel makes them independent of regular schedules, men who take long trips often find this mode of travel exhausting. The American Automobile Association (A.A.A.) is an excellent guide in choosing routes. Gasoline companies furnish free and up-to-date maps of the different states and will route trips. *Lodging for a Night,* published by Duncan Hines, Inc., New York, lists accommodations for the automobile traveler.

Drive-Ur-Self service

Men who do not care to make business trips by automobile often find it desirable to rent cars in the cities to which they go, so that they can cover long distances between local points with ease and at a considerable saving in time. Several car rental agencies issue courtesy cards which enable a businessman to go into any of their branches and rent a car without paying the deposit fee required of a stranger. An increasing number of businessmen who travel are making use of this privilege in distant cities. Arrangements can also be made to have a car waiting for your executive when he gets off the plane or train. Your classified telephone directory lists the service under Automobile Renting and Leasing.

Automobile licenses

One duty which nearly every secretary must perform is the typing of an application for renewal of her employer's license cards. He usually gives the old license card to you, expecting you to copy the data from that. Try to use a little perception in copying this information from year to year. Because a man weighed one hundred sixty pounds when he got his first license is no reason why he could not have gained or lost many pounds later in life. Personal appearance changes from time to time to such an extent that it would be difficult to identify some businessmen from the descriptions on their license cards. It is not uncommon to find a completely gray-haired man who weighs two hundred thirty pounds carrying around a license which describes him as having black hair and weighing one hundred sixty pounds. The ridiculous discrepancy does not impress itself on the man himself because the change has been so gradual. He probably does not take time to think much about the card when it is filled in and handed to him for signature, but he *would* take the time if you brought the matter to his attention by asking him whether he wanted to revise any of the data.

In states where renewal blanks are not sent to former holders of licenses, you will get these blanks from the police department or some other source. If your employer is a member of the American Automobile Association, blanks will usually be sent to him from the local chapter of that association. When a trip is to be taken near the end of the year or near the end of a license period, see that applications are made early enough to get new cards or plates before your employer leaves.

Hotel accommodations

It is usually wise to reserve one of the best rooms at a small hotel, but in the large hotels it is quite safe to accept a medium-priced room. Be sure to include the bath in your reservation request in case the hotel has a limited number of private baths.

Try to get an outside room where the air will be good, and one on an upper floor, to avoid loud traffic noises. Make sure the room is not near a public bathroom or an elevator which would disturb the sleeper during the night. Do not be afraid to ask questions enough to assure yourself that accommodations will be satisfactory.

Confirmations of reservations

All confirmations of hotel reservations should be attached to a typed itinerary so they can be easily found in case your employer needs them upon arrival. If a branch office or a business acquaintance makes hotel reservations for your employer, be sure to have them confirmed by wire.

Choice of hotel

The question of choosing a hotel arises when a trip is to be made into a strange city. The *Hotel Red Book,* published by the American Hotel Association Directory Corp., 221 West 57 Street, New York, N.Y., may be used. Only the most recent issue should be consulted, for hotels change very rapidly. One secretary chose a hotel for her employer from an old list she found in the files. He reached there a little before midnight and went direct to his room. At seven o'clock the next morning he was at the factory with his baggage. As he expressed it: "God alone knew what went on in that hotel during the night." Local residents told him the hotel had deteriorated in the year since the death of the proprietor. It now had an unsavory reputation and was not listed in the newest Red Book.

Branches of a chain of hotels can usually be safely patronized. If your favorite local hotel does not have a branch in the city to be visited, it will have affiliations there. Just call the information department of the local hotel and you will find the people in charge there glad to give you up-to-date information and recommend a hotel that they consider in the class which your employer would wish to patronize.

Payments at hotels

Hotel chains usually issue a credit card to any businessman who is favorably known to the management or is connected with any well-known firm. This credit card will be good in all branches and at most affiliations of the hotel. Such courtesy cards are valuable to take along in case it is necessary to cash checks or otherwise have unexpected credit extended. Your firm may prefer to pay all travel accounts from the main office. Arrangements for forwarding bills should be made at the time of reserving a room.

Foreign travel

Often it is possible to have a foreign representative of your company or a member of some firm which your employer expects to visit take charge of making local arrangements for you. This procedure may eliminate all except direct railway accommodations, and these can be made quite satisfactorily without outside help.

Foreign accommodations

A few considerations must be kept in mind in making foreign reservations. Railroads offer three classes of accommodations—first, second, and third. These grades of service vary accordingly in comfort and price. A first-class compartment contains from four to six seats with excellent appointments. Second-class compartments have from six to eight seats and are recommended for economy. Third class is not carried on most express trains.

European hotels in the larger cities compare favorably in grade and service with American hotels, except that the bath is not so generally included with a room. If the bath is desired, it is wise to say so, even in making reservations for first-class rooms.

Air travel in Europe is as common as in this country, but many travelers prefer to go from one country to another by train, especially when the journey can be made overnight.

Using travel agencies

Unless your employer is familiar with the foreign country he expects to visit, arrangements should be made to have a travel agency care for the details of his trip. He will find it difficult to understand the customs of a new country, especially if he does not know its language well. He may have an experience similar to that of two businessmen who, traveling on their own responsibility, bought railway tickets but neglected to have them stamped. When they got on the train, their tickets were refused and they found themselves stranded at the next station for several hours. Travel agencies have local representatives to take charge of details of this kind, and they can relieve your employer of concern about such matters as taxis, hotels, and tickets. They will send him a typed copy of the complete itinerary, including a map on which the trip is traced, so that he will know exactly what to do next.

Travel agents are listed in the classified telephone directory. Or you may consult the American Society of Travel Agents, Inc., 501 Fifth Avenue, New York, N.Y. A businessman, although not always interested in entertainment while abroad, often combines a business trip with a sightseeing tour. He probably will have little time to devote to planning the pleasure side of a trip before he leaves the office. You can do much to add enjoyment to this part of his trip if you study the advantages offered in the vicinity of cities he will visit: find things which would probably interest him and suggest a list of things he should see. Provide him with books or résumés covering points which might escape his attention. Few businessmen have a broad knowledge of history and pass over many things which would interest them if they knew the significance of these points. One secretary always prepares a little story about each of the sights she schedules for her employer's trips. This memorandum she slips into his brief case.

Travel agencies are of great value in planning group tours. No individual can hope to compete with these companies in securing economy and scope for a trip to be completed in a limited time. However, you pay for the trips of the group, whether you are interested in all the features or not. Often arrangements can be made wherein only a portion of a personally conducted tour is purchased.

Your travel agent will have folders and travel guides your executive might wish to look over before going abroad. Your local bookstore will know of the newest books on points of interest, customs, history, and the like in whichever countries your executive will visit. Be sure any travel book you purchase, especially one that lists hotels, restaurants, or other data that can go out of date quickly, is the latest of its kind.

The itinerary must be complete

A carefully planned itinerary is a guide for the businessman in going about the country, and its carbon copy is a constant index by which you may locate him whenever necessary. Prepare it with accuracy, trying to visualize the trip in order to get in all details. In listing appointments, include initials, title, address, and telephone number of persons to be seen, if you can get these facts from correspondence or other sources. When you have assembled all of your data, start to go over the trip step by step. Roughly account for each moment. After each hour notation, put A.M. or P.M. and be sure to indicate the time division, such as EST, CST, or DST, if the trip is covering several time belts. Leave no detail out.

Here is an example of a prepared itinerary, covering a trip made by Henry F. Brown, a building contractor. An outline of the trip, together with wires confirming hotel reservations, was encased in a blue legal cover, which was easily carried in an inside coat pocket.

5:10 P. M. EST—

Henry F. Brown,
175 Broadway,
New York City

June 9–11, 19—

ITINERARY
New York—Philadelphia—Baltimore—Washington

Tuesday, June 9

2:00 P. M. DST—Leave Pennsylvania Station. Tickets and Pullman reservations (Chair 8, Car 91) in billfold. Contracts and blueprints on Philadelphia job in Envelope No. 1.

3:30 P. M DST—Arrive Suburban Station. Have planned that you go direct to the Sheraton, where R. M. Jones will meet you to talk over the progress of the building. Mr. Jones' office address—1630 Spruce St.—Telephone Spruce 1600.

8:00 P. M. EST—Leave 30th Street Station for Baltimore. Ticket and Pullman reservation (Chair 19, Car 17) in billfold.

9:30 P. M. EST—Arrive in Baltimore. Foreman M. J. Smith will meet you there in his car to drive over to the Lord Baltimore. Telegram confirming hotel reservations attached hereto. Mr. Smith's home address—160 Rockville Blvd. —Telephone Boulevard 8731. Envelope No. 2 contains all Baltimore data.

Wednesday, June 10

8:30 A. M. EST—Mr. Smith will take you on a round of inspection of the five buildings under construction.

11:30 A. M. EST—C. N. Harris, of the Empire Construction Company, will meet you at the Grand Building project to go over the subcontract work before you meet E. R. Preston, president of the company, for lunch.

1:00 P. M. EST—Lunch at the Penn-Sherwood. Subcontracts and blueprints in a large envelope which has been forwarded to the Penn-Sherwood by registered mail.

3:30 P. M. EST—Call Mr. Green here at the home office regarding progress with Empire representatives. Have Mr. Smith's office mail contracts and excess material in large envelope addressed to this office, which you will find in the bottom of the case.

Thursday, June 11

9:00 A. M. EST—Leave Baltimore by bus for Washington. No tickets. Telegram confirming reservations at Mayflower attached hereto. Envelope forwarded by registered mail contains data and figures. Other materials in Package No. 3 in this case.

10:00 A. M. EST—Senator Lane's committee on building will confer with you. Letter giving appointment details in Package No. 3.

3:30 P. M. EST—Take bus to airport. Plane tickets in billfold.

4:00 P. M. EST—Plane leaves for New York.

5:10 P. M. EST—Arrive at La Guardia Airport.

Getting things ready to take on a trip

The purpose of a trip will ordinarily dictate the things you will pack for your employer's use. Any correspondence which you think might be valuable should be included, as well as office forms that might be needed. If you think your employer might want to send out correspondence in the name of the firm, include a supply of the regular office stationery. Personal stationery may be wanted for letters for which hotel stationery cannot properly be used. A clean, well-filled fountain pen, a few pencils with erasers, some memorandum sheets, and a small box containing a few clips, rubber bands, and postage stamps will enable the traveler to work on the train or in his hotel room to advantage. Provide an ample supply of business cards. See that your employer's check book has a sufficient number of blank checks, and put in a new filler if there is any chance that more blanks will be needed before his return.

Files on special interests

Many businessmen have special interests in various parts of the country, such as offices in their fraternities, lodges, or trade organizations, or memberships on boards of directors of different companies. Of course they will want to be able to talk about these affairs intelligently if their trip takes them to these localities. Always keep a special file on each interest and put the ones he might need in your employer's brief case.

Packing files and papers

Label envelopes and packages clearly, putting materials to be used on each call in a separate package. See that your employer's name and a local address, as well as his regular office address, appear on each envelope, so that it can be quickly returned in case packages are lost or misplaced in a strange city.

Pack these envelopes neatly in a case in the order in which they will be used, making a complete list of the letters and documents taken from the office. Do not expect men to carry several small packages. One branch manager was asked to report to the home office and to bring with him a number of important documents. His secretary wrapped these papers in several parcels. Getting off the train one package slipped from under his arm to the floor of the train without his realizing it. Fortunately the conductor returned the package to the manager's office as soon as his train made the return run. The package was forwarded by air mail, but an embarrassing delay could not be avoided. Had the secretary seen that the package was in her employer's traveling case, or had she mailed it on ahead, her executive would have been relieved of responsibility and unnecessary worry.

When part of a trip is to be taken by automobile, you must be careful to seal all packages. Dust enters open packages in traveling any distance and may ruin the contents, so a strip of gummed paper should be pasted across all openings. Line a carrying case with paper or have it covered with oilcloth in order that the envelopes themselves do not become dirty, torn, or wet. Choose a case that will fit into the automobile trunk. If there is no space in the trunk, see that packages are of such a shape that they fit comfortably into available space inside the car.

Forward bulky packages by mail

Bulky packages should usually be sent by parcel post. Be sure that mailed packages are correctly labeled and sealed. If they are mailed to a branch office, see that they are sent in care of some officer. If no one is aware of your employer's approaching arrival, mark mailed packages, *To Be Called for Friday, July 12, or Hold for Arrival.* This designation will preclude any possibility of a package being returned before your employer gets there. Parcel post packages on which you wish quick delivery should be marked *Special Handling.* This marking puts them in a delivery rating with first-class mail. Air express or regular express may be used instead of parcel post if they seem better adapted to your purpose.

Use special delivery on first-class mail when a regular day delivery will not be made, as on Sunday or at night; but if regular day delivery is practically assured, a special delivery stamp often retards receipt. Any special item must be routed through special channels where extra care sometimes consumes so much time that a letter is handled with less dispatch than through regular channels. Do not send materials special delivery to an office if no one will be there to receive a night delivery. Register packages of valuable papers. Insure things which have monetary value.

Financing a trip

Most businessmen use letters of credit if they want to have funds of more than $1,000 available to them. People who carry letters of credit must be substantial citizens, because one must have an account at a bank and be regarded as worthy before these letters are issued. They give a traveler prestige and serve as an introduction to other banking institutions. In thus gaining entrée to banks in a foreign country, a businessman will be extended many courtesies as a result of his affiliation with an American correspondent bank. A small charge is made for a letter of credit. A customer's account is charged with the entire amount at the time such a letter is issued, but any portion not used may be turned in for credit.

Some businessmen cash personal checks or use bank drafts. Money may also be wired to various points or, more economically, be sent by postal or express money orders when time is not limited.

How much cash to take

Few businessmen carry large sums of cash on a trip. Instead of risking the dangers of robbery by carrying enough ready money to defray all expenses of the trip, they prepare to make use of their credit standing. Credit cards make it possible to charge all but the most minor expenses, and have become an indispensable part of the businessman's existence. By using credit cards, he can charge everything from flowers for a hostess to a trip abroad.

For the sake of safety, any money your executive does carry should be in the form of American Express or bank travelers' checks, which are more easily cashed than a letter of credit or a personal check. Generally they are accepted in lieu of cash, especially in foreign shops.

Nevertheless, some money will have to be carried to defray immediate expenses. Details of providing cash for a trip will usually fall to your lot, although your employer will usually cooperate in determining the amount. However, if you are familiar with your employer's needs on such trips, he is often delighted to leave even this decision entirely up to you. Tickets bought in advance eliminate that item in calculations of cash needed. In drawing money from a bank or on a travel advance, be sure to provide a liberal supply of change, such as nickels, dimes, and quarters for telephone calls and tips, and enough one-dollar bills so that taxi fares can be paid quickly. Other bills may be carried in large denominations to avoid bulk.

Try for an unhurried departure

So far as possible try to avoid a flurry at the last minute. Have everything ready in time for a leisurely leave-taking. If your work has been done well, you will be free to fill in gaps left by others. See that office boys are present to carry baggage and call a taxi. Do not hesitate to draw attention to the time, should your employer become engaged by a last-minute caller. By doing this you pave the way for a courteous dismissal or transfer of a customer, since few people are offended by one's leaving to catch a train.

Handling routine business while the executive is absent

Usually you will conduct the business of the office in your employer's absence. Try to do things as you think he would want them handled. Find out what people want and turn them over to someone else in the office if you cannot help them yourself. Nothing is more exasperating than a secretary who says, "Mr. Brown is in Europe for six weeks," and who then hangs up the receiver. Always keep a digest of office activities so that your employer will know what has been done in his absence.

Go over the mail carefully to determine what can wait until your employer's return. Acknowledge routine mail. Some mail you will be able to hand over to others for attention. Be very careful in putting matters away to await your employer's return. If an unusual delay must be made, send a note to the correspondent saying, for example: "Mr. Brown is at present in Europe. He will give your letter of July 9 personal attention upon his return here next Friday."

Giving assistance to substitutes

If another officer takes your employer's place during an absence, you will find it necessary to give him a background for handling many old problems which come up. Keep closely in touch with new matters so that you can help your employer take them up when he returns.

A serious error of secretaries, and of employers, is that of insisting on handling all matters during a vacation or trip, instead of turning some of them over to others. A vice-president in charge of a manufacturing concern has just given several of his officers their choice of delegating their work to another officer in their absence or of seeking employment elsewhere. He said, in describing his problem. "If these fellows are so insecure in their positions as to feel that another could usurp their work in a month, we don't want them. Our men must be sure of their worth." The organization had been much disrupted by secretaries sending important business mail to vacationing officials. Sometimes these documents were overlooked or lost, and the practice always caused delay in the transaction of business.

Communicating with your employer

While your employer is away, you will be a connecting link between him and his office. Communicate with him on all urgent matters, choosing the method best suited from the standpoints of economy and efficiency.

Outline what you want to talk about before you put in a long-distance telephone call. Anticipate any information for which your employer may ask, so as not to cause needless delay after you have secured the connection. Arrange to have special telephone calls put through direct instead of trying to act as an intermediary.

Forwarding a digest of business matters

Your employer will feel more at ease if he knows that his work is being thoughtfully cared for in his absence. Do not hesitate to keep him informed, but do not bother him with unimportant matters. Try to make communications as cheerful as possible. Forward things about which you think he should know, being sure to include in any communication all details which you decide are important enough to bring to his attention. A letter sent to some point to await your employer's arrival would probably read like this:

July 21, 19—

Dear Mr. Brown:

Everything has been going along nicely here. We were able to get the Jones matter settled soon after you left. You will be relieved to hear that he did not object to our handling the final details.

Mr. O'Brien came in with that contract Friday and I turned him over to Mr. Willis. They agreed on a figure of $11,941.57. As this seemed all right, I did not wire you.

Your night letter from Baltimore helped us straighten out those two accounts. Figures were mailed to Mr. Smith at once.

I saw in the paper this morning that R. M. Miller, who handles our account at the First National Bank, has been made a vice-president. Possibly you would like to wire congratulations.

Henry Morgan wanted you to take his son on for the summer. Mr. Laird placed him as a carpenter's helper on the new building.

Attached is a digest of the mail, together with extra carbon copies of letters which I have written.

Sincerely,
(Signed) Marian J. Smith

DIGEST OF MAIL

Letter from F. M. Edwards. Will be here Friday, the 21st. Confirmed appointment.

Contract from Enid Company. Checked thoroughly. Everything OK, so filed it.

Income Tax Return. Reminded Mr. Way to have data ready when you return.

The letters which I am forwarding to you for attention have notes on them showing what has been done and giving data which you may need.

MJS

The employer who gets this communication will have a clear idea of what is being done on all matters needing his attention. Consequently he will find time to read it with interest.

When your executive returns to the office

Free yourself as much as possible so you will be able to spend a great deal of your time in helping your employer get back into office routine. Have everything in order so matters can be gone over quickly. A digest which accompanies each day's work should contain all details with which you did not want to bother your employer during his trip.

Carefully check all materials brought back against the original list of things taken from the office. This double checking will serve as a safeguard against loss during the trip. Early discovery of omitted documents may enable you to have them located. Go over each paper or memorandum carefully to gain an idea of what business was transacted.

If he's returning from a vacation

Vacations are given for relaxation. Good effects should not be worn off by having to work overtime to make up work not done during this period. Don't litter up your employer's desk as a homecoming greeting. Put most matters in a pending file, so they can be taken up several days after his return. In this way the vacationist will not become so discouraged as to lose all the reserve strength he has built up. If a vacation has been much more strenuous than his daily work, some time may be needed to rest after the arduous recreation.

Business trip reports

Many businessmen make a report of their trips, usually compiled from a diary kept in a small book of pocket size. When your employer is dictating from notes and trying to recall events, keep his copy of the itinerary in front of you to check dates and names. Some men use the margins of an itinerary for making notes. Draw attention to these.

An expense voucher is usually attached to a written report. Carefully check all items. If you have some imagination you will ask questions about omitted items, such as meals and taxi or bus fares between stations and hotels. Carefully check all additions and subtractions. You will have a record of the travel advance, so verify the amount of the refund check as being the difference between the money advanced and money spent.

Reports of trips should be written up as soon as possible so that details do not escape your employer's mind. Remember, a good report is not written—it is rewritten. Make a rough draft on which your employer may make corrections or additions. Never feel it an imposition on your good nature to have to copy an entire report several times.

Traveling with your employer

Any businessman can do better work with a secretary who knows his business, so it is often false economy for him to try to work with temporary stenographic help secured in a distant city. When you are called upon to accompany your employer on a business trip, you will be able to render inestimable service if you take the trip seriously.

Usually most of your time is taken up in attending conferences, in transcribing notes, or in arranging details. Be friendly with those whom you meet, for you will have to ask many favors in getting things done in a strange office. Keep your materials packed so they will not be in the way of others. If work must be done at night, see that everything necessary is brought from the office to the hotel, for you may not have access to a strange office after hours. A portable typewriter may be rented so that stenographic work can be done after working hours. This plan will free you during the day for other duties, such as taking notes on meetings, attending to details, and meeting people who desire to consult your employer.

Use of leisure while on a trip

Provide your own entertainment so that your employer will not feel obliged to take care of you. Be sure he knows where you are at all times so he can call you if unexpected work must be done. Guard your conduct at the hotel and office, for your employer will expect you to uphold the dignity of the company you represent. This admonition does not mean that you cannot talk to others—indeed, many very pleasant contacts are made in business without a formal introduction, but you will need to exercise care. The mere fact that you are in a strange city does not give you license to do things you would not do at home. One merchant refused to buy from a firm because he overheard a secretary on a business trip engaged in flirtatious conversation with a salesman in the lounge of his hotel. You never know when people will be judging your company by your social conduct.

In this day and age a woman need have no hesitancy in traveling with her employer, for no reasonable person will criticize them. However, you should be considerate in protecting your employer by removing any chance for suspicion. The wise secretary does this by refraining from being constantly seen with her employer at social gatherings, by reserving rooms on different floors in the hotel, by making friends with others, and by adopting a normal course of conduct.

Travel positions are popular

Most travel positions for secretaries come from having done good work in their home office. On the other hand, some very good positions are found by deliberately seeking them. Indeed the idea of travel has such a fascination for women that they are quick to answer blind advertisements offering travel assignments with a perfect stranger. Beware of the dangers in seeking such positions. Sound businessmen are usually as careful of becoming involved in undesirable entanglements as good secretaries should be. A wise businessman would not accept your services without checking your record, and you should not take a prospective employer's moral integrity and financial responsibility for granted. Your trustfulness might lead to your being stranded in a foreign country without position or money.

A friend informed a college girl that a certain man was advertising for a secretary to go abroad with him one summer. The young woman was admirably equipped for the work so she applied for the job and was selected from one hundred and fifteen applicants. Notwithstanding the apparent honor, her father insisted on an investigation of the man before she accepted the position. "I suppose I am unduly cautious," he told his daughter, "but you will be risking far too much in going abroad with a stranger. We should know something of his background." The report they received showed the man to be wealthy and of keen intellect, but it also revealed a moral record open to much criticism. No casual inquiry would have brought to light the facts which caused the young woman to refuse this man's very liberal offer. If all secretaries were as sensible in checking the standards of employers, they would be sure of fair and honorable treatment, and secretarial work would be placed on a higher plane.

Chapter 9

Care of Money and Bank Accounts

> Money and time are the heaviest burdens of life, and
> the unhappiest of all mortals are those who have more of
> either than they know how to use.
>
> —JOHNSON

Importance of ability and integrity

The care of money and bank accounts is one of the greatest bur-
dens of most businessmen. The amount of help you will be able to give
your employer in this part of his work will depend largely upon two
things—your employer's confidence in your ability and integrity and
his own ability to delegate authority for details of the accounts under
his supervision. Most men do not make the utmost use of secretarial
help, either because of reticence in discussing financial matters with a
secretary or because they have not learned how to take advantage of
the help a secretary is trained to give. However, busy men can not
adequately take care of all monetary details, so a secretary must assume part of this work. Be especially careful never to divulge any
information which you learn from handling your employer's accounts.

Knowledge of bookkeeping essential

Even a businessman who appears proud that his wife or daughter
"does not know a thing about money" usually fails to see the amusing
side of the same impracticality in his secretary. A secretary who had
an excellent personality and came well recommended with five years'
experience went to work for a prominent physician. The first week the
doctor discovered she knew absolutely nothing about keeping accounts

or making out statements. Her employer was astounded; she, on the other hand, seemed at a complete loss when he told her that she was not familiar enough with secretarial work to hold the position. Commenting on this experience, he asked, "Why do girls go into business offices prepared for nothing except to be good company?" This question you must answer if you are unwilling to put forth effort to train for your profession.

Although many schools do not teach accounting subjects in their secretarial courses, you should get some definite knowledge of bookkeeping, for in most offices this lack will be a handicap. Much satisfaction in keeping accounts is lost if you have only learned by rote that certain matters are handled in one way, while others are treated in another manner. When you know why these things are done, you will not be likely to make a mistake in form.

Office accounts

Because business is largely conducted with a monetary motive, secretarial positions demand that you make out many types of vouchers, statements, and records. Even though you may seldom handle actual money or checks, financial records are commonly set up by a secretary.

You may be required to keep an elaborate set of books or merely a journal, or to make out expense vouchers. These records should be typed accurately and neatly. Be sure you check all figures. Nothing will destroy confidence in your work more quickly than errors in addition and subtraction.

Follow office procedure

Work in the accounting department will be greatly facilitated if you understand the principles of accounting enough to comprehend individual methods quickly. Generally someone in a large organization will check you on procedure so that, even with a superficial knowledge of bookkeeping, you can get along passably well if you make a correct copy of each voucher or other form. Keep copies in your desk for ready reference the next time you are called upon to fill in a similar form. Every secretary should take this precaution, but secretaries for salesmen have been known to type up expense vouchers every week for three months and still make the same errors. The word *specimen* should be written in ink in bold letters across each of these reference samples to prevent their being mistaken for legitimate vouchers. Secretarial accounting is not so much a matter of stored-up knowledge of general accounting systems as of intelligent and painstaking study of the particular accounting system with which you happen to be working. Even if you know a great deal about accounting, never try to revise the system in use unless you know the powers behind it want a change.

Special accounts can be problems

Most businessmen are custodians of cash for various purposes, such as lodge and trade association dues, building funds, and miscellaneous odd collections. Because this work is out of their regular daily routine, carelessness in keeping records of such money often develops. How often an employer will come in and say, "I have some extra money here; now I wonder where I got that!" Finally he recalls that John Jones handed him twenty dollars for club dues. How embarrassing if he does not notice the addition to his pocket money before you notify John Jones of nonpayment! Try to get your employer to keep a special purse for such collections. A small pocketbook, with a little notebook and pencil in it, is most convenient. "Brothers in the lodge" may be your employer's friends, but should his accounts become mixed up, friendship might not survive the strain.

An eminent physician was made treasurer of his luncheon club. Every time he collected money, he would mentally note the amount and quite openly stick it in his pocket with his own money. His secretary was careless about asking him to hand this money over as soon as he entered their office, with the result that he sometimes forgot it or used it as his own. A week or so later he frequently could not remember the exact amount. When the time of reckoning came, he was not able to render an accurate account. The amount as shown by his secretary's report was known to be far short of the amount paid in. Although sensible people knew the doctor was not intentionally dishonest, a most disagreeable scene ensued, with some newer members of the club even urging that he be ousted from membership.

Handling payments to special funds

Keep strict records of all payments to any special fund. If you cannot free yourself to record money when it is received, label it most carefully. Clip a memorandum to a bill or check and place cash in an envelope, always indicating from whom received and payment covered. Because such recording is very simple, a secretary has no excuse for slipping up on it. Put the payment in a place where your attention will be drawn to it at your first free moment, but do not leave it exposed where it will become a temptation to those inclined to pick up money or where people with much curiosity may see that John Jones was behind in his dues for a couple of months. Carelessness in keeping financial records private is a serious failing of many secretaries.

In any event, do not borrow from one account to make change in another of these special accounts (or for your own or your employer's needs) without putting a slip in both accounts to show just how they stand. It is always safest not to touch one account for any purpose other than that for which it is intended. In actual practice, however, it is sometimes desirable to make change for someone and avoid an awkward wait, but all accounts should be straightened out as soon as possible.

In giving change, be sure to repeat the amount of money received and count the change back, using the addition method as is done in stores. For example, if a foreman gives you twenty dollars to pay $18.35 which he has collected from his department for the Red Cross, say, "Twenty dollars," as he hands you the bill; then when you hand him the change, say, "Eighteen thirty-five—forty—fifty—nineteen—twenty." Never hand him the change and say, "One dollar and sixty-five cents." Mistakes in counting money are easily detected if both giver and receiver concentrate on making change.

Assisting with personal accounts

Many businessmen need help in caring for their personal accounts. The owner of a business or a professional man is more likely to demand this service than are corporation employees, who often have a natural reluctance to use company secretaries for private business. However, many executives must avail themselves of this assistance, because they spend their private time on company business. Some executives pay a secretary to care for their personal accounts after business hours, or, if the volume of such work is great, they may employ a personal secretary to attend to all private matters.

Handling of personal accounts by secretaries is commonly done in one of three ways—through a petty cash account, through a power of attorney, or through an account in the name of the secretary. An employer who needs little help of this type will maintain complete charge of his own records and only special duties will be delegated to a secretary.

Petty cash fund

Your employer may give you some round sum, say fifty dollars, with which to pay small personal bills as they are presented at the office. With these funds you can buy personal stationery, send gifts and cards, always keeping a careful record of all expenditures. When cash gets low, you should add up the disbursements and request a check for this amount in order to bring the account up to fifty dollars again. A large number of businessmen use only a petty cash fund in allowing their secretaries to care for their bills. This method is very satisfactory when an employer is in his office constantly and has plenty of time to look after most of his personal matters.

When you have power of attorney

In positions where your employer imposes heavy responsibility upon you, he may give you a power of attorney covering certain acts.

You will then be enabled to sign for him. In his absence you can sign his name to checks, and they will be accepted as though he had signed them himself. Because the power of attorney method usually vests more authority in the secretary than mere handling of accounts would warrant, it is being displaced by an account opened in the secretary's name. A joint account opened in the names of both secretary and employer is also widely used but, as a rule, is inadvisable. Two people must keep in very close touch if they are using the same bank account. If you are compelled to use the same account your employer uses, and are allowed to sign checks either on a joint account or with a power of attorney, you will have to be extremely cautious. Businessmen and their secretaries are usually so busy that each finds it difficult to keep accurate records of transactions made by the other. Realizing this danger, you can cooperate with your employer by informing him of your transactions.

The secretary's bank account

The safest method for handling large accounts is that in which your employer establishes a bank account in your name. Such accounts should be opened so that you sign all checks as secretary—never as if they were personal checks. For example, the signature on a check or an endorsement will be "Marian J. Smith, Secretary." This method does not give you access to your employer's bank account, yet it provides a means by which you may be made responsible for seeing that his bills are paid on time.

If you are opening an account in your own name for your employer, be sure that he approves of the bank in which his money is to be kept. You may suggest one which will be convenient for you, but ultimate approval must rest with your employer.

Taking charge of household accounts

Many wives still do not handle household accounts. Turning accounts over to husbands is not an indication that the wives can't keep the accounts. Some have their time entirely taken up in raising families and in creating the proper home background for their husbands. If a husband and wife have independent incomes from which they contribute equally or proportionately to family expenses, they usually prefer to have an outsider manage the account.

Household accounts handled by a secretary should be taken care of in a businesslike manner. When a notice of a $12,000 grocer-butcher bill was served on a prominent New York woman, it was revealed that one wealthy family owed $16,000 and another $21,000 to this same food merchant. The heads of none of these families realized their accounts had been so neglected. Because of credit ratings, many men like to know that their home affairs are on the same business basis as their office affairs. In all cases be prepared to render a clear and accurate account of household disbursements. Do not pay bills just because they are presented to you by a reputable store, unless someone has verified them. Arrange to have a housekeeper or caretaker check receipt of merchandise and services and forward approved bills to you.

Making cash payments

Although a check is the most common means of paying bills, cash may be used to pay small amounts for which a statement is presented. An agent of the company rendering the bill will take the money and receipt the bill. Be sure to have this done, for you have no other evidence of payment. Collectors frequently do not turn in all the money they get. You are protecting the agent and his firm by making it almost impossible for him to be dishonest without arousing suspicion.

Verifying bills

Before you pay a bill, always make sure that it has been verified against goods received. A checkup in one office revealed that secretaries were attaching their "O.K.'s" to bills on which prices were incorrect. Furthermore, mistakes in addition and discounts were not caught, and even non-delivery of billed articles went undetected.

Payment of bills by check

A great advantage is gained in paying bills by check, because a canceled check is a receipt which may be used in any court. (Many checks have a space in which the purpose of the payment can be recorded, but, in any case, information should always be put on the stub.) Because bills paid in cash are not thus protected, receipts must be requested and carefully filed. Some firms require that all payments be made by check because receipts may be lost. Certainly you should reduce cash payments to a minimum.

Collected and uncollected checks

Checks, though they pass in America's small business deals as the equivalent of cash, are really not the same as cash until they have been honored by the bank on which they were drawn. Bankers consider checks as either collected or uncollected.

Collected checks are those drawn on other banks that have passed through a clearing house.

Uncollected checks are those that have not yet cleared. On certain occasions a bank will cash uncollected checks or credit them to a depositor's account. In such a case, the bank charges interest for the number of days it takes for the checks to clear because it considers this advancing of funds as a form of loan.

Kiting checks

Kiting of checks is a pernicious practice and one which will quickly destroy your bank's confidence in you. Kiting is made possible by the fact that checks usually cannot be presented at your bank as soon as they are received by your creditors. If you give a check to John Jones across the street, his secretary will probably present it at the bank in a few hours, but if you send a check to a firm several thousand miles away, some time will be required before it reaches your bank for collection. For this reason it might appear to you to be unnecessary to have all the money in the bank until the check is presented. However, rather strict laws have been enacted which, if invoked to prove that you deliberately played on this time element, might cause you considerable unpleasantness. With the speedy collection of checks through the Federal Reserve System, this type of dishonesty is being made more difficult all the time.

Never pay the month's bills until you have the money actually in the bank. No matter how good your intentions may be, something may happen to make it impossible to have the deposit there when it is needed. In an incredibly short time some of your checks may be returned to the payee marked *insufficient funds,* and your credit rating will be impaired. Some banks, as an accommodation, notify depositors when such checks are received, but they do this only because they believe in the customer's honesty and are willing to take the trouble to call his attention to the deficit.

Protested checks

A check for which there are not sufficient funds may be protested. This procedure makes it necessary to pay legal fees in case the money cannot be collected from the writer of a check.

When a check which you have endorsed is protested, you and all other endorsers will be notified as soon as the maker defaults. You may be called upon to pay the full amount of the check or a proportionate share. For this reason some institutions, such as hotels, which are obliged to accept checks, write the words *no protest* before their signature in endorsing every check, in order that they may not have to pay the protest fee in case a check is not honored. They would be liable anyway, so they assume their liability without question of court proceedings, and risk being able to collect from the maker.

Dangers of fraud

There are two kinds of fraud against which you will have to take precautions—the raising of checks and forgery. An increase in the amount of a check is difficult to detect. A surprisingly large number of checks are so carelessly written that even an amateur might raise them. If you are not writing with a check protector, be sure that your figures are plain. Place them so near the dollar sign that it will be impossible to write another figure in before the first figure. Raise the cents figures instead of merely indicating them by the decimal point. In spelling out the amount, begin at the extreme left-hand edge. Draw a line to fill in all unused space; if a check is typed, the hyphen is generally used to make this line.

Never, under any circumstances, have a check signed and then plan on writing in the amount later. Leaving this blank space is an open temptation to a dishonest person to fill it in for any amount. Some businessmen are prone to sign blank checks, thus placing an added responsibility on their secretaries to see that nothing happens to these checks. They know their bankers would frown on this practice, but if they persist, a secretary can do little but exercise due caution. If such a check is lost, do not allow your employer to make you feel the entire responsibility rests on you.

A less common type of fraud is a forged check, to which a dishonest individual has written another's signature. This type of crime requires considerable writing skill, as bank tellers are extremely apt in detecting a forged signature. Oddly enough, the man who signs his name with a number of odd curls and flourishes is not protecting his signature from forgery. These highly distinguishing characteristics in handwriting are much easier to forge than is a plain signature. And because the flourishes are so prominent, the teller may neglect to make careful scrutiny of an odd signature.

Stop payment orders

Stop payment on checks which you do not want cashed. This may be done by notifying the bank by telegraph, telephone, mail, or direct request. Banks do not usually take orders by telephone except to grant a stop payment request temporarily. Oral requests are customarily honored for expediency, but must be followed by a written request. Do not ask your bank to give you information over the telephone. If it made a practice of doing this, anyone might call up and learn all about your account.

Stop payment orders should be resorted to only in extreme emergencies. Usually the sole legitimate occasion for their use is loss of a check. Keep one or two *stop payment* order blanks among your bank supplies, because they must be used immediately if needed at all. When you have lost a check made out by someone else, ask the person who wrote it to have its payment stopped. If the check is not found soon, the maker will issue a new check at your request.

Certified checks

Sometimes a firm does not know your credit rating or must have certified money in its own account against which to draw checks. It then demands that your check be certified. A certified check is made out exactly like any other check, but it is then taken to the bank on which it is drawn. The bank looks up your account to make sure that you have enough money on deposit to honor the check. If you do, the amount is immediately charged against your account and the bank's certification stamp is placed across the face of the check. The bank then becomes responsible for its payment upon presentation. Even if you do not have a check certified yourself, its recipient may take it to the bank on which it is drawn and have it certified.

If it is desirable to have a transaction covered by a certified check, you should find out whether your employer regards more highly the financial responsibility of the maker of the check or that of the bank on which it is drawn. If your employer considers the maker more responsible than the bank, he will perhaps insist that the maker himself have the check certified before tendering it to him. The reason for such procedure is that, if the bank should become insolvent before actual payment of the check, the maker could not allege that certification was obtained by the holder—in other words, the maker could not say that the holder elected of his own free will to depend upon the soundness of the bank rather than upon that of the maker. If the maker procures certification of his own check, his responsibility to the holder is somewhat greater than if the holder procures certification.

Certified checks are widely used as an evidence of good faith. For instance, if your firm is bidding on a contract, it will generally be required to deposit a certified check with its bid before that bid will be considered. This practice is followed in all government contracts for such projects as county bridges, school buildings, and post offices, and in many private contracts, including the purchasing of security issues.

Cashier's checks

Even if you do not have an account at a bank, you may present money at a bank and have a cashier's check drawn. Sometimes it may seem advisable to pay a certain bill by check in order to get that form of receipt for payment. The signature of the payee on a cashier's check is absolute proof that the bill was paid. If money is held at a bank not regularly used, pending the happening of some event, payment is usually made by a cashier's check.

Drafts as a means of payment

Drafts are really a type of check drawn by a creditor on a debtor, instead of being issued by a debtor to a creditor. For instance, if you do not know the exact amount of a bill of goods which you are ordering, you cannot send a check. However, you may order the goods, at the same time instructing the company to draw on you for the amount. Drafts facilitate payment and are used in many businesses.

Drafts are sometimes resorted to as a means of collection. A debtor may be notified that, unless payment is received by a certain day, the creditor will draw on him. This means of collecting from you is usually considered bad business, and your bank will frown on your account if creditors feel that they must resort to such drastic methods of collection. Protect your account so that you have money enough in it to honor all drafts which may come against it. Your bank will notify you when a draft is presented.

A bank draft is a draft which is drawn by one bank upon another. These drafts usually pass as cash, being generally considered to have greater credit backing than an individual draft. They are sometimes used instead of a cashier's check in paying bills for which a personal or business check might not be accepted.

Drafts may be either sight drafts or time drafts. When depositing drafts, remember that they are not credited until honored. A sight draft may be honored soon, but a time draft will not be honored until a specified period has expired.

Acceptances

Trade acceptances are really time drafts. They are drawn by a seller upon a purchaser of goods. Their use in trade involving large transactions is being displaced by bankers' acceptances. A bank places its stamp on these drafts, thereby guaranteeing their payment by the purchaser. They are usually backed by warehouse receipts for goods or by bills of lading covering goods in transit. Sponsoring of acceptances by a bank makes for marketability and is one of the cheapest methods of financing either foreign or domestic trade. Both trade and bankers' acceptances are sold on a discount basis and may be discounted at a bank, the proceeds being the face amount less discount for the time yet to run.

Notes

A promissory note is backed only by a promise of the individual giving it, plus the responsibility of endorsers, but a collateral note requires the pledging of marketable security, which may be sold if the maker of a note fails to pay. Either type of note may be issued on a demand or time basis and both usually bear interest. If it is necessary to realize cash on them, they may be discounted at a bank. When temporary cash is needed for a bank account, borrowing is usually arranged with the bank on a collateral note.

See that all securities taken back when a collateral note is paid correspond exactly with those deposited at the time the loan was made. As banks usually keep these securities in a separate envelope, there is little danger of their becoming mixed, but there is a possibility that someone may have tampered with the envelope. Dishonesty of bank employees is usually detected by the bank itself, but sometimes even they rely upon the integrity of an employee not worthy of such trust. For instance, a bank employee had a bond which was of the same issue as one held as collateral on a loan to a customer but bearing, of course, another number. The bond in the loan happened to be one of those drawn for redemption that year at a price considerably above its market value. The clerk changed his bond for the one being held as collateral. Ten days later the loan was paid and the collateral bond returned to the owner. Having been notified by his broker of the calling of his bond, the owner asked his secretary to have it cashed. The change in bonds was then discovered. The dishonest act was traced to the bank clerk, who confessed and was dismissed. These things do not often happen, but if you are awake to the possibility that they can, you will help to minimize their occurrence. When redeeming securities held as collateral, check them before leaving the bank. Banks are insured against just such contingencies, but your employer probably will not have insurance against this type of loss or fraud and loss may be complete unless you discover it in time.

Making out a check stub

Every stub provides a place for recording the name, date, purpose, and amount of the check bearing a corresponding number. It usually also contains space for recording deposits and showing the status of the bank account. Always be sure each stub is filled in completely. Transposition of figures is a very common occurrence in copying numbers. A check may have been written for $8.13 and then, in making out the stub, you may have written $8.31. If the amount of the check is only slightly more or less than the bill, the receiver may not bring a small difference to your attention, but you will be unable to reconcile your account if the stub is correct. Try to detect these differences when making out checks, as considerable time will be lost in finding them later. A safeguard against this type of error is to fill out each stub carefully before writing the corresponding check and to compare the amount of each check with the accompanying letter or statement as you enclose them in an envelope.

Making out a check

Erasures and changes of any kind void a check and another should be written out. Banks cannot be expected to protect your money if you do not take ordinary precautions yourself. Always notice whether the written amount corresponds exactly with the figures. Checks should be typewritten whenever possible. Many firms use a check-writing machine, which protects the changing of the amount. Signatures should be clearly written in ink; never use a pencil even though its use will be accepted by your bank. *Mr., Mrs., Miss, Messrs.,* and like titles are omitted.

Cash or bearer checks

A check written to *Cash* and signed by your employer will enable you or any one else to get the money, without positive identification. Sometimes, the word *Bearer* is used. If you receive such a check, be especially careful of it, because anyone might pick it up and cash it. Secretaries are notoriously careless in leaving checks around on their desks. If you are not known to your employer's bank, a check made payable directly to yourself, with your endorsement guaranteed by your employer, is much safer than one made payable to bearer. Such a check is made out by typing the words *Signature Guaranteed* under your endorsement, and then having your employer sign his name under these words. When the check is presented at the bank, you will be asked to sign your name again, so that the signatures may be compared.

Many employers object to having checks payable to their secretaries go through their account and endorsed as though the secretary received the money. For this reason some secretaries who receive checks made out to their order write the words *For Deposit Only* before they sign an endorsement as secretary. This deposit can be checked by inspecting the secretary's account. A bearer check does not mean that the money could not be traced to you easily because it simply means that your name will not appear on the stub of your employer's check book. (The returned check will bear your signature.)

Most secretaries are worthy of the utmost confidence, but as long as a few people do not live up to the rules of the game, employers and secretaries will be subjected to suspicion which must be tolerated, even though it is distressing at times. No matter how unnecessary you may think your employer's precaution is, his experience must have been such as to cause him to use this protection, so do not criticize him or ask questions.

Making a deposit

Always take the bank book with you when you are making a deposit, for it provides an indisputable record of deposits. Duplicate deposit slips or receipts may be lost and amounts not entered. Usually a check book has a place for making entries of disbursements and deposits. Be sure each deposit is entered on the first unused stub before you put money in an account.

When quantities of money are deposited, bills should be arranged in groups of like denomination, large bills being placed on top. When you have a quantity of bills, each denomination may have a loose rubber band or a strip of paper put around it. Roll coins into packages. Your bank will furnish coin wrappers which indicate the number of coins of each denomination to put into a package. Notes, drafts, and acceptances of odd sizes should be carefully labeled. One German bank acceptance was so large that it was folded around the other checks and bills. The teller, thinking it was merely a piece of paper which had been used to wrap up the deposit, threw it away.

A deposit slip

Be sure the name on the deposit slip corresponds exactly with that used on the account itself as evidenced by the bank book. For instance, if an account is opened up in your name, "Marian J. Smith, Secretary," do not make out a deposit slip "M. J. Smith." A seemingly unimportant difference in name may place money in the wrong account.

Totals should be entered for currency and bills, but each check, coupon, acceptance, note, or draft should be listed separately. See that the carbon copy of a deposit slip shows each figure clearly.

Endorsing checks

Every check must be endorsed before it is taken to the bank for deposit. Write the name as near as possible to the top of the blank side so that other matter cannot be written in above it. Several endorsements may be put on one check.

This signature used in endorsing a check should correspond exactly to the name on the opposite side. If a check is made out to a name so different from your usual signature that the bank might not recognize it, write your usual signature below the name used on the check. For instance, if your employer received a nickname as a basketball player in college, a check may come in written to "Slats Brown." You will sign "Slats Brown" and below it "Henry F. Brown, By Marian J. Smith, Secretary." A stamp is frequently used for endorsing checks for deposit.

If your employer must endorse checks and other credit instruments, always see that they are arranged so that the ends on which a signature is to be affixed are together before handing them to him. If an extremely large number of checks must be signed, the secretary may save a busy man's time by withdrawing each check and blotting it as soon as the signature is finished. Several hundred checks can be signed in a few minutes if the signer has to concentrate only on getting his signature written quickly. Of course, this method makes it imperative that you examine all checks most carefully to make sure they are correct.

Certificate of deposit

A certificate of deposit issued for money placed with a bank for a certain length of time is the least common method of making a deposit of money at a bank. The account is not active, the entire amount being withdrawn when needed or at the end of a specified time. These certificates usually bear a certain rate of interest and are often used for temporarily depositing funds in a bank where the depositor does not expect to maintain a checking account.

Savings accounts

Systematic saving of money is encouraged by banks and building and loan associations. When such thrift accounts are opened by your employer, see that payments are made regularly and on time. Entries should be made on a tickler file for several months or a year in advance. Always make one notation at least a couple of days before each payment is due.

If accounts are not systematically built up, but result from an overflow of funds not used for other purposes, they do not require such close supervision. A recent publication by a well-known savings bank revealed that a surprisingly large number of secretaries care for personal and family savings of their employers. Savings banks usually reserve the right to demand notice before accounts are withdrawn, but in actual practice this privilege is seldom invoked.

Reconciliation of bank accounts

You will probably be called upon to reconcile a bank account, even though you are not entrusted with its full charge. Upon receipt of a bank statement, first, verify the amounts of the returned checks against the bank statement. If all the amounts agree, arrange the checks in numerical order. Compare back checks and the amounts against the check book stubs; put a check mark ($\sqrt{}$) on each stub found to be correct. Raised checks are detected by this process of comparison.

Second, make a list of all unreturned checks, listing the numbers and amounts on the back of the bank statement. These are termed "outstanding checks." If a check remains outstanding for any length of time, and you suspect it may have been lost bring it to the attention of your employer. He may be interested in finding the reason it has not been presented.

If a check is lost, returned, or otherwise made void, be sure to add its amount as a deposit on the current stub of the check book with the proper explanation. If you do not make this entry, your account will be "long" by that amount. Never go through several months' stubs, changing figures; that process is one sure way to get the bank book mixed up. If a new check is issued at the same time a stop payment order is given, the new check may be made out without any subtractions on the stub, instead of entering the old amount on the stub as a deposit and subtracting the same amount. An explanation on the stub showing the reason for not subtracting would probably read: "Check issued to take place of Check No. 179 on which payment was stopped 6/7/62."

Total the amounts of all outstanding checks and subtract this sum from the balance you showed on deposit after deducting the amount of the last check for the month. If the resulting figure does not agree with the bank balance, service or collection charges may have been deducted by the bank. If any parts of deposits have been coupons, checks from long distances, or other credit instruments, credit may not yet have been entered.

When an account has been finally reconciled, make a copy of the reconciliation on the back of the last stub issued for the month. This summary should read something as follows:

Balance—Bank Statement		$1,867.19
Balance—Check Book		1,516.14
Difference		351.05
Total Checks Outstanding	$350.05	
Service Charges	1.00	351.05

Enter the $1.00 on the next blank stub as a withdrawal, marking it "service charge." The reconciliation summary should also be copied on the back of the bank statement, where it will be available for ready reference.

If an account does not balance as soon as you have made the necessary adjustments, you will have to start a more detailed search. Nothing but sheer persistence will find discrepancies which sometimes occur. Go over the additions and subtractions on all stubs to see that you have made no errors there. See that you have entered all deposits by checking with the bank statement and your bank book. Recheck canceled checks. Make sure the bank's balance at the beginning of the current month agrees with its balance on hand at the end of last month. Pay particular attention to figures which the bank might have misread. Run over its computations. Banks are not infallible, much as they wish they were.

A cause of much trouble in reconciling accounts is the use of a blank check or an unnumbered check from the back of a check book. Such checks have no stub on which to record data relative to them, and their use may not be known to you. Impress upon a careless employer the importance of telling you when he issues an odd check. If you can do so, avoid this practice at all times; but if you give him one of these extra checks, try to ascertain the amount for which it was made out from your employer as soon as possible. The entry on the stub of the next check should read as follows:

Amount forward		$2,876.41
Amount deposited		179.86
Balance		$3,056.27
Amount blank check issued 5/17 to H. M. Johnson & Co.—March account	$375.00	
Amount of this check	501.17	876.17
Balance		$2,180.10

Payrolls

Making up the payroll in an office which does not have enough employees to warrant hiring a paymaster usually falls to the lot of a secretary in the organization. Great confidence is placed in the person chosen for this work, for it requires honesty, accuracy, and discretion, as well as speed and judgment.

Check payments. Many firms prefer to pay their employees by check, because it takes less time to make out and record the checks than to fill envelopes with cash. Also, paying by check prevents the danger of robbery, an ever present fear at payroll time.

In line with this trend towards paying salaries by check, banks have opened branches in areas, particularly suburban, where factories and offices have been built. Some employers will mail checks direct to their employees' banks.

A special payroll bank account may be opened. A check is drawn on the regular bank account for the total payroll and deposited in the payroll account. Then no matter how many payroll checks have to be written, or how many are not cashed or deposited promptly, they will not affect the reconciliation of the regular bank account.

Cash payments. In making a cash payroll, first figure the amounts from the time records and add the total. The total will give the sum for which you will have to draw a check. Sometimes a list of amounts is typed and sent to the bank, or the adding machine tape is attached to the check so that the bank can make up the amounts which will be needed. The bank makes a charge for this service. Some firms hire banks to make up their entire payrolls, even to putting the amounts in envelopes or making out individual checks.

If you do not have bank service, it will be necessary for you to go down through the columns determining how many pieces of each denomination of bills and change you will need to fill the various envelopes. The total of these amounts must agree with the total of the payroll.

When you make up a cash payroll, go into a place where you will not be disturbed by interruptions; never tend a telephone and try to count money at the same time. However, do not get too far away from protection. Many payroll robberies are made easy by the custodian's going into such a secluded place that he could be bound and gagged without attracting the attention of others around the office. Certainly you should not come back after hours to make up the payroll, unless you are being specially guarded.

After you have counted out the money, check it carefully before it is put into each envelope. Verify each amount with the amount of salary to be received by the individual whose name is on the outside of the envelope. Some employees are honest in returning an overpayment, but you will always be sure of not having a loss if you take necessary precautions yourself instead of relying upon the honesty of others to correct your errors. Never allow people to take any part of your payroll until you have completed it and know that no mistakes have been made. The value of this practice is shown by the experience of a contracting firm in putting up an $11,000 payroll for several building projects. The payroll was handled by the treasurer of the concern and his secretary. For months there had never been a week when they did not have an error. A new secretary came to the office who insisted on checking the entire payroll before releasing any part of it. No error occurred for more than three months; then one day a foreman on one of the jobs, who wanted to get away early, persuaded the treasurer to allow him to pick up his section of the envelopes before the payroll was completed. When the secretary came to the last envelope, the amount was ten dollars short. None of the remaining envelopes contained the extra bill. It probably got into one of the envelopes which the foreman had taken before they had a second checking. Two bills of new money often stick together, making extra precaution necessary on money received from banks which give new bills.

BOOKS ON MONEY AND BANKING

Business Arithmetic (4th ed.), McNelly and Adams, Prentice-Hall, Inc., Englewood Cliffs, N.J.

Managing Personal Finances (3rd ed.), Jordan and Willett, Prentice-Hall, Inc., Englewood Cliffs, N.J.

Secretarial Accounting (6th ed.), Sherwood, Carson, Boling, South-Western Publishing Company, Cincinnati, Ohio

Secretary's Business Review, edited by Nelda R. Lawrence, Prentice-Hall, Inc., Englewood Cliffs, N.J.

Bookkeeping Made Easy, Alexander L. Sheff, Barnes and Noble, New York

Bookkeeping Made Simple, edited by Louis Fields (Garden City), Doubleday, New York

The Management of Bank Funds, Roland I. Robinson, McGraw-Hill Book Company, New York

Accounting for Secretaries, Mayne and Crowningshield, McGraw-Hill Book Company, New York

Chapter **10**

Financial Records and Reports

Gives me some kind of content to remember how pain-
ful it is sometimes to keep money, as well as to get it.
—SAMUEL PEPYS

Importance of financial records

You may often be more occupied in keeping financial records than
in actually handling money and bank accounts. These records differ
widely from accounting records and sometimes prove extremely confusing because an ordinary secretarial course does not lay emphasis
on them. However, they constitute a summary of assets and liabilities,
of income and expense, or other special data necessary to a proper
gauging of the financial status of an organization by officers responsible for its management. Many officers would be as completely be-
wildered by complex accounting records as you might be, but they can
understand figures when they are arranged in readable form. These
résumés of financial matters are sometimes kept in special files, in
books, on charts, or in the form of graphs. Select a method which will
give the clearest picture of any activity when that activity is separated
from a mass of figures. This isolated material can be presented to a
group or kept for purposes of personal supervision. Breaking down of
data into smaller units is highly important in writing up business reports.

It is of vital importance that before you start work on financial
records and business reports you have a thorough understanding of
(1) the reasons for keeping such records and (2) the purpose of the
reports.

Tabulations

Complex tabulations are works of art which must be carefully laid out to show exactly what is desired. In planning a vertical arrangement, consider both length and width of the paper you are using and the size of type on your machine. Standard typewriters are adjusted to six single-spaced lines to the inch, so you will only have to multiply the length of your paper (the number of inches) by six to get the number of possible lines that can be written. Count the number of single-spaced lines needed for your tabulation. Suppose it is forty lines, then subtract forty from sixty-six (six multiplied by eleven) and you will find twenty-six lines of blank space left. Putting half of the blank space above the tabulation and half below will mean that you must begin thirteen lines from the top of the sheet (half of twenty-six lines). In gauging space from right to left, the size of type will indicate the number of spaces to be used—pica type is ten letters to the inch, and elite type twelve letters to the inch.

The title of a tabulation should appear in all capital letters at the top and should be self-explanatory. Side and top headings are arranged so as to clarify meanings of figures in the columns. Side headings are usually long; top headings, short. However, an index of top headings, sometimes termed a "legend," is often placed below the tabulation in order to explain headings which are too long to be put in the table. Boxings of different kinds are used to bring out subheadings. Figures should be arranged in neat and accurate columns. Footnotes sometimes explain variations in data; for instance, an (a) placed before a figure may indicate a footnote which gives the information that quarterly dividends were deducted from figures of companies so marked. Advanced typewriting books give material on arrangement of statistics of this type. You can also find ideas on arrangement in newspaper and magazine compilations.

Graphs

A pictorial way of showing information is to construct a graph which will reveal at a glance the relative standings of different units.

LINE GRAPH SHOWING RESULTS OF ADVERTISING CAMPAIGN

Electric Iron Sales	1	2	3	4	5	6	7	8	9	10	11	12	13	14	15	16	17	18	19	20
1,000																				
900																				
800																				
700																				
600																				
500																				
400																				
300																				
200																				
100																				

——————————— August   ----------- September

Comparison of Sales First Twenty Days Last Month, with Sales, First Twenty Days This Month.

Figure 4. Line Graph

The "pie" and pictorial graphs, which require geometric and artistic ability, are usually the work of an expert, although a secretary might be able to mark off sectors of a pie graph or draw elephants of vary- ing sizes.

Drawing of a line graph and typing of horizontal and vertical graphs usually fall to a secretary.

An executive uses graphs to obtain a clear conception of certain data. He may want to keep a record for his own information as well as for making up financial reports. For instance, an officer of a com- pany using rubber may keep a fairly complete record of the stocks of different rubber companies. These data are kept over a number of years with no apparent use; then a weak rubber company is annexed as a subsidiary to supply the company's rubber requirements. Many possibilities of mergers have been realized because some member of an organization first saw the advantages of the merger by keeping closely in touch with activities of other houses. Things which seem like a hobby often have a very definite use. For this reason absolute

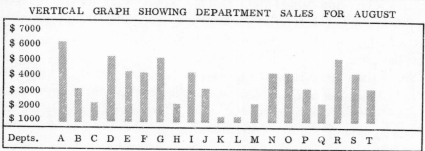

Figure 5.

secrecy about business records which are being kept in your office is essential, unless you are sure that your employer would like people to know he possesses such information.

Financial statements

Many companies issue financial statements at the end of definite periods. These statements may flood your mail at the end of each quarter of the year. They are seldom thrown away but usually are put in a credit file to replace those of the previous quarter, although sometimes, for purposes of comparison, all statements are retained over a period of years. Follow whichever custom your employer desires. If a tabulated résumé is being made of the data on them, see that all captions cover the same items from year to year. For instance, if "Interest and Dividends," carried for several years as one heading, should be suddenly changed to two headings, "Interest" and "Dividends," you may have to add the two items in making an entry on your tabulation; do not enter interest figures and omit those on dividends.

Credit ratings are confidential

Most selling businesses keep a credit record of customers. Large organizations handle such records in one department, but a small business house usually selects some officer to handle this work. Because of the confidential nature of credit reports, they are often placed in the custody of a secretary (a keeper of secrets) who possesses discretion. Typing of this information is seldom entrusted to a stenographic force.

Show these records to no one except those designated to see them. The fact that Bill Huffy, a salesman, comes in all steamed up because a pet customer has been refused a credit extension is no reason for promptly taking out the confidential file and showing him that a report from the Empire Dry Goods Company calls the man a crook. A customer may use your salesman as a witness in a libel suit against the company which was good enough to let you know its unfortunate experience in dealing with him. Likewise, when you give out uncomplimentary information, watch that your employer does not make dangerous allegations. Clever wording of a letter will convey a warning message without committing your firm to any liability of having to defend flat statements.

Dun and Bradstreet's credit rating books are used extensively in general business. Credit rating agencies, working in different trades, also have compiled ratings or will make a special checking for you. These companies (listed under "Credit Rating and Reporting Agencies" in the classified telephone directory) usually have typewritten reports of their findings which they send out, with the provision that they are to be returned within a certain time. Copies of these reports may be made, or data may be taken from them. Always note on this record the date investigation was made, because the financial status of a firm may change rapidly. Your record should show clearly the source of each item of information.

Cards which are to be available for general use should not contain confidential information. Usually such credit cards have only the firm's name and address, together with the names of its officers, and an A, B, C rating indicating the limit of credit to be extended. Colored cards may be used for classification in a box of customers' cards: white for A customers, on whom no limit is placed; blue for B customers, with a $500 limit; yellow for C customers, with a $100 limit; and red for those to whom no credit is to be extended. Colored clips are sometimes used to indicate accounts which are temporarily overdue.

Credit service of banks

Credit departments of banks are excellent sources of information concerning an individual or a firm. Although a bank will not tell you John Jones carries $500 in his account, it will often give you some idea of his rating in a statement such as this: "For the past three years Mr. Jones has carried a checking account with us, averaging a moderate three-figure balance. We have reason to know we are not his only bank account. Our opinion of Mr. Jones's financial responsibility would lead us to give him a high rating. At the time of our last checking, his other banks concurred in this opinion. We would not hesitate to do business with him in moderate amounts."

If a bank or a firm refuses to write a letter about a firm with which it has had dealings, very likely it has a cause for silence. As a rule, extremely derogatory information will not be written out, because banks never wish to become involved in a libel suit. They accept the lawyer's advice to his rather romantic young client: "Don't put anything in writing. Telephone; it's cheap at any price." They will sometimes give such information verbally. In such instances it will be necessary for you to take the report in shorthand over the telephone or to go personally to the bank to talk with one of the officers.

Credit departments of banks have done much toward showing business how to put its transactions on a sound financial basis. Adequate praise can never be given for the masterly way in which they handle these problems, always with an aim to help rather than to restrict business. Even when they feel in duty bound to be a balance wheel to the person who is plunging too deeply, their criticism is couched in terms that hold no rancor. Your firm will probably give its bank detailed information in order to receive advice from and be correctly rated by them. Banks are not hasty in their judgments, but if they have ample reason to be suspicious of the credit of a company, they notify the Better Business Bureaus. Much progress made in cleaning up business has been due to organized efforts of our large banking institutions. Many firms inform their banks of the existence of questionable business enterprises, rather than reporting direct to police or Better Business Bureaus.

An office budget

In all businesses expenditures will likely be under some form of budgetary control.

At the beginning of the year, certain amounts are indicated for each type of expenditure, and an approximate estimate made of amounts which may reasonably be expected as receipts from each source of revenue. Items are arranged under headings of "Income" and "Expenses" and may be subdivided according to departments, branch offices, or other divisions. These records may be kept in a book binder or on loose cards, which are then filed.

You will probably be required to do nothing more with a budget than to set it up in typewritten form. Main headings and limits will be decided by officers and a board of directors. The same headings generally run along from year to year with little change. In preparing a budget for presentation to the board, each officer and head of a department is requested to make out a tentative outline of his needs and prospects. From the budget upon which you are working for the present year, enter amounts allotted and amounts actually spent during each of the past few years. In another column write the figures proposed for the ensuing year. A blank column should follow this one so revised figures may be inserted when allowances have been pared down or increased. Explanations of unusual expenditures should either be inserted with the entries or listed at the bottom of the page in footnotes. Use letters for indicating footnotes in figure work, because a typewritten footnote number may lead to confusion with other numbers. A good book on budgetary control will help you to understand the work of allocating these amounts; it will also make compilation and typing of budgets mean more to you than a mere tapping of figure keys on a typewriter.

When an approved budget has been returned to your department, it will be necessary for you to set up a budget for the new year. On this, receipts and disbursements will be entered under appropriate headings from time to time. Budgets are the bane of the life of some employers. You will be able to do much to help ease this burden if you understand how to allocate costs. Even though you relieve your employer of the details of recording expenses, be sure that he is informed when any part of an allotment is in danger of being overstepped. Care must be exercised in watching proportions, as well as in seeing that entries are made. In times of expanding business, "balancing the budget" may need little thought, but you may see ways of cutting expenses when your business is not prospering.

Household and personal budgets

Some employers require their secretaries to keep personal budgets and household budgets for them. Excellent forms on which to keep records are available, or you can use a sample commercial budget to decide upon headings, and also as a guide in allocation. You will find it worth while to keep one for your own personal accounts. Because income tax requires so much definite data, businessmen, more and more frequently, require secretaries to keep for them records of personal expenses.

Brokerage accounts

A private businessman often keeps a detailed record of his activities in the stock market and requires that his secretary be familiar with investment terms. A businessman is seldom indulgent enough to be amused at your ignorance of the stock market. If you serve as personal secretary to your employer, he will expect you to have a fairly complete knowledge of financial matters. Even if you do not handle his personal affairs, he might ask you to look up yesterday's closing price on a particular stock, or find out for him the current foreign exchange rates. Most small businesses have a certain margin of their working capital in securities against which they can procure a collateral loan for temporary use. In such a company an officer will be in charge of investing for the account of the organization. As secretary to such a man, you would have to aid in keeping clear records.

Interpreting financial pages

Large daily newspapers are an excellent source of day-to-day financial news. Train yourself to read this news every day, in order to develop an awareness and understanding of the world of finance.

Choose a newspaper widely read for its financial news coverage and study its setup to gain an idea of where to look for the news you want of the business world. First, locate the part of the paper in which the financial news regularly appears. By doing this, you won't have to fumble aimlessly through the entire paper should your executive ask you to find, say, the Treasury Statement.

In *The New York Times,* as an example, a page or two of general business and financial news articles usually precede several pages of charts, tabulations and lists of various kinds, such as the one for New York Stock Exchange Transactions shown on page 189.

This is a listing in alphabetical order of each stock sold during the previous day. The highest and lowest prices at which the stock has sold during the year are listed first. Then comes the name of the stock and the dividend it is paying. This is followed by the number of sales for the day in hundreds. Then are listed the day's first bid, high bid, low bid, and last bid. The final item listed is the net change in price, up or down, from the closing price of the preceding day's trading.

Lower case letters following the name of the stock are interpreted in a box at the foot of the page. They are used to give additional information about the stock, particularly its situation in regard to dividends.

In the top center of the New York Stock Exchange transactions appears a boxed graph showing market averages for various dates. Elsewhere in the financial news you will find a listing of Stock Exchange Bid and Asked. In these columns are listed the closing quotations and the asking price for stocks not traded in the day before. Still another tabulation lists recent security issues, the price at which they were offered, and the bid and asked prices at which they were traded.

Bond trading on the New York Stock Exchange also is tabulated, as well as activity on the American Stock Exchange and in Over-the-Counter Securities.

The American Stock Exchange is the outgrowth of curb trading; that is, trading that was done by individuals who were not members of any association and who at one time carried on their trading in the street or on the curb. These so-called "curb brokers" moved indoors and formed their own exchange, the New York Curb Exchange, now known as the American Stock Exchange.

Over-the-Counter Securities are unlisted securities sold on a market

Figure 6. Stock Exchange Transactions

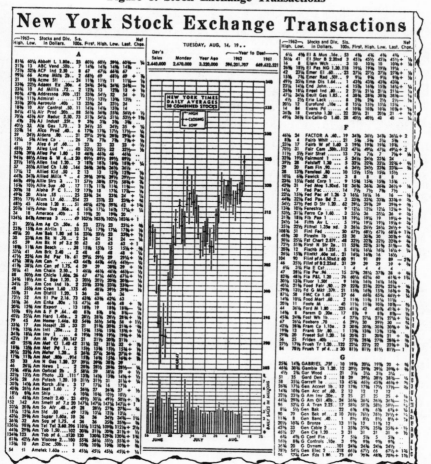

consisting of dealers and brokers throughout the nation who, for their own account and as agents for customers, buy and sell securities among themselves and with the public. They have no exchange and no publicity about individual sales. This is the principal market for Federal, state, and municipal bonds, and for the majority of public utility, railroad, industrial, and foreign bonds, as well as for bank and insurance company stocks.

Stocks and bonds

Stocks are certificates of ownership in some enterprise. Each share represents a proportional part of the assets which you would receive in case of liquidation. Usually a portion of profits for the year is set aside to be paid out to the owners (stockholders) in a form of dividends. These payments are generally remitted quarterly or yearly. Preferred stock may be given preference as to dividends or as to assets, or both. This means that preferred stock, if preferred as to dividends, will be paid its dividend (say, six per cent) before common stockholders receive anything, and if the stock is preferred as to assets, its holders will be paid in full for their investment, in case the company is liquidated, before common stockholders receive anything.

Bonds differ from stocks in that they are loans made to a company without any right of ownership. Interest paid on a bond is a fixed amount or percentage. This interest is sometimes in the form of coupons, which are clipped from a bond and cashed when due. Unlike stocks, bonds have a maturity date upon which the principal becomes due. Notes and certificates are really short-term bonds. (A note is usually evidence of a debt to be paid in from one to five years, and a certificate usually runs only for a period of months.) They also bear interest, as any other bonds do. Trade acceptances, bankers' acceptances, and United States Treasury bills are short-term securities which are bought on a discount basis.

Products such as wheat, cotton, and other produce are bought and sold in commodity markets. These purchases are really contracts for future delivery of produce, but a buyer seldom expects to have the commodity delivered to him. Papers evidencing ownership represent an investment that is much the same as a stock or bond.

Miscellaneous financial news

Reports also appear in the financial pages on Mutual Funds, Commodity Cash Prices, Out of Town and Canadian Exchanges, Foreign Exchange and Free Currency Rates, as well as notices of bond redemptions, security offerings, market averages, and much other information of interest to your executive and therefore to you. For instance, one of your duties will doubtless be to check the list of preferred stocks or bonds being called against your employer's holdings to see if any of his securities are among those called.

Lists of dividend announcements and of dividend meetings also appear in the financial pages and are another item you will want to check against your executive's portfolio.

Portfolio is the word used to describe the entire list of commercial paper and securities your executive owns. The name is derived from a portable case in which papers are carried, usually unfolded.

Placing security orders

Orders for purchase and sale of securities are ordinarily placed with a broker direct or handled through the investment department of a bank. These orders are generally filed as *market* or *limit* orders.

A *market order* is one in which the broker is directed to buy or sell at the best available price when the order reaches the floor of the Stock Exchange. No price limit is set by the buyer.

The majority of investors prefer placing *limit orders*. By this means, a limit is put on the price at which the investor will purchase a stock or the price for which he will sell it. In addition to price, time limits may be specified as follows: An open order, which is good for an indefinite period of time; a G.T.C., or good 'til cancelled order; a G.T.M. (good this month) order, which expires at the close of the last trading day of the calendar month in which the order was placed; G.T.W. (good this week) order, which expires at the end of the last trading day of the calendar week during which it was made; a day order, good only for the day on which it is received by the broker; an F.O.K. (fill or kill) order, which calls for an order to be filled immediately at the stipulated price or else killed; a contingent order, which makes the purchase of a security at a designated price depend on the prior sale of another security (or other securities) at some other price.

The use of stop orders

On certain occasions your executive may ask you to place a *stop order* with his broker. A stop order directs the broker to buy or sell stock as soon as the market price reaches a specified limit. The stop order becomes a market order as soon as the market price reaches the price set by the investor. It is used to protect profits or to limit losses, and in the latter case is called a *stop-loss* order.

Suppose your employer orders his broker to purchase 100 shares of a particular stock and the order is completed at a price of $80 a share. Your employer may then give his broker a *stop order* to sell the stock when its market price rises to $90 (which would give him a profit of one thousand dollars), or when the market price goes down to $77 (which would limit loss, in the event of further price decline, to $300).

Many people have wondered why all investors did not use a stop-loss order at the time of the historic stock market crash of 1929. This was done to a large extent, but in a falling market, these stop-loss orders are uncovered so fast that every time the stock is depressed a point, more stock is thrown on the market. A flood of sale orders tends only to depress prices still further, until it is often impossible to sell all stock at the specified price, or even at any price, in a completely demoralized market. *Stop-limit* orders are similar to stop-loss orders except that they specify a price below which the investor does not want to sell.

Bulls and bears in the marketplace

A market in which stock prices show a very definite upward trend is called a *bull* market; one in which the trend is as definitely downward is a *bear* market. A trader who anticipates a rising market and who buys and sells accordingly is called a *bull*. The trader who anticipates a decline in market prices is a *bear*. Bears generally count on a declining market to make a profit by selling short and buying back at a lower price.

Selling short

A *short sale* is one in which the seller is not the owner or possessor of the security he sells. He must borrow the security, usually from his broker, in order to make the sale. Should his anticipation of a market decline be correct, he then buys back enough shares of the borrowed stock to repay the lender and keeps the difference as his profit. Should the market go up instead of declining, he loses money. For instance, your employer, being a bear on a particular stock, sells one hundred shares of it short at 98. Because your executive does not own any of this stock, his broker borrows one hundred shares from someone who does own it and makes delivery to your employer. A few days later the stock goes down to 94 and your employer buys back one hundred shares to repay the borrowed stock and takes his four-point profit. However, had the stock suddenly gone up to 100 instead of down to 94, your employer would have been compelled to buy the stock at a higher price in order to cover the stock loan, thereby sustaining a loss of two points for his wrong guess on the trend of the market.

Trading on margin

A person who has an account at a broker's need not always have sufficient money to pay for all securities that he buys. He can buy securities partly on credit extended by his broker. This is called margin buying. Brokers finance these transactions out of their own funds or, using the purchased stock as collateral, on loans obtained from banks. The extent to which your employer may buy stock on this basis is subject to regulations of the Federal Reserve System. One of the regulations affects the minimum percentage of the cost of the securities your employer must pay. This percentage—or margin requirement—is changed from time to time to keep up with business cycle trends.

For instance, suppose your employer hears that developments in a certain business will very likely force its stock up within the next month. The price is presently $70 a share and he decides to buy one hundred and fifty shares. Assuming that the percentage the customer must pay has been set at 50 percent of the cost, your executive would have to pay in cash $5,250. The remaining $5,250 would be advanced by the broker, who would hold the stock as security for the loan. In turn the broker could borrow from a bank against the stock he is holding for your executive. Should the stock rise, say, 40 points, your employer may decide to sell. The sale would bring $16,500, giving your employer a gross profit of $11,250, out of which he must repay the broker's loan of $5,250, plus interest, commissions, and taxes.

During the period when the stock is being held on margin, any dividend that might fall due is collected by the broker and credited to the buyer's account.

Also during this period, should the market price of the stock decline the broker may ask your employer to pledge supplementary securities or deposit more cash. This is termed a *margin call*. If your employer is unable to meet this demand, the broker may sell enough of your executive's securities to protect his original loan or to meet the additional margin requirements.

Trading on margin does not mean that your employer is financially embarrassed. It is a matter of reducing his initial cash investment in a stock. Many men are reluctant to take money from a savings account, for instance, or to sell a good mortgage in order to trade on the stock market. If his speculation works out all right, and the stock he buys rises in price, his profits will pay for part of the investment. Of course he takes the chance of having his speculation fail, in which case he might be compelled to withdraw savings or sell other holdings in order to pay off the credit advanced by the broker.

Safeguarding securities

Your executive may leave his stock certificates or bonds in the hands of his broker. However if he should ask that they be delivered to him, guard them carefully until they can be placed in his safe deposit box. While stock certificates are non-negotiable until signed by the owner, should they become lost issuing corporations will insist that a bond for their value be posted. In the case of bearer bonds, possession indicates ownership; be particularly careful to protect them from loss.

Memoranda from the broker

The monthly statement your executive receives from his broker will list only completed transactions. Therefore you should keep a tickler file of *pending* transactions until they are completed and appear in the broker's monthly statement.

In addition, the broker will send confirmation of purchase and sales orders. Sometimes the purchase slip is printed in black and the sales slip in red. These slips are identical except for the words BOUGHT and SOLD. Confirmations list the number of shares bought or sold and at what price; interest (in bond transactions the purchaser is charged and the seller credited with the amount of interest accrued since the last interest payment); broker's commission; Federal and State taxes involved; total in dollars and cents of sale or purchase. The date on which the trade was made also appears on the confirmation, along with the settlement date. The latter indicates to the seller the date on which the securities must be turned over to the broker and to the purchaser the day on which he must pay for the securities.

Check these confirmation slips carefully when they are received, as errors must be reported and corrected within 48 hours.

Keeping accurate records

Both for his own information and for tax purposes your executive should have a record of all securities transactions. Most stationery stores carry forms which will help you maintain records of the following:

- List of investments owned
- Anticipated income

- Dividends received
- Capital gains and loss record
- Individual stock record

Card index of securities

A card index is especially valuable in keeping a record of individual security transactions. Each security is entered on a separate card, and information is recorded on the card from time to time. The card shown below illustrates the type of record used for this work.

	JAN	FEB	MAR	APR	MAY	JUNE	JUL	AUG	SEPT	OCT	NOV	DEC

WOOLWORTH CO., F. W. - 100 shares   Ctf. No. Wt80988

Bot. Aug. 8, 19.. of Orvis Bros. @ 57 1/2- 5767.50
Sold Oct. 24, 19.. to Orvis Bros. @ 64 1/2- 6432.10
NET PROFIT   664.60

Dividends: March, June, Sept. and Dec. 1.

Date	Amt.	Date	Amt.	Date	Amt.	Date	Amt.	Date	Amt.
-/-/..	60. -								

Figure 7. Stock Record

The name of the security is listed on the card. The top of the card should be divided into twelve sections bearing the names of the months. Different colored cards may be used for dividend and interest-bearing securities; colored clips may indicate the month on which various cards are to come up for attention. A movable clip placed on the coming dividend date makes it possible to go through a large file quickly. Cost of a security and date acquired are copied on the card from the broker's statement. Notations of dividend payments are always made at the time they are received.

Coupons, which represent interest on bonds, must be clipped and either deposited in the bank or forwarded to the issuing company for collection.

When a security is sold, *date of selling* and *price received* are entered on the card.

Maintain a separate list of securities your executive received either as a gift or as a stock dividend.

You will need file folders for monthly broker's statements, pending transactions, and security transactions.

If your employer handles investments for other members of his family, maintain separate files and records for each individual.

Reports and notices

Stock right warrants give a stockholder the right to subscribe to a new stock issue. There is usually a time limit on these warrants; be sure to bring them to your employer's attention immediately and make a note of the expiration date of the warrant in the tickler file so that it won't be overlooked.

Annual and interim reports and prospectuses should be shown to your employer, but need not be filed except on a temporary basis.

Dividend notices (unless there is income tax information on them) may be destroyed after your executive has seen them.

Annual meeting notices should be shown to your employer but do not have to be filed. Have your executive sign the proxy so you can send it back.

Notices relating to *changes in corporate structure* are important and should be filed.

Income tax records

Few secretaries are entrusted with the task of making out income tax returns for businessmen or their firms; indeed, few businessmen trust even themselves to do this. However, a secretary can help in keeping records which will aid an expert who prepares the tax returns. Most people do not deduct enough for their exemptions because they have no complete record of them. A busy man cannot be expected to keep an account of every cent he spends. Nevertheless, many businessmen could afford to add several hundred dollars to the wages of a secretary who effects savings by properly setting up records of deductible items.

Individuals who had an income of $600 or more in a calendar year are generally required to file Federal tax returns. Those with incomes below $600 must file returns in order to obtain refund of taxes withheld by employers.

The income tax forms your executive would be most likely to file are as follows:

Individual returns. The individual with an income below $10,000 made up of salary, wages, dividends, and interest (not more than $200 from dividends and interest) may file Form 1040A. All taxpayers who, because of the amount or source of income cannot use 1040A, must file Form 1040. Your employer and his wife may file a joint return. Also, your employer must file an estimated Declaration of Income Tax, Form 1040ES if, as a single man, his total income will exceed $5,000 or, as a married man, his total income will exceed $10,000. If an individual's estimated tax after withholding tax is estimated is less than $40, this form need not be filed.

Partnership returns. Partnerships do not pay Federal income taxes, but a U. S. Partnership Return of Income, Form 1065 must be filed. Partners report their individual Federal income tax returns.

Corporation returns. Those corporations that are not specifically exempted must file U.S. Corporation Income Tax Return, Form 1120. Corporations with an estimated tax liability of over $100,000 for the year are also required to file an estimate of their Federal income tax.

Information returns. Individuals, partnerships and corporations must file an information return, Form 1099, for payments of taxable income of $600 or more or dividend payments over $10 made to others in the course of a trade or business. These returns are used by the Government to make sure that the person getting the income includes it in his tax return.

Withholding tax statement. This statement, which is given to each employee, reports total wages subject to withholding that were paid during the preceding year and the amount of tax withheld on such wages for income tax and old-age benefit tax.

As a secretary you will most likely be required to keep certain records in connection with your employer's individual tax return. Therefore you should familiarize yourself with the sources of taxable income and the exemptions and deductions allowable under the Internal Revenue Code.

Included in taxable income are:

Wages
Salaries
Commissions
Bonuses
Other compensation for services
Dividends
Interest
Annuities
Pensions
Rent and royalties
Profits from business or profession
Gains from sales or exchanges of property
Income from estates or trusts
Prizes or awards won in contests

Records of the various sources of your employer's income may be kept in a card index file or a loose leaf binder.

Tax-exempt income. Excluded from taxable income, wholly or partly, are:

Old-age insurance benefits received from the Federal Social Security program
Unemployment compensation received from a state
Health and accident insurance benefits
Interest on bonds of a state or lower governmental unit
Life insurance proceeds
Personal damages recovered
Bona fide gifts
Bequests and inheritances
Certain specified benefits to members of the armed services.

Allowable deductions. Among the items of expense that are deductible from income taxes are the following:

1. An expense or cost. This includes the expenses of carrying on any trade, business or profession, expenses for production of income, contributions, interest, taxes, medical and dental expense, child care.

2. A realized loss. The principal ones are losses on the sale or exchange of property; losses incurred in a trade, profession or business; losses incurred in transactions entered into for profit though not connected with trade, profession or business; casualty and theft losses; capital losses; bad debts.

3. Depreciation in property value. Included in this classification are depreciation of business property or property held for the production of income; depletion of mines, oil and gas wells; amortization of bond premiums.

Personal exemptions. Income in the amount of $600 for himself and each of his dependents is deductible from your employer's taxable income. Generally a dependent is one who receives over half his support from the taxpayer and whose gross income in a year is less than $600. This limitation of $600 gross income does not apply to a child of the taxpayer who is under the age of 19 or who is a student in full-time attendance at an educational institution for at least five months of the year.

State and local taxes. Most state and local taxes can be included with personal deductions, but Federal taxes may be deducted only as business operating expenses. State and local taxes generally deductible include auto license and driver's license fees, gasoline taxes, income taxes, poll taxes, real estate and personal property taxes, retail sales taxes, school taxes, and cigarette taxes.

State and local taxes *not deductible* include dog license and hunting license fees, estate tax, water taxes (which are deductible as an expense on property from which you receive rent), inheritance, succession, legacy or gift taxes, auto inspection fees.

Records of assets and liabilities. Nearly every firm keeps a record of its assets and liabilities so that new management can begin with little trouble. Sometimes this record is published for the purpose of determining the worth of an organization. Notices of acquisitions of property or discontinuance and destruction of equipment should be reported to the officer who is keeping such a record. A record of smaller items, such as furniture, is requested from time to time. These form an especially important record in determining fire losses and in making insurance and tax appraisals. You will usually find the setup of such an inventory easy to follow.

Employer's personal property

Generally a businessman has such varied interests that it would be quite impossible to settle his estate if some record were not kept of his assets and liabilities. A loose-leaf book is a most desirable form for a record of this kind. When a new property or a new stock is bought, a leaf may be made out showing cost, location of deeds to properties, safekeeping location of stock or bonds, and any other information which might be of value to executors or to an employer himself. When the property is sold, the leaf may be removed and filed for income tax purposes. Many income and estate data may be combined under one common heading. The following is a typical list of headings for estate data:

Assets	Liabilities
Real estate	Loans
Partnerships and business interests	Mortgages
Securities	Notes payable
Loans	Accounts payable
Mortgages	Charge accounts
Accounts receivable	Guarantees
Notes receivable	Miscellaneous liabilities
Bank accounts	
Personal property	
Club memberships	
Miscellaneous assets	

Trust companies will furnish you with skeleton outlines from which you can make up such a list if your employer has not kept one before. If you have sufficient discretion for your employer to trust you with his personal affairs—and you are not worthy of being a secretary unless you can be so trusted—you will be of inestimable help to him in keeping this perpetual inventory.

A periodic inventory of these assets and liabilities should be taken off and a copy filed in a safe-deposit box together with the will, which provides for the ultimate disposition of the estate. You may or may not know the contents of the will, but you will have your records in readable form so that others' work will be made easy. Sometimes much of an estate is lost because only the man who left it knew of an asset.

We laugh at the man who buys a coffin and a harp before his death, but we do not realize that being totally unprepared is equally eccentric. Some heirs are put to considerable inconvenience and hardship when they have to wait for an entangled estate to be settled up enough for them to get some portion of their legacy. Careful men try to save their earnings for those left behind. This saving is best effected by having things in such order that inheritance taxes and executor's fees are reduced to a minimum.

Assisting executors

One of the key people in settling a businessman's estate is his private secretary. Should your employer die while you are still in his service, it will be your duty to protect the estate until his executors take charge. Then you will be called upon to lend much assistance. You are estopped from using bank accounts and power of attorney, and from fulfilling numerous other little duties which you have been in the habit of exercising without your employer's help. The safekeeping box at the bank will not be opened until executors are duly declared in charge. Be sure that anyone who comes into the office to go through papers has a legal right to do so. Keep a strict account of what they do if you have no way of stopping them. Relatives, often through ignorance or willful disregard of the law, make most unjust demands upon a secretary. If you know the trust company which has been made a coexecutor of the estate, it is well to seek its advice in cases where there is reason to think things are not being handled correctly. Be equally honorable in your own dealings with the property of the deceased; if you do not allow others to go through papers in your late employer's desk, you should refrain from doing so yourself.

Trust companies are so accustomed to settling estates that when they are made executors or trustees, they get to work immediately in order to put the business on a running basis without unnecessary delay. Their lawyers and employees are able to instruct you as to just what you can or cannot do. An inexperienced executor may be much harder to work with, not because he is less willing or honest, but because he lacks experience. Your cooperation, however, will be invaluable.

BOOKS THAT WILL HELP IN KEEPING FINANCIAL RECORDS

Analysis of Financial Statements (4th ed.) Harry G. Guthmann, Prentice-Hall, Inc., Englewood Cliffs, N.J.

Credits and Collections, Ettinger & Golieb, Prentice-Hall, Inc., Englewood Cliffs, N.J.

Graphic Approach to Economics, Kapp and Lore, Holt, Rinehart and Winston, Inc., New York

Graphic Presentation Simplified, Rufus R. Lutz, Funk and Wagnalls Company, New York

Statistics as Applied to Economics and Business, Wessel and Willett, Holt, Rinehart and Winston, Inc., New York

Investments (7th ed.), David F. Jordan and Herbert E. Dougall, Prentice-Hall, Inc., Englewood Cliffs, N.J.

Investment Principles and Practices (4th ed.) R. E. Badger and H. G. Guthmann, Prentice-Hall, Inc., Englewood Cliffs, N.J.

Your Investments, Leo Barnes, American Research Council, Larchmont, N.Y.

Chapter 11

Insurance and Legal Problems

> Ignorance of the law excuses no man; not that all men
> know the law, but because 'tis an excuse every man will
> plead, and no man can tell how to confute him.
>
> —JOHN SELDEN

Files that must be kept current

Various types of insurance and legal papers should not be cared for
in a regular annual file. Some of the documents are so important that
they must be stored in a safe; others are so confidential that no one
should leave them in a file which is likely to be opened at almost any
hour of the day. Much material that deals with insurance and legal
matters does not expire with a calendar year; hence the purposes for
which this material is saved are best served if a subject file is kept
current until the policy has expired or the legal case has been settled.

Wide variety of insurance in business

A study of the many kinds of insurance available is invaluable to a
secretary who goes into any business office. A young girl who takes
her first stenographic position has probably heard of life insurance
and perhaps of accident insurance and annuities; however, she probably has very little idea of the various types of policies with which she
may have to deal in the course of her correspondence and office filing.
Be diligent in acquainting yourself with the various insurance policies
your employer carries and the coverage they provide. Also, train yourself to be alert to the need for changes in existing policies.

The Social Security Act

The Federal security program in the United States is divided into several parts. It provides for insurance benefits for old age, unemployment, disability and other contingencies, and also grants-in-aid to the states for certain welfare projects. Originally the Social Security Act included taxing provisions for the payment of these benefits, and these taxes were, and still are, commonly known as social security taxes. However, the taxing provisions of the act have been superseded by the Federal Insurance Contributions Act and the Federal Unemployment Tax.

Unemployment insurance

Unemployment insurance benefits are provided by means of a tax imposed by the Federal Unemployment Tax Act on wages and salaries paid to employees. It is paid by the employer. The insurance benefits are administered on a cooperative basis by the Federal and state governments, and are payable under state unemployment insurance systems. Persons whose employment with your organization has been terminated should be instructed as to how they can register for unemployment insurance. Be sure that forms from the state unemployment office in regard to former employees are filled out and returned promptly, so that the eligibility of a former employee for benefits may be speedily established.

Old-age benefits

A program financed by a tax levied under the Federal Insurance Contributions Act provides old-age, survivor and disability insurance. A Federal program, it is operated by the Social Security Administration for the purpose of providing funds for an individual or his family when earnings cease because of old age, death or disability. The tax is levied in equal amounts on both employer and employee. The program covers wage earners in private industry and commerce, persons self-employed in nonfarm and most professional work, regularly employed agricultural and domestic workers, and, under certain conditions, employees of nonprofit institutions, state and local government employees, and some Federal employees. Principal exclusions are Federal civilian employees under another retirement system, doctors of medicine, and employees of state and local governments and nonprofit organizations that have not come into the system voluntarily. Clergymen, members of religious orders who have not taken a vow of poverty, and Christian Science practitioners have coverage as self-employed persons on an individual elective basis.

Automobile insurance

Your company may have salesmen who travel on business for the company, or it may be engaged in the transportation of its product and employ a fleet of trucks. In your files you will find liability insurance on the cars which are run by employees of the company, even if the cars themselves are owned by the employees who run them. In case of an accident a company may be held jointly liable for life or property damage caused by employees who are engaged in its business. If cars or trucks are owned by the company, fire and theft insurance may also be necessary. The many types of insurance that may be carried to cover one car are frequently a revelation to a beginner.

Theft insurance

Any company which carries a considerable stock of merchandise, particularly merchandise which is portable and of great value, such as furs or jewelry, must carry some type of burglary insurance. Messenger insurance is also a type of robbery insurance which covers safe delivery of anything sent out by a company's messengers. A firm which deals in stocks and bonds or other valuable papers may be forced to take out forgery and check-alteration insurance.

In case of losses from dishonesty or hold-ups of any kind, a tremendous amount of correspondence is usually necessary before payments are effected. You may be requested to take notes at confidential hearings, especially if the matter is not reported to police but is handled quietly by representatives of your own company and the insurance or bonding company. Do everything possible to keep such proceedings strictly private, not only because it is unkind to cast suspicion on an individual, but because information which leaks out from such conferences sometimes makes it impossible to apprehend the real culprit.

Property damage insurance

Fire insurance is a well-known type of protection against property damage or destruction, and practically no business is run without having its property adequately covered in this respect. However, a company which has large stocks of goods usually carries water-damage insurance, or some other type of coverage which will enable the company to recover if its stock of goods is not actually burned but is ruined or decreased in value by smoke or water.

Some businesses carry riot, strike and civil commotion insurance, not only because of damage done to picketed properties but also to adjoining properties.

In sections where storms are common, buildings are frequently insured against windstorms, cyclones, and tornadoes. Use and occupancy insurance is necessary if there is any possibility that business may be seriously handicapped in buildings which cannot be used because of some defect in the building. Occasionally a boiler may break or a flood may make it impossible to get material into a building. Large plate glass show windows are usually insured.

Retirement insurance

Individuals use annuities and endowment policies as a means of saving. These policies are paid at the end of a period of years or at the time when a person reaches a stated age, say sixty years. Similarly, many large companies carry blanket insurance on their employees with which to retire them after a specified age. Usually these policies are the responsibility of the firm itself, but if an employee leaves the concern before his retirement date, he may be privileged to continue the policy on his own initiative. Occasionally you will have to carry on considerable correspondence in effecting such transfers or notify an insurance company of the employment or termination of employment of individuals who may be included in these policies.

Life insurance

Companies which are dependent for their existence or for their proper functioning upon the skill or business acumen of a certain individual may carry insurance on that person's life. The principal of such policies is often paid to the firm as partial compensation for its loss suffered through the individual's death.

Some companies also carry life insurance on employees and officers, the principal being paid to the family or other beneficiaries of the deceased.

Group insurance

Group insurance insures an entire group under one policy at a lower rate than the sum of the premiums which would be charged for separate insurance on the same number of lives. Group policies may include life insurance, accident and health insurance, retirement annuities, and pensions.

Three plans under which group insurance may be written are in common use. The noncontributory plan is one in which the employer pays all the premiums and employees are automatically insured at the conclusion of their probationary period. The contributory plan is one by which premiums are paid jointly by employer and employee. The composite plan is a combination of the contributory and noncontributory plans. Under the latter plan all employees are taken care of to a limited amount, and employees who are interested may, of their own volition, increase the amount of their coverage and pay for it themselves. A group-insurance policy is entirely under the control of an employer.

Business insurance

A business may be protected by insurance much as is the life of an individual. Sole proprietorships, partnerships (general and limited), and closed corporations are especially interested in this type of policy. We have previously spoken of the protection that a business may get from an insurance policy on the life of some tremendously important individual. In addition, credit insurance may be taken out to protect a business from unusual credit losses, a plan which incidentally offers valuable service in credit investigations and collection of accounts. Firms may also be covered by accounts-receivable insurance to protect them against losses of books of account by fire (regular fire-insurance policies specifically do not include losses from destruction of accounts or papers signifying indebtedness).

Many other kinds of insurance coverage are available to the business man. Banks, trust companies and investment houses protect securities and currency against risk. Firms which make frequent shipment by railway or airway express are similarly served by express shipments insurance. Transportation insurance may be purchased by shippers and carriers of almost all lawful goods. Installation transit insurance covers valuable apparatus and equipment which may be damaged or destroyed in the process of transportation. Marine insurance is carried on shipments by water and may also include warrisk clauses.

Fidelity bonds

Secretaries who work in an office where valuables are kept, or who are responsible for any considerable amount of petty cash, are usually required to be covered by a bond. Embezzlement of valuables or of money by employees unfortunately does occur in the business world, and a secretary should welcome an opportunity to have her employer insured against danger of loss. Any person who handles money, stamps, or other valuables must take precautions to see that no breath of suspicion falls on her good name. Once the right to a bond is forfeited because of dishonesty or suspicion in one position, she may find it almost impossible to get a position with another firm.

By all means, keep your personal finances and those of the firm strictly separated. When short of lunch money before payday, you may be tempted to take a dollar from the petty cash box, intending to return it as soon as your check is cashed. However, this is a dangerous practice, because accountants have a discomfiting way of appearing to audit books at most inopportune times. A missing dollar, especially if no slip is found showing where it went, is a reasonably sure way of destroying your employer's confidence in your honesty.

Workmen's compensation insurance

Workmen's compensation (a form of insurance required by law) is carried by employers to cover compensation of employees injured while engaged in their service. This insurance is required for persons employed in almost any phase of industrial work, even those hired temporarily by contract to complete a given piece of work, such as the repairing of a sidewalk in front of a building.

This form of insurance was instituted for the protection of both employee and employer, and your duty as secretary will be to see that reports go out promptly and in correct form. An injured employee must give written notice of accident to the employer, who notifies the Industrial Commission. Be sure to have in your file a supply of blanks for making such reports. Occasionally you will have to persuade an employee to see a doctor, because some persons dislike to admit that they are in pain. For example, a messenger boy might be passing a door which was suddenly opened with such force as to knock the boy off his feet. Boys like to make us think they are "tough," and even though the messenger may be seriously injured, he may very likely stagger off, saying, "Oh, it's nothing." In such cases you will be wise to ask your medical department to send for the boy or, if you have no medical service in the office, you may convey a message from your employer to the boy and make a close checkup to see that the young man really has consulted a doctor.

Usually all correspondence regarding a compensation case is turned over to the insurance company for handling. You should refer all correspondence on claims to someone in authority, rather than risk writing something that might involve the insurance company hired to protect your firm.

Need for accuracy in compensation reports

Reports to the insurance company, to the doctor, and to the state department of labor must be accurate in every respect. As nearly as possible, get the exact time of the accident and statements as to the manner in which the injury was sustained. Make the required reports on time, and be sure they are mailed. For example, the secretary to a doctor was slow in making out a report of treatment. Second reports did not agree with the first one. When the court asked the injured employee to take a new blank to the doctor and bring it back the next time the case was called, the name typed in was "Beatrice" instead of "Bernice" and the date of disability was erased. These facts made the court wonder whether or not the injured employee had changed the date. The doctor who had treated the patient was called to the hearing. Under oath he swore that the injured person could not have done "secretarial work." The court records listed her as a bookkeeper. Such inaccuracies rob an injured employee (who can probably little afford the loss when not working). No one can blame an insurance company for not paying more than is absolutely necessary, but an adjustor will not carry a case into a labor court if records clearly indicate what compensation is due, especially if a client company is watching out for the slightest deviation from fair handling of the policy for which it has paid premiums.

Premium payments

Remittance of premiums on insurance policies is usually scattered over a good many dates, but you will be held responsible for notifying your employer of these dates several days in advance. Whenever a new policy is put into your hands for filing, check to see on what dates premiums must be paid and make a memorandum of those dates. This may be done in a memorandum book or, better still, on cards. Payments should be sent early enough that they reach their destination and can be credited before the date due. Some people take advantage of the days of grace allowed, but if payments are not made before the period elapses, the policy may be forfeited; extra care must be taken if you are running on a period of grace.

Insurance files

All insurance policies should be kept in a vault or fireproof file. Such cabinets should be carefully guarded at all times and should be locked when you are not in the office.

Insurance folders covering individuals contain strictly confidential data regarding age, health, and personal history of the insured person. If this is kept in a general file, a secretary cannot be expected to guard the folder at all times. As a precaution this confidential material should be placed in a properly labeled envelope and sealed by some method which will make it impossible for any curious person to open and reseal the package. If your employer does not insist that a seal be put on these containers, paste a piece of tape across the flap of each envelope as it is handed to you. Arrangement of insurance files is covered on pages 47 and 48 in this book.

Patent files

Closely allied to insurance files are those which contain the patents pertinent to the business of a company. Patent applications and copies of the patents themselves must be carefully guarded. As each patent is granted, it is given a number. If a fairly complete file of copies of patents is kept, numerical filing is generally used. However, in the ordinary business a subject file is much more practical.

Applications for patents

Companies which are engaged in engineering or manufacturing work usually have a research staff. Men are paid to work in these departments and the company nearly always holds the rights to the patents which are developed on its time and at its expense. However, these patents are usually held in the name of an individual and assigned to the company afterward. The legal department of a large company will probably attend to all details pertaining to the application and granting of a patent. However, if you are with a small company, you will have correspondence with a patent attorney and with the Commissioner of Patents, Patent Office, Washington, D.C.

A patent is granted for a period of seventeen years. In drawing up an application for a patent, you must set apart each point that you claim for your patent. These claims are numbered and each one of them passed on separately. If more than twenty claims are made, an extra dollar must be included for each claim you submit. The filing fee for twenty or fewer claims is thirty dollars.

Dictation on patents is always to be treated as a rough draft, and either double or triple spacing should be used to allow for numerous corrections. By the time engineers and patent attorneys get through changing your copy and repunctuating their original ideas, you will probably not know whether your first copy was a frightful mess or not. However, the final copy must be a very careful piece of work. Punctuation is of prime importance and correct setup is a vital necessity. The term which may confuse you if you have never done patent work is *prior art*. The dictator who uses that term is not talking about a picture; he is referring to that body of data which has been assembled on patents. Before a person pays the thirty dollars for a patent he usually has a thorough search made of the records at the Patent Office in Washington. Copies of patents for similar items will be procured for a small sum—usually ten cents—for careful study, and, if he finds nothing in the "prior art" which would lead him to believe that the patent being applied for has little merit, the final application will be drawn up and submitted to Washington.

Value of a postmark

In applying for a patent one must be able to prove that the idea was first thought of by the applicant. Before an invention is perfected, notes are kept on the inventor's progress. These may be kept by the inventor in a notebook or on scraps of paper, but one might later find that the date of the origin of the idea would be hard to prove. Some inventors now dictate their progress, seal the information in an envelope addressed to themselves, and post it by registered mail. When this letter returns in the mails, it is not opened but is kept in a file. Later the postmark can be used as definite proof of the date of some part of a patent's development.

Trademarks

Coined names, emblems, signs, and groups of words written in a distinctive manner may also be registered with the Patent Office. A trademark is good for twenty years and may be renewed at the end of that period if it is in bona fide use. The cost of filing an application for a trademark is twenty-five dollars.

Legal approval of form letters

Few firms could afford to have a legal staff take care of their routine correspondence; however, many cases of litigation could be avoided if the company lawyer went over form letters. By getting approval of an adopted form, many letters could be sent out with only minor changes. Insurance companies and large concerns have a surprisingly small number of strictly original letters.

Pitfalls to be avoided in correspondence

Secretaries are seldom aware of the hazards which must be avoided in letter writing. In politics and business so much is at stake that opponents or competitors are always looking for a flaw which they can turn to their own advantage. Definiteness in naming the subject about which a letter is written is very important. An inventor whose letter to his manufacturers read, "I shall be glad to give you control of the entire production," became involved in a lawsuit because the manufacturers used the letter to gain control of production under later patents. At the time he wrote the letter the man did not realize that he would be responsible for other inventions. Likewise, the politician who wrote, "I think it will be wise to use the money as suggested in our conversation yesterday," became involved in a fraud scandal. The men had talked about two different matters. On one they were in distinct disagreement, but the other was to be held in abeyance until the politician could get further data on it. When he got the needed data he wrote his approval of the matter discussed, but forgot to mention definitely the fund to which he was referring, and his opponents took advantage of his vagueness.

Sometimes a writer purposely avoids definiteness. A statement that "Our product is the best on the market" may expose you to the possibility of having to prove it in court. "Others find our product the best on the market" could probably stand up under a test. "We think" and "we believe" are used to temper positive statements. Do not quote another person unless you know he would approve of your doing so. Men have lost their positions because writers have quoted casual remarks they have made. "Mr. Grant says you are going to put in your copper order next month," is always a dangerous statement to make unless you know Mr. Grant is an employee who has been authorized to give out such confidential information. Credit letters never say anything detrimental to a subject's character, because of the danger of libel suits. Such letters are usually eloquent in what they leave unsaid; if nothing good is said about a firm, you may be fairly safe in reading between the lines that it is a questionable risk.

Having papers notarized

The person who signs a legal paper should sign both the original and the carbon copy. If this is not done for some reason, you should write on the copy who did the signing. This point is one which can be easily overlooked by officers, and later some controversy may arise as to who obligated the firm for some specified amount or for carrying through some certain work. Large contracts usually require the corporate seal. You will be wise to mark each person's initials lightly opposite the place he is to sign. If a person is required to sign in more than one place, a slip may be clipped to the printed form drawing attention to the places where signatures are to be written. An outside notary will be entitled to a fee for notarizing any paper. Signers usually have to appear before the notary public, and it is thoughtful for you to have the blanks fully labeled to avoid mistakes which might necessitate a reappearance before the notary.

The secretary as a notary public

Notary public fees are a source of income to the holders of such a commission, but secretaries are usually unwise to waste much of their own money in applying for a commission. When one thinks of the number of income-tax blanks and other papers which must be notarized, the idea of becoming a notary may seem like a profitable one. However, nearly all banks and large corporations have their own notaries who will do this work for customers, depositors, and employees free of charge, with the result that an individual seldom more than covers expenses.

Notwithstanding this bit of advice on the merits of personally applying for a commission, many secretaries do a quantity of notary work. Should you wish to join their ranks, apply to the Secretary of State at your state capitol for an application. You must be of voting age and a citizen of the state where you expect to use your privilege, and you must register as a notary in the other counties where you expect to use your seal. Full directions for procedure are usually sent with your application blank. If your firm has a legal department, usually all you need to do is forward your application to someone in that department and all of the details will be taken care of until you are notified to go and register in the places designated by your company. If you must do the work yourself, you will want to choose a seal and a stamp which can be carried in your purse. Some notaries also have a rubber stamp made for the place and date, so that they will not have to stop and type this information on the affidavit while their signers wait. This stamp will be appended to any document as follows:

Subscribed and sworn to before me this
. . . . day of . . . . 19 . . .

Notary Public

Form of affidavit

An acknowledgment is the short certification that appears at the end of a legal paper, showing that the paper was duly executed and acknowledged. An affidavit differs from an acknowledgment in that the affidavit attests to the truth or authenticity of the statements made in the paper, or in the affidavit itself; and the affiant usually signs the affidavit.

SIMPLE FORM OF NOTARIZATION OF ABOVE DOCUMENTS

State of ....
County of .... } ss.

On this .... day of ...., 19.., before me personally appeared ...., to me known to be the person ....
described in and who executed the foregoing instrument, and acknowledged that .... executed the same as .... free act and deed.

(Signature of Notary)

(Notarial Seal)

BERNICE C. TURNER
NOTARY PUBLIC
N.Y. Co. Clk's No. 185, Reg. No. 9T226
Bronx Co. Clk's No. 14, Reg. No. 53T39
Kings Co. Clk's No. 32, Reg. No. 9142
Queens Co. Clk's No. 1860, Reg. No. 7092
Commission Expires March 30, 19..

Points to watch in notarizing

Be sure that papers are not dated on legal holidays or on Sundays. Do not notarize papers for people of whose integrity you are not reasonably certain; that is, if you notarize John Brown's signature, you must be reasonably sure he is John Brown. Do not notarize signatures that you do not know are genuine; you do not need to know the contents of the papers you sign, but you must know the signature. In other words, you are not responsible for the facts set forth in a document; all you do is act as an agent of the state to notarize that man's signature when he swears that they are correct.

If you change your place of residence, you must be careful to notify the proper authorities of any change of address. You do not use your business address for notary purposes.

Wills and other typed legal forms

Legal papers over which there is any danger of litigation must be typed without an error, and any change in the original copy must be witnessed. Your honesty as a secretary is of vital importance in typing such a document; if you have become so adept at erasing as to hide your errors completely, you may unwittingly cause much trouble in later years. Suppose a will is contested and they find that a figure has been neatly changed; the suspicion will fall on the person who stood the greatest chance of benefiting by the change. Or suppose you strike $5,000 in a contract and later change is to $8,000; the company for whom the work is done may only want to pay $5,000—and, what is more, they might win out in a court.

Reports on Wage-Hour Law

The Fair Labor Standards Act, or Wage-Hour Law, makes it illegal for any employee to work more than forty hours a week. If one must work overtime in any one salary period, she is entitled to time and one-half for this overtime if paid weekly. If paid bimonthly, overtime in the first week (more than forty hours) may be made up by granting time and one-half time off in the second week of the pay period. That is, if an employee worked two hours overtime on Saturday of the first week, she may be granted three hours off on Monday of the next week (working only thirty-nine hours in the second week) in case your employer does not wish to pay overtime wages.

A salary of seventy-five dollars a week or more may exempt an employee from the provision of the Wage-Hour Law, if that employee does work of an executive or professional nature. If you make reports to the Department of Labor on payrolls, you must be exceedingly careful to see that all reports are correct and that overtime payments are made.

BOOKS ON INSURANCE AND LAW

Business Executive's Handbook (4th ed.) edited by Stanley M. Brown and Lillian Doris, Prentice-Hall, Inc., Englewood Cliffs, N.J.

Federal Tax Course (current year) Prentice-Hall, Inc., Englewood Cliffs, N.J.

Looseleaf Services of Prentice-Hall, Inc.:

Labor Service.

Insurance and Tax Service.

Unemployment Insurance Service.

Chapter 12

Personal Qualifications for Success

> The world is full of willing people; some willing to work,
> the rest willing to let them.
>
> —ROBERT FROST

Starting and finishing work

The ability to carry things through to a conclusion without instruction is the crowning feature of secretarial success. You *may* be a good *starter,* but you must be a good *finisher.* If your employer can sit back calmly and say, "Oh, Miss Smith will notice that and see that it is followed up," you know that you have made yourself valuable to him. Competent secretarial help relieves a superior of all possible details in order that his mind may be concentrated on bigger problems.

Businessmen are usually good starters, having won their recognition through an uncommon faculty of seeing things which others have failed to see. Unfortunately, they are not all equally good finishers. A very brilliant superintendent of schools was severely criticized because he inaugurated so many new ideas and then let them drop because other interests demanded his attention. Unless others were capable of carrying his projects on to a successful conclusion, they never amounted to much. When the school population increased to such a size that an assistant was needed, the superintendent selected a person who possessed tenacity. The chief started things, but his assistant carried them through. A happier combination could not have been found, for each was able to assume a prominent rôle in the work; alone neither would have been conspicuously successful. This same cooperation is needed between secretary and employer. The business-

220

man who says, "I owe a great deal to my secretary," has achieved his utmost success through the ability of that secretary to supplement his efforts. See to it that your employer never has occasion to accuse you of incompetency.

Persistence is a valuable trait

The greatest asset in work of any kind is tenacity of purpose. There are very few things which cannot be done if a person is imbued with a desire to see a matter through. Persistence will mark you as a good worker in any office.

A New York City executive learned accidentally at lunch one day that the daughter of one of his more important customers was in the city en route to Europe. He thought the girl might enjoy meeting his daughter and possibly having dinner with her, but he had no idea how to reach her. All he knew was her name, Trudy Smith, that she was staying in Manhattan overnight, and was sailing the next day. He spoke to his secretary about it when he returned to the office from lunch, but she assured him there was no way to reach the girl. At the same time she made a flippant remark about the number of Smiths in New York City.

Somewhat nettled by her attitude, the executive called in the secretary of his assistant and put the problem to her, saying: "You usually manage to locate what you want; here is one for you to work out." The secretary listened carefully and said she would see what she could do. First she looked up the scheduled sailings in the morning newspaper and found one ship due to depart for Europe the next day. Next she telephoned the steamship company and asked if anyone there could tell her how to reach the girl. They referred her to a travel agent and when she called him she learned he had spoken to the young woman only a half-hour before at her hotel. When the secretary explained why she wanted to reach her, the agent gave the name of the hotel and the telephone number.

By late afternoon, the executive had reached the girl, who was delighted to join his daughter for dinner and the theater. She said she knew no one in New York and had anticipated spending a lonely evening at her hotel.

Sheer persistence, coupled with intelligence and a willingness to serve, had enabled the secretary to track the girl down. The executive's secretary and the one who worked for his assistant demonstrate the two types of workers—those who are willing to work and to help, and those who are willing to let them.

Difficulty in getting people to follow directions

"That girl simply won't do a thing I tell her to do." How often this complaint comes from the businessman! Much as we secretaries wish the charge were not true, we must acknowledge our guilt. This great human failing has not missed us as a group any more than it has missed other groups of American people.

A teacher says, "That class is so dull that fifty per cent of the members put their names in the wrong place on their tests." Then the principal calls teachers to a meeting and asks them to write their names across the top of a card. When the cards are gathered, it is found that half of the teachers have written their names at the bottom of the card. No one would accuse them of being *dull,* but their actions certainly indicate stupidity. In gathering data from businessmen, makers of questionnaires state each question clearly, with a space for the answer following. Even then results show a high percentage of errors.

Why do we have trouble in following directions? Probably our training has put too much emphasis on initiative and not enough on the less spectacular quality of obedience. However, if you would be successful as a secretary, you must have a wholesome respect for law and order. You *may* and *should* "reason why"; but in the final analysis, you must either "do or die." If you fall short of acceptability in your work, it may be because you are too careless in doing what you are requested to do. Blessed is the secretary whose employer never has to give another thought to an instruction after he has given it to her.

Inattention causes misunderstanding

When an employer gives you instructions, *listen* and *think*. Those instructions demand your undivided attention. While receiving instructions you must visualize what is going to be done. Then you can anticipate difficulties and ask questions to iron them out before it is too late. If, instead of taking note of what is being told you, you begin looking over your shorthand or engage in some other occupation, naturally you only half hear what is being said. When your employer is gone, a dozen questions arise in your mind, but you have lost your opportunity to consult him.

Very few people give complete directions, though they may think they are being very explicit. Sit a minute and think: "Have I all the information I need? Is that perfectly clear to me?" In this way you can force your employer to make his directions as clear to you as they are to him. If you rush right off after receiving a command, you may be compelled to return later and to disturb your employer with questions, or make yourself an office pest by asking information of others. People will usually give advice to you whether or not they know any more about the matter than you do. Later you will probably find that because of this free advice the work has been done wrong, and you are held responsible for the error.

Written and oral instructions

When you are given instructions which are to be relayed to another, write them out for the individual concerned. The latter's mind may be so preoccupied at the time you talk to him that he may fail to get the full content of your message. If you say, "Mr. Jones wants you to make up the figures on that new contract for the City," and at the same time hand the man a slip of paper on which you have written:

Mr. Grant:
 Please make up the figures on that new City contract for Mr. Jones before two o'clock tomorrow.
      MJS

there is not much danger that the man will say he did not get the message. A carbon copy of this message may be put on your employer's desk. When instructions are of a long and somewhat involved nature, this custom enables your employer to pick up flaws in your interpretation of his instructions early enough to rectify them.

Keeping an instruction book

Many secretaries maintain a loose-leaf letter-sized book for the purpose of keeping memoranda of instructions. The first part of the book may be a schedule of routine of the day.

The second part of the book may be devoted to samples of filled-in forms, supplemented by full instructions as to where to find the blanks, number of copies needed, disposal of each form, and points on which there is likelihood of making errors.

The third part of the book may contain general instructions which are to be in effect until they are replaced by others.

An instruction book is an invaluable aid to any substitute who comes in to take your place for a day, or to the person who succeeds you in a position.

For future reference

Because forgetfulness is probably the most serious fault a secretary can have, she must keep an accurate record of duties which are to be brought to the attention of herself and others at some future time. Keep a small slip of memorandum paper under the rubber band on the cover of your notebook in order to note down instructions while you are taking dictation. These hastily jotted notes may be transferred to a regular calendar when you return to your desk, if you are not able to carry out instructions at once.

Shorthand notes on a calendar pad have an especial value in not being legible to any casual office caller. However, advance notations are best made in longhand unless someone in the office can read your system of shorthand. One secretary became seriously ill and required a major operation. For several days she could not be disturbed. Her office was in consternation at finding only shorthand notes on her calendar and in the tickler file. No one else in the office knew the same shorthand system as the absent girl. If there is any probability that others may have to read and carry out the instructions you are making note of, write them in longhand.

Manuals of procedure

In nearly every large office you will be given a *secretarial manual,* which is either printed or mimeographed. These manuals present a compilation of the rules which the firm has found useful in eliminating errors and in lessening confusion.

Whatever your personal opinion of this office manual may be, your first and only duty is to show that you have intelligence enough to follow it implicitly. You are hired to do work for someone else, not to do that work as you would have it done. Your way may be perfectly correct in theory, but it will be absolutely wrong if your employer wishes the work done in another manner. Secretaries, like workers in other fields, must develop the tact necessary to subordinate their own ideas to the good of a group.

Even such a simple matter as the proper manner in which to address a senator in a business letter was found, upon investigation of the work of eighteen English authorities, to center around four acceptable forms instead of one hard and fast rule; yet each of several people in an office maintained that his own opinion was correct. This example shows how difficult it is to be unquestionably right, especially in matters of form. Even your employer may not like all the forms given in the manual of procedure which his firm provides; but in a democracy the will of the majority rules, or at least the will of the *ruling majority.*

Making your own standards

In those offices where questions of form are left to the discretion of the workers themselves, most good secretaries are very happy not to be held down to the rules of others. However, there is danger in having no standards against which to measure your work. You will find yourself doing work one way this time and another way the next unless you formulate your own set of rules. Writers usually follow a style manual in order to secure uniformity throughout an entire volume. For instance, they decide always to capitalize certain words, and not to capitalize others. In compiling a set of rules to follow, look up a reason for doing things in a certain way and check up on different authorities in order that you may have a basis upon which to defend your choice. The danger in having no standards was well expressed by one speedy secretary who, after working for several years, returned to a night school to brush up her shorthand theory. When her transscribed letters were returned to her with corrections the first night of school, she exclaimed: "I am amazed at these letters myself. While in school I used to place letters well, but when I went to work I became careless and wrote them any old way. I never realized how far I had strayed from good form until I saw all of those red marks and placement boxes drawn on my work."

Know your company

Many firms also issue employee manuals, containing a résumé of qualities which are considered to be important in each organization. These manuals may include the rules governing tardiness, sick leave, vacations, use of rest rooms, and general deportment. The résumé may be an extensive summing up of those virtues an employee should have, but more often it is just a plain statement of the firm's position on matters of office conduct.

The manual usually contains some idea of the setup of the organization and its methods of remuneration and promotion. A brief history of the company with its purpose often gives beginning secretaries or stenographers some idea of the firm with which they have secured employment. If your company manual does not include a removable sheet containing names of officers, a list of their general duties, their titles, and where they can be located in the building, suggest adding it. A beginner may became very confused when trying to get acquainted in a large office. If someone on the telephone asks you to "get Mr. Smith at once," you do not know whether to look for him in the next office or in the Empire State Building. A map showing locations of departments and of desks also is of great assistance to new employees.

Suggestions for training

Some offices maintain classes for their secretaries and stenographers, and others recommend schools which can aid employees in gaining necessary background or technical training. The attitude of the concern will be outlined in the manual. Occasionally firms pay tuition, or raise the salary of an employee by an amount equal to the tuition paid, when evidence is submitted showing satisfactory completion of approved courses. One Wall Street firm which followed this practice found that a number of its employees were unaware of its policy—not having read the manual—and had never received credit for the evening work they were doing.

Explanation of duties

Special sections of the manual are generally devoted to the firm's rules about opening and sorting mail; handling appointments; reception of callers; telephone supervision; dealing with telegrams, messengers, and expense accounts; filling out various office forms; and other routine work. Treatment of these duties will necessitate an extensive outlining of the company's policy and should anticipate any questions which an employee would be likely to ask. You, as a secretary, can be of inestimable help to the writers of the manual if you try to recall the things which were new or puzzling to you when you first started work with this firm, or elsewhere. From your experience in answering the questions of other secretaries, you will be able to make valuable notes for use in compiling suggestions.

Necessity for standardization

Although hard and fast rules do have a tendency to reduce thinking to a minimum, it is very doubtful whether they tend to destroy initiative to any great extent. Anyone who has asked secretaries to follow a certain standard of practice knows that it is not the occasional person of outstanding initiative who disobeys these rules, but the great mass of those who are too lazy to learn or too careless to heed directions. Rules are generally broken not because an individual has a conscientious objection to doing any one thing in a prescribed way, but because he does not have intelligence enough to reason out the practical value of standardization. Usually the only way management can get employees to follow certain rules of procedure is by periodically checking the work and dismissing those who are not conforming.

Relationship with employer

You will find frequently that your own life must be subordinated to the demands of your executive. Naturally, this shouldn't be overdone, but top-flight secretaries are noted for the consideration they have for their employers. It is in this sense that secretaries have been called "office wives"; not because they attempt to usurp the rights and privileges of their executives' wives, but because they are usually as thoughtful, kind, and helpful in the office as the most ideal wife could be in the home.

When lunch time comes around

Perhaps nothing is a greater disappointment to a businessman than to find that a secretary considers a regular luncheon hour of more importance than his business. The luncheon hour is your own in which to do what you want, and you generally need this respite from the concentration of a forenoon's work, but there is no need for snatching it up as a greedy dog might a bone. You can always slip in a word to your employer before you leave by saying: "Is there anything more you wish before I go?", or you can simply stand in the doorway and nod a goodbye if he is engaged. A man who is not accorded this courtesy may try for fifteen minutes to locate you before it dawns on him that the morning has passed and you are probably out to lunch. This courtesy is equally necessary when you leave the office at night.

Meet friends at noon and forget yourself and your work whenever possible, but you will not be able to do this every day. When you have an important lunch date for which you don't want to be even a few minutes late, insure your getting away promptly by explaining the engagement early in the day. However, it is well to reduce such occasions to a minimum, as a rigid timetable is difficult to adhere to.

Of course an employer who thinks only of himself, causes problems which need individual handling. One man refuses to give his secretary any regular lunch hour. She is to go whenever he goes. Sometimes he decides that he cannot get away, and so at 11:15 he says, "You'd better dash out and get a bite now." The next day he will not leave until 2:30. Occasionally it is 5:00 before he thinks of her. Naturally no one should try to stand up under such irregularity.

When you see time slipping by and little chance of your getting out for lunch, have it sent in. However, your employer should see that a lunch hour so sacrificed is given to you in the form of early dismissal or an occasional half-day vacation.

Employer's lunch hour

If an employer cannot get out for lunch, thoughtfully have lunch sent in for him. Until you learn his tastes, you possibly will have to submit a menu for his approval, but later you will know his desires without bothering him. Busy men sometimes need a secretary who makes them look after their health, not because, as one girl expressed it, "He doesn't know enough to go out to eat unless I tell him," but because they become so involved in work that they forget themselves. One secretary pleased her employer very much by bringing back a well-balanced meal for him when she returned from lunch. The busy trader had never before had time to order more than a ham sandwich and a cup of coffee. His secretary varied the lunches until opening them was much like opening a prize box each day.

Usually your lunch hour will not come at a time when your employer is away from the office. If you go before he does, see that you are back promptly at the end of the hour; that means back in the office and not in the dressing room. Should you follow him, do not leave before he returns. Eat a hearty breakfast so you can stand an occasional postponing of lunch.

Dangers of overwork

Many secretaries endanger their health by taking on too many details. No one could possibly do all the things which might be done in any office. The preceding chapters give many ways in which spare time may be employed, but beware of making rash promises which you cannot carry out. On the other hand, you should never be like the secretaries in a big textile office who spend their spare time addressing envelopes and throwing them away. The office has hired an efficiency man who is dismissing every girl whom he does not find working; and the girls, instead of doing useful things, are putting in their time in this purposeless manner.

See things to do, do them yourself if you have time, and if not get someone else to do them. You cannot load yourself up to the limit with routine work, and yet see other things which are to be done. There is no reason why you should not address envelopes or do any other useful work if you have time, but do not allow yourself to become so involved in this work that you neglect more important duties. A girl in the stenographic department can probably relieve you of straight work and without office interruptions can probably do it exactly as well and faster than you can. Any secretary who becomes so overworked as to lose her sense of humor and proportion is incapable of doing superior work.

Two girls who worked for the same busy executive illustrate the difference between a good and a poor secretary. The first girl used to stand at the window by the hour. She was quick and soon finished the ordinary filing and transcription work. Often she would complain to the secretary across the hallway that she wished she had something to do, but her employer was always so busy that he seldom had time to dictate. The secretary in the other office tried to give her pointers on how to take over some of the tasks which were turning her employer into an exhausted, irritable man. One day she remarked to her own executive, "I wish Mr. X had the right kind of secretarial help; he is so willing that he is becoming overburdened."

When Mr. X's secretary moved away from the city, she was replaced by an absolutely inexperienced college graduate. This girl was as efficient a stenographer as her predecessor, but she found no time on her hands. She would say to her employer, "Now, I could take care of those records if you would stay after hours and explain the details to me." Soon she was relieving him of a tremendous amount of detail. Two mornings a week she and her employer arrived at the office at eight o'clock to get dictation out of the way before others arrived. The executive sent flowers to his fiancée each day and needed gifts for hostesses who were entertaining him. Soon this new secretary had set up a cash fund and was assisting by making these purchases for him. She suggested plays, operas, and entertainments that he and his friends might enjoy. Because she had always mingled in a social group above that in which her employer had been brought up, her judgments and advice were extremely valuable. Soon the man's nerves were quieting down, and he was gaining that poise which is admired in every businessman who is well adjusted to his surroundings. The new secretary assumed so much work that, instead of wishing for something more to do, she found it necessary to send work to the stenographic department. She would not take on more than she could do because she wanted to be free for unexpected duties. One day when she heard her employer say that he would go to a beach from the office if he had time to buy swimming trunks, she jotted a note on her calendar pad. When she went out to lunch she brought back a pair of trunks. Her employer met the secretary from across the hall one day at the elevator and told her about the new girl he had hired. "Perhaps buying men's swimming trunks is not a thing to be taught to secretaries," he said, "but it is often these little things that an employer appreciates. A year ago I used to be haunted by a feeling of inferiority because others seemed to be accomplishing more than I. They always seemed to have time to think of little things, but I was constantly enmeshed in such a web of detail that I thought about unfinished duties when I should have been sleeping. Now I know the value of the help they had. When Miss D told me she was to be married next month, I was crushed; but she is going to stay a while and train the new girl for me." The neighboring secretary, who had watched his struggles, said, "I hope you have learned to take advantage of help; that first girl could have helped you too if you had made her do it."

How fortunate the incoming secretary who is trained by a predecessor who led the way in being a real asset to a busy employer! Often you, like the inexperienced college graduate, will have to be a pioneer in assuming responsibility in your office.

Securing information or data

In order to do your best work, you will have to know where to find material and data. First, know your office, its employees, and their duties. You can solve many business problems by knowing who has materials, where they are kept, or who might know about them. Usually the quickest way out of any difficulty is to ask someone else to solve it for you. Although you should not hesitate to take advantage of any assistance others can give, you must always realize, too, that independent effort is often desirable. A willing person is usually so busy with other people's problems that yours may not be given immediate attention. On the other hand, while it is unfair to ask others to do what you should be able to do yourself, there is no particular virtue in spending half an hour hunting for something that someone else might have been able to tell you immediately.

Use of directories

Scarcely any large body of data exists on any one business that has not been systematized and made available in the form of directories. Each is made up on a general plan which is outlined in the front of the book. Learn to consult these volumes when you are in doubt about your facts or are trying to track something down. By far the most important books of reference in the majority of offices are telephone directories. They are used in checking addresses and for spelling of names, as well as for finding telephone numbers.

Classified telephone directories list groupings of different types of businesses and services. They are valuable in locating a firm with which you are not acquainted, in finding a company for which you have an insufficient name, or in ascertaining the name of a firm for which you have only an approximate address and no name. For instance, if you want to have some multigraphing done and do not know of a firm to which you can send the work, a name may be selected from a classified list of multigraphers. To cite another example—you may know that "Merritt" is one of the names in a firm of lawyers. Going through the classified list, you are able to locate "Logan & Merritt." Or you may know that there is a little glove shop near Thirty-third Street and Lexington Avenue. Under "gloves" you check the addresses until you find a shop that has a corresponding address. City directories supplement telephone directories in locating individuals and business firms. A *Directory of Directors* or Poor's Register are valuable for ascertaining directors of a company. Special trade directories are compiled of firms doing business in one line. These compilations usually contain locations of plants and offices, directors and officers, size and output of each organization, and other special information.

General reference books

Encyclopedias, *Who's Who, The American Year Book, The World Almanac,* and atlases and maps may be used for looking up information of a general character. A large framed map on your office wall, instead of a picture, will prove interesting and helpful. Notice how many callers will stop to study this map.

The Reader's Guide to Periodical Literature is designed to help in locating published material. Files of back numbers of magazines and newspapers may be found at the publishers' or at public libraries. Library files of newspapers and magazines are arranged by years.

Keeping up with the news

Some secretaries limit their knowledge and interests to the point where they know of little beyond their work and the office. An awareness of what's going on in the world will add to your fund of general information, which can be an invaluable asset to your employer.

Reading a daily newspaper and a weekly magazine will keep you abreast of events in a variety of areas.

Reading a daily newspaper thoroughly is not always possible, but you can become adept at skimming through the whole paper page by page, reading headlines and glancing at pictures. Because news stories are written with the most important happenings at the beginning, when you are rushed you can quickly get the gist of a story that catches your eye by reading the first couple of paragraphs. Train yourself to read the obituaries, so that your executive will be informed of the deaths of business acquaintances. Take a look at the financial pages, particularly if your company is listed on one of the exchanges. If you see anything in the news that might interest your employer, mark it—or, better still, clip it, write the date on it, and place it on his desk.

When you are so busy that you cannot find time even to skim through the news, take a minute or two to read the summary of contents that appears in every large newspaper. This summary will give you a rough idea of the news on all fronts.

Nothing provides greater satisfaction to a busy man than to be able to have a question answered correctly. One secretary who had never bothered to familiarize herself with the financial news was asked by her executive to find the listings for out of town exchanges so that he could look up something while on the phone with his West Coast manager. The secretary started at the first page and leafed slowly through the entire paper until she came to the correct page. By the time she did this her employer was in a towering rage. Grabbing the newspaper, he showed the young woman how she could have found the information he wanted in 5 seconds by referring to the index.

The dispatch with which you can find the answers to the questions of your executive will usually pave the way for your being given additional responsibilities. Don't let your stenographic ability be your sole asset.

Remember, too, that the library of a large newspaper is a valuable source of information on questions to which you cannot find an answer, along with university and college libraries, and public libraries.

To keep informed of up-to-date secretarial practices and the latest office equipment and procedures it is a good idea for you to subscribe to the loose-leaf services and magazines that are published just for secretaries. Joining the National Secretaries' Association is another way of keeping up with progress in the secretarial field.

ADDITIONAL BOOKS FOR RESEARCH

Secretaries Who Succeed, Esther R. Becker, Harper and Brothers, New York

How and Where to Look It Up, Robert W. Murphey, McGraw-Hill Book Company, Inc., New York

A thesaurus

A shorthand dictionary (see bibliography at end of Chapter 1)

An unabridged dictionary

PUBLICATIONS

L.S. (Legal Secretaries) and P.S. (for Private Secretaries) published monthly by Bureau of Business Practices, (division of Prentice-Hall, Inc.) New London, Conn.

Today's Secretary (a monthly publication) McGraw-Hill Book Company, New York

The Secretary, published monthly by National Secretaries Association, Kansas City, Mo.

Better Secretaries Series, Prentice-Hall, Inc., Englewood Cliffs, N.J. (*Write for subscription plans*)

Chapter 13

Spelling Difficulties

"Do you spell it with a 'V' or a 'W'?" inquired the judge.
"That depends upon the taste and fancy of the speller,
my lord," replied Sam.

—CHARLES DICKENS

Modern spelling ability

To hear some employers complain about their secretaries' spelling, one would think that spelling had become a lost art. This is really not so, for people today are, generally speaking, much better spellers than were those of the past generation. Secretaries are even better spellers than persons of equal age and experience in other lines of endeavor. Therefore, do not get an inferiority complex over your spelling. Remember, though, that a typewriter makes it imperative that each word you write be absolutely correct. For instance, in writing the word *license* in longhand, the *s* and *c* may be written so that the reader will not notice a mistake in spelling. But typing makes misspelled words stand out clearly.

Detecting others' errors

It is easy to see errors that another has made, because two people are not likely to have a tendency to misspell the same words. For this reason an employer will be much better able to notice your errors than you yourself will. Therefore you must concentrate on your weaknesses. Similarly, when you read proof on material prepared by someone else, you will find it comparatively easy to note defects. When you think you detect a misspelling, never pass over it because you think the other person must be right. If you form a habit of verifying words which do not look correct to you, you will find in time that your spelling has improved.

Technical spelling

Because trade terms are especially confusing, make a rapid study of technical words used in any new line of work. Letters containing incorrectly spelled words of a specialized nature will be criticized by recipients, to whom the vocabulary of their trade has become common knowledge. We must be tolerant with those who forget that new words are always difficult to spell. A young girl from an insurance agent's office volunteered to write some letters for a lawyer in the next office one day when the latter's secretary failed to report for work. Even the fact that he was paying nothing for these services did not deter the lawyer from advertising to the whole building his opinion that the girl couldn't spell because she was ignorant of certain law terms. Although you cannot reach the level of your employer's technical experience at once, never allow yourself to think that you cannot ultimately do so.

Constant use of the dictionary

Spelling is largely a matter of experience. If you have read much, you will ordinarily spell well. You should not be expected to spell all words correctly, but you should be familiar enough with our language to know when you are not sure of a spelling. Then, if you do not verify the word in a dictionary, you are just too lazy to deserve sympathy. A small dictionary on your desk for ready reference and an unabridged dictionary in your office are prime requisites for well-spelled letters.

Rules for spelling

You will find it very profitable to make a careful study of the spelling rules given in the front of a standard dictionary or in any good spelling book. Even though most of these rules have a discouragingly large number of exceptions, they are valuable aids to good spelling. A few of the most helpful are summarized on the following pages.

1. *Doubling the final consonant.* In adding a suffix which begins with a vowel to a word *accented on the last syllable* and ending in a consonant, double the final consonant.

> begin, beginning; compel, compelled; transfer, transferred

When the accent *does not* fall on the last syllable of the word, the final consonant *is not* doubled.

> marvel, marveled; travel, traveled; profit, profited
> jewel, jeweled; focus, focused

When a monosyllabic word ends in a *single consonant* preceded by a *single vowel,* double the final consonant before adding a suffix beginning with a vowel.

> bag, baggage; hot, hotter; plan, planning

When the single consonant *is not* preceded by a single vowel, the final consonant *is not* doubled.

> brief, briefer; act, acted; laud, laudable

2. *Dropping the final "e."* In adding a suffix which *begins* with a vowel to a word ending in e, drop the final e.

> come, coming; shape, shaping; bride, bridal

Final e following c or g is not dropped when the suffix *able* or *ous* is added.

> service, serviceable; manage, manageable; notice, noticeable;
> courage, courageous; advantage, advantageous

All other words drop the final e before adding *able* or *ible.*

> sale, salable; like, likable; sense, sensible

Many secretaries fail to distinguish between words ending in *able* and *ible.* The following list includes most of the words which end in *ible.* Note that very few of them are uncommon words.

accessible
adducible
alible
audible
avertible
cohesible
collapsible
combustible
comestible
compatible
comprehensible
compressible
conductible
contemptible
convertible
convincible
corrigible
corruptible
crucible
deducible
deductible
defectible
defensible
delible
derisible
destructible
diffusible
digestible
dirigible
discernible
discussible
dismissible
dissectible
divisible
edible
eligible
enforcible
exhaustible
expansible

expressible
fallible
feasible
flexible
forcible
fungible
fusible
gullible
horrible
ignitible
illegible
imperceptible
impermissible
impossible
inaccessible
inadmissible
inapprehensible
inaudible
incombustible
incompatible
incompressible
incontrovertible
inconvincible
incorrigible
incredible
indefeasible
indefensible
indelible
indigestible
indivertible
indivisible
inducible
inexhaustible
inexpansible
infallible
infeasible
inflexible
insensible
insuppressible

insusceptible
intangible
intelligible
intercontrovertible
inventible
invertible
invincible
invisible
irascible
irreducible
irremissible
irrepressible
irresistible
legible
negligible
omissible
ostensible
partible
perceptible
permissible
plausible
possible
prescriptible
reëligible
reprehensible
resistible
responsible
reversible
sensible
suppressible
susceptible
tangible
tensible
terrible
thurible
transmissible
undigestible
unintelligible
visible

In adding to words ending in *e* a suffix which begins with a consonant, do not drop the final *e*.

hate, hateful; manage, management; move, movement

However, if a word ends in *dge,* the *e* is dropped before *ment* is added.

judge, judgment; acknowledge, acknowledgment

In adding any suffix to a word ending in two *e*'s, do not drop the final *e.*

agree, agreement; guarantee, guaranteeing

3. *Forming plurals of nouns.*   When the final *y* is preceded by a vowel, simply add *s.*

attorney, attorneys; survey, surveys

When the final *y* is not preceded by a vowel, change the *y* to *i* and add *es.*

entry, entries; delivery, deliveries; annuity, annuities

Note: The same rules hold when *s* or *d* is added to a verb ending in *y.*

survey, surveys, surveyed; try, tries, tried

When the final *o* is preceded by a *consonant,* add *es.*

veto, vetoes; cargo, cargoes; tomato, tomatoes

When the final *o* is preceded by a *vowel,* or when the word is a musical term, add only *s.*

portfolio, portfolios; radio, radios; rodeo, rodeos; piano, pianos; solo, solos; cello, cellos

For most nouns that end in *f* or *fe,* change the *f* to *v* and add *es.*

shelf, shelves; half, halves; knife, knives
Common exceptions: belief, beliefs; brief, briefs; chief, chiefs; proof, proofs.

Many nouns that have been adopted from foreign languages retain their original plural endings.

um to *a*
   datum, data; memorandum, memoranda
is to *es*
   analysis, analyses; crisis, crises; thesis, theses
us to *i*
   alumnus, alumni (masculine); terminus, termini
a to *ae*
   alumna, alumnae (feminine); formula, formulae
on to *a*
   criterion, criteria; phenomenon, phenomena
eau to *eaux*
   beau, beaux; tableau, tableaux
ex or *ix* to *ices*
   index, indices; appendix, appendices

Note: Nevertheless, a few foreign nouns have accepted English plurals which are more widely used than the Latin forms:

   indexes, appendixes, memorandums, formulas

4. *Combinations of "i" and "e."* The *e* comes before the *i* when the combination follows *s* or soft *c*.

   receive, seize, conceit
   Exceptions: siege, sieve, financier

Following other letters, the *i* precedes the *e*.

   wield, believe, grieve, shield, piece, conscience
   Exceptions: neither, leisure, weird, counterfeit, surfeit, forfeit

When a combination has the sound of long *a* or long *i,* the *e* precedes the *i.*

   weight, skein, sleigh, sleight, Einstein

5. *Terminations "sede," "ceed," and "cede."*

   One word ends in *sede*—supersede.
   Three words end in *ceed*—exceed, proceed, succeed.
   All other words ending in this sound are spelled cede—precede, decede, etc.

Memorizing spelling of words

Notwithstanding the fact that a few rules do help, spelling is largely a matter of memory. Hence overcome your weaknesses through study.

The following list of words is made up of those often misspelled in transcription. Test yourself to see if you can spell them correctly. The following rules have been observed in dividing the words into syllables: Never divide a word so that one letter is left alone at the end of a line; never carry over to the next line a final two-letter syllable, a three-letter one if the third letter is an *s* which forms the plural of a word, or the three-letter syllable *ble* if it follows a single-letter syllable consisting of only *a* or *i*. Omission of a hyphen between syllables of a word indicates that the word may not be divided at that place.

ab-sence	al-read y	at-ti-tude
a bu-sive	al-ter-nate	at-tor-neys
ac-cede	al-to-geth er	at-trib-ute
ac-cel-er-ate	a mus-ing	au-di-ence
ac-cept-a ble	a nal-y-sis	a vi-a-tor
ac-cept-ance	an-a-lyze	aw-ful
ac-cli-mate	an-ni-ver-sa ry	
ac-com-mo-date	an-nu al	bal-ance
ac-com-pa-ny-ing	an-tic-i-pate	ba-na na
ac-cred-it ed	a pol-o-gize	bank-rupt cy
ac-cu-rate	a pol-o gy	bar-gain
ac-cus-tomed	a pos-tro-phe	be-gin-ning
a chieve	ap-pa-ra-tus	be-lieve
ac-knowl-edge	ap-par el	ben-e-fit
ad-mi-ra-ble	ap-pre-ci-ate	be-siege
ad-ver-tise-ment	ar-chi-tect	bril-liant
ad-vis-a ble	ar-gu-ing	*Britain
ad-vo-cate	ar-gu-ment	*British
a ër-o-nau-tic	ar-range-ment	*Buffalo
af-fi-da-vit	as-cer-tain	bul-le-tin
a gainst	as-sign ee	bu-reau
ag-gra-vate	as-sign or	
a li as	as-sist-ant	cal-en-dar
all right	as-so-ci-a-tion	can-cel-la-tion
al-most	at-tempt	can't

ca-pac-i ty
cau-cus
ceil-ing
cen-sus
charge-a ble
chas-tise-ment
choc-o-late
choose
clear-ance
col-lat-er al
colo-nel
com-ing
com-merce
com-mer-cial
com-mit-tees
com-mod-i-ties
com-par-a-tive ly
com-pet-i-tor
con-ceal
con-cise
*Connecticut
con-science
con-sign ee
con-sign or
con-ta-gious
con-tin-u-ance
con-trac-tor
con-ver-sant
corps
coun-se-lor
coun-ter-feit
cou-ra-geous
cour-te-ous
cour-te-sy
cre-den-tials
crit-i-cism
crit-i-cize
cur-ing
cur-rent
cus-tom-a ry

de-ceive
de-ci-sion
de-ci-sive
de-fend-ant
def-i-nite
del-e-gate
del-i-cate
de-lin-quent
de-mur-rage
de-pend-ent
de-scrip-tion
de-sir-a ble
de-sir-ous
de-spair
de-vel op
di-lem ma
dif-fer-ence
dis-ap-point
dis-as-trous
dis-ci-pline
dis-pense
dis-tri-bu-tion
dis-turb-ance
doc-ile
don't

ear-nest
e co-nom ic
ef-fi-cient
e lec-tri-cian
el-i-gi-ble
e lim-i-nate
em-bar-rass
en-deav or
en-gi-neer
en-ve-lope
e qual-i-ty
e qual ly
e quipped
e rup-tion

es-sen-tial
et-i-quette
ex-ag-ger-ate
ex-cel
ex-empt
ex-er-cise
ex-ist-ence
ex-pe-ri-ence
ex-qui-site
ex-ten-sion
ex-tra-ne-ous
ex-trav-a-gant

fa-cil-i-ties
fa-mil-iar
fas-ci-nate
fa-vor-ite
*February
fi-nan-cial
fore-head
for-eign
fore-sight
for-feit
for-mal ly
for-mer ly
for-ti-eth
for ty
four-teen
fourth

gauge
gen-u-ine
gram-mar
grate-ful
guar-an-tee
guar-an ty

hand-some
haz-ard
hes-i-tate

*Proper nouns should never be divided into syllables. Carry the entire word to the next line rather than divide a name, which is a unit.

ig-no-rant

il-leg-i ble

il-lus-trat ed

im-ag-ine

im-mense

im-par-tial

im-prov-ing

in-ad-vert-ent ly

in-as-much

in-au-gu-rate

in-ces-sant

in-con-ven-ient

in-de-pend-ent

in-dict

in-dis-pen-sa-ble

in-ef-fi-cien cy

in-i-tial

in-no-cence

in-no-cent

in-struc-tor

in-sur-ance

in-ter-est

in-ter-pret

in-ter-ro-gate

in-ter-rupt

in-tol-er-a ble

ir-rel-e-vant

ir-re-sist-i ble

ir-rev-o-ca ble

is-su-ing

i tem-ize

jan-i-tor

judg-ment

jus-tice

jus-ti-fy-ing

ju-ve-nile

knack

knowl-edge

lab-o-ra-to ry

lei-sure

le-ni-en cy

li-brar-i an

li-cense

lieu-ten-ant

lim-it ed

lu-bri-ca-tion

ly-ce um

mag-a-zine

mail-a ble

*Massachusetts

med-i-cine

me-di-o-cre

mile-age

mis-cel-la-ne-ous

mis-chie-vous

mort-gage

mu-nic-i-pal

nec-es-sa ry

nick el

†ninety-ninth

nui-sance

nul-li-fi-ca-tion

ob-serv-ance

oc-ca-sion

oc-cur

oc-curred

oc-cur-rence

of-fered

o mis-sion

op-por-tu-ni ty

op-po-si-tion

or-di-na-ri ly

ow-ing

pam-phlet

par-al-lel

par-cel

*Paterson (N.J.)

pe-cul-iar

per-ma-nent

per-sist-ent

per-son-nel

per-suade

piece

*Pittsburgh

plain-tiff

plan-ning

pol-i cy

po-lit-i-cal

pre-cede

prec-e-dent

prec-i-pice

pref-er-ence

prej-u-dice

prep-a-ra-tion

pre-scrip-tion

pres-i-dent

pro-ceed

pro-fes-sor

prom-is-so ry

punc-tu al

qual-i-fi-ca-tions

quan-ti ty

ques-tion-naire

qui et

quite

ra-di-a-tor

re-ceipt

re-ceive

rec-i pe

rec-ol-lect

rec-om-men-da-tion

re-frig-er-a-tor

re-hearse

re-luc-tance

re-mit-tance

re-mu-ner-ate

rep-e-ti-tion

rep-re-sent-a-tive

† Hyphenated words are divided only at the hyphen.

re-spon-si-ble
ret-i-cence
re-verse

sac-ri-fice
safe ty
sal-a ble
sal-a ry
sat-is-fac-to ry
scis-sors
sec-re-ta ry
seize
sep-a-rate
serv-ice-a ble
sher-iff
ship-ment
shipped
siege
sim-i-lar
sin-cere
sou-ve-nirs
spe-cial
sub-tle

suc-ceed
suf-fi-cient
sug ar
su-per-flu-ous
su-per-in-tend-ent
sur-prised
sus-pense

tap-es-try
tar-iff
ten-an cy
ten-ant
ten-ta-tive
ter-mi-nal
ter-mi-nate
ter-mi-nus
ter-ri-to ry
their
thief
trans-ferred
trav-el er
treas-ur er
trea-tise

un der-signed
u nique
un-til
u su al

va-can-cies
va-ri-ous
ve-he-ment
ve-hi-cle
venge-ance
ver-i fy
vi-cious
vil-lain
vis-i ble
vol-umes

ware-house
wheth er
whole-sal ers
with-draw al
won-drous

yield

You should add to this list any other words which you have found particularly difficult to spell. In this way you can make the list your very own.

Syllabication

The words given in the sample list (pages 242–245) have been divided into syllables for you in order that you may study syllabication at the same time you are studying spelling. Many words are frequently misspelled, simply because they are not pronounced correctly. Whenever you look up the spelling of a word in a dictionary, check on the pronunciation at the same time.

Syllable division of unfamiliar words must be checked with a dictionary, but it should not be necessary to look up division of words containing *over, anti, com, tion, tial, ous, ble, ment, ing,* or similar forms. To divide *ack-nowledge* or *assig-nment* into such obviously in-correct syllables as those indicated is inexcusable.

1. A word of one syllable, a two-syllable word containing five or fewer letters, or a proper name, should not be divided. (Initials and titles should also go on the same line with the name to which they belong.)

> freight, sensed; poem, using; Shenandoah, T. C. Brown
> Dr. Brown

2. At least two letters and a hyphen must appear at the end of a line and at least three letters must be carried to the next line, or a word should not be divided. (The hyphen is never carried to the second line.)

> *Wrong: a-bout, o-bliged; chos-en, like-ly, preced-ed*

3. Divide words between double letters, provided, of course, that there will be a full syllable on either side of the hyphen. If there will not be, the word cannot be thus divided.

> intel-ligence, il-lustrate, bag-gage, begin-ning
> trans*ferred, stressed, equipped, propelled, rebuffed*

Hyphenation

Aside from its use in the division of a word at the end of a line, a hyphen is used as a part of the spelling of many words. Because of the lack of standardization in spelling forms in common business usage, much confusion exists regarding hyphenation of compound words. Even dictionaries are not always in agreement on the use of the hyphen. However, modern usage tends to eliminate rather than over-use the hyphen.

1. Many words which are combinations of two nouns are now written as one word, without a hyphen.

> textbook, notebook, blackboard, billboard, viewpoint, football, masterpiece, policyholder, saleswoman, spokesman, turnover, busi-nessman, bylaws

If you are in doubt about the use of the hyphen in a certain word, consult your dictionary to see whether a hyphen is necessary. (Note that, because the hyphen is used in many dictionaries to divide words into syllables, a double hyphen is used to indicate the hyphen itself.) If a noun cannot be found in an unabridged dictionary as a hyphenated word it is probably safe to write two separate words.

2. Adjective modifiers which include a combination of two or more parts of speech used to express a single idea are hyphenated.

> up-to-date merchandise, hard-headed financier, middle-aged woman, law-abiding citizen, hit-and-run driver, so-called essentials, round-the-world fliers, well-to-do clients

It is well to note that these same expressions are not hyphenated when they are not used as direct adjective modifiers.

> The *short-story writer* wrote that *short story.*
> The *well-known* speaker is not *well known* to me.
> The *worth-while* article may not be *worth while* to you.

Note: Common business usage, as well as editorial usage in some of our best newspaper and magazine offices, would seem to sanction the custom of writing the adjective form of *worthwhile* as one word.

3. A hyphen is used to connect various members of a group of words which are used as a single noun.

> son-in-law, *tête-à-tête,* four-in-hand, secretary-treasurer

4. Titles with *ex, vice,* and *elect* are hyphenated.

> ex-treasurer, vice-president, president-elect

Note: The hyphen after the prefix *vice* is so often left out that some authorities consider the omission proper usage.

> vice president *or* vice-president

5. A hyphen is not generally used with the suffixes *like, hood, self, selves,* and *ship.*

> lifelike, childhood, yourself, themselves, partnership

6. A hyphen is not generally used with the prefixes *ante, anti, any, bi, co, down, every, fore, grand, great, hyper, no, non, off, out, pre, post, semi, some, step, sub, trans, ultra, under, up,* and *when.*

antedate, antislavery, anybody, bipartisan, copartnership, downtown, everywhere, foreground, grandfather, greatcoat, hypersensitive, nobody, nonessential, offset, outfield, predigest, postdate, semicolon, somewhere, stepsister, subway, transcontinental, ultramarine, undertone, upright, whenever

Note: Combinations involving proper nouns are hyphenated.

pro-German, un-American, anti-Semitic

7. The prefixes, *self, well, by,* and *cross* are usually used with the hyphen.

self-sufficient, well-worn, by-products, cross-examination

Note: Note that all "manufactured" compound words are hyphenated, even though the prefixes come under those listed in 6. A few of the less common words also require the hyphen.

ultra-violet

A common practice is to use a hyphen in typewriting where the dieresis is used in printed matter. Avoid handwritten marks.

preëminent,   pre-eminent
coöperation,   co-operation

Note: There is a tendency to omit both the hyphen and the dieresis in *cooperate* and *cooperation:* of course, you will follow the style required in your office.

A hyphen is also used in instances in which doubling of letters, caused by adding a prefix or a suffix, is typographically objectionable.

intra-atomic, *not* intraatomic; snail-like; *not* snaillike; bell-like, *not* belllike

Foreign words and phrases

Foreign words and phrases are put in italics in printed matter. The proper way to indicate an italicized word in typing is to underscore it; but underscoring is often objectionable because it puts undue emphasis on the foreign phrase, which is usually a comparatively un-important part of the correspondence. Consequently, foreign phrases in business letters are usually written exactly like other words in the letter.

Use of foreign phrases is open to much criticism. Some people as-sert that it shows a dearth of English vocabulary; others, that it is a vehicle by which a writer seeks to exhibit his superiority; and still oth-ers look upon it as a means by which a writer tries to conceal trickery. No matter how sparingly foreign terms are used, one must be abso-lutely certain the reader will be thoroughly familiar with the form so employed. One can safely say that most foreign phrases are not read at all. For example, a secretary transcribed a letter her employer wrote to a client in which *per se* was used three times. The next time she saw the man she said, "I never knew you were a Latin student until I went to work for Mr. B." The man confided that her employer's letters an-noyed him immeasurably. His comment on the practice was: "Tell me, what is the idea of putting Latin in a letter? I was going to look up *per se,* but someone had borrowed the dictionary. Then I noticed that the letter made perfectly good sense without those words, and so I knew they didn't mean anything." Certainly a busy man reading, "This contract *per se* is not important . . . ," might be forgiven for thinking that the Latin was put in merely as a filler of space—dead wood from a dead language. An automobile salesman has volunteered the information that most people who ride in *de luxe* models of cars think the foreign phrase means *"The looks."*

In writing their own letters, few secretaries will use terms from a foreign language, because it has been fully impressed upon them to use only English in their correspondence. However, many secretaries have to take dictation which contains foreign words and phrases, and they frequently have to read them in letters from correspondents. Re-cording foreign words will naturally not be difficult if you are familiar with the foreign tongue used, but few secretaries know Latin, German, French, Italian, and Spanish—the languages from which commonly quoted forms are taken. For this reason familiarize yourself with a few frequently used terms in order that you may recognize them when you meet them in your work.

Be careful to see that your employer is accurate in his use of foreign phrases. Check over your notes to be sure that he is using the correct part of speech. A foreign adjective should be used only as an adjective; yet, many times an adjective is dictated for a noun or for a verb. In our language we do not have occasion to differentiate between genders of adjectives modifying nouns, but this point must be carefully watched in foreign phrases (*bonne amie;* never *bon amie*). Prepositions are frequently confused, too, since quotations are often taken from a language of which the dictator has only a superficial knowledge (*post meridiem* for *ante meridiem*).

Mispronunciation of foreign words is often very confusing to a secretary. For example, in a letter to a representative who had been transferred to a German territory, the sales manager dictated: "I suppose you can say 'We Gates' to the best of them now." The secretary wrote the words as she heard them dictated, although they meant nothing to her. Her executive was astounded because the phrase did not come back to him written *"Wie geht's?"* especially since the secretary had formerly been employed as a German interpreter. Though such mispronunciations are difficult to take down in shorthand, they can never be so perplexing as correctly pronounced phrases from a language with which you are not familiar. For example, French pronunciation of certain English letters differs widely from English pronunciation of those same sounds. Consequently it is almost impossible to spell unfamiliar foreign words correctly simply from sounds you hear in dictation. Knowing how to spell certain terms you have learned from a book may not help you much, either, when a man reels off phrases in perfect French. Admit your defeat and ask for the spelling, for you would probably not recognize the word in a dictionary merely by its pronunciation.

Foreign words and phrases not found in the following list may usually be found in the appendix of an unabridged dictionary. Bracketed letters after the phrases indicate the language in which the expressions are found. Uncommon terms may be found in a foreign-language dictionary. Many words in this list have become Anglicized and therefore need not be set in italics in printed matter.

ab officio [L.], from office
ad arbitrium [L.], at discretion

ad infinitum [L.], endlessly

ad interim [L.], in the meantime

ad libitum [L.], at pleasure

à la carte [F.], according to the card or menu; with a stated price for each dish

à la mode [F.], in the fashion

Alma Mater [L.], fostering mother; the university or college from which one has been graduated

anno Domini [L.], in the year of our Lord

ante bellum [L.], before the war

ante meridiem [L.], before noon

a priori [L.], prior to, or distinct from, experience; from general laws to particular instances

apropos [F.], to the purpose; by the way; pertinently; in connection with

auf Wiedersehen [G.], until I see you again; goodbye; goodbye for the present

au revoir [F.], until we meet again; goodbye for the present

beau geste [F.], a fine gesture

beau monde [F.], the fashionable world; society

beaux-arts [F.], the fine arts

bel-esprit [F.], a fine, or brilliant, mind; a wit

belle dame [F.], fair lady

belle vue [F.], fine view or prospect

bijou [F.], a jewel; something small and choice

bona fide [L.], in good faith, without fraud

bon ami, bonne amie [F.], a good friend; a lover or sweetheart

bon enfant [F.], a good child

bonhomie [F.], good nature, unaffected affability

bonhomme [F.], a good, simple fellow

bon jour [F.], good day (used in salutations)

bon marché [F.], a good bargain

bon mot [F.], a clever saying

bon voyage [F.], a good journey or voyage

bourgeois, bourgeoise [F.], middle-class; common

bourgeoisie [F.], the bourgeois class

carte blanche [F.], a blank card; full discretionary power

casus belli [L.], an occasion, or cause, for war

caveat emptor [L.], let the buyer beware

coup d'état [F.], a stroke of state; a sudden political stroke

cum laude [L.], with honors (a phrase of commendation on diplomas)

de luxe [F.], a luxury; of especial fineness or elegance

démodé [F.], no longer in fashion

de trop [F.], too much; too many; in the way

en masse [F.], in a mass, or body; all together

ensemble [F.], together; taken as a unit

et cetera [L.], and others; and so forth

ex cathedra [L.], from the chair, or seat of authority

exempli gratia (*e. g.*) [L.], for the sake of example; for instance

ex officio [L.], by virtue of office

ex parte [L.], from, or on, one side only; in the interest of one party

faux pas [F.], a false step; a breach of etiquette, or propriety

femme de chambre [F.], a lady's maid; a chambermaid

femme de lettres [F.], a literary woman

fête [F.], a feast or festival; a celebration or an entertainment

fiesta [Sp.], a feast, or festival; a holiday

finis [L.], the end

finis ecce laborum! [L.], behold the end of our labors!

fra [It.], brother; monk; priest

frères [F.], brothers (*Lazard Frères,* a firm title)

grand homme [F.], a great man

grand merci [F.], a many thanks; much obliged!

grand monde [F.], a great, or fashionable, world

grand prix [F.], the chief prize

grande dame [F.], a great lady

gratis [L.], free, without cost

habeas corpus [L.], (that) you have the body; a common law writ for bringing a person before a judge or court

Hausfrau [G.], a housewife

hoc tempore [L.], at this time

hoi polloi [Gr.], the multitude

homme d'esprit [F.], a man of intellect or wit

homme de fortune [F.], a man of fortune

homme de lettres [F.], a literary man

hors-d'œuvre [F.], outside of work; something unusual; a light supplementary dish, as a relish, served at a meal

ich weiss nicht [G.], I do not know

idem [L.], the same

id est (*i.e.*) [L.], that is

in fine [L.], in the end

in memoriam [L.], in memory (of)

in re [L.], in the matter of

in se [L.], in itself or themselves

in toto [L.], on the whole

jawohl [G.], yes, indeed

jeu d'esprit [F.], a play of wit

Kirche, Küche, Kinder [G.], church, kitchen, children (recommended by William II as proper objects for a woman's attention)

laissez faire [F.], let them do as they please; a policy of non-interference

le brave des braves [F.], the bravest of the brave

lettre de crédit [F.], a letter of credit

magna cum laude [L.], with great honors (used on diplomas)

maison [F.], a house or building

maître d'hôtel [F.], a hotel landlord; steward, or head waiter

maîtresse d'école [F.], a schoolmistress

mala fide [L.], in bad faith; with, or by, fraud

mater [L.], mother

materia medica [L.], medical material; a branch of medical science concerned with studying this material

memorabilia [L.], things worthy to be remembered

ménage [F.], a domestic establishment

mère [F.], mother

modus operandi [L.], the manner, or mode, of operation

mon ami, mon amie [F.], my friend

mon cher, ma chère [F.], my dear

mon Dieu! [F.], my God! (a mild interjection) good heavens!

mon vieux [F.], old fellow

n'est-ce pas? [F.], isn't that so?

nein [G.], no

nom de plume [F.], a pen name

nom de théâtre [F.], a stage name

non [F.], no; not

nota bene [L.], note well; take notice

nouveau riche [F.], one newly rich

objet d'art [F.], an object of artistic worth

omnia vincit labor [L.], labor conquers all things

O tempora! O mores! [L.], oh, the times! oh, the customs!

oui [F.], yes

parlez-vous français? [F.], do you speak French?

pater [L.], father

per capita [L.], by heads; for each individual

per centum [L.], by the hundred

per diem [L.], by the day; daily

persona grata [L.], an acceptable person, especially one acceptable to the government

petit, petite [F.], small

pièce de résistance [F.], the most substantial dish of a meal; the main feature of anything

post meridiem [L.], after noon

post mortem [L.], after death

prima facie [L.], at first view or appearance

pro forma [L.], as a matter of form

pro rata [L.], in proportion

pro tempore [L.], for the time being; temporarily

quasi [L.], as if; as it were

re [L.], in the matter of

répondez, s'il vous plaît [F.], R.S.V.P.; answer, if you please

robe-de-chambre [F.], a chamber robe; a dressing gown

robe-de-nuit [F.], a nightgown or nightshirt

rue [F.], a street

salle [F.], a hall; a room

sans façon [F.], informally; without ceremony

sans souci [F.], without care; free from care (properly applied to a hotel furnishing complete service)

schola cantorum [L.], school of singers

sic semper tyrannis [L.], ever thus to tyrants

sine qua non [L.], without which not; indispensable; absolutely necessary

sotto voce [It.], in an undertone; aside

status quo [L.], the state in which anything was or is; without change

sub rosa [L.], under the rose; in strict confidence

summa cum laude [L.], with highest honors (used on diplomas)

table d'hôte [F.], a meal with prearranged courses

terra firma [L.], the solid earth; land as opposed to air or water

ultra vires [L.], beyond the legal powers

verbatim et litteratim [L.], word for word and letter for letter

versus [L.], against

via [L.], highway; by way of

vice versa [L.], the other way around; conversely

wagon-lit [F.], a sleeping car

Wanderlust [G.], the impelling desire to wander or travel

Wie geht es? [G.], How goes it? (greeting) How are you?

ADDITIONAL REFERENCE BOOKS

Any standard dictionary

Secretary's Speller (revised), Mary Elizabeth Chute, Holt, Rinehart and Winston, Inc. New York

The University Spelling Book, Pollock and Baker, Prentice-Hall, Inc., Englewood Cliffs, N.J.

Chapter **14**

Capitalization, Abbreviation, and Number Problems

Read not my blemishes in the world's report; I have not kept the square, but that to come shall all be done by the rule.

—SHAKESPEARE

Judgment open to criticism

Any work which calls into play individual judgment is always open to criticism, for no two people see things in exactly the same light. In no place in secretarial work is there a greater necessity for the exercise of careful judgment than in deciding these three transcription problems: whether to capitalize or to use lower case, whether to abbreviate or to write in full, and whether to use a figure or to write a number out in words. In the last analysis, capitalization, abbreviation, and number problems are a matter of good judgment, which is built up on a knowledge of your own business. The kind of writing you are doing and the purpose you have in mind will usually determine the procedure.

Purposes of capitalization

Capitalization is used for emphasis. We capitalize names because we want to segregate them from common words; we capitalize titles because we want to emphasize the dignity which we attach to them; and we capitalize special words because we want to show our reader

255

that we consider them important. Capital letters are a platform upon which we seat the dignitaries of written language. A rule of most businesses is: "When in doubt, capitalize. You seldom make a mistake by according too much honor, but you can offend by being too sparing in bestowing your favors." At the same time, incorrect capitalization indicates that the writer is naïvely impressed by the importance of the events about which he writes, or is striving to place false emphasis on a matter which he realizes is incapable of attracting a reader's attention through the regular medium of ordinary type. Publishing houses, newspapers, and magazines use capitals very sparingly.

Words with all letters capitalized are confined to advertising, to billing (where size is important), and to other uses which demand overemphasis.

Rules for capitalization

The following rules for capitalization must not be considered as limitations beyond which one dare not step. They are designed as guides to general usage. They may be followed rather safely in regard to what *not* to write in the lower case, but they do not attempt to outline the bounds within which business may properly employ capital letters.

Capitalize:

1. The first word in every sentence, or in every group of words used as a sentence.

> The man is fair in his judgments.
> Try this over on your piano.
> Where will I find personal stationery?
> Down with the rebels!

2. The first word in every line of poetry.

> O pray you, noble lady, weep no more;
> But let my words—the words of one so small,
> Who knowing nothing knows but to obey,
> And if I do not there is penance given—
> Comfort your sorrows; for they do not flow

From evil done; right sure am I of that,
Who see your tender grace and stateliness.
                                                —*Guinevere.*

    Higher still and higher
      From the earth thou springest
    Like a cloud of fire;
      The blue deep thou wingest,
    And singing still doest soar, and soaring
        ever singest.
                                                —*To a Skylark.*

Note: Line indentations are usually employed in poetry to accentuate rhymed lines; when such emphasis is not desired, then lines begin on an even margin. If a line of poetry must be carried to a second typewritten line, the forwarded part should not be capitalized, and should begin farther toward the center than does any regularly indented line.

3. The first word in a direct quotation.

She said, "Unless you are young and very pretty, we usually advise against trumping your partner's ace."

4. Every proper noun.

James, Jacksonville, The First National Bank, *The New York Times,* China

5. Every proper adjective.

American, Italian, Germanic, Indian, Venetian, Swiss

6. Titles of courtesy.

Her Majesty, Queen Elizabeth; The Honorable Governor Smith; Judge Smith; Your Royal Highness

7. Designations of members of religious, political, and fraternal organizations.

The Democrats and the Republicans are evenly divided.
The Mormon choir broadcasts a delightful program.
President Kennedy is a Roman Catholic.
The Methodists and the Masons united in having a picnic.
He is a Delta Sigma Delta.

8. All references to the Deity.

> God; Father, Son, and Holy Ghost; His; Light of the World; Love; Star of Bethlehem

Note: The word *god* is not capitalized when it refers to heathen or non-Christian gods.

Note: References to Mary, the mother of Jesus, when made in the Catholic sense, are also capitalized.

> We pray for Her intercession.
> Holy Mother, hear our needs.

9. Official titles when they precede a name, but not when they follow it.

> President John M. Brown presided and Secretary L. M. Jones spoke.
> Officers present were John M. Brown, president, and L. M. Jones, secretary.

Note: This rule applies only to titles in the body of a letter or other written matter. When the title is used in the address, it is capitalized.

> John M. Brown, President,
> F. X. Smith, Advertising Manager
> Thomas A. Jones, Treasurer

10. Family titles used with a name or in direct address. (If used in other constructions, they are not capitalized.)

> I suppose you will offer me the proverbial excuse that you were attending your aunt's funeral.
> No, Uncle John died this time.
> He doubts my excuse, Mother.
> Would you like to talk to my mother?

11. Political titles used to refer to a specific person.

> the Secretary of Commerce, the Prince of Wales, the Mayor, the Governor

Note: If it is not quite evident that a following name has been omitted, the word is not a capitalized title.

> The Judge says bridge is an important game.
> (The person spoken to knows you mean Judge Woodward.)
> The judge was not interested in our case.
> (The person is not interested in which judge tried your case.)

12. All words, except conjunctions, prepositions, and articles, in titles of literary works and in names of firms or organizations.

> *Review of Reviews; Capitalization and Abbreviation;* John Doe and Company; The American Association for the United Nations

However, some authorities prefer to capitalize all words of more than two or three letters (against, with, before, etc.).

> *The Man Against the Sky*
> *Two Years Before the Mast*
> *The Man With the Iron Mask*

Note: When an article *the* is used before a corporate name, it should be capitalized if it forms a part of the registered name; otherwise *the* should be written in lower case, or omitted if it adds nothing to the fluency of the expression.

> Our organization is The First National Bank.
> Our organization is the First National Bank.

13. A descriptive name preceding a special name.

> Lake Placid, Hotel Brighton, University of Pennsylvania, Club Marshall

Note: Two common styles are in use when special names precede descriptive names. Usually, business prefers the "up style" of capitalization in letter writing, but a few men require the "down style" in the body of a letter (never in the address). The "down style" is used in journalistic writing.

> *Up Style:* Our Wall Street Office is being closed.
> *Down Style:* Our Wall street office is being closed.
> *Up Style:* He is attending Colgate University.
> *Down Style:* He is attending Colgate university.

14. Names of courses, but not of subjects themselves—unless the latter are derived from proper nouns.

> We registered for History I and Latin II.
> We are studying history and Latin.
> I enjoyed Professor Brown's course, Problems in American Democracy.

15. Names of special products in business, especially those which are registered as a trade-mark.

> Pepsi-Cola, Esso, Fels, Shoecraft, Buttercrust, Coca-Cola

16. The first word and the title in a salutation, but only the first word in a complimentary closing.

> My dear Neighbor:
> Most sincerely yours,

17. Names of things personified.

> It seems that Fate is against me.
> Big Business demands loyalty and hard work.
> We are convinced that Prosperity is just around the corner.

18. Days of the week and months of the year, but not the seasons.

> Sunday, January, spring, summer, fall, autumn, winter

19. Points of the compass when they refer to a section of the country, but not when they indicate direction.

> We cater to people who spend their winters in the South.
> A strong south wind retarded our speed.
> Persons with a Middle West point of view are likely to be interested primarily in America; those from the East, in European problems.
> The trip east will be a very fast one with very few stops at airports on the route.

20. Capitalize *Federal, Constitution, Government, National,* and *State* when they refer to the United States or to the state in which you live.

> The Government is trying to offer flood relief.
> The State ticket is all prepared now.
> The Constitution is our guide.
> We are interested in school government.
> Every one of our states has its own laws, but did these laws not merge into a national policy, we should have conflicts similar to those now prevalent in Europe.
> The constitution of the society was well planned.

21. Such general terms as *club, society, company, association, school, college,* and others when used instead of the entire name of some special organization.

Will you drive up to the Club with me?
The Bank does not favor this policy.
I am writing this on Corporation time.
We shall see you on the Continent (an abbreviated reference to the European Continent).

22. Names of holidays.

Veterans Day, Washington's Birthday, Labor Day, Christmas

23. The interjection *O,* but not *oh,* unless its use comes under some other capitalization rule.

Our yearning is, O for a thousand hands!
We are, oh, so tired!

24. Foreign prefixal terms placed before foreign names, when not preceded by a given name.

Eleanor von Schoenberg
The Von Schoenberg family

Note: When foreigners become naturalized American citizens, they often Americanize such names by capitalizing the prefixal term or omitting it altogether. However, if a person prefers to retain the foreign form, he is given that privilege, and you should follow his choice.

Alta De Rose
Alta Rose
Alta de Rose

25. Any noun followed by a Roman numeral.

Chapter II
Section IV

Purposes of abbreviation

Abbreviation is a shortening process. One may shorten his forms in writing either because of haste or because of limited writing space. In hasty types of writing, abbreviation may be employed freely, but in leisurely styles of writing shortening is not desirable. Billing, listing, and tabulating are usually done in abbreviated form. Of course, final consideration must always be whether a reader will easily comprehend the shortened form. Surely little time is saved in writing an abbreviated memorandum to a person who does not understand the terms you are using. When writing to people with technical training, you may quite properly make maximum use of abbreviations, because shortened forms aid in quick scanning. Real danger in the use of abbreviations comes from a tendency to fail to consider the layman; in letters to him, technical terms should not only be written out in full, but they should also be explained.

A minimum of abbreviation is advisable in solid forms of writing. Letters which are designed to reflect leisureliness use complete terms. Businessmen are usually loath to give an impression of slighting even an unimportant note; therefore, in writing business letters they frequently avoid even accepted abbreviations. Portions of a letter which can be tabulated in the body of a paragraph may quite properly contain abbreviations.

Rules for abbreviation

A few guides regarding standard practice will help you to become acquainted with abbreviations which will be easily understood by your readers. Your attention is directed to the following:

1. A good general rule for abbreviating is: Shorten as many words as possible in billing and tabulating (always keeping in mind that the abbreviations must be understood by the reader), but use abbreviations sparingly in letters and solid matter. For example, in a statement you would say:

> Your memo, 8/18. Shipped via Penna. RR.
> 817 lbs. Phila. Cement to Messrs. Smith & Jones,
> 21 S. Marion St., Bethlehem, Pa.

A letter regarding the same instructions would read as follows:

> In compliance with your memorandum of August 18, we are shipping by way of Pennsylvania Railroad 817 pounds of Philadelphia Cement to:
>
> > Messrs. Smith and Jones,
> > 21 S. Marion Street,
> > Bethlehem, Pennsylvania.

2. Names of cities and streets are not abbreviated, even in the address of a letter.

Philadelphia, Pa., *not* Phila., Pa.; Washington Ave., *not* Wash. Ave.

Note: Although the words *street* and *avenue* and names of states are best written in full in a letter, they may be abbreviated in informal types of business letters if they form a part of the address. They are never abbreviated in any other instances.

3. Do not abbreviate given names unless the persons to whom the names refer write them that way.

Geo., Chas., Wm., Jos., Jno.

4. A few abbreviations have become so commonly used in certain phrases that they are seldom written out in full, even when the forms are used in dignified writing.

Ft. Collins, Mt. Morris, St. Cloud, No. 18

Note: Include in this classification the titles Messrs., Mr. Mrs., Dr. when they appear before a name, and Jr., Sr., Esq., and initials for degrees when they follow a name.

I inclose the note of Mr. J. E. Carl, Jr.
He is several years my junior.
We live in St. Paul.
He is a saint.

5. Degrees, in abbreviated form, follow a name and are separated from it by a comma. When copying degrees, arrange them in the inverse order of their importance.

Harold M. Kinn, B.S., M.A., Ph.D.

Note: When two degrees of approximately equal rank are included in a list, the one of most importance in connection with what is being written will be reserved for the last. Writers often list their degrees of equal importance in the order in which they were conferred.

In a banking article, one would probably write:

Harold M. Kinn, Ph.D., D.C.S.

6. While it may be permissible in the body of a letter to abbreviate titles and the name of the state when quoting an address, these same terms should never be abbreviated when used in other constructions in the letter.

We are shipping the circulars to Dr. James M. Grant, 18 W. Fourth Street, Allentown, Pa. The doctor will see to the distribution of these circulars in his section of Pennsylvania.

7. Do not repeat title abbreviations which mean the same thing. Two abbreviations which indicate different titles of offices may be used.

> Dr. James Smith, *or* James Smith, M.D. (*never* Dr. James Smith, M.D.)
> Major J. T. McDonald, M.D. (titles do not overlap)

Note: When an abbreviation follows a name, it should be set off by commas, but no commas are used when it precedes the name. A few writers do not set off *Jr.* and *Sr.,* but the majority of business houses require the comma.

8. When degrees appear alone in the body of a letter, they are not abbreviated.

> John M. Baker, B.S.
> He was granted a bachelor of science degree.

9. In formal writing, *Honorable* and *Reverend* may be either abbreviated or written in full before a name, but they must be preceded by the article *the*.

> the Hon. Felix Frankfurter *or*
>   the Honorable Felix Frankfurter
> the Rev. James Levings *or*
>   the Reverend James Levings

Note: If the given name is omitted, then include another title in the body of a letter.

> the Honorable Justice Frankfurter
> the Honorable Doctor Copeland
> the Reverend Father Levings

10. In mentioning a man and his wife, or a woman and her husband, do not use the expressions "and wife" or "and husband."

> Mr. and Mrs. John White, *not* John White and wife
> Dr. and Mrs. E. H. Frain, *not* Mrs. Frain and husband

11. In repeating a reference to a person already named in a letter, use only his title and his family name. In referring to a man for the

first time, write his full name without the title *Mr.*, but see that any title of distinction precedes his name. *Mrs.* or *Miss* must always precede a woman's name.

> James F. Harvey (never use *Mr.*) will call on you tomorrow. Mr. Harvey (do not repeat *James*) has been with us for the last ten years.
>
> Dr. H. M. Brown is to be at our clinic tomorrow. Dr. Brown has devoted many years of his life to treating crippled children.
>
> We have just been conferring with Mrs. Anna Wilson in regard to her sweeper. Mrs. Wilson tells us that it tears her carpets.
>
> The Rev. J. M. Lane will preside. Will you assist Mr. Lane?

12. In the body of a letter, it is generally advisable to spell out *company, corporation, association, brothers, street, avenue, boulevard, park, general, president, secretary, captain, professor, father,* and similar terms; this is not necessary in an address, in footnotes, or in billing, tabulating, and listing.

Note: President, when referring to the President of the United States, is never abbreviated.

13. Avoid the following abbreviations in the body of a letter.

> namely—*viz.*
> that is—*i.e.*
> for example—*e.g.*
> and other things—*etc.*
> and—&

Note: In a company name the ampersand (&) is used if its use has been adopted by the firm itself; but if the firm uses the word *and,* you should follow that form. Letterheads or directories should be consulted to verify such forms.

14. Do not abbreviate *United States* in ordinary writing.

> A citizen of the United States is welcome.
> The United States will be represented.

Note: The fact that newspapers use the abbreviation *U.S.* in some constructions makes use of the form permissible in business English:

> U.S. Navy, U.S. Marines, U.S. Steel

Note: The abbreviation *U.S.A.* would be used in giving your address to a foreign correspondent:

James M. Smith & Co.
1166 Locust Street
Philadelphia, Pa.
U.S.A.

or in referring to a person in the United States Army:

Gen. A. R. Smith, U.S.A. *but*
Are you in the U.S. Army?

15. Never abbreviate *Christmas. Xmas* is highly objectionable to some readers.

16. Lastly, be sure that you are using the correct abbreviation when you finally decide the shortened form would be sanctioned as good usage.

Days of the week

Days of the week are never abbreviated in a letter. In billing, these forms are used:

Sun., Mon., Tues., Wed., Thurs., Fri., Sat.

In certain forms of tabulation, names of the days must be inserted in a very limited space. When you cannot type column headings vertically on a table or allot five spaces to the daily column (the number necessary for the abbreviation of Thursday), each abbreviation is often cut to two or three letters, with no period following the forms.

Su Mo Tu We Th Fr Sa

or

Sun Mon Tue Wed Thu Fri Sat

Months of the year

Months are never abbreviated in the body of a letter and seldom in the date line. In billing, these forms are used:

Jan., Feb., Mar., Apr., May, June, July, Aug., Sept., Oct., Nov., Dec.

If tabulation makes it necessary to reduce names of months to three spaces, the regular abbreviations are used, except for these necessary changes: *Jun, Jul, Sep.*

States and territories of the United States

One should always either follow abbreviations sanctioned by the United States Post Office Department or write names of states in full. "Manufactured" abbreviations cause no end of trouble. Learn the following thoroughly:

Ala.	Ill.	Mont.	P.R.
Alas.	Ind.	Nebr.	R.I.
Ariz.	Iowa	Nev.	S.C.
Ark.	Kans.	N.H.	S.D.
Calif.	Ky.	N.J.	Tenn.
Colo.	La.	N.M.	Utah
Conn.	Maine	N.Y.	Tex.
Del.	Md.	N.C.	Vt.
D.C.	Mass.	N.D.	Va.
Fla.	Mich.	Ohio	Wash.
Ga.	Minn.	Okla.	W. Va.
Hawaii	Miss.	Oreg.	Wis.
Idaho	Mo.	Pa.	Wyo.

Note: Observe some of the dangers of poor abbreviation. The abbreviations for *California* and *Colorado* were changed because of difficulty in distinguishing between many a handwritten *Cal.* and *Col.* There is little danger of "mis-striking" a key in writing *Ga., La., Pa.,* and *Va.,* because different fingers are used in reaching for the first letters of these words. Some writers always spell out *N.H., N.J.,* and *N.Y.,* because *H, J,* and *Y* are all struck with the same finger. Abbreviations often written incorrectly are *Ky., Mo., Pa., Vt.,* and *Va. Idaho, Iowa, Maine, Ohio,* and *Utah* are not abbreviated. Although it is possible to abbreviate *Puerto Rico* (*P.R.*), most writers don't.

Business abbreviations

Although an unabridged dictionary gives a fairly complete list of abbreviations, it is sometimes hard to find the abbreviation for a certain phrase which does not follow an alphabetic arrangement of the word itself. The following list of abbreviations has been compiled with a view to its general secretarial usefulness. Certain abbreviations are given in one way in the dictionary but are used in a different way in billing, where they are probably most frequently encountered. In the list given, business usage has been followed. For example, the dictionary gives *b. l.* for bill of lading, but most secretaries are required to write *B/L*. Though it must not be supposed that *b. l.* is never used, the other form is given here in order to acquaint you with current business usage. A lack of knowledge of abbreviations used in business will cause much confusion for a beginner. Periods are commonly eliminated in repeating the name of a bureau which is commonly abbreviated, but courtesy to readers demands that the title be written in full the first time it is mentioned in an article or letter.

A.A.A.   American Automobile Association
A.B.A.   American Bankers Association
a/c or *acct.*   account
a. c.   alternating current
A.D.   in the year of our Lord
Adj. Gen.   Adjutant General
adv. or *advt.*   advertisement
agcy.   agency
agt.   agent
alt.   alternate
A.M.   Master of Arts; before noon (also a.m.)
A.M.A.   American Medical Association
Am. or *Amer.*   America; American
amt.   amount
anon.   anonymous
ans.   answer
AP   Associated Press
A/P   accounts payable
approx.   approximately
A/R   accounts receivable
arr.   arrives; arrived
art.   article; artillery
assn.   association
asst.   assistant; assorted
att. or *atty.*   attorney
ave.   avenue
B.A.   Bachelor of Arts; British America
bal.   balance
B/B   bank balance

bbl.   barrel

B.C.   Bachelor of Chemistry; before Christ; British Columbia

bd.   board; bond; bound

bdl.   bundle

B/E   bill of exchange

bet.   between

bg.   bag

bk.   bank; book

bkg. or *bank.*   banking

bl.   bale

B/L   bill of lading

bldg.   building

bldr.   builder

blk.   block

blvd.   boulevard

B.M.E.   Bachelor of Mechanical *or* of Mining Engineering

B/P or *B. pay.*   bills payable

B/R or *B. rec.*   bills receivable

B/S   balance sheet; bill of sale

B.S.   Bachelor of Science

bu.   bushel; bushels

B/V   book value

bx.   box

C.   centigrade

c. & f.   cost and freight

C/B   cash book

cc.   cubic centimeter

cf.   compare

c.f.i.   cost, freight, and insurance

c.i.f. & c.   cost, insurance, freight, and commission

c.i.f.c. & i.   cost, insurance, freight, commission, and interest

cm.   centimeter

Co.   county; company

c/o   care of

c.o.d. or *COD*   cash, *or* collect, on delivery

Com.-in-chf.   Commander-in-chief

con.   consolidated

cont.   continuing; continued; contract

conv.   convertible

coop.   coöperative

cor.   corner

corp.   corporation

Corp.   corporal

cp.   compare, coupon
c.p.   candlepower; chemically pure
cr.   credit; creditor; creek
ct.   cent
ctf.   certificate
ctge.   cartage
cts.   cents
cu.   cubic
c.w.o.   cash with order
cwt.   hundredweight
D/A   deposit account; drawing account; documents upon acceptance
D/B or *D.B.*   day book
d.c.   direct current
dept.   department
dis., disc., or *disct.*   discount
dist.   district
div.   dividend, division
do.   ditto
doz.   dozen
dr.   debtor; debit
Dr.   doctor
E.   east
ea.   each
e. & o.e.   errors and omissions excepted
ed.   editor; education; edition
e.e.   errors excepted
e.g.   for example
eng.   engineer; engineering
engr.   engraver; engraving
esp.   especially
est.   estate; estimated
estab.   established
et al.   and others; and elsewhere
etc.   and other things
exch.   exchange
exec.   executive
F.   Fahrenheit
f.a.s.   free alongside ship
fin. sec.   financial secretary
f.o.b. or *FOB*   free on board
fol.   following
frt. or *fgt.*   freight

ft.   foot; feet; fort
fwd.   forward
gal.   gallon; gallons
gen.   general
gov.   governor
govt.   government
g.t.c. or *GTC*   good till canceled or countermanded
gtd.   guaranteed
h.c.l.   high cost of living
hdkf.   handkerchief
HOLC   Home Owners Loan Corporation
Hon.   honorable
h.p.   horsepower
hr.   hour
hrs.   hours
I.B.A.   Investment Bankers Association
I.C.C.   Interstate Commerce Commission
id.   the same
i.e.   that is
in.   inch; inches
inc.   incorporated; increase
incl.   inclosure; including
ins.   insurance; inspector
inst.   instant—of this month; instalment
int.   interest
I.O.U.   "I owe you"—used as an acknowledgement of a debt
J/A   joint account
Jr.   junior
k.   karat; knot
kg.   keg; kilogram
km.   kilometer
kw. or *k.w.*   kilowatts
kw.-h. or *kw.-hr.*   kilowatt-hours
l. c.   lower case
L/C   letter of credit
LL.B.   Bachelor of Laws
l.t.   long ton
Lt. or *Lieut.*   lieutenant
Lt. Gov.   Lieutenant Governor
ltd.   limited
lv.   leave; leaves
m.   meter
M.A.   Master of Arts

mag.   magazine
Maj. Gen.   Major General
max.   maximum
M.B.A.   Master of Business Administration
M.C.S.   Master of Commercial Science
M.D.   Doctor of Medicine
mdse.   merchandise
meas.   measure; measuring
memo.   memorandum
Messrs.   Messieurs
mfg.   manufacturing
mfr.   manufacturer
mgr.   manager
mi.   mile; miles
min.   minimum
misc.   miscellaneous
mkt.   market
Mlle.   Mademoiselle
Mlles.   Mesdemoiselles
m.m.   the necessary changes being made
Mme.   Madame
Mmes.   Mesdames
M/O or *M.O.*   money order
mo.   month
M.P.   member of Parliament
m.p.h.   miles per hour
Mr.   Mister (pl. Messrs.)
Mrs.   Mistress; "Missis" (pl. Mmes.)
MS.   manuscript
MSS.   manuscripts
Mt.   mount
mtg.   mortgage
mts.   mountains
Mus. B.   Bachelor of Music
M/V   market value
N.   north
N.A.   North America; North American
Natl. or *Nat.*   National
N/B   National Bank
N.B.   note well
n.g.   no good (colloquial)
No.   number
Nol. pros.   to be unwilling to prosecute

Nos. numbers
N.Y.C. New York City
o.e. omissions excepted
O.K. all right
O/R or *O.R.* owner's risk
O/S or *O.S.* out of stock
oz. ounce, ounces
p. page
pat. patent, patented
payt. payment
pd. paid
pfd. preferred
pk. peck
pkg. package
pkt. packet
P/L or *P & L.* profit and loss
P.M. postmaster, afternoon (also written p.m.)
pop. population
pp. pages
P.P. parcel post
pr. pair; pairs
Pres. president
P.S. postscript
pt. pint; part
qt. quart
R.D. rural delivery
recd. received
ref. reference; referred
reg. register; registered
rep. representative; representing
r.p.h. revolutions per hour
R.R. or *RR* railroad
R.S.V.P. reply, if you please
rt. right
Ry. railway
S. south
S.A. South America
S/B savings bank
s.c. small capitals
Sc. B. Bachelor of Science
sec. secretary
sect. section
Sgt. Sergeant

sh.	share

shpt.	shipment

S/O	seller's option

Soc.	society

SOS	a distress call

sp. gr.	specific gravity

Sr.	senior

ss.	namely; to wit

SS.	steamship

St.	street; saint

s.t.	short ton

sta.	station

stet	let it stand

stk.	stock

str.	steamer; strait

supt.	superintendent

syn.	synonym

synd.	syndicate

t.	ton

t.b.	tuberculosis (colloquial)

T/B	trial balance

T/C	trust company

TNT	trinitrotoluene (a highly explosive substance)

tr.	transpose; trust; trustee

Treas.	treasurer, treasury

twp.	township

ty. or *ter.*	territory

u.c.	upper case

ult.	ultimo—of the last month

U.S.A.	United States of America; United States Army

U.S.M.	United States Mail

U.S.N.	United States Navy

UPI	United Press International

viz.	namely; to wit

vol.	volume

V.P. or *Vice Pres.*	vice president

vs.	versus

W.	West

W/B	waybill

w.f.	wrong font

whf.	wharf

w.i.	when issued

wk. week
wt. weight
W/W warehouse warrant
yd. yard
Y.M.C.A. Young Men's Christian Association
Y.M.H.A. Young Men's Hebrew Association
yr. year
Y.W.C.A. Young Women's Christian Association
Y.W.H.A. Young Women's Hebrew Association

Reading of numbers

One accountant who was checking shipments involving millions of dollars tested nearly fifty girls before he found one who knew how to read numbers correctly. The decimal point should be read "and" in quoting numbers. Although this is the only time *and* should be used in reading figures, some secretaries insert the word a number of times. This habit makes their reading very confusing to the person who is writing down or checking figures.

$116,947.25
> *Read:* One hundred sixteen thousand nine hundred forty-seven dollars *and* twenty-five cents.
> *Never intersperse your reading with useless "and's" like this:* One hundred *and* sixteen thousand *and* nine hundred forty-seven dollars and twenty-five cents.

Suppose a man asks you to read to him a tonnage report while he puts down the figures. In order not to have any transpositions or inaccuracies, he will try to keep right up to your reading. In reading *587.6 T.* correctly, you will phrase *five hundred eighty-seven,* then say *and* for the decimal point, and continue *six-tenths tons.* Were you to say *five hundred and eighty-seven,* the man would have written 500 before you got to the *eighty-seven.* Such inaccurate reading necessitates erasures and causes much confusion. If no decimal point is written, as in mixed numbers, the *and* is read before the common fraction.

8¾
> *Read:* Eight and three-quarters

Mathematical ability

One special grievance of employers is that letters lack mathematical correctness. A businessman will sometimes state in an interview that he expects you to know "a little eighth-grade arithmetic." Such a warning should alert you to review an arithmetic book. Many things in it will be much clearer to you now than they were ten years ago. Children learn much of this valuable background by rote, with little idea of its practical application.

The main cause for mathematical errors does not lie so much in a lack of knowledge·of the comparatively small number of arithmetical processes involved in secretarial duties as in a lack of sufficient care in checking work. Secretaries seldom check their work to such a point that it does not contain errors they might have eliminated themselves. Your chief danger will lie, not so much in your inability to figure discounts, wall paper, floor space, or any other kind of problem, as in your neglect to prove, in typing a letter, that a payment of $25.00 on a $48.76 account does not leave a balance due of $13.76, or even of $23.67.

Remember that unless your letters reflect your ability to add, subtract, multiply, and divide correctly, the fact that you may know when to write a number in full and when to write a figure will not impress a businessman in the least.

Advantages and dangers in writing figures

Figures are short and easy to read. Business letters, being designed to be read quickly, make much wider use of figures than do other types of writing. Your final test for determining whether or not you should write a figure or a word will be whether you think that the reader will be likely to refer to the number after he has finished reading the material in which it is contained. One danger must always be kept in mind in sending out work containing figures; that danger is lack of correctness. Few secretaries know the bank of number keys on a typewriter; hence, they strike wrong keys or else, in looking up to see that they are striking the right key, they lose their place on the page they are copying. A figure that is insignificant from a typewriting point of view may be vitally important from the reader's standpoint. It *does* make a slight difference whether we get to a place on May 8 or May 9.

Rules for writing figures

These rules are compiled to acquaint you with good usage. Only a few of them are such hard and fast rules that they cannot be varied to suit your employer's preference.

1. Years are almost never written in full, except in the wording of formal invitations or in legal documents.

He moved here in 1913.

2. Months are never written in figures in a letter. However, in billing or tabulation the following forms are widely used:

8/17/..   8-17-..

3. Days are usually written in figures in a letter. When the date is given to include figures for the year, figures must be used for the day also. If the year is missing, some secretaries prefer to write the day in words.

All of these forms are correct: March 1, 19..
March 1
March first
the first of March
the 1st of March

Note: When the month directly precedes the day, the *st, d,* or *th* are not written with the figure; but when the foreign order is used, the letters do follow the figure.

He will be here March 21.
He will be here the 21st of March.

4. Hours are written in full if the written form is very short; but if the written form would be too long for easy reading, figures are used.

I shall see you at two o'clock
We shall expect you at 9:15 p. m.
I take the 8:27 every morning.

5. Figures which indicate the year of graduation are placed in abbreviated form after the name of the graduate or his school.

Write to James M. Brown, '60. He was a graduate of Harvard Law School '60, and took postgraduate work in social work.

6. Never use a number at the beginning of a sentence. Rearrange the sentence, if necessary, to avoid such a use.

Wrong: 19.. was a good year for us.
Right: The year 19.. was a good one for us.

7. When one number follows another, a choice must usually be made as to which one can best be spelled out.

Buy 75 five-cent apples.
There will be two 75-yard dashes.

Note: When it seems best to write both numbers in figures, a comma may be used; however, it is generally preferable to rearrange the sentence.

In 19.., 87,694 letters were dispatched from this office.
In 19.. this office dispatched 87,694, letters.

8. Ages are usually written in full in a letter, unless they include months and days.

I am thirty years of age.
He was 71 years, 8 months, 22 days old.

9. Write figures for temperature readings.

62° F.   24° C.

10. Approximations should be spelled out.

We have about two hundred patients here now.
The dress costs nearly fifty dollars.

11. Do not spell out four-figure numbers as hundreds instead of thousands (even in dates).

Wrong: Fourteen hundred ninety-two
Right: One thousand four hundred ninety-two

12. No period follows *per cent* today, though it formerly was treated as an abbreviation of the Latin *per centum.* In very informal business letters, the per cent sign may be used where it is desirable to have quotations stand out prominently.

Fifty per cent of our stock is gone.
The price is $875, 20% off for cash.

13. Quantities which are followed by a word indicating weight or measure are given in full in the more formal types of writing; but figures are used in a business letter when one might be interested in later referring to the quantity only. Usually the measure is not abbreviated, except in a letter giving quotations.

They have a ten-pound son.
Send us 10 pounds of flour.
Flour prices are: 10 lb., 67¢; 25 lb., $1.47.

14. In reporting athletic events, election returns, and other statistical matter which will be referred to hastily, always use figures.

His time was 2:45:27.
The score is 14–6.
He won by a majority of 6,749 votes.
Mr. Jones got 10 votes; Mr. Smith, only 6.
They produced an average of 35 letters an hour.

15. In writing dimensions in a letter, it is usually considered best to write the numbers in full; but when it is desirable that the measures stand out for comparison or quick reference, they may be written in figures. In writing to the technically trained, signs may be used for inches and feet.

In an article on decoration: The rugs were nine feet wide by twelve feet three inches long.
To a woman customer: We now have the rug which you admired last week (No. 18) in the size you need, 9 ft. by 12 ft. 3 in.
To a rug merchant: We are shipping Pattern No. 18 in size 9′ × 12′ 3″.

16. Sums of money which cannot be expressed in two words should be written in figures.

> Twenty-five dollars
> Two hundred dollars
> Eighty-seven cents
> $175 $19,747.23

Note: If the price will be needed for comparison or reference, it should always be written in figures.

17. Do not use extra ciphers to indicate no cents. Omit the decimal point.

> Our tables are now selling for $37.
> We are crediting you with $7.
> We offer you $650 for the car.

Note: When figures are used in comparisons in a letter, the ciphers should be used to indicate cents if the next amount cannot be written without a decimal point.

The price will now be $51.00 instead of $59.50 as previously quoted.

18. A dollar sign should not be used in writing sums of money less than one dollar.

> The toy costs eighty-seven cents.
>   *or*
> The toy is quoted at 87¢.
>   *but not*
> The toy costs $.87.

19. Sums of money spelled out should be followed by the figures in parentheses only in legal writing, or in a letter of the legal type. When figures are repeated after a written sum or a written number, they should directly follow the expressions which they repeat.

> *Right:* The sum of fifty-seven dollars ($57) is to be paid.
> The sum of fifty-seven (57) dollars is to be paid.
> We guarantee to enlist the help of eighty (80) persons.
> *Wrong:* The sum of fifty-seven ($57) dollars is to be paid.
> We guarantee to enlist the help of eighty persons (80).

20. Write in full all numbered streets and avenues when the figure is 10 or lower. Use figures for numbers above *tenth*. In formal types of

writing, such as invitations, the street number is spelled out, regardless of its length.

281 Fifth Avenue
187 West 18th Street

Note: If no letter of direction appears between the house number and the street number, it is advisable to write the street number in full, unless it is too long. In the latter instance, a dash is used to separate the house number from the street number.

18 Thirteenth Avenue
917—210th Street

21. House numbers should always be written in figures, with the possible exception of a house numbered "1."

9 East 87th Street
One Fifth Avenue

22. Roman numerals are usually capital letters and do not need to be followed by a period, unless it is needed for a purpose other than that of indicating abbreviation.

I—1	VIII— 8	LX— 60	D— 500
II—2	IX— 9	LXX— 70	DC— 600
III—3	X—10	LXXX— 80	DCC— 700
IV—4	XI—11	XC— 90	DCCC— 800
V—5	XX—20	C—100	CM— 900
VI—6	XXX—30	CC—200	M—1000
VII—7	XL—40	CCC—300	MM—2000
	L—50	CD—400	

MCMXXXII—1932

Note: When *M* is used as an abbreviation for 1,000, as in references to quantities of lumber or bonds, a figure is used before the *M* instead of additional *M*'s being added.

2 M ft. White Pine Flooring (not MM ft.)
3M Fourth Liberty 4¼'s (not MMM bonds)

23. Common usage has settled upon certain types of designations which require Roman numerals and others which require Arabic numbers. References to sections of writing are:

Vol. I	Vols. I & II
Book I	Books I & II
Part I	Parts I & II
Chap. I	Chaps. I & II
Art. I	Arts. I & II
Sect. 1	Sects. 1 & 2
col. 1	cols. 1 & 2
p. 29	pp. 29 & 30
v. 29 (line of poetry)	vv. 29 & 30
l. 29	ll. 84–97
No. 1	Nos. 1 & 2
Fig. 1	Figs. 1 & 2
Ill. 1	Ills. 1 & 2
Table 1	Tables 1 & 2
Chart 1	Charts 1 & 2

Note: When a listing of articles or sentences is made in tabulated order, a period follows the Arabic number. In the body of a paragraph, the number is enclosed in parentheses.

I am listing below the points in my general background which may have a bearing on this position:
1. Age—28 years
2. Education—Palmerton High School '52
            Swarthmore College '56
            Peirce School of Business '57
3. Religion—Episcopalian
4. Experience—Secretary for two years to
            Hon. M. M. Brown,
            1616 Broad Street,
            Philadelphia, Pa.
5. References—My former employer

We are giving you three choices: (1) a black with silver trimmings, (2) a blue with silver trimmings, and (3) a tan with brown trimmings.

BOOKS THAT WILL GIVE YOU A BASIS FOR JUDGMENT IN

CAPITALIZATION, ABBREVIATION, AND NUMBER PROBLEMS

Any standard dictionary (abbreviation and capitalization lists in back)
The Secretary's Handbook (8th ed.) Taintor and Munro, Macmillan Co., New York
Business Executive's Handbook (4th ed.) Brown and Doris, Prentice-Hall, Inc., Englewood Cliffs, N.J.
Handbook of English, McPeek and Wright, Ronald Press Co., New York

Chapter **15**

Sentence Structure and Punctuation

True ease in writing comes from art, not chance.
—ALEXANDER POPE

Punctuation dependent upon structure

Good punctuation is dependent upon good sentence structure; no amount of punctuating can make a poor sentence correct. Voice, gesture, facial expression, and pauses make a dictated sentence clear. Punctuation, in writing, must supplant these physical aids to interpretation. Properly punctuating a letter as it is being transcribed is comparatively easy if the thought to be expressed was perfectly clear in the mind of the author as he dictated. However, if he did not know just what he was going to say, he may have wandered around in his dictation to such an extent that he failed to express his ideas clearly. A reader of a letter expects a direct and concise statement of the matter involved. Often a letter must say in three hundred words what a man would take fifteen minutes of conversation to discuss. A style which is too conversational may be very difficult to punctuate, not because it is incorrect grammatically, but because its unexpected appearance in a letter puts a severe burden of interpretation upon punctuation marks. Good sentence structure helps us express accurately the idea we want to convey.

Punctuation consciousness

The chief trouble with most secretaries is not that they do not know how to punctuate their transcriptions, but that they are not conscious of punctuation while taking dictation. Consequently they omit periods, question marks, commas in unusual constructions, and other aids to interpreting notes. When a secretary goes back to read over her notes, she may have forgotten the inflection in her employer's voice when he was dictating. If the end of a sentence has not been indicated, the first phrase of the next sentence may fit right onto the unmarked end of the sentence she is writing. Transcripts reveal a surprisingly large number of such errors.

> *Wrong:* We immediately filled their order. While they waited, they expressed appreciation of our prompt service.
> *Right:* We immediately filled their order while they waited. They expressed appreciation of our prompt service.

Sequence of ideas

In constructing sentences we should aim chiefly to place our thoughts before the reader in the precise order needed to enable him to comprehend the message. If his mind must rearrange items before it is possible for him to get our meaning, reading will be slow. Important ideas may be lost sight of before their full importance is grasped. For this reason a business letter which does not have a subject heading should include in the first sentence some mention of the subject.

> *Poor:* Your order of March 15 is being filled by our Detroit branch because our stock here is temporarily exhausted.
> *Better:* Because our stock here is temporarily exhausted, our Detroit branch is filling your order of March 15.

Arrangement of a sentence is often dependent upon a dramatic element. That portion of a sentence which the author wishes emphasized is placed in a position where it will make an impression upon the mind of the reader. In the following sentence, the writer wishes to emphasize the date of starting a new policy.

> Starting next Monday, but not applying to orders previously filed with us, a cash policy will be instituted at this store which will enable us to sell all goods four per cent below present price standards.

Types of sentences

The type of sentence to be used in any given place is largely dependent upon the kind of writing being done. Short sentences are not necessarily better than long ones; a long sentence may be the proper medium for conveying a number of closely knit ideas. A letter composed of too many short sentences sounds choppy; a series of long and involved sentences taxes the reader's power of retention. Short sentences should be used to speed up the tempo of writing when a writer's object is to get quick action; longer sentences are used in explanations.

Advertising letters are usually good examples of business writing. They are written with a definite purpose in mind. Some letters are more interesting if complex constructions are used; however, simple constructions are most effective in an ordinary letter, because the reader does not then find interpretation burdensome.

The author of a book on English wrote a test advertisement for a firm. The members thought that it was excellent, but it failed to bring in tangible results. The firm then tested the "pulling power" of a letter written by a successful young salesman. That letter was not a model of sentence structure, but the response it brought forth was astonishingly good. The young man knew his product and his customers; therefore, he had an effective message. You will have to guard against having a purely literary interest in letters you write for your employer. Just because a letter does not appeal to you as being a model of good English is no reason for condemning it. Business is looking for letters which will bring in profits. Language should never be the master; it must always be the servant of the writer.

Simple sentences

A sentence which has one subject and one predicate ordinarily needs little attention.

Furs are now *selling* at the lowest prices in history.

Although either subject or predicate, or both, may be compound, the sentence remains simple in structure. However, the problem of agreement between subject and verb is always present.

> *Furs* and *dresses* / *are bought* and *sold* at low prices.
> Either *profit* or *loss* / *is* sure to be small.

A simple sentence which is overburdened with modifiers sometimes becomes a real problem in punctuation. Usually, the thought is much more clearly expressed if the ideas are recast into a complex sentence structure.

> *Poor:* Being overburdened by home worries and cares, a secretary and her employer, generally so congenial, became irritable and allowed their peace of mind to be marred, quite unnecessarily, by their mutual criticisms of each other.
> *Better:* A secretary and her employer were generally congenial, but an unusually heavy burden of home worries and cares caused them to become irritable; their peace of mind was marred, quite unnecessarily, by their mutual criticisms of each other.

Although sentences may become too involved, a number of short sentences can be combined into one sentence through judicious handling of subjects, predicates, and modifiers. This joining of related ideas avoids useless repetition. Watch your employer's dictation for opportunities to connect thoughts which are better expressed as a unit.

> *Poor:* We have not received your remittance. We have also not heard from you.
> *Better:* We have neither received your remittance nor heard from you.

Compound sentences

Compound sentences are those composed of two or more clauses of equal grammatical value.

> Prices went down, competitors undersold us, and we were obliged to assume a loss on the stock.

Any one of these clauses would, if written alone, make a complete thought. Combining them into a compound sentence merely makes reading smoother and adds unity to the letter. The fact that dictators have a way of stringing letters along in a series of loosely connected ideas should not blind one to use of the compound sentence. A compound sentence is not necessarily a long one.

> Customers withdrew deposits, and banks failed.

Words, phrases, and clauses may be used as modifiers, and the sentence may be several typewritten lines in length. If ideas are closely connected and easily comprehended, do not try to make a sentence division. Your duty will be to see that extraneous ideas do not mar sentence unity.

Businessmen often lament that the ordinary secretary doesn't know a sentence when she *sees* one. Frequently this is true, but any shorthand writer will tell you that, more often, there are no sentences to be found in dictated matter. Of course it is hard to see a sentence when it isn't there! Nevertheless, constructing good sentences out of a conglomeration of words is part of the work of a good secretary. A poor secretary will stuggle over the punctuation of such passages as the following; a good secretary will get out her grammatical ax and start chopping before she begins to type.

> In regard to the changes you suggest in the wheels of our large sedans, we are running these under a special contract, as they are not made in our own factory, and will not be able to make any change at this time, but will be very glad to consider this suggestion at our next salesmen's meeting.

Some good writers limit all sentences to not more than four or five typewritten lines. Sentences of greater length usually demand careful analysis.

Complex sentences

Sentences which contain clauses subordinate to the main idea are complex. There must always be at least one main, or independent, clause to which a dependent clause should be joined.

> They found the folder *where they had left it*.

The fact that one or more *dependent* clauses are used in a complex sentence should warn you of pitfalls for which you will have to watch. The dependent clause modifies, or is dependent upon, some part of the main clause; therefore, its placement must be such as to eliminate any possibility of its being construed to modify another word. A reader should have the qualifying idea when he needs it for clear and accurate comprehension. Careful scrutiny is needed to make certain that thoughts are going to be carried logically by the sentence.

> *Poor:* Humor is appreciated which is not tinged with sarcasm.
> *Better:* Humor which is not tinged with sarcasm is appreciated.

Means of coordination

Clauses of equal rank are connected by coordinating conjunctions. Great care must be taken to choose the proper conjunction for connecting independent clauses. The use of *and* for *but* is a common error in compound sentence structure.

> We knew our error, *but* (not *and*) they thought the goods were perfect.

The following list of conjunctive words and phrases which may be used to avoid repetition of *and* is submitted for your ready reference: *but, though, although, still, however, yet, nevertheless, so, as, then, therefore, hence, accordingly, since, on the contrary, at the same time, for all that, on the other hand, as a result, as a consequence, at any rate, in any event, for this reason.* Sometimes connectives are used in pairs, for example: *either.....or; neither.....nor; as..... so; although.....nevertheless; though.....yet; both.....and; if..... then; not only.....but also.* These are called correlatives.

Means of subordination

Clauses which are dependent are nearly always introduced by a special term. This word may be merely a connective, or it may have definite grammatical value in the clause itself. Connectives which introduce a dependent clause may be subordinating conjunctions, conjunctive pronouns, or conjunctive adverbs. In all events, they form a tie between the modified word or portion of the sentence and the clause itself. Among the most common subordinating words are: *that, if, while, when, where, what, who, whose, whom, for, because, like, such as, but that.*

Purposes of sentences

Sentences are used to state facts, to give commands, or to ask questions. The same idea may be conveyed in each of the three forms of sentences.

> We shall appreciate your giving this matter your prompt attention.
> Kindly give this matter your prompt attention.
> Will you kindly give this matter your prompt attention?

The form of a sentence may be changed to avoid a sameness in construction, to secure emphasis, or to convey a difference in your attitude toward the reader.

Any one of the sentence forms—declarative, imperative, or interrogative—may be used to express such strong feeling as to demand an exclamation mark after it.

Use of modifiers

The main parts (subject and predicate) of any sentence may be limited in their meaning by the addition of modifiers. These modifiers may take the form of simple adjectives and adverbs, or of prepositional phrases and participial phrases having the uses of adjectives and adverbs. Often an entire sentence or a clause can be changed to a simple modifier which gives the meaning more clearly. This possibility of improving dictated material makes it desirable for you to read through a letter completely before transcribing it. Necessary changes and punctuation marks can be inserted in notes to avoid loss of time when typing; however, these revisions are not so important as is proper organization of ideas, which cannot be effected a sentence at a time.

Choppy: Your report for January pleased me. It was excellent. I am recommending that you be rewarded accordingly.

Better: Your excellent report for January pleased me so much that I am recommending that you be rewarded accordingly.

A series of sentences beginning with *we* should usually be changed by subordinating the less important of the complete thoughts. Other words which, when used in a series, are equally indicative of poor combination are *they, it, I, you,* and *your.* In dictated material one may find half a dozen sentences beginning with the same word.

Poor: We will ship your order at once. We know you are in a hurry for the goods. We are inclosing the bill with this letter.

Better: Because we know you are in a hurry to have the goods, we are shipping your order at once. The bill is inclosed with this letter.

Points of emphasis

The beginning and end of any form of expression leave a deeper impression than intervening parts. Our introduction to a person and our farewell to him usually remain in our minds after we part company. Likewise, the beginning and the ending are the most effective parts of a sentence.

Beginning and ending weak: Nevertheless, in trying to avoid winter skin difficulties, you will need to consider a choice of soap *to some extent.*

Better: In trying to avoid winter skin difficulties, you will need to consider a choice of soap.

A like rule for placement of important thoughts should be observed in arranging sentences in paragraphs. The first paragraph should be strong; hence, the first sentence in it should be positive. You should work out an arrangement of words that will be a written reflection of ideas of a vigorous personality. Just imagine the impression your firm makes by using some such opening sentence as:

Your letter of the 9th inst. received, and contents duly noted.

How much better to say:

> Your letter of October 9 brings to our attention an error that we shall attempt to rectify at once.

In writing to a large firm, however, the wording "an error" would not be sufficient explanation; you would need to explain the error so fully that the reader would not be compelled to look up a previous letter in order to refresh his memory as to its content.

The first sentence of a paragraph should be a key to the idea which is to be expressed. Sentences which follow a strong opening sentence should be a clear and logical development of that idea. Transitions between paragraphs should be smooth; the reader should not be asked to make a mental leap from one paragraph to another. Some writers accomplish this easy transition by allowing the sentences in a paragraph to taper off in force. By lessening a reader's concentration at the end of one paragraph, his mind is so cleared that he can easily grasp a new idea presented in the next paragraph. However, the final sentence must be one of the strongest in the letter—one which will remain in the reader's mind. Any sentence beginning with a word which ends in *-ing* should be avoided either as the first or as the last sentence in a letter, because a participially introduced sentence is a very weak construction. For this reason, the open closing (a sentence ending without punctuation) is not a forceful concluding sentence.

> *Weak:* Hoping we may hear from you by next Tuesday, we are
> *Stronger:* May we hear from you by next Tuesday?

Paragraphs

Arrangement of sentences into paragraphs should be determined before you begin your transcription. In school you were taught to paragraph ideas. Because most business letters, for filing convenience, cover only one topic, many a secretary is prone to make but a single paragraph of a letter, not realizing that it is possible and permissible to paragraph *parts of ideas.* If a letter is a little long, a careless secretary may decide it ought to have another paragraph and arbitrarily indent some sentence without regard for its relation to the preceding matter.

You must learn to paragraph business letters, not only to make them look better, but to bring out ideas. There is no excuse for making a new paragraph unless such arrangement is going to make the thought clearer or more easily read. Good short paragraphs are preferred to long ones only because they make the context easy to grasp.

Poor paragraphing in transcriptions has caused many businessmen to form the habit of saying "paragraph" as they dictate. If paragraphing is dictated to you, in the name of common sense, use it! One secretary actually told her employer that her system of shorthand had no symbol to indicate a paragraph, and so she never marked divisions when he dictated them. Needless to say, her paragraphing of his letters was a constant source of vexation to him.

Changing of sentence structure

English teachers are continually telling secretarial students to revise dictated matter. Many a secretary goes out to her first position with this admonition thoroughly grounded into her consciousness, but she soon finds there is little time in the ordinary business office to put the theory into practice. She has probably never before come in contact with dictated material which was not reasonably clear. If sixty letters a day must be produced, a secretary cannot waste too much time trying to decide what to do with a conglomeration of ideas.

The rush of business leaves little time to worry about lack of perfection; passably good letters are all that can be hoped for in most offices. However, the majority of letters that have been transcribed exactly as dictated would not be passed by an employer. You will have to do some revising as you transcribe. Some men are very happy to have their letters changed; they feel that you are not doing your duty unless you construct from a poorly dictated background of notes the best letter you can devise. Other men resent your trying to improve their work; any corrections that you make for such an employer will have to be executed so skillfully that he will not detect them. Sometimes this antagonism is a matter of stubbornness, but more often it arises from a misinterpretation of your motive. Too thorough a job of correcting his letters, leads a man to think you believe him incompetent or yourself overwise. You cannot build up an employer's writing or dictating ability by tearing down every sentence he utters.

Any letter could be criticized. For this reason, do not feel compelled to waste your time struggling to make a masterpiece of every letter you transcribe. Under most circumstances the more nearly you follow your notes, the happier everyone will be. You must understand clearly what you are taking down in shorthand; then you can put the burden of content on your employer.

Revamping of sentences to cover up shorthand defects is a pernicious practice. You can sometimes change a sentence in such a way as to cover up a portion of omitted dictation or unreadable notes. Such an omission may not be easily detected in the course of the employer's hasty reading of your typewritten letter. However, if he does notice he may be very much annoyed to find that a portion of a dictated letter was lost in transcribing, either through your carelessness or through your deliberate effort to cover up your inability to read illegible notes or to fill in missing portions.

This warning for you to be practical rather than overzealous in recasting dictation should not deter you from taking every opportunity to reconstruct letters in order to improve them. If you have tact and a clear head, your employer will gain confidence enough in your ability to let you have your own way with letters. If he is a very busy man, he must rely on letters being so accurate that he can sign them with confidence. This faith, which many businessmen repose in a secretary's ability, places the burden of good construction on you personally.

Rules for punctuation

In order to gain anything resembling an adequate knowledge of punctuation, it is necessary to keep firmly in mind some general rules. A few minutes of concentrated study will enable you to master them thoroughly. Take one punctuation mark at a time and learn its uses.

Punctuation is designed to make reading easy. The present tendency is toward the elimination of all punctuation which is not essential to clearness. However, never get the idea held by the secretary who said to her employer: "They aren't using commas any more." Business *is* using commas, but to use one in the wrong place is as dangerous as to omit one where it is needed. The disposition of vast fortunes has sometimes depended upon the omission or insertion of a comma in a will. After a person is dead, the meaning of a will, if not clear, may have to be settled by the courts. Likewise, a letter which you send to a customer must be so self-explanatory as to leave no possibility of misinterpretation.

The period

The period is the most fundamental of all marks of punctuation. It is the traffic light that appears on the written highway and makes the reader stop to comprehend one thought before speeding on to another.

The chief uses of the period are in the following connections:

1. After either a declarative or an imperative sentence. (Two typewriting spaces follow this period.)

> Bacon is now selling at fifty cents a pound.
> Send me half a pound of round steak.

Note: A period is used after any expression which takes the place of a sentence, even though it is not grammatically a complete thought. Though there is no doubt that a complete sentence is to be preferred, many businessmen in recent years have adopted the incomplete sentence.

> And now for bad debts. I have decided to send Mr. Payne over your entire territory during the next month.

2. After an abbreviation. (Only one typewriting space follows this period.)

> Rev.   f. o. b.
> Fla.   SS.

3. As a decimal point in figures. (No spacing is permissible.)

> $97.16   2.8 lbs.

4. As an indication that certain words have been omitted in quoted material.

At least three periods (leaders) must be used to indicate omission. More periods may be used if it seems desirable so to indicate the omission of long passages. When leaders show the omission of

words at the beginning of a quotation, a capital is not used to introduce the quoted portion unless the author has used a capital in the
original. No punctuation follows directly after quoted material if
leaders are used to indicate that the sentence is not complete. If a
question mark is absolutely necessary, it may follow the periods which
indicate omission.

> All of us would like to be able to
> ". . . look into the seeds of time,
> And say which grain will grow and which will not."

> Some of us believe so implicitly that ". . . it would be miserable
> . . . to have no will but that of another . . ." that we are afraid
> not to have our will in constant battle with that of others.

> "He that hideth hatred with lying lips . . . is a fool."
>
> —Proverbs 10:18

Note: A period marks the end of any quoted material which is the end of a
declarative or imperative sentence. If other words follow the quotation, the period
is displaced by a comma. (A period or comma is typed before quotation marks at
all times.)

He said, "Sunco is a delightful breakfast treat."
"Sunco is a delightful breakfast treat," says the businessman.

The interrogation point

Use of the interrogation point is so simple that one hesitates to
mention it. How surprising, then, to find omission of interrogation
marks among the foremost errors of careless punctuation! When you
are transcribing, your mind will be concerned with context, and it will
be easy not to realize you are copying a question. The proper time to
punctuate a question is when it is being dictated, for a rising inflection
of the dictator's voice will indicate interrogation. However, by reading
over every letter before releasing it from your machine, you should
discover any period which has been wrongly placed after a question.

A question mark, or interrogation point, should be used as follows:

1. After every statement that you wish a reader to understand as a
question.

What are you planning to do about our order?

Note: An interrogative sentence to which no answer is demanded may be followed by a period.

> May we hear from you in a few days.
> May we have the pleasure of serving you again.

(There is no reason why a question mark should not follow this type of sentence, and businessmen frequently require it. Many writers, however, avoid the question form when they do not expect the reader to regard the sentence as requiring a reply.)

2. After any quoted question.

> Our customers ask, "Is this cough mixture free from drugs?"
> "Is this cough mixture free from drugs?" our customers ask.

An indirect question is followed by a period.

> Our customers ask whether this cough mixture is free from drugs.

Note: A question mark is placed inside quotation marks if it belongs to the quoted matter, but it is placed outside quotation marks when the quoted matter is a part of the question.

> "Are you interested in biographical plays?"
> Have you seen "The Barretts of Wimpole Street"?

3. After expressions which should be indicated as doubtful or uncertain. (A question mark is placed in parentheses directly following the questionable portion of the sentence.)

> When the reports are all in next Tuesday (?), I shall make a tabulation of the results.
> What is the price of that 75 lb. (?) size sack of sugar?

Note: Irony may also be expressed by questioning a term.

> May I suggest that your efficient (?) secretary probably still has the message for you.

The exclamation mark

An exclamation mark is sparingly used in business because it indicates that the writer is being governed by emotions rather than by reasoning. However, its occasional use provides relief from the monotony of business routine. Some types of advertising make exaggerated but quite effective use of exclamations in working up an appeal which is purely emotional. Most businessmen avoid an exclamation in ordinary correspondence because they feel it "too collegiate";

you will probably be much more inclined to use exclamation marks in your own writing than in transcribing letters of your employer.

An exclamation mark is made by holding down both the *shift key and the space bar* while the period and the apostrophe are struck. Holding the space bar on some typewriters eliminates the necessity for backspacing. At the end of a sentence the exclamation mark is followed by two spaces; in the body of a sentence, by only one space.

Uses of the exclamation mark may be summarized as follows:

1. An exclamation point may follow any word, group of words, or sentence which is expressed with strong feeling.

> Hurrah! (Word)
> Done for the day! (Group of words)
> That telephone is ringing again! (Statement)
> Shut the door! (Command)
> Why does he do that! (Question)

Note: Very strong feeling may be indicated by a number of exclamation marks. And he expects a businessman to believe that!!!

2. An exclamation mark follows either an interjection or an entire sentence, depending upon the meaning to be conveyed. The entire sentence may be used to express emotion; or the interjection may express emotion and the rest of the sentence may be used as an explanation of that feeling.

> Ouch! that is where the good business shoe pinches.
> Well, can you imagine such lack of business ethics!

Note: A comma replaces the exclamation mark after an interjection when only mild emphasis is desired.

> Ah, I thought you were wrong.

3. An exclamation may be used to show derision.

> And you think you are a salesman!

The comma

A comma, the most common mark of punctuation within a sentence, is always followed by one typewriting space, except in figures, where no spacing after commas is allowed. (At the end of a quotation, a quotation mark is written after the comma and before the space.)

Uses of the comma are as follows:

1. To indicate inverted order.

> Weaver, James M.
>
> Complying with your request, we have shipped the goods today.
>
> Prices having advanced, it is impossible to fill your order at our June quotations.
>
> Like all other houses, we have been obliged to curtail our production.
>
> Upon receiving your report, Mr. James will make up the tabulation of results.
>
> If you are not satisfied, return the goods to us at our expense.
>
> While you are busy getting orders, every effort will be made to prepare goods for prompt shipment.

Note: If any sentence begins with *if, though, while,* or any of the other subordinating conjunctions, you should look for an opportunity to place a comma before the main clause. Sentences beginning with a word which ends in *-ing* should give you the same warning.

2. To set off intervening or parenthetical expressions and modifiers.

> You understand, of course, that we cannot give this reduction unless you pay cash.
>
> We find, therefore, that it is impossible to fill our contract.
>
> We cannot believe, Mr. Simpson, that you would take advantage of an unfortunate situation.
>
> Absolute honesty, if he possesses such a thing, is surely a matter of degree.
>
> Detroit, the home of the automobile, is a beautiful city.
>
> The report, which came shortly after you left, verified your convictions.

Note: A common secretarial error is the insertion of only one of a pair of commas which set off intervening or parenthetical expressions. A comma almost never comes before a verb unless another comma, the first of a pair, has been previously used in the sentence. If you find you must put a comma before a verb, make sure that the other comma of the pair is also inserted. When you have omitted the first comma by mistake, you can insert it so skillfully that a reader will not notice the lack of uniform spacing.

The boy trying to get his tackle free, fell into the water.

The boy, trying to get his tackle free, fell into the water.

(Notice in the above illustration how, by slightly depressing the backspacer, the typist inserted the omitted comma. No erasure was necessary.) Not all phrases and clauses occurring between a subject and a predicate are set off by commas, but if one comma is used the other is absolutely necessary. *No commas are inserted when a restrictive modifier is used.*

The report *that I lost* has been found.

3. To separate members of a series.

Pens, pencils, and notebooks are needed.

To write legible notes, to transcribe rapidly, and to understand context are fundamental to a secretary's rapid production of good letters.

The wage level was raised, people bought more goods, and production had to be increased.

He bought a beautiful, lemon-yellow, sweet-songed canary for the invalid.

Note: Some authorities permit omission of the comma before *and,* but this causes confusion in listing combinations. For example, dresses are sometimes ordered in a combination of colors, such as blue and white, or blue and yellow. A comma placed between all members of the series makes directions clear.

Send the prints in blue, red and white, yellow and brown, and green.

Note: Commas always precede and follow *etc.* when the latter is used in a series. No *and* is necessary, since *etc.* means *and other things.* The abbreviation *etc.* is much used in business but is to be avoided in strictly literary writing.

Peaches, pears, apples, etc., are sold here.

4. To set off an appositive modifier that is not absolutely necessary to the meaning of the sentence. (No commas are used if the appositive is closely connected with its antecedent.)

Two of my brothers, John and Henry, are brokers.

My brother John is a broker.

The messenger, a very capable boy, detected the error.

I myself can see no reason for the change.

The other members of the committee, those who insist on his removal, are influenced by hearsay.

5. To set off a nominative of address.

No, sir.

Go West, young man.

Housewives, you will appreciate Sunco for dishwashing.

O Lord, remember not our transgressions.

You will find, Mr. Investor, that our services are complete.

6. To indicate omission of words.

> January 1 *in* 1960
> January 1, 1960
> Albany *in* New York
> Albany, New York
> Oranges are forty cents; tangerines *are* twenty-five cents.
> Oranges are forty cents; tangerines, twenty-five cents.
> The factory located *at* 79 Broadway *in* Yonkers is to be torn down.
> The factory, 79 Broadway, Yonkers, is to be torn down.

7. To set off introductory words and phrases, or their abbreviations.

> *Well,* what do you think of our offer?
> We are offering three colors, *namely,* red, green, and black.
> The man was dazed; *that is,* he did not realize he had been in an accident.
> This is a straight six per cent reduction; *for example,* sixty-dollar suits are now $56.40.
> Our line of vegetables is complete; *e. g.,* kale, spinach, strawberries, and green peas form part of our daily stock.

8. To separate whole numbers into groups of three figures each, beginning at the left of the decimal point.

> $40,879 . 85
> 1,875,942 . 7497632
> 1,000 lbs.
> No. 8,476 .

Note: When a serial number is given, the comma is omitted.

> #2M47653

9. To punctuate the salutation of a friendly letter.

> Dear John,
> Dearest Mother,

10. To make a break in long breathless sentences, or to insure clearness in unusual passages.

> Our large stock enables us to give to every customer the very best products available, and those types of merchandise best suited to his individual needs.
> Those things that show, show plainly.

Note: When *and* connects items—words, phrases, or clauses—there is usually no comma (unless it is needed to indicate a stopping for breath), because *and* indicates unity. Such conjunctions as *but* and *so* demand a comma before them, because they indicate not unity, but contradiction.

Stocks are large now, but they will not be complete in another week.

11. To separate direct quotations from the rest of a sentence.

"I am coming," said the clerk.
The clerk said, "I am coming."
"I am coming," said the clerk, "as soon as I finish with my customer."

Note: An indirect quotation requires no comma.

The clerk said he was coming.

Note: Some authorities allow the omission of the comma when a verb directly precedes a quotation, but most books do not follow this custom. However, if your employer demands this style, he has authority behind his desires.

The customer replied "The goods are very much misrepresented."
I said "No."

The semicolon

A semicolon could be employed much more often in business letters than it now is. A secretary will do well not to neglect a study of this form of punctuation. Only one typewriting space follows the semicolon.

The chief business uses of a semicolon are:

1. To indicate omission of a conjunction between independent clauses of a compound sentence.

Some of your order is being shipped today, *but* some of it will not go forward until next week.
Some of your order is being shipped today; some of it will not go forward until next week.

2. To connect two statements closely related in thought.

We mail a large number of catalogues; last year we sent out over five thousand.

3. To replace commas that separate items in sentences in which some commas are used in other constructions.

Please send us three of Pattern #10, black and yellow; five of #16, green and white; eight of #150, green and tan; and seven of #177, blue and white.

Our officers are listed as follows: James M. Briggs, president; U. H. Hines, vice-president; Anna Smith, secretary-treasurer; and M. A. Lyons, manager.

4. To introduce clauses beginning with *such as, however, therefore, accordingly, for example (e.g.), that is (i.e.), namely (viz.), hence, consequently, also,* and other words which indicate that the second clause explains the preceding part of the sentence.

Our sedans are strictly up to the minute in their mechanism; for instance, they have a steering-wheel gear lever.

The colon

The most formal mark of punctuation is the colon. Two typewriting spaces follow it.

The chief uses of the colon are:

1. To introduce a listing which is tabulated, or one written in run-on form, if it is introduced by such words as *the following, as follows, namely,* or any other word or group of words which indicates formality.

You are given the following colors from which to choose:

red	pink	black	brown
green	blue	orange	cream
yellow	white	purple	tan

Send the goods in the following shades: red, blue, black, and pink.

Note: If a listing is not formally introduced, no colon is used.

My brothers are Matthew, Mark, Luke, and John.

2. To introduce a long quotation, one of two or more sentences, or one which is too formal to be preceded by a comma.

He spoke thus: "My friends and customers . . . ."

The second paragraph in your letter reads: "I am in no hurry for the goods at this time, but in another month our spring rush will start. Then we want to be completely stocked up so as not to lose trade."

3. To follow formal or business salutations.

Dear Mr. Smith:
Ladies:
Mr. President:

Note: No dash follows the colon after a salutation.

4. To indicate balance.

He did not see: they did not hear.
A 13:7 football score.

5. To indicate divisions in *Bible* and time references.

They remembered his text—Proverbs 10:2.
We go to work on the 8:40 Special.

The dash

Two hyphens struck one after the other are used for a typewritten dash. No spacing is used before, after, or between these hyphens. Overworking of the dash is not in favor with businessmen, but a dash does have its legitimate uses, among which are the following:

1. To set off inserted or parenthetical expressions. We have noted that the comma has also been used for this purpose. When a break is noticeable but the new thought is not sufficiently unrelated to the rest of the sentence to demand the use of parentheses, a dash is used.

The papers which you sent—the bill of lading and the drayman's receipt—will be sufficient.
If you consider price—and price only—we cannot hope to convince you.

2. To indicate a quick change of thought, or an afterthought.

We were sure of their trade—they didn't tell us of any dissatisfaction with our deliveries.

We shall see you during next week end—and on Washington's Birthday.

3. To denote a sudden breaking off or interruption in a sentence.

You will not see us unless—.
He started to explain, "We didn't think you would—"; but he seemed to reconsider, and stopped talking.

4. To indicate faltering or hesitancy in speech.

Well—er—I didn't have—I couldn't get the money.

Parentheses

No typewriting space should be left between a parenthesis mark and the matter it encloses; but a space should be left between it and preceding matter, or between it and following matter. (Two spaces should be left between sentences.) Punctuation should be included in the parenthetical portion of a sentence if it is absolutely necessary to the meaning of the enclosed matter; otherwise, punctuation follows a parenthesis mark.

Parentheses are used to indicate that an expression is quite disconnected from the rest of the sentence. Illustrations follow:

1. Statements which in a play would be marked "Aside."

His credit is not good (we suspected as much), and so all orders must be accepted on a cash basis only.

2. Explanations necessary to make comprehension certain.

They (Mr. Jones and his secretary) seem quite sure that our agent was at fault.

3. Instructions as to reference.

You will be responsible (see "Owner's Liability," page 7) for damage of this nature.

4. Citations in the body of a sentence.

We read (Doris: *Corporation Meetings, Minutes, and Resolutions,* page 24) that it is immaterial how a notice is served on a director if he attends the meeting.

5. Figures verifying a written number.

You will pay us the sum of three hundred dollars ($300).

Note: This legal form is not usually followed in writing a business letter unless there is danger of misinterpretation. Figures alone are used in most routine letters.

6. Dates indicating a span of life or time.

Robert Browning (1812–1889)
During Madison's presidency (1809–1817)
You will be hired for the days of the sale (January 8–11).

The apostrophe

Some glaring punctuation errors are made in the use or omission of the apostrophe. A study of the following uses of an apostrophe may prove helpful:

1. To form the possessive case of nouns. Ownership is designated in all singular nouns that do not end in *s* by the addition of an apostrophe and *s*.

boy's, firm's, secretary's, Moody's

If a singular form ends in *s,* modern usage adds an apostrophe and *s,* but the possessive *'s* is sometimes omitted in words that end in sounds that cannot easily be pronounced with an additional *s*-sound, especially when the word following begins with an *s* or *s* sound.

Barnes's book, Woods's farm, King James's Version, for goodness' sake, for conscience' sake, Moses' secret

To form a plural possessive, add an apostrophe only to the plural form that ends in *s.* If a plural form does not end in *s,* the plural possessive is formed by adding an apostrophe and *s.*

boy's, boys'; man's, men's; customer's, customers'

Note: An apostrophe may or may not be used in titles. Consult a firm's letterhead to find the style that has been adopted.

　　Farmers National Bank, Farmer's National Bank

Note: No apostrophe is used with pronouns; a special form of the pronoun is used to show possession.

　　my, our, your, yours, his, theirs, its, whose

(*It's* means *it is* and is not the possessive form of the pronoun *it.*)

2.　To form plurals of figures, letters, and some words.

　　Pile up your money by separating the 1's, 5's, and 10's.
　　How many *e*'s are there in *agreeable?*
　　Be careful not to use too many *and*'s.
　　I am surrounded by I.O.U.'s.

3.　To indicate omission of letters.

　　did not, didn't; telephone, 'phone; I will, I'll; it is, it's; would have,
　　would've (never *would of*); 1960, '60; it is, 'tis; until, 'til; of
　　clock, o'clock.

Quotation marks

Like parentheses, quotation marks include all punctuation belonging to the matter they enclose. They do not include punctuation which does not refer to enclosed matter, unless the punctuation is a comma or a period. No space is left between a quotation mark and enclosed matter; but one space, at least, separates a quotation from the rest of the sentence (a colon or a period preceding or ending a quotation makes two spaces necessary).

　　"Where are you going?" he asked.
　　"I am going south," he replied.
　　"They are interested," he said, "in seeing portraits."
　　"Murder!" screamed the man.
　　Did they read "Ode to Spring"?

Quotation marks are used to enclose:

1.　A direct quotation.

　　"If you will only be patient and give me time to learn," said the secretary, "I will not disappoint you."

Note: An indirect quotation is not included in quotation marks.

Her employer said his office was not a training school.

2. A saying borrowed from another author.

Secretaries find themselves "toiling, rejoicing, sorrowing," but always gaining in the esteem of the employer they faithfully serve.

3. Titles of plays, articles, books, or magazines.

In a sentence references are usually enclosed in quotation marks, but in compiling a list quotation marks are not used. The name of your company publication should be capitalized, but not in quotes. Widely read papers and magazines, such as *The New York Times* and *The Saturday Evening Post,* do not need quotation marks.

4. Poor grammatical construction or slang.

We "ain't got no" Sunco today.
Everything is "putrid" here now.

Note: It is usually considered poor taste to label slang or your own humor in a business letter, unless the term might not be understood. The same is true in the use of nicknames. It is better to write a straight sentence saying: "It's too darned bad Joe DiMaggio didn't make a home run today," than to accentuate the slang and nickname by quoting them.

5. A word used with a special meaning.

Even if you are not a "lady," you appreciate the courtesy you find in polished company.

A quoted paragraph is sometimes written in smaller type (single-spaced in a double-spaced letter) and not enclosed in quotation marks. If a passage is enclosed in quotation marks, the mark must appear at the beginning of each paragraph, but *never at the end of any paragraph except the last one.*

Single quotation marks

Single quotation marks, made by striking the apostrophe, are used to quote matter within another quotation.

He said, "I am reading 'To Celia.' "
She said, "He said, 'No,' with emphasis."

The brace

A penned brace is so noticeable in a typewritten document that its use is to be avoided whenever possible. Several other forms may be used, chief of which are:

```
McAndrews  )
    vs.    )ss.
Adams      )

                        (J. H. Byren, Chairman
                        )M. P. Ryan
            Board  of   (E. H. Phillips
               Directors.  )Emory O'Rourke
                        (D. P. Scoville

                        : Tan sedan
            $2,485 . : Blue coupe
```

Figure 8. Brackets Made on Typewriter

The hyphen

No space is used before or after a hyphen in compound words *when both parts of the compound are expressed*. Its chief uses are:

1. To combine closely allied words or phrases.

   long-lost brother, catch-as-catch-can methods of selling, brother-in-law, two-foot rule, twenty-five

2. Instead of the word *to* when a span is to be indicated.

   1959–1962, pp. 85–89, Psalms 23: 1–7

3. To avoid repetition in compound terms.

Did you say Postmaster- or Attorney-General?
The word *it* might refer either to spinning-mill or -jenny.
They are a hard- and fast-working force.

4. To combine numbers and letters.

Call 224-R. Invoice No. M-217429.

BOOKS THAT WILL HELP YOU WITH PUNCTUATION

Handbook of English, C. W. Roberts and others, Oxford University Press,
New York
English for Business (3rd ed.), Charles C. Parkhurst, Prentice-Hall, Inc.,
Englewood Cliffs, N.J.
Effective English, Philip T. Gerber, Random House, Inc., New York
Practical Business Writing, Farley and Schnell, Prentice-Hall, Inc., Engle-
wood Cliffs, N.J.
How to Build a Better Vocabulary, Nurnberg and Rhodes, Prentice-Hall,
Inc., Englewood Cliffs, N.J.
Any standard text on English will contain rules on punctuation, and may
treat just the problem that is confronting you.

Chapter 16

Common Mistakes in Grammar

Grammar, which knows how to control even kings.
—MOLIÈRE

Grammatical foundations

Some businessmen say they prefer a foreign-born secretary because she has learned our language properly through a knowledge of grammatical rules. True, an American-born secretary first learned the language by rote, and consequently she may regard a thorough study of the rules of grammar as unnecessary. This lack of foundation on her part frequently makes her unaware of many incorrect constructions which she uses. English is based upon principles, just as is every science. Grammar is the science of language, and a knowledge of its rules is essential to correct usage.

Modern youth's lack of knowledge of grammar is a mystery to an older employer. Thirty years ago much time was spent in the classroom in diagramming sentences, with the result that executives who had such training usually know technical grammar. (Naturally, students could not diagram a sentence if they did not know the parts of speech and the relative values of phrases and clauses.) Knowledge of principles did not always carry over into speech and writing, and some educators began to condemn grammar as useless. Then followed the educational fad of omitting a formal study of grammar. In the firm belief that good usage would be absorbed from the reading of good literature, teachers assigned innumerable books for student reading, with little thought of the adolescent's interests. Though the *reading class* did give to the student a fluency of speech not gained in the old *language dissection class,* this form of instruction did not wholly meet his language needs, for it failed to build for him the foundation upon which to construct what he wanted to express.

Educational policy has been reversed recently, and textbooks on grammar are again making their appearance in school markets. If your language instruction was received in the "anti-grammar" era, you will probably profit by reading a good book on English grammar. Your work as a secretary, more than any other, demands a background knowledge of grammar.

Parts of speech

The eight parts of speech will be reviewed in this chapter, not with an aim to teaching their uses, but rather that you may become conscious of the mistakes for which you will have to search before transcribing dictated matter.

Nouns and pronouns

Because pronouns are words which are used instead of nouns, they are grouped with nouns in this analysis. Trouble with nouns and pronouns is largely confined to antecedents, number, and case. In defining a noun, never use the word *to* as the beginning word in your definition. *To* is the sign of a verb definition. *The act of, the process of,* or *the quality of* is the sign of a noun definition. For example, *cancellation* means *the act of making void.* It does *not* mean *to make void.*

Antecedents. Pronouns are used instead of nouns in order to avoid repetition. Obviously, there can be no repetition until the noun has first been used; consequently, a pronoun is not employed unless it has a stated antecedent which first names the thing about which you are writing. (The pronoun *I* is the only exception to the foregoing generalization; its antecedent is clearly understood to be the individual speaking.)

1. *Indefinite use of "we," "you," and "they."* Many a man has been in a quandary because a business associate has written: "Will *you* attend the theater with *us* this evening?" If the man finally decides

to play safe and go alone, he frequently finds that the wives of the other men are attending the party, and that he is a fifth spoke in the evening's wheel. On the other hand, if he asks his wife to accompany him, he may find that the *us* in the invitation referred to members of a stag party. A most objectionable form of alibi is that which employs the indefinite *they*. For example, who is meant by *they* in such a sentence as: "They aren't abbreviating any more?"

2. *Adjective pronouns.*   The group of words that are commonly used as demonstrative adjectives may be used occasionally as adjective pronouns that enable a writer to avoid repetition of nouns which they modify.

> *Demonstrative adjective: This* man is my father.
> *Adjective pronoun: This* is my father.

So much confusion has resulted from indiscriminate use of adjective pronouns that many writers never employ that form of the pronoun to begin a sentence.

> *Ambiguous:* We are going to move. *This* will enable us to reach the office on time.
> *Clear:* We are going to move. *This change* will enable us to reach the office on time.

The following words are included in the list of commonly used adjective pronouns: *this, these, that, those, many, few, little, much, either, neither, both, each, the latter, the former, some, several, any.* Great care must be taken to see that antecedents of such words (when used as adjective pronouns) are clearly expressed.

The opening sentence of a business letter which employs *this* as an adjective pronoun is a flagrant violation of the rule that every pronoun should have an expressed antecedent.

> *Wrong: This* is in response to your inquiry.
> *Right:* We are answering your inquiry.

3. *Inferred antecedents.*   Occasionally, pronouns may be used where the reader can reasonably be expected to infer what the unexpressed antecedent is. This usage is most common in referring to the weather.

It is twenty below zero today.

Although this sentence may be understood in most cases, the reader might be confused by indefinite use of the pronoun in a paragraph such as the following:

The room is very cold today. It is twenty below zero.

Does *it* refer to temperature of the room or to general atmospheric temperature? Obviously, you must make clear in the reader's mind whether *it* refers to *outside temperature* or *room temperature*.

4. *Proximity of antecedents.* Most secretaries believe and follow the rule that states: Place a pronoun immediately after its noun antecedent if there is another intervening noun to which the pronoun might refer.

The executive told his assistant that *he* did not know the rules of English grammar.

Anyone reading this sentence would naturally infer that the executive was confessing his own failings. A tendency to depend upon context for meaning rather than upon proximity of an antecedent in interpreting the writer's choice of a pronoun makes rewording of such sentences imperative. The art of changing ambiguous sentences of this type is so difficult to acquire that many secretaries abandon the struggle as vain and write material as it has been dictated. Often reconstruction of two or more sentences makes it possible to write a smooth, clearly expressed thought. A single sentence is difficult to reword. Test your own ability to reconstruct the ambiguous sentence above. The possibilities of changes are not exhausted by the following corrected sentences:

The executive did not think his assistant knew the rules of grammar and told him so.
Because the assistant did not know the rules of grammar, his employer reminded him of his lack of knowledge.

Number. Verbs agree with their subjects in number. Choice of a verb is consequently dependent upon a clear knowledge of number in nouns and pronouns. While most nouns form their plurals by adding *s* or *es,* pronouns express number by a difference in form. Become familiar with the following table of pronouns in order to employ the correct forms.

Personal Pronouns

	SINGULAR			PLURAL		
	Nomi-native	*Posses-sive*	*Objec-tive*	*Nomi-native*	*Posses-sive*	*Objec-tive*
First Person (*speaker*):	I	my mine	me	we	our ours	us
Second Person (*one spoken to*):	you	your yours	you	you	your yours	you
Old form	thou	thy thine	thee	ye	your	you

Third Person		(*Feminine gender*)			(*All genders*)	
(*one spoken of*):	she	her hers	her	they	their theirs	them

(*Masculine gender*)

he   his   him

(*Common, or neuter, gender*)

it   its   it

THE RELATIVE PRONOUN *who*

who   whose   whom   who   whose   whom

Note: The other relative pronouns are *that, which,* and *what. Who* refers to persons only; *that,* to persons, animals, or things, or to a group of mixed objects; *which,* to animals or things. *What* is not properly used with an expressed antecedent. In general, *that* is preferable in restrictive clauses; *which,* in nonrestrictive clauses. Occasionally *whose* is used as the possessive of *that* or *which.*

The *man* and the *dog that* just passed are close friends. (Never *who.*)
Tell me *what* you want. (Antecedent not expressed.)
The horse *whose* leg was injured will not enter the race. (*Whose* as possessive of *that.*)

Agreement.   Among the perplexing problems of number are those which involve agreement of pronouns with their antecedents and agreement of verbs with their subjects. The following rules are worthy of study:

1. A singular collective noun must be followed by a singular pronoun.

The *company* is dedicating *its* new building. (Never *their*.)
The *committee* was divided in *its* opinion.

Note: The word *majority* has three meanings, and it is these which determine the number of the verbs or pronouns used.

1. The *majority* (plurality) *was* small but sufficient to effect the passage of the bill.
2. The *majority* (single group) *was* determined to have its law enforced.
   Or
   The *majority* (members of group) *were* determined to have their law enforced.
3. The *majority* (individuals) *were* elated over the passage of the bill.

2. The impersonal *he* is used when a singular pronoun refers to either of two antecedents.

Either *John or Frank* will be awarded the prize that *he* coveted. (Never *they*. In cases of mixed gender, *each* may be substituted for *he*.)

3. A compound subject composed of two singular forms takes a plural verb if the forms are connected by *and;* a singular verb, if connected by *or*.

Mary *and* he *are* going.
Mary *or* he *is* going.

Note: If one member of a compound subject is singular and the other is plural, the subject nearer the verb governs the number of the verb.

Either Max or *they are* wrong.
They or *I am* wrong.

4. Some few nouns are always used in the plural and consequently take plural verbs and plural pronouns.

scissors	tidings	valuables
shears	thanks	riches
oats	goods	fireworks
clothes	victuals	eaves
bellows	odds	ashes

The *scissors are* dull, and *their* points are broken.

Other nouns are plural in forms, but singular in meaning; hence they take singular verbs and singular pronouns.

economics	athletics	ethics
mathematics	civics	measles
physics	statistics	mumps
politics	news	aëronautics
series	species	acoustics

Note: When not used as the names of sciences some of these words, such as *statistics, politics,* and *acoustics,* take plural verbs.

Statistics is an interesting study.
These *statistics* are not clear.

Because some nouns have the same form for the singular and plural, the number must be indicated by verbs and pronouns.

deer, sheep, series, species, corps
The *deer was* shot in *its* head.
The *deer were* feeding on *their* favorite knoll.

5. A subject always governs the number of its verb, even though one or more other nouns or pronouns may be nearer to the verb than the subject itself. A common error is that of making a verb agree with the object of a preposition because the phrase, of which that noun object forms a part, intervenes between the subject of the sentence and the verb.

One of the papers *is* missing. (Never *are.*)

Note: Either, neither, each, and all forms of *one* and *body* always take singular verbs.

Either rule *is* correct.
Everybody thinks he did *his* work well.
Not *one* of the subscriptions *is* missing.

Note: Some, few, many, both, all, and *more* are plural and take plural verbs.

Few were interested in his remarks.
Many of the men *are* on vacations at this time.

Note: Though *none* means *no one* or *not any,* it must not be supposed that it cannot be used in a plural sense. Its meaning will determine the number of verb and of pronoun. This common misconception of the word *none* was revealed when a young banker in an officers' training group wrote up the results of his inspection of a department. The sentence *"None* of the men *are* especially fitted for *their* work" was criticized from a grammatical point of view. When several American texts revealed that his sentence expressed the thought he had in mind, the critics suggested that the singular use must be "pure English." The *Oxford English Dictionary* proved the fallacy of this theory by stating that the plural use was the more common. If use of the word *none* comes up, substitute *not one* or *not any* for it.

Correct: None of the men *is* wiser than Mr. Jones.
    Not one of the men *is* wiser than Mr. Jones.
Correct: None of the men *are* fitted for the work.
    Not any of the men *are* fitted for the work.

6. Fractions are dependent for number upon the sense in which they are used and their verbs are governed accordingly.

Two thirds of the *work is* done.
Two thirds of the *men are* on vacations.

Case. Nouns use the same form for both nominative and objective cases and require study only for methods of forming the possessive case; but pronouns, as indicated in the table of personal and relative pronouns, have a different form for each one of the three cases. When one has studied how to form the possessive case of nouns, there is little excuse for leaving out the apostrophe. No thought need be given to the nominative and objective cases of nouns. However, the use of pronouns demands constant vigilance of the form in all three cases.

1. The possessive case of a noun or pronoun is used when the form modifies a gerund (a verbal noun ending in *ing*).

I do not approve of *his being* sent West. (Not *him.*)
Mr. Smith's trying the post meets with our approval.
We do not like *their having* lunch so late.

2. A clause interjected between a subject pronoun and its verb does not change the case of the pronoun.

Who *do you think* is responsible for the error? (Never *whom.*)

3. Both of the objects of a preposition or of a verb must be in the objective case.

Divide the letters *between Miss Smith* and *me.* (Never *I.*)
He *gave Miss Smith* and *me* the letters.
Let them and *me* try.

4. An interrogative pronoun that is an object of a preposition or of a verb must be in the objective case.

Whom did you give the letter *to?*
Better form: *To whom* did you give the letter?
Whom did they *ask?*
Whom will they *see?*

5. The nominative case of a pronoun is used with certain forms of the verb *be* when the pronoun is a predicate substantive.

It *is I.*
It ought *to be she.*
That can't *be they.*
It *was he.*
You never can *be we.*

6. Compounds of *who, which,* and *what* with *ever* are indefinite, are used with no antecedent, and are inflected to show case.

Nominative: Whoever was trying to get in left before I could answer.
Possessive: I spilled ink on *whosever* coat was on this desk.
Objective: Choose *whomever* you like.

7. The nominative case must be used after a conjunction that introduces an independent clause, even though the verb in the latter clause is not expressed.

He is taller than *I* (am).
We are faster than *they* (are).

Verbs and verb phrases

A verb declares or asserts something about a subject which is either expressed or understood. Verb forms include the simple verb and the compound verb, or verb phrase. The latter consists of a participle and some auxiliary form of a verb. An intransitive verb does not require an object, but a transitive verb requires one. Regular verbs are those which form their past tense and past participle by adding *d* or *ed;* irregular verbs have special forms.

Conjugation.   Conjugation of both a regular verb and an irregular verb may help to refresh your memory on mood and tense.

REGULAR VERB: *play*   IRREGULAR VERB: *go*

PRINCIPAL PARTS

Present:	play	go
Past:	played	went
Present Participle:	playing	going
Past Participle:	played	gone

INDICATIVE MOOD
Present Tense

Singular:

I play	I go
you play	you go
he plays	he goes

Plural:

we play	we go
you play	you go
they play	they go

Past Tense

Singular:

I played	I went
you played	you went
he played	he went

Plural:

we played	we went
you played	you went
they played	they went

Future Tense

Singular:

I shall play	I shall go
you will play	you will go
he will play	he will go

Plural:

we shall play	we shall go
you will play	you will go
they will play	they will go

Present Perfect Tense

Singular:

I have played	I have gone
you have played	you have gone
he has played	he has gone

INDICATIVE MOOD (*Cont.*)

Plural:

we have played	we have gone
you have played	you have gone
they have played	they have gone

Past Perfect Tense

Singular:

I had played	I had gone
you had played	you had gone
he had played	he had gone

Plural:

we had played	we had gone
you had played	you had gone
they had played	they had gone

Future Perfect Tense

Singular:

I shall have played	I shall have gone
you will have played	you will have gone
he will have played	he will have gone

Plural:

we shall have played	we shall have gone
you will have played	you will have gone
they will have played	they will have gone

SUBJUNCTIVE MOOD

Present Tense

Singular:

if I play	if I go
if you play	if you go
if he plays	if he goes

Plural:

if we play	if we go
if you play	if you go
if they play	if they go

Past Tense

Singular:

if I played	if I went
if you played	if you went
if he played	if he went

SUBJUNCTIVE MOOD (*Cont.*)

Plural:

if we played	if we went
if you played	if you went
if they played	if they went

IMPERATIVE MOOD

Present Tense Only

Singular and Plural:

(you) play	(you) go

INFINITIVES

Present:

to play	to go

Past:

to have played	to have gone

PARTICIPLES

Present:

playing	going

Past:

played	gone

Present Perfect:

having played	having gone

Notice that the verb form does not change throughout the conjugation in which it appears, except in the third person singular in the present and present perfect tenses. This explains why it is incorrect to say "he don't," which is *he do not*. The same rule applies, of course, to *she* and *it*—*she doesn't* and *it doesn't*. The past tense is always the same throughout. You can see why it is wrong to say "he done it," for *done* is a past participle and must be used with an auxiliary in a verb phrase. *Shall* is used in the first person, both singular and plural, to indicate future or future perfect tense; *will* is used with the other two persons. The order of *shall* and *will* is just reversed to express determination. Therefore, *I will go* means that I am determined to go, while *I shall go* simply indicates expectation; *he shall go* expresses determination on the part of the speaker to force another to act, and *he will go* merely expectation.

Misused verbs. In a dictionary certain indications (*v.t.* and *v.i.*, or *tr.* and *intr.*) call your attention to the fact that verbs are transitive or intransitive. Following these abbreviations, the parts of the verb will be given. For example: *lie, v.i., lie, lay, lain;* and *lay, v.t., lay, laid, laid.* Because *lie* is intransitive, it cannot take an object; but *lay* will have to be followed by an object, because it is transitive. Consequently, the conjugation of *I lay* and *I lie* will be as follows:

I lay the book here.	*Present*	I lie here.
I laid the book here.	*Past*	I lay here.
I have laid the book here.	*Present Perfect*	I have lain here.

A similar distinction exists between *sit* and *set*. *Set* being a transitive verb, it is impossible to *set* unless you *set something*.

I *sit* here. They *set* the *dishes* on the table.

Hanged is applied to persons; *hung,* to objects. Both are past tenses of the verb *hang*.

They *hanged* the *man* for the murder.
They *hung* a *map* in the office.

Though *got* and *proved* are today preferred to *gotten* and *proven,* if an employer insists on saying *have gotten* or *has proven,* do not feel that you must persuade him to change his wording. However, in your own writing, follow modern practice by writing *have got* and *has proved*. A flagrant error in the use of *got* is its confusion with *have*. *Have,* aside from being an auxiliary verb in the present perfect tense, denotes possession. *Get* denotes the act of going after a thing.

I *have* five dollars. (The money is in my possession.)
I *got* five dollars. (I was successful in procuring that amount.)

Consequently, *I have got five dollars* is wrong, not because you cannot say *have got,* but because you probably mean possession rather than the act of procuring.

May means permission; *can,* ability.

May I go? (Will you permit me to go?)
Can I go? (Would I be able to go?)

Ought is not a verb but an auxiliary. Consequently, it is impossible to construct a good sentence by putting another auxiliary before *ought*.

> *Never:* I *had ought* to go.
> *But:* I *ought* to go.
>
> *Never:* I *should ought* to try.
> *Either:* I *should* try.
> *Or:* I *ought* to try.

Irregular verbs. A study of some of the common irregular verbs will be profitable. It should be noted that verb forms in the second column do not need a helping word to express past time, and therefore are not found in verb phrases. Consequently, *had went, has did,* and *have saw* are wrong. The verb forms in the third column must have a helping verb; they are never correct if used alone as independent verbs. Hence, *I seen him* and *they done it* are wrong.

Present	Past	Past Participle
abide	abode	abode
am	was	
is	were	been
are		
arise	arose	arisen
awake	awoke, awaked	awaked
bear	bore (*archaic,* bare)	borne
beat	beat	beat, beaten
beget	begot (*archaic, begat*)	begotten, begot
begin	began	begun
bend	bent, bended	bent, bended
beseech	besought	besought
bet	bet	bet
bid (to offer a price)	bid	bid
bid (to invite *or* greet)	bade	bidden
bind	bound	bound
bite	bit	bitten, bit
bleed	bled	bled
blow	blew	blown
break	broke (*archaic, brake*)	broken

Present	Past	Past Participle
breed	bred	bred
bring	brought	brought
build	built (*archaic,* builded)	built (*archaic,* builded)
burn	burned, burnt	burned, burnt
burst	burst	burst
buy	bought	bought
can	could	. . . .
cast	cast	cast
catch	caught	caught
choose	chose	chosen
cling	clung	clung
clothe	clothed, clad	clothed, clad
come	came	come
cost	cost	cost
creep	crept	crept
crow	crowed, crew	crowed (*archaic,* crown)
cut	cut	cut
deal	dealt	dealt
dig	dug, digged	dug, digged
dive	dived (*colloq.,* dove)	dived
do	did	done
draw	drew	drawn
dream	dreamed, dreamt	dreamed, dreamt
drink	drank (*archaic,* drunk)	drunk
drive	drove (*archaic,* drave)	driven
eat	ate	eaten
fall	fell	fallen
feed	fed	fed
feel	felt	felt
fight	fought	fought
find	found	found
flee	fled	fled
fling	flung	flung
flow	flowed	flowed
fly	flew	flown
forbear	forbore (*archaic,* forbare)	forborne

Present	Past	Past Participle
forbid	forbade, forbad	forbidden (*archaic, forbid*)
forget	forgot (*archaic, forgat*)	forgotten, forgot
forgive	forgave	forgiven
forsake	forsook	forsaken
freeze	froze	frozen
get	got (*archaic, gat*)	got, gotten
give	gave	given
go	went	gone
grind	ground	ground
grow	grew	grown
hang (to kill)	hanged	hanged
hang (to suspend)	hung	hung
have	had	had
hear	heard	heard
heave	heaved, hove	heaved, hove (*archaic, hoven*)
hew	hewed	hewed, hewn
hide	hid	hidden, hid
hit	hit	hit
hold	held	held
hurt	hurt	hurt
keep	kept	kept
kneel	knelt, kneeled	knelt, kneeled
know	knew	known
lay	laid	laid
lead	led	led
leap	leaped, leapt	leaped, leapt
learn	learned, learnt	learned, learnt
leave	left	left
lend	lent	lent
let	let	let
light	lighted, lit	lighted, lit
loose	loosed	loosed
lose	lost	lost
make	made	made
mean	meant	meant
meet	met	met
mow	mowed	mowed, mown
pay	paid	paid

Present	Past	Past Participle
plead	pleaded (*colloq.*, plead *or* pled)	pleaded (*colloq.*, plead *or* pled)
prove	proved	proved, proven
put	put	put
quit	quit, quitted	quit, quitted
read	read	read
rid	rid, ridded	rid, ridded
ride	rode (*archaic,* rid)	ridden (*archaic,* rid)
ring	rang, rung	rung
rise	rose	risen
run	ran, run	run
say	said	said
see	saw	seen
seek	sought	sought
sell	sold	sold
send	sent	sent
set	set	set
shake	shook	shaken
shear	sheared (*archaic,* shore)	sheared, shorn
shed	shed	shed
shine (to glow forth)	shone	shone
shine (to polish)	shined	shined
shoe	shod	shod
shoot	shot	shot
show	showed	shown, showed
shrink	shrank, shrunk	shrunk
shut	shut	shut
sing	sang, sung	sung
sink	sank, sunk	sunk
sit	sat	sat
slay	slew	slain
sleep	slept	slept
slide	slid	slidden, slid
sling	slung (*archaic,* slang)	slung
slink	slunk (*archaic,* slank)	slunk
slit	slit, slitted	slit, slitted
smell	smelled, smelt	smelled, smelt
smite	smote	smitten, smit, smote

Present	Past	Past Participle
sow	sowed	sown, sowed
speak	spoke (*archaic,* spake)	spoken
speed	sped, speeded	sped, speeded
spend	spent	spent
spin	spun (*archaic,* span)	spun
spit	spit (*archaic,* spat)	spit (*archaic,* spat)
split	split	split
spread	spread	spread
spring	sprang, sprung	sprung
stand	stood	stood
stay	stayed, staid	stayed, staid
steal	stole	stolen
stick	stuck	stuck
sting	stung (*archaic,* stang)	stung (*archaic,* stang)
stink	stank, stunk	stunk
stop	stopped (*poetic,* stopt)	stopped (*poetic,* stopt)
stride	strode	stridden
strike	struck	struck (*poetic* or *rhetorical,* stricken)
string	strung	strung
strive	strove	striven
swear	swore (*archaic,* sware)	sworn
sweat	sweat, sweated	sweat, sweated
sweep	swept	swept
swell	swelled	swelled, swollen
swim	swam, swum	swum
swing	swung (*archaic,* swang)	swung
take	took	taken
teach	taught	taught
tear	tore	torn
tell	told	told
think	thought	thought
thrive	throve, thrived	thrived, thriven
throw	threw	thrown
thrust	thrust	thrust
tread	trod	trodden, trod

Present	Past	Past Participle
wake	waked, woke	waked, woke
wear	wore	worn
weave	wove	woven, wove
wed	wedded	wedded, wed
weep	wept	wept
wet	wet, wetted	wet, wetted
win	won	won
wind	wound	wound
work (to toil; to operate)	worked	worked
work (to fashion by labor)	wrought	wrought
wring	wrung (*archaic*, wringed)	wrung (*archaic*, wringed)
write	wrote	written

Errors in tense. Most errors which directly concern verbs are those of tense. The present tense is often used where the past tense is required.

> *Wrong:* Says I, "We are not interested in your proposition."
> *Right:* I *said,* "We are not interested in your proposal."

> *Wrong:* He *says,* "Our car is better than yours."
> *Right:* He *said,* "Our car is better than yours."

Another common error is substitution of the past tense for the present perfect or past perfect tenses.

> *Wrong:* I *transcribed* the letter already.
> *Right:* I *have already transcribed* the letter.

> *Wrong:* I was idle when he came in, though I *was* busy before that time.
> *Right:* I was idle when he came in, though I *had been* busy before that time.

Tenses of infinitives are also confused.

> *Wrong:* I planned *to have written* that letter first.
> *Right:* I planned *to write* that letter first.

An incorrect knowledge of the auxiliary verbs which form perfect tenses causes such errors as the following:

> *Did* you *finish* my letter?
> > *for*
> *Have* you *finished* my letter?

> *Wrong:* If I *would have known* you wanted the letter, I would have written that one first.
> *Right:* If I *had known* you wanted the letter, I would have written that one first.

> *Wrong:* He *was waiting* at the door half an hour when I arrived.
> *Right:* He *had been waiting* at the door half an hour when I arrived.

Errors in the use of the subjunctive mode are usually a result of misunderstanding the difference between a statement which is true, or was possibly true, and one which is impossible.

> If I *were* you, I should get here on time.
> If I *was* ill, I don't remember it.

The first sentence is correct because *were* is used in a statement obviously not true; it is self-evident that *I* am not *you*. The second sentence is correct because *was* is used in a statement that is true, or possibly might be true. Though I do not remember, it is possible I was ill that day.

Infinitives, participles, and gerunds. Infinitives, participles, and gerunds are verbal in form and are treated under verbs. Errors most often associated with them are: the use of the objective case instead of the possessive case before the gerund (as explained on page 317), the split infinitive, the dangling participle, and the dangling gerund.

The split infinitive is grammatically incorrect. If one is dictated, it is usually safe and desirable to correct it. However, your employer may belong to that school of thinkers who believe the split infinitive form places more emphasis on the interposed word than does the form generally thought of as correct. In this case it is unwise to annoy him by making changes in word order.

> *Split:* I am trying *to* quietly *remove* the file.
> *Closed:* I am trying *to remove* the file quietly.

Some writers consider a split verb phrase equally bad form, but most authorities do not object to the insertion of an occasional word.

> *Split:* I *am* quietly *trying* to remove the file.

A dangling participle is (a) a participle which *dangles* between two words, either of which it might be supposed to modify; or (b) a participle that has no word to modify. Much ambiguity is caused by sentences with dangling participles.

> (a) *Ambiguous: Having finished* for the day, *we* told the *secretary* to go home.
>   *Better:* We told the secretary to go home when she had finished for the day.
> (b) *Wrong: Having finished* for the day, the office was closed.
>   *Right: Having finished* for the day, *we* closed the office.

Note: In the first sentence under (a), one is not sure whether the employers or the secretary was finished for the day. In the first sentence under (b), one does not know who finished for the day—certainly not the office.

Dangling gerunds are similar in construction to dangling participles. When a gerund is used as the object of a preposition, the agent, or word the gerund phrase modifies, must be expressed and must be placed as near as possible to the modifying phrase.

> *Faulty:* In *preparing* this book, an *attempt* has been made to organize the material to best advantage.
> *Right:* In *preparing* this book, the *author* has attempted to organize the material to best advantage.

Adjectives and adverbs

Words which add color to writing are adjectives and adverbs. Though many adjectives may be turned into adverbs by adding *ly* (*calm—calmly*), one must not suppose that the same forms may not sometimes be used for both classes of words. The real difference between adjectives and adverbs is in the kinds of words which they modify: an adjective modifies nouns and pronouns; and an adverb modifies verbs, adjectives, or other adverbs.

The natural position of an adjective is before the noun it modifies, but it may be placed directly after the noun or after the verb (as a predicate adjective).

>The *capable* and *efficient secretary* was a great asset.
>The *secretary, capable* and *efficient,* was a great asset.
>The *secretary* was *capable* and *efficient.*

When an adjective modifier is a participial phrase, great care must be taken to see that the phrase is placed near the noun it modifies.

>*Being capable and efficient,* the *secretary* was a great asset.
>*Never:* The *secretary* was a great asset, *being capable and efficient.*

The same principle holds true when an adjective modifier is turned into an adjective clause.

>The *secretary, who was capable and efficient,* was a great asset.
>*Never:* The *secretary* was a great asset, *who was capable and efficient.*

The rule of proximity governs adverbs as well as adjectives; adverbs must be placed near the verb, adjective, or adverb which they modify.

>*Poor:* She *typed* as the afternoon wore on *very rapidly.*
>*Better:* She typed *very rapidly* as the afternoon wore on.

(The adverb *rapidly* modifies the verb *typed;* the adverb *very* modifies the adverb *rapidly.*)

>*Poor:* She is a typist in a brokerage office handling large accounts, *very rapid and efficient.*
>*Better:* She is a *very rapid* and *efficient* typist in a brokerage office handling large accounts.

(The adjectives *rapid* and *efficient* are adjectives modifying the noun *typist;* the adverb *very* modifies the adjective *rapid.*)

When an adverb is placed at the beginning of a sentence, or out of its natural order, the comma may be omitted only if the meaning will be perfectly clear without punctuation.

>*Brightly shone* the sun.
>*Brightly* the sun *shone.*
>Fortunately, skating became a possible outlet for their energy.

Adverbs denote time, place, manner, and degree.

> We shall *go now.* (Time)
> We shall *go there.* (Place)
> We shall *go slowly.* (Manner)
> We shall *go very* slowly. (Degree)
> We shall now go there very slowly. (A combination of all the types of adverbs in one sentence.)

When a number of adverbial ideas are to be expressed, especially when some ideas are cast into adverbial clauses or adverbial phrases, great care must be taken to arrange the elements in logical order.

> We tried to see you at the office *last Saturday when we were in the city.*
> *Never:* We tried to see you *last Saturday* at the office *when we were in the city.*

Confusion in use of adjectives and adverbs.   A predicate adjective is often confused with an adverb.

> *Predicate adjective: She* looks *beautiful.* (Not *beautifully.*)
> *Adverb:* She *looks down.*

Any form of the verb *be* and such verbs as *look, feel, sound, smell,* and *taste* may be followed by a predicate adjective.

> The *girl* is *charming.*
> *We* were *happy.*
> The *child* looks *bright.*
> The *secretary* feels *capable.*
> Her *voice* sounds *clear.*
> The *perfume* smells *cheap.*
> The *apple* tastes *sour.*

In the above sentences the predicate adjectives modify the subject nouns or pronouns. However, if the verb were the part of the sentence that needed to be expanded in meaning, an adverb would be required.

> The whistle *sounded shrilly* through the night.

Again, the adjective might be needed to describe the condition produced on the object of the verb.

> She kept the *files clean*.

Often an adverb is placed before the verb if a named object would otherwise intervene. This arrangement may be used, also, when the object of the verb has modifying clauses or phrases following it.

> She *arranged* the files *carefully*.
> *Preferable:* She *carefully arranged* the files.
> She *carefully arranged* the files that were in our office.

Though most words ending in *ly* are adverbs, a few adjectives also have this form. *Friendly, orderly, gentlemanly,* and *lonely* are examples. Certain adverbs, depending upon their emphasis and meaning in the sentences in which they appear, are also correctly used with or without the *ly;* for example, *slow, slowly; quick, quickly.*

> *Either:* Drive *slowly*.
> *Or:*   Drive *slow*.

Double negatives.   Some secretaries are noticeably careless in not avoiding use of the double negative. Unbelievable as it may seem, one medical secretary who was earning more than one hundred dollars a week always asked patients when they left the office: "You *don't* want *no* appointment, do you?" She certainly should have asked such a question in the positive form, "When do you wish another appointment?" but to have used the double negative was inexcusable.

Among common double negatives are:

ain't no	aren't none	could not scarcely
couldn't hardly	doesn't want no	cannot barely
aren't but	wouldn't never	do not nearly

Comparison.   Adjectives and adverbs may be written in three degrees—positive, comparative, and superlative. The positive degree merely assigns the quality to the object or person named; the comparative degree compares the quality possessed by one object or person with that of some other possessor; and the superlative degree gives to the possessor outstanding rank among any number of other possessors of the same quality.

> *Positive:* She is a *good* secretary.
> *Comparative:* She is *better* than my last secretary.
> *Superlative:* She is the *best* secretary I ever had.
> *Positive:* His spelling is *poor.*
> *Comparative:* His spelling is *poorer* than mine.
> *Superlative:* His spelling is the *poorest* I have ever seen.

Dictionaries usually give the comparative and superlative forms of an adjective or an adverb. These forms are worthy of study:

Positive	*Comparative*	*Superlative*
full	fuller	fullest
wealthy	wealthier	wealthiest
well (*adverb or adjective*)	better	best
good (*adjective*)	better	best
bad	worse	worst
little (*quantity*)	less	least
few (*number*)	fewer	fewest
much (*quantity*)	more	most
many (*number*)	more	most
beautiful	more beautiful	most beautiful
annoying	less annoying	least annoying

Certain points must be noted in the comparison of adjectives:

1. Some adjectives cannot be compared; for example, *accurate, supreme, wrong, superior, complete, unique, perfect,* or *absolute.* A thing can never be *more accurate* or *most supreme.*

2. *Less* applies to quantity; *fewer,* to number.

> The old typewriting tests should have read, "Tests are eligible with five or *fewer* (not *less*) errors."
> We have *less leisure* than you have.

3. An incomplete comparison really tells nothing.

> We sell *better* groceries. (Better than what?)

4. Only things of equal grammatical rank may be compared.

> *Wrong:* The *needs* of your customers are *greater than* these people.
> *Right:* The *needs* of your customers are *greater than those* of these people.

5. The comparative degree is used to compare not more than two objects or groups of objects. If more than two things are considered in a comparison, the superlative must be employed.

> *Comparative:* Our prices are *lower than* those of any other store in the city. (Comparison of two groups of prices.)
> *Superlative:* The prices at our store are the *lowest* in the city.

The articles. Grammar often groups the articles as adjectives. A few uses of these three words—*a, an,* and *the*—demand special attention.

1. The article is not repeated if one person is designated by two terms, but it is necessary to repeat the article to indicate two persons.

> *The* secretary and treasurer (one person) was present.
> *The* secretary and *the* treasurer (two persons) were present.

Note: If predicate nouns refer to the same person, the article is not repeated.

I am the janitor, office boy, telephone operator, timekeeper, and paymistress around here, in addition to being chief stenographer.

2. *The* should be used only to point out definitely; *a* and *an* are used in indefinite constructions. Most writers try to be too definite and consequently overwork *the.* Can you see clearly the difference in meaning in the following sentences?

> Send me a book on finance.
> Send me the book on finance.

3. In general *a* is used before any word beginning with a consonant and *an* is used before any word beginning with a vowel (*a, e, i, o, u*). However, even though a word may begin with a vowel, if the vowel has a *y* or *w* sound, *an* is not used.

> *a* unique plan
> *a* ewe lamb
> *a* one-sided argument
> *a* humorous incident

4. If *h* is silent, the word is preceded by *an;* otherwise, use *a* before words beginning with *h* as before other words beginning with consonants.

an hour	*a* hoarse voice	*a* historical event
an honest day's work	*a* hideous reptile	*a* humble servant
an honorable man	*a* humorous smile	*a* hundred
	a half-peck	

Some authorities make certain exceptions to the above rule; they prefer *an* to *a* with the words *historical, humble,* and *hundred.* This use is permissible.

An indefinite article may be used instead of the words *each, every, for,* or *per.* Occasionally one finds the definite article used in this sense also, but Americans are not particularly fond of such expressions as *fifty cents the bushel.*

three times a week	twice a year
two dollars an hour	two hundred miles an hour
fifty dollars an ounce	eighty revolutions a minute

Demonstrative adjectives. *This* and *that* are used to point out single objects; *these* and *those,* to point out a number of similar objects.

this boy	that boy
these boys	those boys
this kind of ink	that kind of ink
these kinds of ink	those kinds of ink

This and *these* point out things which are near at hand; *that* and *those,* things which are distant. Consequently, following words with *here* and *there* is repetition. A personal pronoun must never be confused with (and used for) a demonstrative adjective.

> *Wrong:* This here, these here, that there, those there, them there things, them things.

A demonstrative adjective becomes an adjective pronoun when its noun is omitted to avoid repetition, but unless the antecedent is contained in the same sentence, the meaning is likely to be ambiguous.

A demonstrative pronoun must have a definite antecedent and must not be used to refer vaguely to the whole idea expressed by the preceding sentence.

> *This* makes it necessary for me to change our rules. (What does?)
> *This evasion* makes it necessary for me to change our rules.

Prepositions

Prepositions govern the case of and show the relation between a following noun or pronoun and some other part of the sentence. Consequently, one should always see that a preposition does have an object. A dangling preposition is a source of confusion.

> *Wrong:* Where are they going *to?*
> *Right:* Where are they going?

> *Poor: Whom* shall I give the letter *to?*
> *Better: To whom* shall I give the letter?

Two prepositions are seldom used together before one object unless, of course, they are used in parallel constructions and are connected by a conjunction.

> *Wrong:* I am not *near to* his desk.
> *Right:* I am not *near* his desk.

> *Wrong:* He was put *off of* the committee.
> *Right:* He was put *off* the committee.

> *Correct:* We shall be there *at* or *near* tne hour.
> *Correct:* We have a government *of, by,* and *for* the people.

The following colloquial combinations should be avoided:

> in around; at about; on to; near at; in between; around among; off from; of about; around about; in among; for to; near by; in on; in at; up to

Prepositions are frequently used redundantly after verbs. Some grammarians contend that the use of superficial or unnecessary words is the chief sin of "American" English. Whether the preposition has taken on the use of an adverb or not, it is redundant in such expressions as *return back, climb up, descending down,* and *invade into.*

Special uses of prepositions. Certain fine distinctions are made in the uses of different prepositions. For example, *between* is used when speaking of two objects; *among,* when speaking of more than two objects.

> There is not much choice *between* the *two* words.
> Your choice must be made *among three* synonyms.

Into suggests direction toward an object; *in,* merely location.

> We moved *into* our new office Thursday.
> We have been *in* this office fifteen years.

In is used in referring to cities; *at,* to smaller places.

> He resides *in* Chicago, but he was born *at* Paris, Illinois.

Besides means *in addition to; beside* means *at the side of.*

> Do you need anything *besides* the file?
> I work *beside* him every day.

Around should not be used for *about* in approximating time.

> I shall reach there *about* three o'clock. (Not *around.*)

Though *in front of* is considered correct for *before, in back of* is not sanctioned for *behind.*

> He stood *in front of* me; they stood *behind* me.

Idiomatic uses of prepositions. Certain prepositions follow certain words as night follows day. For instance, the prepositions which follow the verb *differ* are *with* and *from* (not *to* and *than*). We *differ with* a person in opinion; we *differ from* him in appearance. One thing is *different from* another, not *different than* or *different to* it.

When in doubt as to what preposition to use, consult a dictionary. The preposition will be found in parentheses after the meaning of the verb with which it is used.

Example: cater—to purvey food (for); to provide requisites (for); to supply means of gratification (to).

The following list of approved prepositional idioms is worthy of study:

acceptable *to*

accommodate *to* (what we cannot help)
accommodate *with* (what is desired)

in accordance *with*

accountable *to* (a person)
accountable *for* (a thing)

adjust *to*

advantage *over* (an adversary)
advantage *of* (benefits)

agree *with* (a person)
agree *to* (something which is proposed)
agree *upon* (something already determined)
agreeable *to*

angry *with* (a person)
angry *at* (a thing)

appropriate *to* (assign to)
appropriate *for* (set apart for)

ask *of* or *from* (a person)
ask *for* (something desired)

betray *to* (a person)
betray *into* (a thing)

call *at* (a house)
call *for* (something desired)
call *on, upon,* or *for* (a person)

charge *against* (a person)
charge *with* (a thing)

compare *to* (to liken to)
compare *with* (to examine in the same relationship)

concur *with* (a person)
concur *in* (an opinion or a course of action)
concur *to* (something already in effect)

conversant *with* (a person)
conversant *in* (a topic)

copy *after* (an act)
copy *from* (a thing)

correspond *with* (things which are consistent)
correspond *to* (things which offer fulfillment)

die *of* (a disease)
die *for* (a person or cause)
die *by* (an act or means of violence)

differ *with* (a person)
differ *in* (an opinion or manner)

disappointment *of* (something denied)
disappointment *in* (something obtained)

grateful *to* (a person)
grateful *for* (a gift or favor)

look *on* (in order to see)
look *for* (in order to find)
look *after* (in order to follow)

protect (ourselves) *against*
protect (other persons) *from*

reconcile *to* (to adjust differences, or to bring to acquiescence)
reconcile *with* (to make consistent)

skillful *in* (before a noun)
skillful *at* (before a gerund)

unite (a thing) *to*
unite *with* (a thing)

Conjunctions

In the chapter on sentence structure, both subordinating and co-ordinating conjunctions were treated (page 288). However, a few common errors should be brought to your attention.

Prepositions are often incorrectly used as conjunctions.

Wrong: Do *like* I do.
Right: Do *as* I do.

Wrong: I cannot go *without* you do.
Right: I cannot go *unless* you do.

Subordinating conjunctions are not used to introduce noun clauses (*where, when, because, on account of,* and *as* may not take the place of *whether* or *that*).

Wrong: The reason is *because* I am too busy.
Right: The reason is *that* I am too busy.

Expletives

The expletive *there* is not a part of speech. Its only function is to throw the subject of a sentence into the predicate, thereby making the approach less abrupt.

Weak: There are *certain rules* to be followed in the playing of any game.
Stronger: Certain rules must be followed in the playing of any game.

The pronoun *it* is sometimes used in a similar sense, but the words that might be the subject are considered an explanation of the pronoun.

Weak: It is necessary *that I get this out at once.*
Stronger: I must get this out at once.

Unrestricted use of the expletive tends to make writing weak.

BOOKS FOR VERIFYING POINTS OF GRAMMAR

Descriptive English Grammar, House and Harman, Prentice-Hall, Inc., Englewood Cliffs, N.J.
A Dictionary of Modern English Usage, H. W. Fowler, Oxford University Press, New York
Fundamentals of English Grammar, Nellie S. Riherd, Exposition Press, New York
English Grammar, George O. Curme, Barnes and Noble, New York
English Grammar Simplified (revised), James C. Fernald, Funk and Wagnalls Company, New York

Chapter **17**

Letter Writing Skills

Polonius: What do you read, my Lord?
Hamlet: Words, words, words.
—SHAKESPEARE

How to gain a knowledge of correspondence

You have no right to a secretarial position unless you know the fundamentals of English and letter writing. If this knowledge were made a requisite for obtaining any secretarial work, many who are now holding jobs would be eliminated and the labor market would be cleared of a great number of inefficient people. It is not an uncommon experience for an employer to test out a dozen or more applicants without finding one who knows even the rudiments of correspondence. After trying several candidates, one woman exclaimed, "These girls have prepared themselves not for secretarial positions, but for positions as companions, and their spoken English is so poor they fail even in that capacity."

Read a variety of English texts

Get a dozen books on English grammar, not to study but to read as you would a magazine. This reading will give you a broad concept of the field; you will see that authorities themselves do not put equal emphasis on the same things. All texts emphasize outstanding business errors; finding these incorrect forms in different dress in a number of books will tend to stamp them indelibly upon your memory. The trouble with many a secretary is that she wants to memorize from cover to cover every book on English that she reads. The result is that she does not read far into any book before she becomes tired and puts it aside.

Listing errors for which you must watch

Compile a list of those errors you commonly make and, more important still, list the errors your employer commonly makes. The practice will help to impress these failings on your mind so that you will detect them when you are taking dictation or transcribing. As you read through each new book, you will discover that different things are emphasized. If you try to adopt all the suggestions, you will find you are revolutionizing your correspondence, which is never a good thing. As one girl said after reading an English text, "They tell you not to use so many words that there just aren't any words left." This excess of negative advice is unfortunately true of the majority of textbooks—they tell you what *not* to use, but fail to give you suitable substitutes. Many secretaries come out of school knowing that they should avoid *trust, hope, instant, beg, state, recent date, yours to hand,* and numerous other stereotyped words and phrases, but they do not know what to substitute for these expressions. Nevertheless, they criticize employers who use them. Try to supply a better construction, but remember also that your employer knows his business and that age, even though it may develop undue conservatism, gives a man much valuable experience from which to draw his words.

Suggestions for the setup of correspondence

Men who have been fortunate enough to have had good secretaries may not have felt the need to delve deeply into the skills of good correspondence, because they have learned much by observation. You, as a secretary, however, must not rely on observation alone to give you a knowledge of correspondence. Wide and constant study of this field is your duty. You will not be expected to be an expert in engineering or dentistry, economics or manufacturing, but you will be held responsible for a thorough knowledge of English and of correspondence techniques.

No rules can be given for setting up the letter forms to be used in any office. A standard will have to be decided on by the heads of the committee which formulates the rules for your firm's manual. A few of the general ideas listed in the following pages may suggest points that are worthy of consideration in determining a policy. Many of them, if adopted, would eliminate some disadvantages of manuals that have been compiled without consideration of the typists' angle.

The mechanical setup of a letter is of much importance in making office correspondence attractive. Often the form used will be largely determined by the type of letterhead in use.

Carbon copies.   Before starting to write a letter, determine the number of carbon copies that will be required. (Many secretaries think about this matter after a letter is finished.) Would it be well to send a copy of this letter to a branch manager, a salesman, a department head, or someone else? Will more than one copy be required for the filing system, because several topics are covered by the letter? Holding a few extra copies in reserve is always better than not having enough. In making a large number of carbon copies, be sure to use thin carbon paper.

When you are told to send a carbon copy of a letter to another person, make a note of this at the foot of the page, flush with the left-hand margin and below the identification initials and any other notations, such as "Enclosure." The abbreviation *cc* may be used or the words *Copy to,* followed by the name of the person to whom you are sending a copy.

Date.   The date line should be written to space well with the general plan of the letterhead, as well as the style of letter used and the length of the letter. Usually the date line is typed four or more spaces below the letterhead and, depending on the style of the letter, flush with either the right- or left-hand margin. Type it conventionally, all on one line. It is doubtful whether anything is gained by the freak date lines affected by some secretaries. The date is put on a letter for a utilitarian purpose and should not distract the reader or cause the person who has to file it to hunt through the letter for it. Do not use *d, nd, rd, st,* or *th* after the day of the month. The name of the month should not be abbreviated or written in figures. Except in replies to very formal invitations, the day of the month or the year should not be spelled out.

Letter forms in general use

There are half-a-dozen styles of letter forms from which to choose, if no hard and fast rules have been laid down by the company for which you work. They are full block, block, semi-block, indented, official, and simplified.

In the full block style there are no indentations and the date, address, salutation and closing all begin flush with the left margin. Paragraphs are not indented, but begin flush left also.

In block style, the address, salutation and paragraphs are all flush with the left-hand margin but the date line and the closing are aligned with the right-hand margin.

Except for indented first lines of each paragraph, semi-block is the same as block.

Indented style has each line of the address indented five spaces more than the preceding line and if a signature or title is used it is typed three spaces from the start of the complimentary close. First lines of paragraphs also are indented.

The distinguishing feature of the official style is that the address is placed below the signature, flush with the left-hand margin, instead of before the salutation. Type identification initials and any other notations two spaces below the address.

The simplified letter form omits the salutation and complimentary close. All parts of the letter begin flush with the left-hand margin. Instead of a salutation a subject line in capital letters is placed between the address and the body of the letter. Also, the words "Copy to" are omitted before the names of persons to whom carbon copies are to be sent.

Attention lines

In writing to a large firm it is often desirable to direct your letter to the attention of some individual. Type the name of the person two spaces below the address, as shown in the following two examples:

The X.Y.Z. Broadcasting Company
30 Rockefeller Plaza
New York 20, N.Y.

Attention Mr. James R. Smith
Legal Department
or
Attention Mr. A. M. Jones

It is permissible to use only a man's last name if his initials or given name are not known. When an attention line is used, the salutation is *Gentlemen.*

Use of subject headings

A line of convenience to both the writer and the reader is the subject heading. Because it is really a part of the letter, it is placed a line below the salutation, and is thereby linked to the body of the letter. Subject titles are included for the convenience of readers and not for your own filing purposes. A title written for filing use should be placed above or under the date, so that it will be seen quickly by whoever does the filing. This reference title may be put only on the carbon copies, because the receiver of a letter seldom uses the same filing title that you have adopted. When you answer letters containing a file number or title, it is courteous to refer to it in your reply, placing it about four spaces below the date.

Length determines spacing

Single space all letters, unless they are very short. However, even short letters should be single-spaced if your firm uses half-sheet letterheads as well as the conventional size.

Always leave a double space between paragraphs in a single-space-letter.

The indented style of letter form should be used with double-spaced letters; otherwise it is difficult to tell where new paragraphs begin.

Typing addresses

After determining the type of letter form to be used, adjust the line-space gauge, the marginal stops, and the tabulator stops, and then move down at least two double spaces (but never more than twelve) below the date line. The address should not extend beyond the center of the page; and when the block style is used an extremely long firm name should be carried over to a second line which is indented three spaces. Even though the body of the letter is double-spaced, the address should be single-spaced.

Use the official name of the company to which you are writing. If there is no street address, put the city and state on separate lines. If both a street address and a post office box number appear on a letterhead, it is preferable to use the box number when replying. A business title or position should not be abbreviated; if it is long, place it on the second line. It may be omitted if by placing it on a separate line it makes the address run over four lines.

Numbered streets and avenues up to and including *twelfth* should be spelled out. Above *twelfth,* figures are used and they should not be followed by *d, st,* or *th.* Numbers of houses (with the exception of One) should be written in figures. A house number and the numerical name of a street or avenue should be separated by a space, a hyphen, and a space.

The postal zone number follows the name of the city. If there is no street address, put city and state on separate lines.

In the indented style of letter, each line of the address is indented five spaces more than the preceding line.

Examples of addresses:

The First National Old Colony Corporation,
   100 Broadway,
      New York 6, N.Y.

Dr. A. A. Turner, President
Venus Space Ships, Inc.
11 Worth Street
New York 13, N.Y.

Mr. Charles G. Jones
926 W. Vanderbilt Avenue
Perth Amboy, New Jersey

Dr. James Smith
Paris
Illinois

Mr. A. W. Campbell
916 West Street
Philadelphia, Pa.

Mrs. John Keane
One Fifth Avenue
New York 3, N.Y.

Mr. James L. Brown
Empire Corporation
506 – 79 Street
Newark, New Jersey

Abbreviations

Be sure you use the correct abbreviations of the states, if you do not spell them out. (See list on page 267.) Do not abbreviate names of streets or cities. *East, West, North,* and *South* may be abbreviated when they precede street names—never when they are the names of streets themselves.

Reference Captions:

Your File #376141

Our order of March 5

European Tours

Salutations

In a business letter the salutation should always be followed by a colon; in a friendly letter a comma is used. Only the first word and the title with which you address the receiver should be capitalized.

Examples:

> Dear Sir:
> My dear Sir:
> Dear friend James,

Dear Sirs is used instead of *Gentlemen* by some conservative banking houses. A list of all titles and salutations used in United States Government correspondence is a good guide in addressing an occasional dignitary, though some authorities advise the use of *Dear Sir* for all business letters, regardless of the rank of the recipients. The Department of State publishes a style book of the forms of address it uses, called "Correspondence Handbook."

PROPER MANNER OF ADDRESSING CORRESPONDENTS

Firm of men:

> Brown Advertising Agency
> 918 W. Fourth Street
> New York 12, N.Y.
> Gentlemen:

Mixed groups in which it seems advisable to recognize the women members:

> National Republican Club
> 54 West 40 Street
> New York 18, N.Y.
> Ladies and Gentlemen:

Firm of women:

> Smith College
> Northampton, Mass.
> Mesdames:

Note: Some writers prefer to use *Ladies* in this instance, but the form *Mesdames* is more widely accepted for addressing a group of women.

A man and his wife:

> Mr. and Mrs. John Fisher
> 2121 W. 280 Street
> New York 32, N.Y.
> Dear Mr. and Mrs. Fisher:

Two unmarried women:

> Misses Esther and Lona Kester,
> Lightstreet Road,
> Bloomsburg, Pa.
> My dear Misses Kester:

An unmarried woman:

> Miss Aula Holter
> 210 E. Fifth Street
> Bloomsburg, Pa.
> Dear Miss Holter:
> *or*
> Dear Madam:

A married woman:

> Mrs. O. B. Bennett,
> Hamilton, N.Y.
> Dear Mrs. Bennett:
> *or*
> Dear Madam:

A widow:

> Mrs. John Smith
> *or in business*
> Mrs. Della Smith,
> 1212 Fifth Avenue,
> New York 29, N.Y.
> Dear Mrs. Smith
> *or*
> Dear Madam:

A divorcee:

> Mrs. Armstrong Smith (her maiden name combined with her married name)
> > *or in business*
>
> Mrs. Della Smith
> 1212 Fifth Avenue
> New York 29, N.Y.
> Dear Mrs. Smith:
> > *or*
>
> Dear Madam:

Two men:

> Messrs. James Smith and Joe Robbins
> 1212 Fifth Avenue
> New York 29, N.Y.
> Gentlemen:

The President of the United States:

> The President,
> The White House,
> Washington, D.C.
> The President: (Very formal); Mr. President: (formal); My dear Mr. President: (informal)

Some form of *respectfully* is used in the complimentary closing. Business letters addressed to high officials should aim at quiet dignity rather than the ostentation used by those seeking political favor.

The Vice President of the United States:

> The Vice President,
> United States Senate,
> Washington, D.C.
> Sir: (formal); My dear Mr. Vice President: (informal)

A senator:

> The Honorable John Doe,
> > The United States Senate,
> > > Washington, D.C.
>
> Sir: (formal); My dear Senator Doe: (informal)

A representative:

> The Honorable John Doe,
>> Speaker of the House of Representatives,
>>> Washington, D.C.
>
> Sir: (formal); My dear Mr. Speaker: (informal)

A cabinet officer:

> The Honorable John Doe,
>> Secretary of the Treasury,
>>> Washington, D.C.
>
> Sir: (formal); My dear Mr. Speaker: (informal)

A justice of the Supreme Court:

> Mr. Justice Doe,
>> The Supreme Court,
>>> Washington, D.C.
>
> Sir: (formal); My dear Mr. Justice: (informal)

A governor:

> The Honorable John Doe,
>> Governor of New York,
>>> Albany, N.Y.
>
> Sir: (formal); My dear Governor Doe: (informal)

A mayor:

> The Honorable John Doe,
>> Mayor of New York,
>>> New York, N.Y.
>
> Sir: (formal); My dear Mayor Doe: (informal)

For all of the above the forms of complimentary close would be:

> Very truly yours, (formal); Sincerely yours, (informal)

Professional titles

Titles of educational distinction should always be correct, for it is embarrassing to a person to be accorded a title to which he has no right. Although the title *Professor* may be used in addressing the majority of educators, the initials of the professional degree or degrees may be placed after the name instead.

To the president of a university:

>John Doe, LL.D., Ph.D.
>>President, New York University
>>New York 12, N.Y.
>
>Sir: (formal); My dear Dr. Doe: (informal)

To the dean of the university:

>John Doe, LL.M., Jur. Sc.D.,
>>Dean, Law Department,
>>>New York University,
>>>>New York 12, N.Y.
>
>>*or*
>
>Dean John Doe,
>>Graduate School of Business Administration,
>>New York University,
>>>New York 12, N.Y.
>
>Sir: (formal); My dear Dean (or Dr.) Doe: (informal)

To a professor:

>John Doe, M.A.,
>>*or*
>
>Professor John Doe,
>>Department of Economics,
>>New York University,
>>>New York 12, N.Y.
>
>Sir: (formal); My dear Mr. (or Professor) Doe: (informal)

If someone has been granted a doctor's degree in any subject, whether medicine, dentistry, education, finance or any of the other numerous branches of study, it is permissible either to address him as Dr. or to add his degree initials after his name. In a list where it is desirable to make a distinction between veterinarians, educators, medical doctors and chiropodists, it is wise to use the initials.

Ecclesiastical forms of title and address are complex, so you would be well advised to check carefully before writing to any member of a religious organization.

Paragraphs

A double space should be made above and below the salutation in a singled-spaced letter. If the indented form is used for paragraphs, line-space after the salutation and begin the paragraph directly below the finishing point of *Gentlemen:* or *Dear Sirs:*, because ten spaces are used in writing those salutations. The starting point for the paragraph can be reached by spacing once after *Dear Sir:*. Paragraph indentations should be uniform throughout. The body of a letter should always be uniformly spaced. If marginal stops are carefully adjusted, the bell will enable you to keep the right-hand margin fairly even.

Quotations and other centered items

Deep indentation makes quoted matter stand out clearly. Few secretaries take time to look over their notes in order to determine those parts which might be effectively centered. Often the ease with which a letter is read depends upon whether facts are buried in the reading matter of a paragraph or whether they are centered, indented, or tabulated, so that they can be comprehended at a glance.

Tabulations, which are often extremely effective in a letter, sometimes require boxings to emphasize certain parts. Various characters on the machine may be used to make these boxings— the period, the hyphen, the quotation mark, the underscore, the *x*, the *o*, the oblique line, and the parenthesis. To make unbroken horizontal lines, strike the underscore very lightly. To make a vertical line, put the shift lock on and depress the apostrophe with force at the spot where you wish to begin. Turn the thumb wheel until the line is the desired length. Should the ink become dull, release the key and find a new space on the ribbon. In making any vertical boxing, keep the thumb of the left hand pressed tightly down on the space bar, and turn the cylinder with the right hand. This precaution will prevent the machine from spacing and will thus eliminate the danger of uneven lines which result from neglect to backspace correctly each time.

Additional pages

In letters of two or more pages, there is danger in marking a second sheet with only a figure 2, for the two pages of a letter may become separated. The recipient's name and the date of the letter will serve to identify second sheets. A balanced arrangement can be made by putting the name of the addressee on one side and the date of the letter on the other. Notice that no time is lost in centering this form of heading.

R. M. Jones Company—2   August 8, 19. .

Try to carry over a fair portion of your letter to the second sheet. This may be accomplished by avoiding any writing on the last inch of the first sheet. Never put only the complimentary closing and signatures on a second sheet; at least two lines of the body of the letter must be forwarded.

Complimentary closings

The complimentary close should be typed two spaces below the last line of the letter, slightly to the right of center, except in the full block style. It should never extend beyond the right-hand margin. Capitalize only the first word and follow whatever closing is used with a comma. The degree of formality used in the closing should agree with the salutation, as well as the general tone of the letter itself, and the degree of friendship that exists between the writer and the addressee.

The closings used generally in business letters are *Very truly yours, Yours very truly, Yours truly* and *Sincerely*. The first three are more formal, the last one informal. In writing to a superior or a person of high position, or an older person to whom you wish to show respect, the very formal *Respectfully yours* or *Yours very respectfully* may be used. A somewhat personal closing that many executives use when writing to business friends of long standing is *Cordially*. If your executive insists that you use the open closing, place no punctuation at the end of the line before the complimentary closing.

Example:

> Trusting this meets with your approval, we are
>
> Very truly yours,

Many authorities contend that a secretarial manual should contain no example of this weak type of closing, since it should be eliminated from business usage. We all agree to this in theory, but the secretary who has never worked for a man who insists on its use is indeed fortunate.

Signatures

Always have a letter signed in ink. Be sure that you leave ample space (usually two double spaces) for the signature. The amount of space will depend, of course, on the size of your employer's handwriting, but at least three single spaces must be left.

When a letter is being written for a firm, the name of the firm may be typed above the signature. A double space below, the word *By* may appear where the signature of the person signing for the firm will be placed. In writing *By* you relieve the signer of individual responsibility for the contents of the letter, as this word clearly indicates that the signer is acting as the agent of his firm. Efforts to eliminate Latin forms from business correspondence have nearly succeeded in replacing the old form *Per* with the English word *By*.

Regardless of the penmanship of the person signing, signatures are likely to be hard to read. Most men are not consistently good writers, and their signatures fit into the description given by the son of a famous mill owner: "Dad gets an idea, writes the first three letters, and then finishes with a wavy line." Odd and poorly written signatures may easily be forged. Unless the name appears elsewhere in the letterhead, always type it under the signature. This practice will save needless searching on the part of the person answering the letter.

The title of the signer should be typed under his name, if this title does not appear in the letterhead. Unless departmental stationery is used, departments in a large organization may be designated. If the department is to be mentioned, it should be typed under the signature also.

(1)   Yours truly,
           GRAHAM and NELSON
               (Signature of E. H. Nelson)
               President

Note: Letterhead carries names of partners.

(2)   Yours truly,
           GRAHAM and NELSON
           By (Cashier's signature)
             M. B. Grant, Cashier

(3)   Very truly yours,
              GRAHAM AND NELSON
               (Manager's signature)
               D. H. Dell, Manager,
               Collection Department

Identification marks

The initials of the dictator and the secretary should be typed flush left several spaces below the title following the signature. Many types of identification are used, but one general rule covers them all: the dictator's initials precede those of the stenographer.

Examples:

    BCT:SMM
    BCT/SMM
    BCT-SMM
    BCT——SM
    Bernard C. Taylor—SMM

The first form has an advantage in that the shift lock on the typewriter can be locked and the entire annotation written as one word. The other forms necessitate shifting to write the dividing character.

The author has a personal aversion to the use of lower case initials for a secretary. If the person dictating is also the signer of the letter, the name written in full in the identification makes it unnecessary to type it under the signature. Writing the full name in this manner may be an advantage, if names of titles and departments which are typed under the signature are very long:

> Yours very truly,
> GRAHAM and COMPANY
> (Mr. Taylor's signature)
> Vice-President and General Manager,
> Statistical and Sales Departments
> Bernard C. Taylor—SMM

Where a man signs letters that he does not dictate, it is sometimes wise to conceal this fact by omitting the identification from the original copy. This is done by typing the initials on a sheet of paper placed over the original, so that they will appear on the carbon copies only.

Enclosures

Read through your letter for mistakes while it is still in the typewriter. If you form this habit of checking over your work, your letters will usually be free from typographical errors. As you read through the letter, note the number of enclosures. A single space below the identification, write *Encl.* to indicate that you will have one enclosure. *Encl.—2* will indicate that you will have two enclosures, and so on.

Postscripts

Place a postscript about two spaces below the identification. Begin at the left-hand margin, writing *P. S.* The postscript may include something that has been forgotten in the body of the letter, or some thought that the writer wishes to emphasize in the reader's mind by placing it outside the letter proper. Men frequently prefer to add a postscript in handwriting; they think it gives the letter a personal touch. These additions should be written on the carbon copies also, if they are not of a wholly personal and extraneous nature. The dictator's name or initials should be signed in *ink*.

Corrections should be made in pencil

If your employer must make corrections in your letter, try to get him to do this in pencil. Usually pencil corrections can be erased and the correction can be so neatly made on the typewriter as to preserve a neat-looking letter. Some men have a habit, which is very annoying to a careful secretary, of sending out a letter with corrections marked on it in ink. Such a method of revision spoils the appearance of the letter.

Consistency an evidence of secretarial intelligence

The foregoing points are cited to aid you in thinking about letter forms and must not be taken as rules which cover all good letter writing. If your employer favors any special form, or if a firm has compiled a manual for setting up correspondence, the only thing for you to do is to follow that form accurately—and at all times. Most secretaries are not consistently careful workers; they may follow a form well a few times, but sooner or later they wander away from it. The dictator who wants the word ATTENTION written in capital letters will become exasperated at finding this practice not uniformly followed. Though an employer is seldom so heartless as to make a busy secretary recopy a letter each time it varies slightly from given directions, he may become very much annoyed by continued repetition of the same error. Such minor matters may mean nothing to you, as a secretary, but they often impress your employer as evidence that you are not a consistently careful worker.

See page 381 for a list of helpful books.

Chapter **18**

Content and Form of Letters

When I read your letters, I hear you talk.
—COWPER

Personal character of letters

A common criticism which the businessman levels at his secretary is that she cannot put his own style into letters which she writes for his signature: "The letters lack individuality and life—in fact they are much like form letters chosen to fit the occasion." Let us face this criticism fairly and see just why you cannot write letters for him that are more expressive of his personality.

Looking over good letters, we must be impressed with the fact that each is a very personal thing. Even though a similar message is to be conveyed to two people, it is scarcely safe to write identical letters to both of them. Your employer's attitude toward a certain correspondent may be reserved; therefore, a restrained attitude will have to be maintained in letters you write or they will have a false note.

The secretary to the president of a large corporation writes nearly all of her employer's letters. People often comment: "Isn't that remark just like the old fox? His letters are the cleverest things one could hope to read." Close acquaintanceship with the woman who was so cleverly imitating her employer permitted us to ask the secret of her success. Her belief was that the confidence her executive had in her was the key to her understanding. She said: "Whenever a caller leaves, Mr. B. will quite frankly tell me what he thinks of the man and often will give a little outline of his acquaintance with him. Naturally I am interested. After a stranger comes in, Mr. B. usually looks at me quizzically and asks what I think of that man. This habit of his has taught me to observe office callers. We may not always agree on a person; but, at least, I am aware that my employer has very definite opinions of him. This complete understanding of his appraisal of people helps me to write to them from his angle."

Development of your employer's personal characteristics in writing cannot be effected in a day. In acquiring this almost intangible ability, you will find help in studying your employer's vocabulary, his dictated letters, the individual letters he receives, and his conversation with correspondents, whether in the office or over the telephone.

Relationships with correspondents

No secretary has the right to feel it incumbent upon her superior to see that she is given a formal introduction to every stranger who happens to call. However, your executive's attitude toward you, and his opinion of your ability, can easily be sensed by the people you deal with and will often serve to make it possible for you to relieve your employer of much work. In a paper given by a businessman, this value was clearly brought out in these words:

> My pleasure and gratitude for her loyal and able coöperation prompted me, quite unthinkingly, to freely express to my customers my appreciation of her. Their reactions taught me I was benefiting myself in doing this. The customers liked and respected Miss Smith; many of them were her friends. That I had the discernment to appreciate her fine qualities raised me in their estimation. I also found that in praising her, I was indirectly commending myself and the resources of my establishment. It is a natural inference that a high-class firm will employ only a high type of secretary, and that a high type of secretary will accept employment only in a high-class office. Therefore, in increasing the prestige of my secretary, I was raising my own status. My expressions of appreciation also had considerable value in reënforcing Miss Smith's authority in the execution of her responsibilities. The customers felt that if I had such complete faith in her judgment and character, they also could rely upon them without question. The benefit of this, in view of the type and scope of the executive secretary's duties, is obvious.

If office guests are introduced to you and you are given an opportunity to listen to office conversations, you should find it easy to insert a personal touch in business letters you might have to write. A joke may be made of some point previously discussed, or individual interests judiciously referred to. Of course, this practice is impossible if your office is in a room apart from that of your executive, or if he regards you as a menial who is not worthy of being introduced to callers.

Sometimes the reason an executive does not introduce his secretary to all callers has nothing to do with snobbery on his part. We might as well be brutally frank here, because employers find it hard to explain the problem to offenders. *Not all secretaries have learned to listen.*

You would soon notice if your mother, upon being introduced to one of your friends, spent much of a valuable afternoon in conversing with him on subjects in which neither you nor your guest had any interest. Such selfishness would be almost as embarrassing as to have her skulk around in other parts of the house when someone called at your home. You do not expect to slink about the office as an intruder might, but you must avoid monopolizing the conversation simply because your employer has been courteous enough to introduce you to a caller. When presented to your employer's guests, acknowledge the introduction with a friendly and unembarrassed, "How do you do," or "Good morning," and then continue with your work. Always remember that the caller is primarily interested in your employer and that any contribution you may make to the conversation should be directed through your employer or, in any event, should include him. Only in case your employer must withdraw from the conversation is it permissible for you to assume a positive role.

Extraneous thoughts in writing

The inclusion of extraneous thoughts in writing business letters is one of the brightening contributions to dull routine, if not overdone.

A remarkable friendship was developed between a certain branch office and its home office because in writing a résumé of conditions in Cleveland for the week, the secretary inserted the following: "If this report sounds *flighty,* it is due to environment. Cleveland is so much *up in the air* this week that it is quite impossible to get customers to think of business." The reply from the district supervisor showed a keen interest in the city's first air meet. His clever ending to his reply put the responsibility for renewed effort up to the manager: "since you are down in the dirt of Mother Earth again, I know you are just *plowing* in the sales this week." The manager, pleased by the human attitude taken by the district supervisor, inspired his salesmen to turn in a recordbreaking number of sales. However, numerous instances can be cited in which a secretary's usefulness has been undermined by her efforts to be original. Better make your letters conventional, rather than appear ridiculous in attempts at humor.

Where to start in writing letters

Most secretaries could write much better letters than their employers if they were not afraid to make the start. Naturally they should be able to write better letters, for the secretary has been trained in writing good letters, while most businessmen are not accomplished correspondents. However, the fact that you can write good general letters is no reason to suppose you will be a "howling success" in taking over the letter writing of some special office. You will have to learn the policies of your firm, of its customers, and, most of all, of your employer. Once your executive learns to trust your judgment, he will note on many of the letters he receives each day the type of reply you can make to them. A system of this kind saves him the time it would take to dictate these answers.

The first week you should be able to start on a few letters such as those drawing attention to errors in accounts or those covering payment of bills. Hunt carbon copies of previous correspondence and note the wording used. Put your answers on your employer's desk with the bills; if they are satisfactory, he will sign them and is likely to be relieved that he does not have to dictate them. Should anything be lacking, or wrong, you will find out wherein you failed. Choose short letters for your first efforts. The following letter is one that represents a good type on which to begin:

January 7, 19—

Bradford Plaster Works,
    984 East 17 Street,
        Philadelphia, Pa.

Gentlemen:

On your December statement you have charged us $24.60 a ton for white sand purchased on the fifteenth. This price should be $2.46. Please send us a corrected invoice.

Very truly yours,
ATLAS CONTRACTING COMPANY
(Signature)

EBF:BCT   President

In writing to routine departments, it is always best to cut a letter down to the fewest possible words. Members of these departments are busy and have no time to read long letters. Statements about getting a new invoice "so we can send you a check" simply fill space. Firms naturally expect you to pay your bills, and any elaboration either means nothing to them or causes them to wonder why such a thought came into your mind.

Sometimes men like to bring a little laughter into these dull departments. This can be done if your employer is so clever in making friendships that routine workers do not think him sarcastic. The following letter was written in this jesting tone by a contractor who knew how to deal with people:

January 9, 19—.

Bradford Plaster Works,
    948 East 17 Street,
        Philadelphia, Pa.

Gentlemen: DECEMBER STATEMENT

I notice that you have charged me $24.60 a ton for *white* sand purchased on December 15.

Please send me at once your lowest quotation on *gold* sand.

Very truly yours,
ATLAS CONTRACTING COMPANY
(Signature)
M. J. Friend, President

MJF:BCT

Two days later a corrected statement came in with a typed card clipped to it:

Mr. Friend,

Just to show you we are not "gold diggers."

Horribly sorry,
Jane R. Daniels

Acknowledgment letters, also, are easy to write. When you are able to serve a customer, he is usually not critical of you. For this reason it is well at first to choose letters which are not likely to stir up adverse feeling in the minds of their recipients. The following is a letter which might be written by you in the early stages of your rôle as correspondent:

December 1, 19—.

Mr. O. B. Mason,
410 Watson Boulevard,
Green Springs, Va.

Dear Sir:

Your order of November 9 will be given our early attention. Thank you for the opportunity you have afforded us to show you the type of service we can give to merchants in your locality.

Owing to a reduction which we were able to make in the price of Sunshine Corn, we are sending a check to you for the difference between your remittance and the present price of the corn.

SUNSHINE CORN—2 dozen crates

Old price	$124.00
New price	119.64
Amount of check	$ 4.36

We hope to serve you again.

Very truly yours,
(Signature)
James M. Smith, Vice President

JMS:C
Encl.

Most letters of this type are clearer if certain portions of them can be centered and tabulated. Explanations should always be made as definite as possible.

As you become better acquainted with the business, it will be easy for you to take over a greater amount of its correspondence.

Social letters present problems

Letters of a social or semisocial type are usually a greater problem to a businessman than are straight business letters. Even a secretary may find it hard to get into the spirit of social letter writing. For this reason, some businessmen who have a large number of allied social interests engage both a business secretary and a social secretary. This so-called "personal secretary" has charge of all letters of a fraternal, social, semi-business, or personal nature. A girl handling this work must be capable of dealing with people who have time to do things in a leisurely and socially correct manner.

A girl who is personal secretary to an important bank official has given a clear picture of this phase of secretarial work. Her employer is on the directorates of many corporations; is treasurer of the Y.M.C.A., the Red Cross, the Community Chest Fund, two hospitals, and his church; is grand master of his district lodge; is national chairman of his fraternity; is a committeeman of his political party; and is the holder of other posts. He is so busy that he seldom knows all that is being done in his name. The accounts are turned over to clerks, who assume full charge as though they were handling any other individual bank account. When the man must go to a meeting or receive a caller relative to one of these outside interests, his personal secretary supplies him with a complete written report, and hastily goes over with him any important points of development.

Most people are inclined to think men dislike sentiment. When asked whether she found men slighting letters of a social nature, this young woman replied: "Don't you ever think it! No crime is so great as to fail to reply to a letter. Men thrive on 'patting each other on the back.' Mr. Blank does some simple little thing for another man and receives a long letter which would indicate that the man feels himself indebted to him forever. Mr. Blank then writes a letter telling the man what a pleasure it has been to serve him, and back comes another complimentary reply. Sometimes half a dozen sets of letters are exchanged over that one little thing."

Letters written over a secretary's signature

When you write a letter to which you append your own signature, you should not try to make it sound as though your employer had written it. It is your own letter and should reflect your personality. A vast number of letters in a busy office can be written over your own signature. A few illustrations will serve as a key to the various types of useful secretarial writing.

(1)

March 1, 19—.

Dear Mr. Kellar:

Mr. Brown deeply regrets that funds will not permit making a contribution to the Reforestation Society this year.

Urgent demands from other sources have been very heavy and, though amounts set aside for contributions have not been curtailed, it is necessary to confine gifts to those calls which have a strictly human appeal.

When conditions are more settled economically, Mr. Brown will be happy to help your organization again in its very worthy work.

Sincerely yours,

(Signature)

Secretary to Mr. Brown

Fred J. Kellar, Secretary,
Reforestation Society,
Albany, New York.

(2)

January 14, 19—.

Dear Mr. Zeiper:

Mr. Brown wishes me to say that it will be a pleasure for him to speak to the New York Educational Society at the February meeting.

As probably suited to your interests, Mr. Brown has chosen for his topic, "Coöperation between Businessmen and their Secretaries."

Unless we hear from you to the contrary, Mr. Brown will be at the Statler Hilton Hotel, Saturday, February 5, at two o'clock. However, it will be necessary for him to leave promptly at 3:15 in order to keep another appointment. This engagement will make it imperative for his twenty-minute talk to be fitted into your program before that time.

If you cannot arrange your program in this way, please let us know.

Very truly yours,

(Signature)

Secretary to Mr. Brown

Dr. James M. Zeiper,
　　New York Educational Society,
　　　　Prince School,
　　　　　　Pelham, New York.

(3)

July 23, 19——.

Mr. William D. Deane, Jr.,
　　18 Grand Court,
　　　　Beverly, N.J.

Dear Mr. Deane:

Mr. Brown is on his vacation at this time, but will return the first of next month.

In order that he may have before him upon his return complete information regarding your application, I am sending you the regular form that we require from all men making application for positions with us. The enclosed booklet will help you to understand the scope of our organization.

When your application form is returned, it will be attached to your letter, which I am holding for Mr. Brown's attention. You should hear from us definitely within the next two weeks.

Very truly yours,

(Signature)

Secretary to Mr. Brown

Encl.—2

Notice that in these letters the secretary has taken the initiative in writing. As a basis for writing the first letter she may have received only a curt "No" from her employer, or she may have known that the contribution budget had already been apportioned. In the second letter observe how cleverly she has avoided much likelihood of her employer's becoming entangled in a long, tiresome meeting in which he has little real interest. She can now go ahead and complete her employer's calendar for the day without having to make allowance for the possibility of his being tied up for the entire afternoon. In the last letter she makes no rash promises that her employer will "doubtless have a place" for the young man, yet she gives him definite assurance that his letter is not going into the wastebasket. Letters written by a secretary must be models of tact and thoughtfulness.

Formal and informal invitations

An informal invitation is answered in an equally informal manner. A strictly formal invitation (unless the sender is extremely well known to your employer) requires that the formal wording be followed almost exactly in sending acceptance or regrets.

Businessmen are besieged with invitations of various kinds and they usually find it good business to mix with people. The number of invitations accepted by her employer is a revelation to any secretary who comes from a home where evenings are spent in reading and recreative pursuits. She frequently keeps a social calendar as well as a business calendar, as this record is a great aid in answering invitations.

In sending regrets, one need not state a reason for not being able to attend a certain function; it is not supposed that everyone invited will be able to come. Often men have very good reasons for not wanting their business engagements known. Information given in a note of regrets may cause a competitor to surmise developments in the absentee's business affairs. If a man feels like giving a reason for failing to accept an invitation, he may do so, but there is no necessity for resorting to falsehood in writing regrets. Do not be at a loss to know how to reject an invitation which is returned to you by your employer with this notation, "Regrets—no reason."

(1)

January 7, 19—.

My dear Mr. and Mrs. Brown:

On Friday evening Mr. and Mrs. A. L. Johnson, of Chicago, will dine with us informally. It would be a pleasure to have you join us and renew your acquaintance with our old friends. We are planning to serve dinner at seven-thirty.

Very sincerely yours,

(Signed) Dorothy Weekley

Mr. and Mrs. James L. Weekley,
  Weekley Manor,
    Bough Creek, N.Y.

Note: On monogrammed paper, or that on which the home address does not appear, write your own address at the bottom of the letter.

(2)

January 8, 19—.

Dear Mr. and Mrs. Weekley:

Everything about your invitation pleases us—even the hour—and we shall be happy to accept your hospitality. It will be delightful to recall the happy days when Chicago was our home. Mrs. Brown joins me in thanking you for so kindly remembering us.

Very sincerely yours,

(Signed) J. H. Brown

Mr. and Mrs. James L. Weekley,
  Weekley Manor,
    Bough Creek, N.Y.

Note: Of course, where we have used (Signed) we have meant simply to indicate that the following signature is written with a pen. One would never write the word *Signed* on a letter to be given to an employer for his signature.

(3)

January 8, 19—.

Dear Mr. and Mrs. Weekley:

Mrs. Brown and I regret that it will be quite impossible for us to dine with you next Friday evening. Your thoughtfulness in arranging the hour to suit our convenience makes us feel that the Fates have not been kind in denying us this privilege.

We recall many pleasant memories of those days in Chicago, among the most pleasant of which are joys shared with Mr. and Mrs.

Johnson. The next time our friends are in New York City we hope to be more fortunate in the disposal of our time. Thank you for so kindly remembering us.

Very sincerely yours,

(Signed) J. H. Brown

Mr. and Mrs. James L. Weekley,
　Weekley Manor,
　　Bough Creek, N.Y.

(1)

January 3, 19——.

Dear Mr. Price:

The First Corporation will have a table at the annual meeting of the American Acceptance Council at the Hotel Roosevelt at seven o'clock on the evening of March 23. We shall be pleased to have you join us as our guest at the dinner.

In order that our people may enter the dining room as a unit, we are asking that they assemble in Room K, at six-thirty, for a short informal reception.

Our travel department will be happy to attend to hotel reservations or make other arrangements for you relative to your stay in New York.

Very sincerely yours,

(Signed) J. H. Brown

Graham M. Price, President,
　The Unity Banking Company,
　　810 Canal Street,
　　　New Orleans, La.

(2)

January 7, 19——.

Dear Mr. Brown:

I shall be pleased to attend the Acceptance banquet as your guest. Under such able guidance as that of your company, I anticipate a perfect evening, starting with that informal reception in Room K.

Your kind offer leads me also to accept the services of your travel department and to ask that they reserve a double room with bath for me at the Commodore. My wife and I shall arrive in New York on Sunday evening at eleven o'clock.

Very sincerely yours,

(Signed) Graham M. Price

Mr. J. H. Brown,
　11 Maiden Lane,
　　New York 38, N.Y.

(3)

January 7, 19—.

Dear Mr. Brown:

Just two days ago I accepted another invitation to be a guest at the Acceptance banquet. This makes it quite impossible for me to avail myself of your hospitality. However, it is a pleasure to know that I am going to see you during that week.

Thank you for so kindly remembering me in arranging your table.

Very sincerely yours,

(Signed) Graham M. Price

Mr. J. H. Brown,
11 Maiden Lane,
New York 38, N.Y.

(1)

THE FIRST TRUST COMPANY
requests your presence
at a formal tea and dance
to be given in its new quarters
at three o'clock
on Saturday afternoon
January tenth
prior to its opening for business
on the following Monday.

(2)

Mr. and Mrs. J. H. Brown accept with pleasure the invitation to a formal tea and dance to be given by the First Trust Company, in its new quarters, at three o'clock on Saturday afternoon, January tenth.

(3)

Mr. and Mrs. J. H. Brown regret that they are unable to accept the invitation to a formal tea and dance to be given by the First Trust Company, in its new quarters, at three o'clock on Saturday afternoon, January tenth.

Cards and letters of introduction

Introductions are made by letter or by card when a mutual acquaintance thinks strangers will have a common interest. Nothing is more discourteous than to foist upon some friend or business acquaintance the company of a person who will be a bore to him. Most employers are very careful in giving out cards of introduction, yet they try not to miss an opportunity to use this means of widening their business influence.

Introductions are quite properly given to business acquaintances who are traveling in a part of the country where a branch office of your firm is located, to a person who is consulting a friend of your employer in a business capacity, or to other persons who your employer feels reasonably certain will welcome acquaintance with the person introduced. Business should, no doubt, be done with that firm best qualified to do your work, but in actual practice much of it is thrown toward, or diverted from, a company simply because of friendships that its officers make.

Letters of introduction should not be sealed. This courtesy reveals your good faith in the person to whom you have given the letter, since he may then feel assured that the introduction is friendly. In business many an introduction is written on the back of an ordinary business card.

(*Typed on the reverse side of Mr. Brown's business card*)

Graham M. Price, President,
Unity Banking Company,
New Orleans, La.
Introducing
Allan M. Lane
(Signed) J. H. Brown

Large firms often use for this purpose a card of correspondence-card size, engraved with the firm's name. Below the name is a space for the address of the person to whom the caller is referred, the printed word *Introducing,* with a space below for the caller's name, and lines for the signature of the officer sponsoring the introduction and the date. These cards are enclosed in an unsealed envelope when handed to the caller. Sometimes an indication of the reason for the introduction (whether it is a business proposition or merely a common interest) is given on the card. Because unsolicited canvassing is usually barred from a first-class office, unscrupulous men have made wide misuse of the card of introduction as an opening wedge to get in to try to sell insurance, books, and various items. A card which explains a business mission is much more courteous than a blind introduction.

> Dear Mr. Rice:
>
> Mr. Green is keenly interested in public utility bonds. I assured him you could tell him *all* about them.
>
> Truly yours,
>
> (Signed) J. H. Brown
>
> May 5, 19—.

By far the most polite of all methods of introduction is that in which you forward a letter to the person in a strange city whom you wish your other friend to meet. The letter enables the recipient of the letter to take the initiative in meeting the traveler, if such an acquaintance seems desirable. This procedure overcomes any embarrassment which your traveler friend may be inclined to feel in intruding upon the privacy of an unknown person. If you are awake to your opportunities, you can do much to help your employer widen the scope of his firm's business friendships. Don't hesitate to bring ideas of this kind to your executive's attention. Such a letter as either of the following is an example of thoughtfulness:

(1)

November 21, 19—.

J. M. Royal & Company,
   899 Cedar Street,
      Minneapolis, Minn.

Gentlemen:

   Mr. R. A. Trent has been a good customer of ours for years. Now he has moved to 1194 Pearl Street, in your city. We have recommended that he consult you in regard to any repair work on jewelry that he may need to have done while he is in the West.

> Very truly yours,
>
> (Signed) J. H. Brown

(2)

November 21, 19—.

Dear Mr. and Mrs. Gray:

Mr. and Mrs. R. A. Trent are spending Friday and Saturday of the first week in December in Chicago, making their headquarters at the Blackstone Hotel.

These friends of mine have devoted much time to art and travel. This interest, which you have in common, makes me think you might find them very congenial. May I suggest that you arrange to make their acquaintance while they are in your city.

Very sincerely yours,

(Signed) J. H. Brown

Mr. and Mrs. L. M. Gray,
11 Shore Drive,
Chicago, Ill.

Such letters will help your friends to become more pleasantly acclimated to a new environment. The first letter gives the firm receiving it an advertising lead and usually results in a reciprocal courtesy being extended the writer by the managers of the firms so recommended. The second letter often paves the way to a lasting friendship; at the least it affords a pleasant evening for people with common interests. Receipt of the following letter from Mr. Gray will certainly make Mr. and Mrs. Trent feel that Mr. Brown had their interests in mind:

November 30, 19—.

My dear Mr. and Mrs. Trent:

Our mutual friend, Mr. J. H. Brown, has written us that you will be in Chicago this week. Will it be possible for you to have lunch with Mrs. Gray and me at the Commerce Club Friday noon?

You can reach us by calling either my office (Loop 7179) or our home (Hyde Park 2034).

Very sincerely yours,

(Signed) L. M. Gray

Mr. and Mrs. R. A. Trent,
Blackstone Hotel,
Chicago, Illinois.

Notes of congratulation

Businessmen who are much interested in people are careful not to overlook an opportunity to recognize the joys and achievements of others. You can do much to help in this work by calling to the attention of your employer news items, rumors, and happenings of an interesting type. There will be many occasions when your executive will want to send a note of congratulation or praise to a friend or acquaintance; even to a total stranger.

Most people find it comparatively easy to compose letters to people they know, but they are inclined to be stilted in writing to strangers, or to individuals whom they do not know intimately. The following letters were selected by the author because they are not models but actual letters which brought joy in an accomplishment. They reflect a uniformly friendly note, though they were written to her by a close friend, a mere business acquaintance, and a perfect stranger, respectively.

(*From a close friend*)

December 24, 19—.

Dear Bernice,

The autographed copy of your book reached this desk an hour ago and confirmed my conviction that there is a Santa Claus. Its bright red cover is very appropriate to the Christmas season and would make a financial volume tempting to me even if the name "Turner" in gold letters were not an added attraction.

A rather hurried glance at the volume reveals the work to be a finished production. I compliment you on a job well accomplished.

May your Christmas at home be the beginning of that happy time when, your writing troubles over, you reap an author's benefits in the form of congratulations and royalties. (Our bank has ordered a copy for its library.)

Most sincerely,

Miss Bernice C. Turner,
368 E. Eighth Street,
Bloomsburg, Pa.

(*From a business acquaintance*)

December 24, 19—.

My dear Miss Turner:

I wish to express my sincere thanks for the autographed copy of "The Federal Fund Market" received today.

Although I have not yet had time to look through the book very searchingly, I am sure that you, as its author, have done yourself proud, and I extend my felicitations. I trust that the treatise will be fruitful of the sort of results you desire. At any rate, it should be decidedly helpful to the large and growing class of readers who are interested in the subject.

With renewed thanks and kind regards, I extend to you hearty Yuletide greetings.

Yours sincerely,

Miss Bernice C. Turner,
First National Old Colony Corporation,
100 Broadway,
New York 6, N.Y.

(*From a total stranger*)

January 2, 19—.

My dear Miss Turner:

I simply want to add my note of congratulations to the many which you must be receiving on the publication of your book, "The Federal Fund Market."

It always requires a great deal of courage to be the first to commit one's self in writing on any subject, but I feel sure yours is the forerunner of many other books on Federal Funds which will be much more voluminous and complicated, and not nearly so direct and practical as yours.

Very sincerely,

Miss Bernice C. Turner,
1060 Park Avenue,
New York 28, N.Y.

Letters of a congratulatory character are sent by businessmen to those who have received promotions, to those who have distinguished themselves by outstanding achievement, to those who have had honors bestowed upon them or members of their family, and to those in whose families have occurred births, marriages, graduations, or other events of direct concern. One of the customs which has grown up among business houses is that of sending flowers or a letter of congratulation to the officers of a firm which is opening new offices. Your employer will probably think of these courtesies several days after the event unless you do some anticipatory thinking for him.

Notes of sympathy

More appreciated than the note of congratulation is the friendly remembrance which comes to one at a time when he is meeting reverses. Sickness, accident, death, or any disaster usually leaves one with a feeling of dependence. Just at these times of greatest need, many friends and acquaintances are likely to forsake us, not so much because they prefer to know only a successful person but rather because they are at a loss to know what to say in a case of adversity.

A Pollyanna attitude should be avoided, because it conveys to the person a lack of sympathetic understanding. However, a perfectly hopeless note is seldom advisable. In writing of a death, the word *death* is not to be used, because many persons have a conscientious objection to its finality. The word *loss* is much less open to criticism. Most businessmen send telegrams of sympathy because they can seldom think of more than ten words of condolence. Nevertheless, a letter is generally sufficiently appreciated to merit the extra effort which its composition entails. Naturally, if a secretary has never heard of the deceased nor his family, any letter she might write for her employer would lack individuality. Some men overcome this difficulty by giving the secretary an outline of the acquaintanceship. The secretary then writes one letter and the employer composes another. By combining the two letters in the employer's words, a fairly good result may be obtained.

Suppose one of the officers in your organization met with a fatal accident. If neither you nor your employer is acquainted with the family, it will probably fall to your lot to compose the letter of sympathy.

June 1, 19——.

Dear Mrs. Blaine and Children,

Just yet I am a little too shocked to realize that we are to be denied Mr. Blaine's guiding influence in this organization. He was a rock upon which we all built confidently, knowing that his unbounded sympathy and good judgment would help us steer our course aright.

The sympathy of this entire office force goes out to you and your family in this time of bereavement. You have assured us that there is nothing more we can do for you just now, but I invite you to consult me at any time in the future if you ever need the assistance of one whose close business association with Mr. Blaine may enable him to help you who must carry out his ideals and ambitions.

Very sincerely yours,

(Signed) J. H. Brown

Mrs. M. H. Blaine and Family,
Greenport Boulevard,
Newport, Rhode Island.

Many businessmen send letters to those who are called upon to meet life's reverses. The following letter sent to a man who has lost his position would probably give the searcher for work just the confidence he needs for that ordeal.

December 2, 19——.

Dear Fred,

The news that you lost your position just reached me when I went to call on you today. Having suffered a similar experience myself about two years ago, I want you to know that I understand the feeling of defeat which accompanies dismissal from an office to which one has gone with visions of success.

During the long days of job hunting, nothing would have meant so much to me as tangible proof that I had not become one of life's failures. Even yet I shudder when I think of the black despair which engulfs a man who has no work. You are a good worker; never allow yourself to doubt that. Some firm is going to be made richer by the circumstances which have made you available to them.

Any help I might give you will bring me pleasure, too. Do not hesitate to call on me.

Most sincerely yours,

(Signed) Jim

A different type of loss might call for the following letter:

May 14, 19—.

Dear Mr. and Mrs. Deiver,

Announcement of the fire which destroyed your home just came to me in the form of a clipping from your local paper. What a sense of disappointment it must have brought to you who had so carefully planned that home!

Accept my sympathy in your loss. Your splendid hospitality had endeared the house to your friends, though even a humble hut would be fascinating to us so long as it housed your family.

Very sincerely yours,
(Signed) J. H. Brown

Mr. and Mrs. E. A. Deiver,
827 Avenue of the Americas,
New York 1, N.Y.

Legal and other pitfalls

In the final analysis, you must be awake to possibilities of interpretation and of misinterpretation. Be definite if you want to avoid misunderstanding, and avoid committing yourself if you are not perfectly sure of your ground. Each letter must be considered on its own merits. The letter that someone could not criticize has never been written. A writer must think about a letter of importance and revise it many times before he is satisfied with it. When a safe and complete form has been written for one letter, future correspondence may be modeled after that pattern. Few people can make all letters original because of the time element; they may use phrases or even whole paragraphs over and over again simply because the wording is safe. A secretary must see that these form-letter crutches are not used so often that office correspondence loses the elasticity of adaptability.

BOOKS THAT HELP TO FORM JUDGMENTS IN LETTER WRITING

Babenroth's Modern Business Communication, A. C. Babenroth. Edited by Charles C. Parkhurst, Prentice-Hall, Inc., Englewood Cliffs, N.J.
Actual Business English (revised), P. H. Deffendall, The Macmillan Company, New York

Effective Business Writing (2nd ed.), Williams and Ball, The Ronald Press Company, New York

The Book of Etiquette, Emily Post, Funk and Wagnalls Co., New York

Business Writing Theory and Practice, Charles Chandler Parkhurst and Roy Davis, Prentice-Hall, Inc., Englewood Cliffs, N.J.

Smooth Sailing Letters, L. E. Frailey, Prentice-Hall, Inc., Englewood Cliffs, N.J.

Business English In Practice (2nd ed.), Handy and Clifton, Pitman Publishing Corp., New York

Business Letter, I. E. Dwyer, Houghton Mifflin Co., Dubuque, Iowa

Business Letter Writing at a Glance, G. Peterson, Ottenheimer Publishers, Inc., Baltimore, Md.

Business Writing, Harold J. Janis and Others, Barnes and Noble, Inc., New York

Chapter 19

Minutes and Reports of Meetings

Report me and my cause aright.
—SHAKESPEARE

Knowledge of parliamentary procedure

Businessmen often assert that secretaries know nothing about parliamentary procedure. To hear lawyers direct the same criticism at businessmen is highly amusing. One corporation attorney says: "I spend two-thirds of my time trying to fix up the blunders that the officers of this organization make, simply because they do not know what they are doing and are too careless to consult legal authority before they act. One would think that even a child might be able to see as irregular some of the ridiculous things they do." But abysmal ignorance of the formal way a business meeting is conducted is common to both secretaries and their executives.

The first thing you must learn is that a business meeting is a serious thing. Business must be transacted exactly according to law, or else opposing factions may try to invalidate much of the work accomplished. One could hardly deem the ordinary school, church, or club meeting a fit pattern on which to model a business meeting. Certainly there is no objection to having a *strictly legal* meeting of a fraternal organization, but usually formality is less necessary at a meeting in which matters causing profit and loss are not involved.

The kinds of corporate meetings are: annual stockholders' meetings; special stockholders' meetings; regular meetings of directors; special meetings of directors; committee meetings.

Methods of reporting meetings

A secretary usually writes up minutes of meetings. The report may come to her through her employer, or she may be asked to attend the meeting for the purpose of doing the reporting. In either case, in order to write a good report, some concept of the general procedure of the meeting must be gained. This knowledge may often be gleaned from reading over old minutes of the organization.

If a new organization is being effected, you will have to be a pioneer and plot out your own trail. The following models of order of business may serve as a guide to you.[1]

1. Election of temporary chairman and secretary of the meeting.
2. Oath of office of temporary officers.
3. Presentation of notice of meeting or waiver if notice has been waived.
4. Report that certificate of incorporation has been filed as required by statute.
5. Order that certificate of incorporation be made a part of the record of the meeting.
6. Adoption of by-laws.
7. Election of directors. Generally, where the board of directors is named in the certificate of incorporation, no election takes place at the first incorporators' meeting. In a few of the states, however, the practice is for the incorporators to go through a formal approval of the directors named in the certificate of incorporation. If "dummy" directors have been named in the certificate of incorporation, these directors resign at the incorporators' meeting and an election is held by the incorporators to fill the vacancies. If the statute, charter, or by-laws permit the remaining directors to fill vacancies, the resignation of a director named in the certificate of incorporation may take place at the first directors' meeting and the vacancy may be filled at the same meeting.
8. Authorization for opening the books for subscriptions.
9. Report of subscriptions to capital stock.
10. Order that subscriptions be made a part of the record of the meeting.
11. Presentation of transfers of subscriptions. This step is necessary

[1] Doris and Friedman, *Encyclopedia of Corporate Meetings, Minutes, and Resolutions* (1958, Prentice-Hall, Inc., Englewood Cliffs, N.J.)

where temporary or "dummy" incorporators have been used in incorporating the company.

12. Authorization for board of directors to issue stock.
13. Fixing the terms and conditions of the preferred stock, where this is required to be done at the incorporators' meeting, or permitted to be done under the statute.
14. Election of officers.
15. Oath of office of permanent officers.
16. Call for bond from treasurer. (Bonds may, of course, be required from other officers.)
17. Approval of bond.
18. Adoption of corporation seal.
19. Adoption of form of corporate stock.
20. Authority to purchase corporate record books.
21. Appointment of principal office and resident agent in the state of incorporation, if one is required by statute.
22. Order that proper officers or directors execute and file any reports or records that the statute requires.
23. Appointment of regular date for directors' meeting, if by-laws do not provide for one.
24. Authorization for treasurer to open a bank account. If by-laws do not provide for the signing of checks and other instruments, the directors by resolution will assign the duty to some officer or officers.
25. Authorization for treasurer to pay the expenses incident to the organization of the company.
26. Transaction of any other business that is within the power of the persons meeting to transact.

The order of business in a regular stockholders' meeting is much more simple:

1. Call to order.
2. Election of a chairman and the appointment of a temporary secretary, if necessary.
3. Presentation of proofs of the due calling of the meeting.
4. Presentation and examination of proxies.
5. Announcement of a quorum present.
6. Reading and settlement of the minutes of the previous meeting.
7. Presentation of list of stockholders.
8. Reports of officers and committees.
9. Appointment of inspectors of election.
10. Opening of polls.

11. Election of directors.
12. Closing of polls.
13. Report of inspectors.
14. Declaration of election of directors.
15. New business.
16. Adjournment.

Directors' meetings are still more simple in order:

1. Call to order.
2. Announcement of a quorum present.
3. Reading and approval of the minutes of the previous meeting.
4. Reports of officers and committees.
5. Unfinished business.
6. Election of officers, if there is to be an election.
7. Declaration of dividend, if there is to be a dividend declared.
8. Other new business.
9. Adjournment.

The order of business to be followed in a committee meeting is usually outlined in the by-laws. In order to gain some idea of what any meeting of this type is like, you will do well to read the general rules on procedure for a directors' meeting.

Outline, summary, and verbatim reports

If your employer brings you a report of the meeting, he will probably have the notes in outline form. You will be expected to expand them into complete sentences. Naturally, your expansion of notes without first-hand knowledge of the events which took place at the meeting makes it necessary that your employer read and correct the minutes you have written before they are copied into the minute book. If he dictates the report himself, he will do the expanding, and there will not be much danger of errors creeping into the record. Occasionally one finds a man who wants the permanent record written in outline form, though this practice is not a good one to follow. Expanding an outline into complete sentences does not mean, of course, that you are to write fiction in order to make an interesting tale of the events; it merely means that the items are to be clearly stated in complete sentences.

Notes: Call to order 10:15.

        Minutes approved.

        Treasurer's report.

Expanded minutes:

April 15, 19——.

The regular meeting of the directors of the Van Dine Corporation was held at the Hotel Woods today. The meeting was called to order by the president, H. H. Wills, at 10:15 a.m.

Minutes of the last meeting were read by the secretary, J. J. Daniels, and were approved.

The treasurer, M. D. Smith, made his report to the directors. A copy of this report is made a part of these minutes.

If you are asked to go to a meeting for the purpose of reporting it, you should understand clearly just what you are expected to get. If a summary report is all that is necessary, you will record only those things which are of vital importance. Should it be necessary to make a verbatim report, you will have to have attained a reporting speed in taking notes. Though verbatim reports are seldom written in the form of minutes—because a summary is much more satisfactory— a full report is sometimes handy for reference. Many firms preserve the shorthand notes of a verbatim report in order to be able later to verify certain interpretations of actions taken. Occasionally, in a heated controversy, complete notes are required (including even swear words).

Importance of hearing and understanding

Something that a beginning reporter often does not realize is that when an employer sends an employee in to get a report, he expects the report to be complete, regardless of circumstances. Naturally, good hearing faculties are a prime requisite for reporting. However, if you do not hear something, or do not understand it, you may be unwise to let the matter drop or to skip over that part. Observation of business secretaries who report meetings of large trade organizations for the purpose of writing the minutes is a real education. If a man speaking from the floor cannot be heard, the secretary is on her feet in a second asking that he speak louder. If he uses a term she does not understand or a name she cannot spell, he is asked to repeat the remark. Should it be impossible for him to speak loud enough to be heard distinctly, she asks that he come to the platform. Because her success depends upon the accuracy of the report, she takes no chances with her reputation. If you are the official reporter of a meeting, you must follow her example. Of course you will never speak directly to anyone except the chairman (unless the chair is temporarily vacant). Usually it is not necessary for your voice to ring through the meeting room, for you can arrange a system of signals with the chairman. A raising of the pen above your head will indicate that you cannot hear. The chairman, if alert, can then quickly ask the speaker to repeat his remarks. If you are not the official reporter of the meeting, it may not always be possible to interrupt. Then you will need to mark your notes so that you will be able to verify doubtful matters with as little loss of time as possible. Sometimes this checking can be done by consulting the speaker himself; sometimes it is best to have your employer consult the man for you; and sometimes the spelling, statistics, or reference will have to be verified through other channels. A question mark with a circle around it will remind you of points you want to check when you read back your notes.

Some years ago a girl was sent to report a business meeting that took place at a banquet at which a noted scientist spoke. Because the girl knew nothing about scientific terms, the talk on nuclear fission made her feel totally inadequate. Each sentence brought her nearer the border of despair. No one at her table could help her out. Her employer had requested that she send a report of the meeting to the newspapers, so with grim determination, she took down everything she could and marked her notebook at the places where she was uncertain. At the close of the talk, the girl rushed up to the speaker and asked him to clarify these points, which he graciously consented to do. Because he knew the girl would be sending the report of his speech to the press, the scientist was anxious for her to have complete details of his message, and carefully explained points she had missed.

The newspapers were so pleased with her detailed report of an important speech that they printed it in full in a prominent place. When officers of the trade association which had sponsored the banquet congratulated the secretary on her wonderful shorthand ability, she chuckled to herself in satisfaction over the fact that she had not lacked courage to seek by drastic means what she was expected to get.

This experience should teach you that, when you know you are expected to get a report, you must put down some kind of outline for everything you hear, even though you are almost in despair because you know your forms are wrong. Corrections are easier to fill in than omissions.

Content of minutes

Minutes should always include three items: the kind of meeting (regular or special), the place, and the date—whether or not these items are contained in the notes you receive. The following reports are submitted as models:

MINUTES OF MEETING OF FINANCE COMMITTEE

A meeting of the Finance Committee of the Board of Directors of . . . . was held at the office of the Company, ... Street, ... City, on the . . . . day of . . . . , at . . . . o'clock in the . . . . noon.

Present: Messrs. . . . . , ... , ... , constituting a quorum.

Absent: Messrs. . . . . and . . . .

Mr. . . . . presided at the meeting.

The minutes of the previous Finance Committee meeting, held on . . . . , 19 . ., were read and approved.

The Chairman of the meeting reported that this Corporation had been requested to make an appropriation toward the expenses necessarily incident to the campaign of a leading politician who is a candidate for reëlection. Since the right of the Corporation to make contributions of this kind had been questioned, the Chairman recommended that the opinion of the Corporation's attorney be secured, so that the members of the Committee might feel certain that they were observing the full requirements of the law on the subject.

After the motion was duly made and seconded, the matter was referred to the Chairman for proper disposition.

The special committee, appointed by the Chairman at the meeting held . . . . , 19 . ., to consider the question of making future contracts for sales of semifinished products to competitors of subsidiary companies, made a special report, which was approved and adopted. The report was ordered to be made a part of the minutes of the meeting.

(*Insert copy of report here.*)

The President reported the purchase of 8,000 tons of pig iron for September delivery.

The President submitted a letter from . . . ., under date of . . . ., 19. ., in regard to building a plant in Canada to manufacture all lines of products that the Corporation is exporting to Canada. The letter was accompanied by six statements giving data in regard to the proposition.

After the motion was duly made and seconded, the Secretary was directed to send a copy of the correspondence to each member of the Committee.

No further business coming before the meeting, the same was adjourned after a motion to that effect had been made, seconded, and carried.

. . . .
Secretary of the Meeting

MINUTES OF MEETING NOT HELD FOR LACK OF QUORUM

There being no members of the Executive Committee present at . . . ., ... Street, City of . . . ., State of . . . ., on (day of week) . . . ., 19. ., at . . . o'clock . . . . M., ...,
the time and place set for a regular meeting of the Committee, no meeting was held and no business was transacted.

A true record.

. . . .
(Notary's signature)   Assistant Secretary

Attest: . . . .

MINUTES OF MEETING ADJOURNED TO A FIXED DATE

At the time set for the regular meeting of the Board of Directors of . . . . Corporation to be held at the offices of the Company, ... Street, City of . . . ., State of . . . ., on (day of week)
. . . ., 19. ., at . . . . o'clock . . . .M., there were present . . . ., ..., and . . . .

Since no quorum was present, the meeting was adjourned, under the provisions of the by-laws, to (day of week) . . . .,
. . . .,
19. ., at . . . . o'clock . . . . M.

. . . .
Secretary

Indexing of minutes

The minutes of some organizations are so voluminous that it is necessary to keep an index, and even a cross index, of them. This index is divided into different headings, such as:

Duties of president
Duties of secretary
Duties of treasurer
Financial obligations
Purchase and sale of real estate
Sales policies
Statistics of organization

As many other headings may be used as will make the material less cumbersome for the various departments that use it for ready reference. This reference may be put in the back of the minute book, but it is occasionally made in the form of a card index. Frequently, minutes are written up with a wide left-hand margin, and marginal headings are used as a basis for indexing.

As indicated in the minutes of the finance committee meeting used as an illustration of the content of minutes, various reports, resolutions, and correspondence are often made a part of the records. Although it may sometimes be possible to insert these extra sheets in the minute book, business offices seldom allow this to be done. Instead of saying "Insert copy here," many firms write, "Copy on file in Folder #17." Then all extraneous documents are placed in a special file, which is carefully labeled:

Treasurer's Reports
In Memoriam Resolutions
Oaths
Bonds
Affidavits, and so on.

This practice keeps the minute book in good condition, provides a place for keeping documents which usually vary in size, and makes it possible to allow reference to certain portions of the official record without disclosing confidential materials.

Correcting minutes

Minutes should never be written into a minute book until they are free from errors. Nevertheless, minutes are not always "approved as read." A slight correction may be made, in red ink; that is, a line may be drawn through a word or phrase and the correction written above. If longer corrections are made, they should be written on a separate sheet. The old record is deleted by striking a red line through the paragraph and making a marginal indication of the page on which the correction will be found. Never tear a sheet out of a minute book, and never rewrite minutes in full.

Motions and their amendments

Motions should always be written verbatim. Then if it is necessary to amend them, the amendment must be voted on just as though it were an original motion. Extreme care will be necessary to get the exact wording of these corrections. This caution must be observed, also, with any original motion. A correction amendment, whether passed or defeated, should be made a part of the minutes. The correction would probably read somewhat as follows:

> Minutes of the last regular meeting were read by the Assistant Secretary, A. M. Brown.

DEFEATED MOTION

R. J. Brown moved that the instructions regarding the hiring of an architect be amended to read "verbal or written applications to be tendered to the Secretary or any member of the Board." The motion was not seconded, and so was not put to a vote.

AMENDED MOTION

R. J. Brown moved that the instructions regarding the hiring of an architect be amended to read "written applications to be tendered to the Secretary or any member of the Board." The motion was seconded by E. L. Jones and put to a vote.

In Favor	Opposed
Brown	Graham
Smith	Elwood
Jones	Freis
Frye	

President Freis then instructed the Secretary to change the minutes as amended.

When the minutes of a previous meeting have been amended, changes on the original entry must always indicate the page on which the motion for amendment can be found. References to later changes are made usually in the form of marginal notes. Of course, the minutes of the meeting will not now read "approved as read," but "approved as amended," and if the vote for approval is not unanimous, it will be necessary to record the vote.

Records of attendance and votes

In a small meeting a secretary is expected to keep a record of the attendance. If possible, take the roll while the men are gathering, in order that you may have a full record of those present when the meeting is called to order. However, it is necessary sometimes to record the entrance of tardy members. If some man knows nothing about a certain action, it may be that the business was transacted before his arrival. In a case in which a man is known to be opposed to a course of action and is influential enough to alter the result of a vote, other members sometimes take advantage of his tardiness to push a measure through. If your minutes read, "The motion was unanimously approved," and do not contain a later record of the entrance of an opponent of the measure, his sanction of the measure is wrongly taken for granted. Men do like to have a record in black and white of their stand on each measure, especially if later events prove they were right and the world was wrong. A few men do not have the courage of their convictions and think if they slip out of a meeting just before a vote is taken, they can swing to the proper side later. For this reason a record should also be kept of those men who leave a meeting during the time it is in session. A scrupulously careful record of all votes on any question of more than trifling importance must be kept. At a large meeting an adequate system is usually provided for the recording of attendance and votes; at a small meeting this is usually your responsibility.

Care of corporate records

Should your employer have the custody of the corporate books, the corporate seal, or the corporate files, you will have to share in the responsibility of protecting them. So long as your employer is in the office, you can usually consult him in regard to giving out materials. The problem of deciding what to do when he is not there is often puzzling.

One girl was asked for the corporation seal at a time when her employer was away. The man who requested it had no right to the seal, but was trying to take advantage of the custodian's absence to accomplish some "dirty work." Still another secretary gave out the combination of her employer's safe to a man who later used that knowledge in having records changed and destroyed. Such incidents as these are fair warning that you must know who is to be given access to each type of record. Then it is your duty to see that no one, except those authorized, is allowed to see confidential materials. In extreme cases you may be compelled to act contrary to orders, but your employer should be notified of any deviation from his instructions.

Some years ago a young woman was given the combination to a safe in which a corporation seal was kept. She asked who was to be given the privilege of using the seal and was told, "Absolutely nobody, unless I first give permission!" Some months later her employer was in a hospital when a corporation meeting was held. The president came in to get the seal. The secretary said: "Mr. F. has told me never to give that seal to any person. However, I know this is an exceptional case. If you will get another officer to come with you, I shall give it to you." The president was surprised at the request, but he went to find a vice-president. When he reëntered her office with the vice-president, he asked the girl to accompany them to the meeting and to make a record of the places in which they had used the seal. When she returned the seal to the safe, she knew for what it had been used, and was able to communicate the information to her superior after his health had improved. Some weeks later the young woman was promoted to a position of responsibility, because the officers of the company had been much impressed with her trustworthiness.

Preparedness necessary to conduct of a meeting

Nothing could be more futile than some business meetings at which no one has seen fit to make the necessary preparations for putting each motion through with dispatch. A mad rush to make last-minute plans, and to get materials in shape before the opening of a poorly planned meeting, usually plunges responsible officers into a nervous frenzy (to say nothing of the secretaries who must bear the brunt of such a situation). Naturally, a meeting is not a success if uncalled-for haste makes the men in charge mentally unfit for association with human beings, much less for leadership.

Let us look at two types of meetings to see what a secretary can do toward making things move smoothly. The drawing of some foreign bonds for payment every six months takes place in a large investment house on Wall Street. Representatives of participating banking houses are present while a girl draws these numbers in the presence of a member of the consulate from that foreign country. A young woman who had just graduated from college was secretary to the man in charge of this drawing. The night that the notices were to be sent out the man came in at just about five o'clock and told the girl to stay after hours to write the letters. Practically nothing more was done until the hour for the meeting. Then there was a mad flurry to get material in the files relating to the drawing. The responsible officer had not provided a suitable box for the bond numbers; this matter had to be attended to while members of other banking houses waited at the meeting. An unscheduled meeting which was being held in the conference chamber had to be disbanded to make room for this regular event. No one had been chosen for the drawing, so a last minute selection had to be made. Because the officers were not familiar with the terms of the contract, the provision for drawing bond numbers had to be read at the meeting. The member of the foreign consulate had not arrived half-an-hour after the time the drawing was scheduled to have taken place. No attention had been paid to the notice until the consulate was called, and then a representative summoned a taxicab and hurried to the meeting. A climax of the comedy seemed to have been reached when not one man in the assembled group had a clean handkerchief which might be used to blindfold the girl who was to draw the numbers; however, the worst was yet to come. A three-page legal form had to be typed without error, and then signed by the persons present. The first time the form was typed an error in computation was discovered; the second time it was found that the next date for drawing could not be scheduled because that date fell on a Sunday. By the time this second mistake had been discovered, the secretary was so nervous that she could not type a third copy without making an error. The men paced impatiently up and down in her office. At length, another girl had to be commandeered to make the final copy of the record, which was submitted in signed form one hour and fifteen minutes after it had been begun.

A secretary who witnessed the whole irrational procedure made a note that she would study the situation and save any other girl from becoming a nervous wreck. When the next October drawing took place, notices were prepared three days before they were to go out. When no word had been received from the foreign consulate by the day before the meeting, a telephone call was made to ascertain if arrangements were being made to have a member present. The much-dreaded legal form was completely typed a week before the meeting, so that the secretary had time to be sure everything was all right. Space was left on the form for inserting the numbers of the drawn bonds. Before two o'clock the conference room was prepared for the meeting, including such supplies as the box of bond numbers and a blindfold for the girl who was to make the drawing. The result was that in a very few minutes signatures were attached to the legal document, and the men went merrily on their way. The new secretary had no reason to look back on the events of the day as a nightmare.

Notices of meetings

The task of sending out notices of a meeting will nearly always fall upon a secretary. The first thing you should do in equipping yourself for this part of your work is to make up a list of the meetings which are to be held under the jurisdiction of the man for whom you work. Look over the by-laws during your leisure hours to determine the dates for mailing out meeting notices, the matter of their form, and the persons to receive them. This digest can be put on a memorandum which will be easy to follow. Two or three days before each group of notices is to be sent out will generally allow you ample time for preparing the envelopes and other materials. Your calendar should be made up accordingly. Unless attendance is optional, you will do well to ascertain whether or not notices have reached those concerned. When proxies are returned by nonattending members, a numerical arrangement of these voting powers should be made. Reservations of the meeting room should always be made ahead of time, to avoid last-minute confusion as to the place.

Materials to be taken to a meeting

The procedure followed at a meeting can be correct and orderly only if all materials are on hand and in shape for quick reference. You will want to see that your employer takes the following things with him:

1. An envelope containing any correspondence or memorandums likely to be required.

2. A copy of the corporation law of the state in which the company is organized.

3. The certificate of incorporation, with marginal notations of amendments.

4. The by-laws, with marginal notations of amendments.

5. A carefully prepared "Order of Business" (known as the *agenda*).

6. Blank forms, such as oaths, affidavits, and so forth.

7. A memorandum pad on which to record matters which must be followed up after the meeting.

8. The corporation seal.

9. Stationery and envelopes for sending out newspaper reports and other messages which must be dispatched at once.

10. Pen, pencils, ink, eraser, ruler, clips, rubber bands, paste, and pins.

Copies of resolutions

Many secretaries are confused by the use of the word *copy* with regard to sending out resolutions. This term does not necessarily mean "carbon copy." Expressions of sympathy and similar actions taken at a meeting are incorporated into the record of the meeting. The minutes must contain a copy of the resolutions so passed. An exact copy of the content of these resolutions may be written on paper of good quality, encased in a legal cover properly inscribed, and sent to the proper persons. In case of death it is customary to send to the relatives of the deceased a copy of the resolutions encased in a white cover. Note that in writing resolutions and minutes, the following expressions are written in capital letters: RESOLVED, BE IT FURTHER RESOLVED, WHEREAS, and KNOW ALL MEN BY THESE PRESENTS.

BOOKS THAT HELP IN WRITING UP MINUTES AND REPORTS

Report Writing (3rd ed.), C. G. Gaum and others, Prentice-Hall, Inc., Englewood Cliffs, N.J.
The Secretary's Handbook (8th ed.), Taintor and Munro, The Macmillan Company, New York.
Business Writing, S. Roland, McGraw-Hill Book Company, New York.
Communication Through Reports, P. Douglass, Prentice-Hall, Inc., Englewood Cliffs, N.J.

Chapter **20**

Manuscripts and Proofreading

Print it as it stands—beautifully.
—HENRY JAMES

Cooperation with printers

Secretaries, as well as those who write for publication, are guilty of many sins against printers, who are expected to turn out perfect work with utmost speed, regardless of the condition of copy or proofs. A few rules will enable a secretary to work more intelligently with the printer or publisher and thus obtain better and quicker results—whether her problem be the preparation of a letterhead or of a 500-page book.

Typing a manuscript

Your work will be concerned largely with the preparation of manuscript for the printer. All work should be submitted on standard 8½ by 11-inch sheets of white, unglazed, bond paper of good quality. Use double spacing, and write on one side of the paper only. Leave margins of at least one and a quarter inches on all four sides of the paper to allow room for editor's and proofreader's marks.

Indent paragraphs five spaces. Page numbers should be written in the upper right-hand corner of each sheet and should be placed in this position consistently throughout an entire article or book. The printer should receive the original copy of a manuscript, or if that is impossible, the first carbon copy may be sent to him. Always preserve in your files at least one clear carbon copy to be used in case the original is lost. If the manuscript is being sent to a publisher, send both the original and a carbon copy, but mail each separately.

Do not fold or roll a manuscript, because doing so makes it hard to handle. Manuscripts should never be permanently bound; use removable clips or pins if some binding is necessary to fasten together parts of smaller articles or pages of chapters of a book. Voluminous manuscripts which cannot be sent flat in a big envelope are wrapped, or submitted in a paper brief case.

Types of headings to use

A chapter heading should be written in capital letters. If a subheading is centered, capitalize the first letter of every word in it except the prepositions, articles, and common conjunctions. In the preparation of texts, a side heading may be used for the sake of clarity. Only the first letter of the first word of a side heading should be capitalized. A side heading may be followed by a period and a dash.

A wavy line below a word or group of words indicates that the printer is to use boldface type; straight line underscoring means that the words are to be printed in italic type. Questions of setup can safely be left to the discretion of the publisher or printer.

Label illustrations carefully

Great care should be taken to mark illustrations clearly so that they will appear in their proper positions in the final published material. Tabulated material and charts should be carefully checked for absolute accuracy. A caption that is to appear below an illustration should be typed on a piece of paper and attached to the bottom of the photograph or sketch. It is usually better not to include illustrations in the typed manuscript. Keep them separate and indicate their positions in the manuscript by means of a numbering system. Do not paste or staple illustrations to the manuscript or to extra sheets of paper. Illustrations should be mailed separate from the manuscript.

Reproduction of illustrations

Roughly speaking, the photo engravings used to print illustrations may be divided into two classes: line or half-tone. Perhaps the best way to explain the distinction between the two, without going into detail, is to say that half-tone engravings reproduce photographs and line engravings reproduce pen and ink drawings, charts and graphs, typewritten material, and so forth. However, if any of the latter possess shading which has been gained by any means other than the use of lines, a combination of half-tone engraving and line engraving is necessary to reproduce the grey tones as well as the solid lines.

In submitting photographs, always try to obtain the original. Glossy prints, rather than soft finishes, reproduce best. Photographs clipped from other publications rarely give good results. If a photostat is to be used, be sure to submit the positive, or black on white; not the negative, or white on black. To obtain best results from typewritten material, prepare your copy with a silk or carbon paper ribbon on a pica type machine. Be sure your type is perfectly clean; if the letter *o* and the letter *a* are filled up with ink and lint, the reproduction will appear spotty and slipshod.

Illustrations containing a great deal of minute detail should never be reduced to more than half their original sizes. Some illustrations cannot stand even a half reduction.

All illustrative material should be plainly marked with the number of the page in the manuscript where it is to appear. Also, if any of the photographs or drawings require special treatment, full instructions should be written and attached.

Footnotes

Footnotes are placed at the bottom of the sheet on which the reference is made. A straight line of about 15 spaces should separate the footnote from the rest of the page. Notes to a table should appear directly beneath the table. A straight line also sets off the footnote from the preceding and following text. When there are many footnotes they should be typed double space, separate from the manuscript, chapter by chapter.

Unless only a very few footnote references are necessary, number the footnotes and follow the same sequence throughout the entire article; in a book the number sequence of footnotes may be followed throughout each chapter only. Variations of the asterisk and dagger marks may be used to indicate occasional footnotes. For reference marks in a table, use italicized lower case letters or numbers in parentheses in order to prevent these notations from being confused with letters and figures which appear in the tables.

The purpose of the footnote is to give the authority for a statement or quotation, to refer to a more complete work, or to give additional information or comment. It must always be remembered that footnotes distract the reader's attention from the article itself, and their unrestrained use may destroy interest in the work. Material which is meant to be gone over hurriedly should never include footnotes, because they slow up the reading process. References in this type of writing should assume the conversational tone and should appear in the body of the article, as follows: "Brown and Doris in their 1947 edition of *Business Letters and How to Write Them,* stress in these words the importance of getting the reader's point of view: . . ."

In a work designed for a slower type of reading, a quotation may be separated from the preceding text and followed by a small number. (Use the variable line spacer on your machine to raise the number above the regular alignment.) This number is repeated at the bottom of the page to indicate the source of the reference:

[1] Brown, S. M., and Doris, Lillian, *Business Letters and How to Write Them,* Englewood Cliffs, N.J., Prentice-Hall, Inc., 1947.

Footnotes which are law citations have this form:

Treadwell *v.* Clark, 114 App. Div. 493, affirmed 190 N. Y. 51.

Front matter

Each section of the front matter of a book or pamphlet should start on a separate sheet. Roman numerals may be used to number these sheets. The sequence of front matter pages usually runs as follows:

half title, frontispiece (if any), title, copyright, dedication (if any), preface or foreword, and table of contents. (A half title is nothing but the title itself, repeated in somewhat smaller type than the title proper, and placed alone on the right-hand page directly preceding the title page.) The frontispiece should of course face the title page.

The title page should be arranged with the typing centered, just as it is to appear in the book or pamphlet. The preface, foreword, or introduction may be typed in the same form as the body of the manuscript. The table of contents should be typed in the form in which it will appear, except that page numbers cannot be inserted until page proofs are received from the printer. A lengthy table of contents is often not set until after the book is paged, so that you are able to insert the numbers right in the typed copy. A specimen of a table of contents follows:

CHAPTER   PAGE

    VI. Social Letters ....
       Invitations ....
         Formal ....
         Informal ....
       Acceptances ....
       Regrets ....

Bibliography

A bibliography may follow each chapter of a book, or it may be assembled at the end of the book following the last chapter. The author's name comes first, followed by the title, the place of publication, the publisher, and the copyright year of the book.

> Doris, Lillian, *Real Estate Office Secretary's Handbook,* Prentice-Hall, Inc., Englewood Cliffs, N.J., 1953.

In listing several works by one author, it is not necessary to repeat the author's name; a typewritten line of about four spaces serves as a ditto mark.

> Doris, Lillian, *Business Finance Handbook,* Prentice-Hall, Inc., Englewood Cliffs, N.J., 1953.

——————— *Real Estate Office Secretary's Handbook,* Prentice-Hall, Inc., 1953.

When reference is made to an article in a magazine or newspaper, give the full title of the article, the author's name, and the date of the issue, the name of the publication, section (if any), page number, and column.

Hamburger, Edmund A., "New Departure in Fiduciary Security Transfers."
The Business Lawyer, p. 428, January, 1962.
The New York Times, March 4, 1962, sec. 4, p. 10, col. 4.

Note: Occasionally, where it seems desirable to place emphasis on the title of the book, and where nothing would be gained by attempting to make an alphabetical arrangement according to authors, the title may come first. This practice has been followed in the listings made at the ends of the chapters in this book.

Appendix

Pages of material which is to go in an appendix should be numbered separately. Appendix material may quite properly be a glossary of terms; long, quoted passages; forms; answers to questions which appear in the body of a work of textbook character; or matters of a reference nature. The appendix should never be used as a depository for illustrations; the latter are far more effective when they accompany their references in the text.

Editing the manuscript

Most writers are compelled to have their work retyped many times. First, a rough draft is made; then, the thoughts are gone over and rearranged in better form. Glaring mistakes in grammar and punctuation are corrected this time. A second copy is subjected to further refining. When each revised draft becomes so complicated with revisions that it cannot be read easily, another typing must be made. At last, the final polish may be given. Unless you are extremely interested in the work you are doing and are trying to help in making corrections, this repeated typing of manuscript work will become a deadly grind.

On the other hand, if you try to see improvement in each revised copy, you will be fascinated by the work. It has been said that books are not *written,* but *rewritten;* who should realize that fact better than the secretary to an author!

Final editing of a manuscript before it is submitted to the printer will be up to you, whether your employer joins with you in the work or not. Check the various headings to see that they correspond with the titles in the table of contents. All typographical errors and spacing errors should be corrected. Spelling, capitalization, hyphenation, punctuation, and grammar will have been pretty well straightened out in the earlier readings. Make sure that all inserts, cuts, and extraneous materials are correctly labeled and are included in the manuscript folder. References to previous or following portions of the work should be checked as you read, since revisions may have made your first references incorrect. For example, you may have written, "In Chapter V you will find . . ." only to discover that revision has changed Chapter V to Chapter VIII.

When correcting a manuscript, make corrections of a few words between the lines. Do not try to use the proofreader's marks shown on page 409 and do not write corrections sideways on the manuscript or on the backs of pages.

When a correction is longer than a few words, or when material must be added to a finished sheet, or an insertion is needed to insure clarity of much-corrected material, the new portions should be typed on full sheets of paper. These extra sheets should be the number of the page to which the insertion will be added plus a lower case letter; for instance, if an insertion is to be made on page 8, the correction sheet is numbered 8a. Cross out the portion of the manuscript for which the insert is to be substituted and write in the margin in a circle, *Insert 8a.* If the correction takes up less room than the original copy, the old material may be crossed out and a strip of paper bearing the correction pasted over the deleted lines.

Advertising and special copy

In writing straight matter for a publisher you do not need to concern yourself with the size of type or general setup of the material, for editors generally have much better judgment than a novice can have in regard to these matters. However, when you prepare copy for the local job printer, it is advantageous to be acquainted with the different styles of type. If everything you send him is clearly and correctly marked, it will save time for the printer and money for your firm.

In preparing advertising copy, the layout for the ad should be approximately the size of the advertisement to be used. You will need to know the sizes and kinds of type in order to plan the best arrangement for your material in the allotted space. Emphasis and subordination can be worked out clearly if you make use of various sizes of type. (See pages 406, and 407.)

Typing can seldom be put in the layout, as spaces will be limited. Typing goes on a copy sheet. The layout sheet and the copy sheet must be accurately labeled so an operator will experience no trouble in matching the copy to its appropriate place in the advertisement.

Notices of meetings, letterheads, signs, name cards, bills, and other office printing are subject to size analysis. If printed forms are made up, be sure that ample blank space is left for typing all data ordinarily required in each particular space. Some forms are so poorly designed that the space in which a customer's name is supposed to be typed is not large enough to accommodate comfortably even such a short name as A. B. Zee.

Type faces and their sizes

Following are three tables that illustrate some of the various sizes and kinds of type. The first shows the same line set in sizes ranging from 6-point to 48-point. (A point is $\frac{1}{72}$ of an inch.) Note that, beginning with 24-point, the entire sentence in one line across the page of this book cannot be set.

The second table shows a line of 10-point type set in seven different ways. The important thing to note here is the fact that even though only one size is used, seven varieties are possible. However, all these combinations are not always available with every type face.

The third table shows a few of the various families of type set in 14-point. (The line of typewriter type is of course 12-point or pica.)

While there are many others, the few printed will illustrate the fact that all type does not look like.

Space between lines of type is called leading. The lines that you are reading now are leaded two points. If you are ever tempted to instruct the printer to set a piece of copy solid, that is, with no leading between the lines, remember that type set in this way is hard to read. Type matter leaded one, two, or even three points is always easier on the eyes. *The larger the type, the heavier the leading* is a good rule to follow.

I

This line is set in 6-point type.

This line is set in 7-point type.

This line is set in 8-point type.

This line is set in 9-point type.

This line is set in 10-point type.

This line is set in 11-point type.

This line is set in 12-point type.

This line is set in 14-point type.

This line is set in 18-point type.

This line is set in 24-point type.

This line is set in 30-point type.

This line is set in 36-point type.

This line is set in 48-point type.

II

THIS LINE IS SET IN CAPITALS (OR CAPS).

Tʜɪs Lɪɴᴇ Is Sᴇᴛ ɪɴ Cᴀᴘs ᴀɴᴅ Sᴍᴀʟʟ Cᴀᴘs.

ᴛʜɪs ʟɪɴᴇ ɪs sᴇᴛ ɪɴ sᴍᴀʟʟ ᴄᴀᴘs.

This Line Is Set in Caps and Lower Case.

this line is set in lower case.

This line is set in italic.

This line is set in boldface.

III

This line is set in Caslon lightface.

This line is set in Caslon bold.

This line is set in Caslon Italic.

This line is set in Scotch Roman.

This line is set in Garamont.

This line is set in Kennerley.

This line is set in Cheltenham bold.

This line is set in Century.

This line is set in Bookman.

This line is set in Bodoni.

This line is set in Bodoni Bold.

This line is set in Sans Serif Bold No. 330.

This line is set in Cloister.

This line is set in French Round Face.

This line is set in Script.

This line is set in typewriter type.

Proofreading

After a manuscript has been accepted and set up, it will have to be proofread. Galley proofs consist of long, narrow sheets approximating three pages of the finished book, depending upon the size of the page. Two sets of proofs, together with the manuscript, will be sent to you by the publisher or printer. Read the set which contains the printer's corrections, carefully marking any errors not caught by his proofreader.

Have someone read the original manuscript slowly while you check the proofs, in order that you may detect omissions and variations, as well as typographical errors. Check figures very carefully.

Go over the proofs once more yourself, watching form and spelling. When you are satisfied that all necessary corrections have been made, copy all corrections onto the duplicate proof sheets.

Keep this latter set for your files and return the other set of proofs and the manuscript as quickly as possible to the publisher or printer. Manuscript not yet in type should be sent by American Express insured or by registered mail. Insure all proofs sent through the mails.

In the case of magazine articles, the first, or galley, proofs are all that will be sent to you; but with a book, you will receive page proofs also, after the corrected galleys have been returned to the printer. This practice gives you one more opportunity to check proofs. Page proofs also give you a chance to check the placement of footnotes, illustrations, and other reference material. Content changes can be made on proofs, but the cost is usually charged to the author; content is supposed to be correct on the manuscript. However, if a change is important, do not hesitate to call your employer's attention to the necessity for correction on proofs. Try to make inserts the same length as deletions; that is, six words can seldom be put in where one is taken out.

PROOFREADER'S MARKS

∧ Insert marginal addition.

Stet Retain crossed-out word or letter; let it stand. Dots may be placed under crossed out material you wish to have retained.

✗ Type appears battered; examine.

≡ Align type.

eg.# Unevenly spaced; equalize spacing.

no¶ No paragraph; "run in."

out See copy Here is an omission; see copy.

¶ Make a paragraph here.

tr Transpose words or letters as indicated.

ℐ Take out matter indicated; dele.

⊃ Upside down; reverse.

◡ Close up; no space.

Insert a space here.

⊥ Push down this space.

⊡ Indent line one em.

⊏ Move this to the left.

⊐ Move this to the right.

ld. Insert lead between lines.

⌐ Raise to proper position.

⌐ Lower to proper position.

wf Wrong font; change to proper font.

Qy? Is this right?

lc Put in lower case (small letters).

Draw slanting line through letter.

Put in small capitals. Draw double s.c. lines under letter.

Put in capitals. Draw triple lines Caps under letter.

Change to Roman type. Underscore or circle text with straight line. rom.

Change to Italic type. Underscore text with straight line. ital.

Change to bold face type. Underscore text with wavy line. bf

Insert comma. ∧

Insert semicolon. ;/

Insert colon. :/

Insert period. ⊙

Insert interrogation mark. ?/

Insert exclamation mark. !/

Insert hyphen. =/

Insert apostrophe. ✓

Insert quotation marks. ℓℓ/''

Insert superior letter or figure. (Specify.) ⌄b

Insert inferior letter or figure. (Specify.) ⌃2

Insert brackets. ⊏/⊐

Insert parenthesis. (/)

One-em dash. 1/em

Two-em parallel dash. /2 em/

Figure 9. Proofreader's Marks

A PIECE OF CORRECTED PROOF

S.C. It does not appear that the earliest printers had any method of e/

eg.# correcting errors before the form was on the press/ The learned The ⊙ e

e learned correctors of the first two centuries of printing were not

#;/ proof readers in our sense/ they were rather what we should term e/9

not/ office editors. Their labors were chiefly to see that the proof corre /=/

sponded to the copy, but that the printed page was correct in its

Caps/; latinity/ that the words were there, and that the sense was right. Stet

lc They cared but little about orthography, bad letters or purely printer's tr errors, and when the text seemed to them wrong they consulted fresh

authorities or altered it on their own responsibility. Good proofs in ∧

not# the modern sense, were impossible until professional readers were e ld

1/em employed men who had first a printer's education, and then spent tr many years in the correction of proof. The orthography of English, which for the past century has undergone little change, was very fluctuating until after the publication of Johnson's Dictionary, and capitals, which have been used with considerable regularity for the past 80 years, were previously used on the miss or hit plan. The approach to regularity, so far as we have, may be attributed to the growth of a class of professional proof readers, and it is to them that we owe the correctness of modern printing. More errors have been found in the Bible than in any other one work.   For many generations it was frequently the case that Bibles were brought out stealthily, from fear of governmental interference. They were frequently printed from imperfect texts, and were often modified to meet the views of those who published them. The story is related that a certain woman in Germany, who was the wife of a printer, and had become disgusted with the continual assertion of the superiority of man over woman, which she had heard, hurried into the composing room while her husband was at supper and altered a sentence in the Bible, which he was printing, so that it read Narr instead of Herr, thus making the verse read "And he shall be thy fool" instead of "and he shall be thy Lord." The word not was omitted by Barker, the king's printer in England in 1632, in printing the seventh commandment. He was fined £3,000 on this account.

Figure 10. Corrected Proof

Indexing

Return one set of page proofs at once, and from the other compile your index. This work will bring into play all you have learned about filing, indexing, and making cross references. Each topic should be put on a 3 by 5-inch card and the page number should follow it. If a number of cross references must be made, make out a separate card for each reference:

Topics:
Filing, 27
Types of filing, 27
Filing and office routine, 27
Filing, secretarial duties in, 27

Note: In order to have complete cross references, you will have to make seven cards to list each of the following items separately:

Filing, 27
Filing and office routine, 27

Filing, types of, 27
Filing, secretarial duties in, 27
Types of filing, 27
Office routine, filing and, 27
Secretarial duties in filing, 27

The cards carrying the above inscriptions should be filed alphabetically, by first letters only, in a box. When the entire book has been gone through in this manner, the cards are taken from the alphabetic divisions of the box and the topics under each letter arranged in further alphabetic sequence. Duplications are eliminated and all necessary editorial work is completed, after which the cards may be numbered with an automatic numbering stamp and sent to the printer. In cases of unusual arrangement of an index, the items on the cards may be typed, double space, on 8½ by 11-inch sheets of paper. Note the following:

Filing, 27
    and office routine, 27
    secretarial duties in, 27
    types of, 27
Office routine, filing and, 27
Secretarial duties in filing, 27
Types of filing, 27

In smaller indexing problems, twenty-six columns are prepared on a large sheet of paper. Spread this sheet out on a table and go through your reading matter page by page, indexing and cross-indexing under the various letters. When you have finished, alphabetize the headings under the various columns by numbering them in the order in which the topics should appear. Letters may be used to indicate the order of the subdivisions under the topics. Typing from such a numbered list makes arrangement easy.

(*Numbered list*)
[3] Statistical charts, 18
[1] Secretarial duties, 34, 72
  [b] shorthand, 27
  [a] filing, 45
  [c] telephone supervision, 75
[2] Statements of account, 41

(*Rearranged list*)
Secretarial duties, 34, 72
  filing, 45
  shorthand, 27
  telephone supervision, 75
Statements of account, 41
Statistical charts, 18

In checking the final copy of the index, cross off each subject that conforms to one on the original list; in this way, you will be able to detect any omitted items.

Copyright

In preparing material for publication, be careful not to use copy-righted passages or illustrations without written permission from the publisher.

When you prepare the front matter for your book or pamphlet, you will, of course, include a copyright notice. This notice should read as follows: *Copyright, 19—, by* ———————. *All rights reserved. Printed in the U. S. A.* It should appear on the title page or on the reverse side of the title page, preferably the latter.

To copyright a work, obtain an application blank from the Register of Copyrights, Washington, D. C. (When requesting a blank, indicate whether the work is being published for the first time in the United States, whether it is a new edition of an old publication, or whether it is typewritten manuscript that has not yet been set in type and printed.) After filling out the application blank, send it to the Register of Copyrights, together with a certified check for $4 and two copies of the book or pamphlet you are copyrighting.

BOOKS THAT HELP SOLVE MANUSCRIPT AND PRINTING PROBLEMS

Printer's Type Book (most printing companies).
Manual of Style, University of Chicago Press, Chicago.
Style Book for Writers and Editors, Thomas Y. Crowell Company, New York
Proofreading and Copy Preparation, Joseph Lasky, Mentor Press, New York

Chapter 21

The Office Beautiful

I believe . . . in the might of design, the mystery of color, the redemption of all things by Beauty ever-lasting . . .

—George Bernard Shaw

Making the office livable

The office is your home away from home; the place where you spend most of your waking hours. It stands to reason, then, that the more comfortable and attractive your office is, the happier and more pleasant will be your working day.

Of course, it's possible to get carried away by the home away from home idea. For instance, if your personal taste runs to ruffled organdy curtains, cute bric-a-brac, and lots and lots of green growing things, then you'd better confine your decorating to home. Leave the office decor to a professional interior decorator.

Your office can be attractive and relaxing, but it must be business-like and efficient. From your office, and your executive's, clients or customers form an impression of your firm. Whether this impression is good or bad depends, in large measure, upon you.

How the office reflects your characteristics

You may not fully realize how much the office reflects your personal traits. Your dress may be the latest fashion, your hair well kept, and your makeup perfect; but if you're fundamentally lazy and untidy, the office will reveal these basic characteristics. An atmosphere of neglect quickly grows up in an office where the desk tops are never

413

dusted and ashtrays never emptied unless the cleaning force has performed its duties; where flowers and plants are allowed to wilt and die for lack of care and then just left where they are; where the air is stale and musty, and where piles of unfiled material have been allowed to accumulate.

The tidiness of the office is your responsibility, as it is in your own room or your own home. By adding just a few minutes to your day at the office you can make sure everything is in order. Try to get to the office every morning a little ahead of time. Dust desk and furniture tops and tidy your employer's desk. Make sure he has a supply of freshly sharpened pencils, scratch pads, paper clips, and so forth. Put fresh water in the carafe by his desk and polish the drinking glass. If your employer has a private bath, see that used towels are replaced by clean ones and the necessary essentials are at hand. All this takes perhaps ten minutes of your time. Then while you're waiting for the first mail delivery, water the plants and change the water in the flower vases.

Don't overdo tidiness

Even a good thing can be carried too far, and some people carry neatness and tidiness to the point where they become slightly ridiculous. Emptying ashtrays during the day is one thing, but doing so every time a visitor drops an ash in one is unnecessary and annoying. One area in which you must never overdo tidiness is your executive's desk. Some men are naturally neat. Others prefer a cluttered desk on which everything builds up in layers into which they can burrow at will and find exactly what they want. Let your executive keep his desk any way he wishes, and don't register disapproval if he's the untidy type. It's irritating to a man to sense that his secretary is silently putting up with what she considers his faults and eccentricities.

Nagging has no place in business

No matter how much room for improvement you see in your own and your executive's offices, don't make too big an issue out of it. The average man is averse to change; he likes things to stay where he's used to seeing them. You may think a chair or table should be moved somewhere else, but be wise and leave it where it is until you have consulted your employer. If he says no to the move, don't bring it up again. A man can be extremely sensitive to any intimation that feminine fancy led to changes in his office arrangement. He will feel much more secure in his position as commander of the office if he can readily answer any comment on a change with, "Yes, the light was not good on Miss Smith's desk" or "We found we needed more room for that new cabinet." For this reason, if you want to move anything, think out a sensible reason for doing so, one that your employer can use should a fellow officer remark on the change.

When decorating becomes a "must"

The time does come, however, when even the most disinterested man realizes the office needs to be painted, furniture renewed or replaced, and perhaps the lighting improved.

If the work to be done is not too involved, you will probably be in charge of it. However, even if a top-notch decorator is called in to do the place over from top to bottom, you will undoubtedly be appointed to coordinate your employer's preferences and the decorator's ideas. Either way, knowing a few basic facts about the complexities of interior design will be helpful to you.

Sensitivity to color

Most of us are totally unaware of the ways in which color affects our lives. It influences our moods and attitudes in ways we never suspect. Offhand, you would never think of your meals in terms of color. Yet the Color Research Institute of America has conducted tests in which the colors of food served to people were changed by means of lighting effects into dark, muddy, sickly shades. Most of the guests were unable to eat; others tried to swallow the food, but became ill. Still other tests by the Color Research Institute have proved how color influences work production.

One young woman found her head ached after every visit to one of her friends. As she wasn't the type to get headaches, this puzzled her. One day she read a Color Research Institute pamphlet which said bright yellow could be head-splitting. She thought of the vivid yellows her friend had used to decorate her living room and realized what caused her head to ache whenever she was a guest in that room.

The office atmosphere you would like to have depends on the colors you select for the walls, flooring, upholstery and draperies. Unless you have a sure sense of color, use a color wheel when working out the color scheme for your office or your executive's. Be sure to consult your employer about his tastes in color so that he doesn't find himself surrounded by a hue he dislikes or that makes him nervous and restless.

How to choose colors

A color wheel is an indispensable aid to working out a satisfactory color scheme, the majority of which are derived from four basic methods of selection. You probably remember from school days that the *primary colors* are red, blue and yellow. By mixing any two of the primary colors equally we get three *secondary colors*—purple, orange, and green. When a primary color is mixed with a secondary color, *tertiary colors* are produced; for instance, red plus orange in varying proportions can result in such shades as russet, burnt orange, coral and the like.

The four fundamental color schemes are these: the complementary, the triad, the split complementary, and related.

Complementary.   Using a color wheel, choose direct contrasts; that is, the pair of colors that are exactly opposite each other on the wheel. Use one in a bright tone for smaller areas, the other in grayed tones for larger areas.

Triad.   Draw an even-sided triangle on the color wheel, say from yellow to blue to red, to find the basic colors for this scheme. Use only one hue in a strong bright tone in small areas, with the other two in grayed tones.

Split complementary.   Select a color on the wheel and, as you would for the complementary scheme, find the opposite color on the wheel then move to each side of it for the hues you want. As an example, if you pick yellow you will find that it may be used with blue-violet and red-violet. The true violet shade, directly opposite yellow, may also be used.

Related. This scheme is developed by using colors which are related because they are side by side on the wheel. Any group can be used, all around the wheel. A contrast color opposite any one of the group you select can be used as an accent. For instance, in the yellow-orange to red group complementary blue could be used for accent.

Black, white, gray, and other definitely neutral tones can be used with any combination of colors.

To work out whichever color scheme you decide on, make one color the dominant one. It may dominate by covering a large area or by strength of hue in a smaller area. If it is to cover a large area, the color should be in a light or grayed tone. If it is to dominate by strength, then use a small amount of it in bold, strong tones. Key your other colors to the dominant one, softening or lightening them as necessary. Use as your guide the rule to avoid too many colors and too strong tones except in accents, which should be well distributed and not spotty.

Tone is the relative strength of a color as it approaches black or white. Tints are the light tones resulting when white is mixed with a color; shades are the dark tones derived when black is added to a color.

Choose color with a purpose

Aside from affecting your emotions, color can make a room look smaller or larger. In general, light colors are best in small rooms and dark colors in large ones, because light tints tend to enlarge an area and dark colors to diminish it.

Relate color also to the amount of light and sun your office gets. The warm colors, yellows, reds and oranges, are stimulating and excellent for offices facing north or east. The cool, retreating colors, such as the violets, blues and greens, are best used in southern and western exposures. Offices facing either east or west can also take divided color schemes, because they get sun part of each day. As eastern exposure gets the comparatively cool morning sun, more warm than cool colors can be used. The warm afternoon sun reaches western exposures and therefore more cool than warm colors are advisable.

Suggested color schemes

You may be hesitating to choose a color scheme for your own office or that of your executive. Perhaps these ideas will be of some help in making up your mind.

• Chartreuse and yellow upholstery combined with brown carpeting, a matching print in the draperies and mahogany wood paneled walls.

• Orange-rust vinyl upholstery combined with a brown and orange tweed carpet, pale beige walls and striped draperies in matching hues.

• Olive green and beige upholstery, beige carpeting, one wall white the others pale green, white draperies. A desk of olive green with a white top would be effective in this office.

• Cinnamon brown and green upholstery, pale green carpeting, and walls of a paler green with light yellow window draperies.

• Gold, orange and yellow-beige upholstery, golden yellow vinyl flooring, off-white walls, matchstick blinds with bands of matching colors.

How light affects color

Incandescent and fluorescent lighting affect colors differently. Study colors and fabrics under the lighting you have in your office, or plan to have installed, as well as in daylight. Although your office is used mostly in the daytime, winter nights start early and the lights are put on in the afternoon. If your office has no outside light at all, you will have to be even more particular about selecting colors and fabrics which will show up well under constant artificial light.

Light and your eyesight

While lighting is important in a decorating scheme, the principal function of correct lighting is protection of your eyesight. Work performance improves in direct relation to lessening of eyestrain and fatigue. The electric utility in your area has experts in modern lighting who will be glad to advise you on ways to modernize your office lighting. Good general, or background, lighting, plus adequate local lighting for close work, are of the utmost importance.

Other phases of decorating

If your decorating task includes new floor covering, and you are not using a decorator, select a reliable dealer in floor coverings and talk the problem over with him. Carpeting remains popular for excellent reasons, such as wear, acoustics, and the warmth and richness of its appearance. If you are interested in smart and attractive tile flooring, investigate the various kinds, and their advantages and disadvantages, before you decide. Keep in mind that a light color floor affords interesting contrast to dark furniture, as does a dark floor to light woods.

Draw draperies, either full- or sill-length, are by far the most popular form of window decoration. In most instances they are used with blinds or shades of some kind, or with sheer glass curtains, depending on the view from the window and the amount of sun that comes in.

You can match the upholstery of one or two pieces of furniture to the fabric in the window draperies. Go easy on patterns. If the draperies are patterned, be sure any other pattern you decide to use complements it. For instance, a stripe or small abstract line print might be used with a large floral or scenic print; whereas floral and scenic prints together would add up to too much of a good thing. In general, one print in a room is enough. Use textured plain fabrics, plus vinyl or leather, elsewhere in the room.

Arrangement of the office

Redecorating the office gives you a perfect excuse for rearranging furniture and office equipment. This should be done, however, not so much with the idea of making the office look a little different as with the thought of saving time and energy in daily tasks and getting the most out of your space and equipment. Study the placement of furniture, files and other equipment. Are the files close to the person who uses them most. Do you have to dodge around chairs or tables to reach any of the equipment you use constantly? Does your office serve also as a reception room? Does your employer need a conversation grouping in his office where he can confer informally with visitors? Do you need more storage space?

Your answers to these questions will influence any changes or additions you might wish to make. One of the first things decorators do is to plan use of the space they are to decorate. You can do this yourself, and the answers to the questions above will aid your thinking along this line.

To start, measure the office and, reducing the measurements from feet to inches, draw a sketch of the space you have. Be sure to include on the drawing such things as radiators, doors, windows, electrical outlets, and closets. A well known decorator did over the office of a prominent executive and the result was attractive and entirely satisfactory. However, the decorator had forgotten to sketch on her space plan a closet in one corner of the office. She had purchased a beautiful chair for this corner. It looked fine, but the executive stored in the closet behind it records and papers to which he frequently referred. Every time he opened the door he had to move the chair. Needless to say, the chair had been moved from that spot within a week.

Draw on your floor plan the path of each routine work procedure, such as going to the files, trips to the supply cabinet, and so forth. From this sketch you can decide what arrangement of furniture and equipment would cut down on these trips or shorten the distance between the files and supplies and you. Then with cutouts or by drawing, place the furniture and equipment where you think it would make better use of space and simplify certain daily tasks. This is a good time to think of adding wall units that will hold books, TV, a small refrigerator, even a compact office kitchen Although custom-made units are expensive, they cut down on the amount of furniture needed in an office and at the same time give a substantial, well-furnished look to the room.

The importance of accessories

Lamps, ashtrays, pictures, desk sets, clocks, paperweights, and all the other office accessories, often attract more attention than the other furnishings. These are the little things (although not necessarily small in size) that make the biggest impression because they express individuality. Don't clutter the office up with cheap bits of bric-a-brac; choose a few good items that are handsome and functional.

Hiring an expert

Do-it-yourself decorating takes a great deal more time than the average secretary has to spare. Although you might enjoy decorating your own office or your executive's, this is a task that takes hours of thought, planning, and shopping. It isn't something you can take care of in a few lunch hours. For this reason, many executives insist that their secretaries hire an interior decorator when the office has to be done over or a few articles of furniture purchased or reupholstered. If you are moving your offices, by all means consult a decorator. The ones who specialize in office decorating have space planners on their staffs who study the offices being considered and advise whether the space is adequate and how it can be used to full advantage. With office rents so high, it's smart to plan and utilize every expensive square foot of space.

There are three types of decorating service you can call on: that furnished by a dealer in office furniture, that of the contract division of a furniture store's decorating department, and that of the independent interior designer. There's a common misconception that decorators want to do only the most expensive things they can think of. This isn't so. A competent decorator will handle your money as carefully as he would his own. Decorators do a great deal that can't even be included in their fees; such as saving you valuable time and working out all the details that are involved in a decorating job, to say nothing of saving you from expensive errors of taste and judgment. Don't be afraid to tell a decorator what you want done and how much you want to spend.

Possibly the degree to which the decorator tries to reflect a client's individuality is the chief difference among the several types of decorators. If you are undecided as to which type of decorator to use, ask to see photographs of their work. In this way you will be able to see the kind of job each one does and determine which is best suited to your needs.

Flowers and plants as accents

Flowers and plants are charming accessories in any office. Tall green plants, generally clinging to a piece of tree bark, are effective with either traditional or contemporary furnishings. A full, healthy-looking plant delights most people, but be sure to discard plants that become straggly and pitiful-looking, for they add nothing to a room.

A number of attractive green plants grow in water as well as soil. In case you are the type who forgets to water plants until they are shriveled and dying, philodendron, Chinese evergreen, dracaena and dieffenbachia are among the plants that grow well in water.

Spray the leaves of green plants weekly or wipe them with a cloth moistened in water or milk. Wipe the underside of the leaf as well. Don't use oil or wax to make leaves shine.

Large square or rectangular planters, metal lined, which you can fill with pots of flowers or plants, enable you to change displays with the seasons. The planter might be filled with pots of chrysanthemums in the fall, geraniums in summer, poinsettias at Christmas time, and coleus or calladium in the spring.

Many artificial flowers, leaves, and plants are excellent for office use. Be careful to select only the ones that look most like the real thing. Whatever you do, don't let them become dust catchers. Nothing looks worse than a dusty, tired-looking arrangement of artificial flowers and plants.

Fresh flowers at a price

If your executive enjoys fresh flowers in his office, you can arrange with a local florist to supply arrangements on a regular basis for a flat fee. Perhaps this expense is out of line with the office budget. In that case, it is possible for you to purchase from one to seven flowers and make a delightful arrangement whenever you find yourself in the mood. Branches of flowering shrubs, or even attractive foliage, brought it by you or your executive or any other staff member, can be used to supplement the office flower budget.

Making your own arrangements

Keep in a small box or basket several kinds of needle and wire holders, a small pair of flower shears, floral clay, a watering bulb. A few containers of different sizes are nice to have, but you can get along with just two. The best all-purpose container is a shallow rectangular dish 10–12 inches long and 1½ to 2 inches deep. A tall rectangle (known as the pillow vase) or a tall columnar vase 9 to 12 inches in height make good containers for branches and leaves. When you start an arrangement work on newspaper or paper towels. This makes cleaning up a simple matter of rolling up the paper.

A carload of flowers isn't necessary for an enchanting arrangement. Visualize one lovely rose nestling among lemon leaves in a low container; two roses of different heights with their own foliage in a goblet or bud vase; one large peony and some leaves in a shallow metal ashtray or dish; two iris with spears of iris foliage in a tall slim vase; or two day lilies with their own foliage. A lengthy list could be made up, but these few are mentioned only to convince you that it doesn't take a lot of money or dozens of blossoms to decorate the office with flowers.

There are several excellent books on the market on the subject of flower arranging. Buy one, perhaps an inexpensive paperback to start, and study it in your spare moments. There is much pleasure to be found in creating floral designs, and how thrilling it is to hear people praise them.

Basic designs that are simple to do include the triangle and side triangle, the circular, the perpendicular, and the horizontal.

Triangle. This symmetrical arrangement is made by first establishing height and width with foliage and flowers. Then fill in the center with the largest flowers you have. This type of arrangement is one that does require lots of flowers, as it should look generous and expansive.

Side triangle. This can be either a right or left triangle and is most effective in shallow rectangular containers. It is a good design for areas where it will be viewed from both sides.

Circular. Visualize a circle as you place the flowers in the container. Round flowers are best for this type of arrangement, but to avoid monotony use foliage that offers contrast.

Perpendicular. This is an excellent design for limited space. Use a tall container and make the arrangement straight up and down. Gladioli and their foliage are excellent for this type of design.

Horizontal. This design is best used on a long flat area, such as a side table or chest. It is actually an adaptation of the perpendicular line, having center interest and a spike flower such as gladioli or heather extending out at either side.

Gaining rapidly in popularity is the Japanese type of flower design. Slightly more difficult to do, it is particularly effective in contemporary settings. The Moribana arrangement emphasizes nature; the flowers symbolizing heaven, man, earth, mountain, meadow. Place a needlepoint holder in the corner of a shallow rectangular container, insert the flower representing heaven, which should be 1½ to 2 times the width of the container, in the center of the holder towards the rear; man, ⅔ the height of heaven, is placed to the left; earth, ⅓ the height of heaven, juts out to the right; mountain is placed slightly behind and lower than heaven; meadow is placed forward as the lowest point in the design. Extra blossoms, called helpers, can be placed between man and mountain, heaven and meadow, and meadow and earth. The stems must not cross.

Arrangements of dried flowers are popular in the winter time. They are fun to try and your florist will have the supplies and suggestions needed to get you started. Popular in Colonial times, these dried ar-

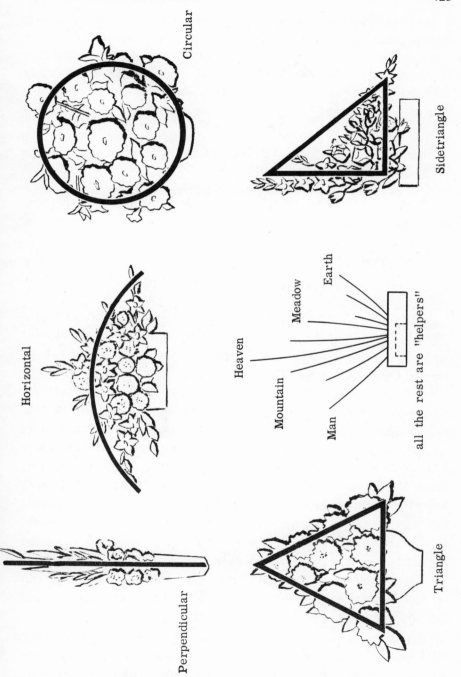

Figures 11–16. Flower Arrangements

rangements look equally well against traditional and contemporary backgrounds.

Points to remember

When you use a tall vase the height of the flowers above the rim should be equal to 1½ to 2 times the height of the vase. In low containers the tallest stem should equal 1½ to 2 times the length or diameter of the bowl.

Contrast color, texture and form to achieve an interesting arrangement.

Care of cut flowers

Use clean containers and holders. Make fresh cuts in the stems and remove all foliage that would be under water. Don't put flowers into cold water; it should be tepid. To revive drooping cut flowers, slice the stem ends and plunge into a container of hot water. The cut flower preservatives your florist has also encourage flowers to last longer. Other aids to lasting bloom are changing the water daily and keeping arrangements in a cool, draftless place if possible.

A word of warning. Attractive though plants and flowers are, just be sure you don't place them where they can easily be tipped over or where they will get in someone's way.

Flower calendar

Each month has a flower of its own. If you do your own arrangements, you might want to use the flower of the month for at least one of them.

January	— Carnation	July	— Larkspur
February	— Primrose	August	— Poppy
March	— Jonquil	September	— Aster
April	— Daisy	October	— Calendula
May	— Lily of the Valley	November	— Chrysanthemum
June	— Rose	December	— Poinsettia

RECOMMENDED BOOKS ON FLOWER ARRANGING

Flower Arranging, Editors of Better Homes and Gardens, Meredith Publishing Company, Des Moines, Iowa

Flower Arrangements Anyone Can Do Anywhere (a pocket book), Matilda Rogers, New American Library, New York

Flowers: Their Arrangement, J. Gregory Conway, Alfred A. Knopf, Inc., New York

Flower Arrangement (a pocket book), Betty Massingham, Penguin Books, Inc., Baltimore, Md.

Stepping Stones to Japanese Floral Art, Rachel E. Carr, David McKay, Inc., New York

Index